A VOICE IN THEIR OWN DESTINY

A Volume in the Series

CULTURE AND POLITICS IN THE COLD WAR AND BEYOND

Edited by

EDWIN A. MARTINI AND SCOTT LADERMAN

A VOICE IN THEIR OWN DESTINY

REAGAN, THATCHER, AND PUBLIC DIPLOMACY
IN THE NUCLEAR 1980S

ANTHONY M. EAMES

University of Massachusetts Press
AMHERST AND BOSTON

ISBN 978-1-62534-709-1 (paper); 710-7 (hardcover)

Designed by Sally Nichols
Set in Minion Pro and Impact
Printed and bound by Books International, Inc.

Cover design by Sally Nichols
Cover photo: (top) Levan Ramishvili, *Ronald Reagan, Alexander Haig and Margaret Thatcher outside No. 10 Downing Street*. CC1.0;
(bottom) Martin Argles *Nuclear weapons protest at Greenham Common airbase, Americans at the blockade holding sign*. Copyright Guardian News & Media Ltd 2022.

Library of Congress Cataloging-in-Publication Data
Names: Eames, Anthony M., 1988– author.
Title: A voice in their own destiny : Reagan, Thatcher, and public diplomacy in the nuclear 1980s / Anthony M. Eames.
Other titles: Reagan, Thatcher, and public diplomacy in the nuclear 1980s
Description: Amherst : University of Massachusetts Press, [2023] | Series: Culture and politics in the Cold War and beyond | Includes bibliographical references and index.
Identifiers: LCCN 2022044970 (print) | LCCN 2022044971 (ebook) | ISBN 9781625347091 (paper) | ISBN 9781625347107 (hardcover) | ISBN 9781685750091 (ebook)
Subjects: LCSH: United States—Politics and government—1981–1989. | United States—Foreign relations—1981–1989. | Great Britain—Politics and government—1979–1997. | Great Britain—Foreign relations—1979–1997. | Antinuclear movement—United States. | Antinuclear movement—Great Britain. | Nuclear disarmament. | Propaganda—History—20th century. | Cold War.
Classification: LCC E876 .E236 2023 (print) | LCC E876 (ebook) | DDC 973.927—dc23/eng/20230105
LC record available at https://lccn.loc.gov/2022044970
LC ebook record available at https://lccn.loc.gov/2022044971

British Library Cataloguing-in-Publication Data
A catalog record for this book is available from the British Library.

For Kelly and Owen, Mom and Dad

CONTENTS

FIGURES

ACKNOWLEDGMENTS

While writing this book, I have been enlightened and encouraged by many colleagues, friends, and family members. My mentors, Kathryn Olesko and David Painter, deserve more credit than I can give them for helping turn my raw ideas and enthusiasm for nuclear history into a study worth reading. They modeled the roles of world-class scholar and generous teacher. I thank them for all of their intellectual, professional, and personal support. I am thankful to Toshi Higuchi, Bill Burr, and Matthew Grant for offering valued insights that brought greater nuance to my work. Without their outstanding contributions to the field of nuclear history, I could not have conceived of this book.

I am grateful for my colleagues and teachers who invested their time and energy in my work. I could not have completed this book without support from the community of historians at Georgetown University, including Jackson Perry, Tom Foley, Chad Frazier, Thom Loyd, Andrew Ross, Kate Steir, Cory Young, Katherine Benton-Cohen, Alison Games, John McNeill, Clark Alejandrino, Carolina Madinaveitia, John Maurer, Greg Brew, Robynne Mellor, Oliver Horn, and Anand Toprani. Many others have freely shared their time and thoughts in service of my work, especially Henry Nau, Sarah Robey, Nicholas Cull, Christian Ostermann, Marty Sherwin, Bruce Gregory, Mike Schneider, Carnes Lord, Roger Zakheim, Luke Griffith, Frances Burke, Chris Campbell, Craig Harrington, and Alex Pappas. I owe a debt to the editors and archivists who invested in my project, including Matt Becker, Rachael DeShano, Ira Pemstein, and Jennifer Newby.

The Ronald Reagan Presidential Foundation and Institute, the Harry Truman Good Neighbor Foundation, the American Institute of Physics, and the Georgetown University History Department and Graduate School generously funded writing sabbaticals and research trips across the United States and the United Kingdom.

My family has been my most important source of inspiration and comfort. My wife, Kelly, has given so much of herself and kept me inspired, motivated, and focused throughout the writing of this book. Her support has been unending and deeply needed. My son Owen's arrival energized me precisely when I needed that boost to finish this book. My mother, Angeles, and my father, Marshall, instilled in me a love of learning. My sisters, Luisa and Briana, have supported me in ways big and small since I first set out to become a historian. Thanks to Bill, Maryann, Agnes, Pat, Archie, Brendan, Stephanie, Declan, Everett, Jason, Ross, and Woodley for keeping my spirits high throughout the many years of research and writing.

GLOSSARY OF ABBREVIATIONS, ACRONYMS, AND TERMS

ABM: antiballistic missile, designed to target and destroy incoming ballistic missiles

ACDA: Arms Control and Disarmament Agency (United States)

AFL-CIO: American Federation of Labor Unions–Congress of Industrial Organizations (United States)

AFSC: American Friends Service Committee (United States)

ASAT: antisatellite weapon, designed to destroy satellites in space

BAC: British Atlantic Committee (United Kingdom)

ballistic missile: multiphase missile that does not rely on aerodynamic lift and follows a ballistic trajectory

BBC: British Broadcasting Corporation

BMA: British Medical Association (United Kingdom)

BMD: ballistic missile defense, a system for defending against incoming ballistic missiles (see *ABM*)

CALC: Clergy and Laity Concerned (United States)

CLW: Council for a Livable World (United States)

CND: Campaign for Nuclear Disarmament (United Kingdom)

CoE: Church of England (United Kingdom)

counterforce: nuclear targeting doctrine that prioritizes enemy military targets

countervalue: nuclear targeting doctrine that prioritizes enemy population and economic centers

CPD: Committee on the Present Danger (United States)

CPI: Committee on Public Information (United States)

CPS: Coalition for Peace through Security (United Kingdom)

CRD: Conservative Research Department (United Kingdom)

cruise missile: guided missile that uses aerodynamic lift; usually slower than ballistic missiles

dense-pack: concept for basing the MX missile (see *MX ICBM*)

CSIS: Center for Strategic and International Studies (United States)

DS-19: Defence Secretariat 19 (United Kingdom)

END: European Nuclear Disarmament (United Kingdom)

ESR: Educators for Social Responsibility (United States)

FAS: Federation of American Scientists (United States)

FBS: forward-based U.S. weapons (United States); e.g., systems based outside of the United States capable of striking targets within the Soviet mainland

FCO: Foreign and Commonwealth Office (United Kingdom)

FOR: Fellowship of Reconciliation

freeze: concept for checking the arms race by first freezing the size of the U.S. and
  Soviet nuclear arsenals and then freezing other aspects of nuclear programs,
  including testing; also, *Freeze,* the largest antinuclear organization in the United
  States in the 1980s
FV '84: Freeze Voter '84 (United States)
GCW: Greenham Common Women (United Kingdom)
GLCM: ground-launched cruise missile
hardened site: site constructed to withstand a nuclear blast
ICBM: intercontinental ballistic missile, a fixed or mobile missile that can deliver war-
  heads farther than 5,500 kilometers and follows a suborbital ballistic trajectory;
  ranges defined by SALT and SALT II treaties
IEDSS: Institute for European Defence and Strategic Studies (United Kingdom)
INF: intermediate-range nuclear forces, land based missiles and aircraft with a range/
  combat radius between the battle field and 5,500 kilometers
JASONS: technical advisory board of civilian experts for national security issues
  (United States)
JCS: joint chiefs of staff (United States)
JWP: Jobs with Peace (United States)
KGB: Soviet Union's primary security agency
kiloton: nuclear yield equal to 1,000 tons of dynamite
LATB: London after the Bomb Working Group
MAD: mutual assured destruction, a concept of strategic stability under which rivals
  are deterred from launching a nuclear attack because each possesses the nuclear
  capability to destroy the other in a counterattack
MCANW: Medical Campaign against Nuclear Weapons (United Kingdom)
megaton: nuclear yield equal to 1 million tons of dynamite
Midgetman: small highly accurate and mobile ICBM carrying a single warhead
MIRV: multiple independently targeted reentry vehicles, carried on a ballistic missile
  that can be directed at separate targets
MoD: Ministry of Defence (United Kingdom)
MP: Member of Parliament (United Kingdom)
MRBM: medium-range ballistic missile
MX ICBM: intercontinental ballistic missile capable of carrying ten nuclear warheads;
  renamed Peacekeeper by Reagan administration
NATO: North Atlantic Treaty Organization
NCCB: National Conference of Catholic Bishops (United States)
NSC: National Security Council (United States)
NSDD: National Security Decision Directive (United States)
NSPG: National Security Planning Group (United States)
NST: Nuclear and Space Talks
NVDA: nonviolent direct action
NWFZ: Nuclear Weapon Free Zone movement
OTA: Office of Technology Assessment (United States)
Pershing II: intermediate-range ballistic missiles (United States)
PSR: Physicians for Social Responsibility (United States)
RAF: Royal Air Force (United Kingdom)
RAGE: Ratepayers against the Greenham Encampments (United Kingdom)

SALT: Strategic Arms Limitation Talks

SALT II: Strategic Arms Limitation Talks, negotiations after initial treaty

SANA: Scientists against Nuclear Arms (United Kingdom)

SANE: National Committee for a Sane Nuclear Policy; also, papers of SANE (United States)

SCC: Standing Consultative Commission, a permanent U.S.-Soviet commission to implement and maintain SALT agreements

SCLC: Southern Christian Leadership Conference (United States)

SCOPE-ENUWAR: study from the Scientific Committee on Problems of the Environment on the environmental effects of nuclear war

SDI: Strategic Defense Initiative, a defense project comprising the development and future deployment of multiple types of ABM capabilities

SDIO: Strategic Defense Initiative Organization (United States)

SDP: Social Democratic Party (United Kingdom)

SfP: Science for the People (United States)

SLBM: submarine-launched ballistic missile

SSOD: U.N. Special Session on Disarmament

SS-20: U.S. designation for Soviet intermediate-range ballistic missile deployed in the late 1970s

START: Strategic Arms Reduction Talks

throw-weight: The weight of all components on a missile, excluding the rocket(s) that power the missile.

TGWU: Trade and General Workers Union (United Kingdom)

Trident I (C-4): submarine-launched ballistic missile (United States)

Trident II (D-5): submarine-launched ballistic missile with improved range and accuracy over the Trident I (United States)

TTAPS: initials of the authors of the nuclear winters study, often used as an acronym to reference the study: Turco, Toon, Ackerman, Pollack, and Sagan

TUC: Trade Union Congress (United Kingdom)

UCS: Union of Concern Scientists (United States)

USIA: United States Information Agency

VOA: Voice of America

WAND: Women's Action for Nuclear Disarmament (United States)

warhead: explosive component of a nuclear weapon

WFD: Women and Families for Defence (United Kingdom)

WILPF: Women's International League for Peace and Freedom

WPA: Women's Pentagon Action (United States)

WPC: World Peace Campaign (international/Soviet Union)

WPS: Women's Party for Survival (United States)

yield: energy released in an explosion, usually expressed in terms of dynamite equivalent

A VOICE IN THEIR OWN DESTINY

INTRODUCTION

THE EMINENT BRITISH historian and antinuclear activist E. P. Thompson opposed U.S. Secretary of Defense Caspar Weinberger in a heavily promoted debate at the Oxford Union on February 27, 1984. It was a time of peak Cold War anxiety, and organizers billed the event as historic. Not only was Weinberger the first sitting U.S. defense secretary to participate in an Oxford Union debate, but this would be the first direct confrontation between an official representative of President Ronald Reagan's administration and the British antinuclear movement. The motion on that evening was broad—"there is no moral difference between the foreign policies of the USA and the USSR"—but both Weinberger and Thompson refocused the debate on the competing merits of nuclear deterrence and nuclear disarmament. Thompson argued that the development of deterrence had pushed the United States into a belligerent military posture that eroded the moral differences between the superpowers that once existed at the beginning of the Cold War. Now, in 1984, he claimed, "there is no morality." Weinberger countered that deterrence had in fact guaranteed U.S. moral superiority over the Soviet Union. Weinberger justified the U.S. nuclear buildup as a way to maintain the credibility of deterrence, suggesting that it was based not on U.S. aggression but on a calculation of what would deter the men in the Kremlin from asserting their immoral philosophy over Western Europe and the rest of the free world. By a margin of 271 to 232, the Oxford Union voted against the motion and in favor of Weinberger's argument that deterrence was moral because it secured western freedoms.[1]

The encounter was the centerpiece of wider debates on issues of deterrence and disarmament in the United States and the United Kingdom. After his appearance at the Oxford Union, Weinberger remained in Britain to discuss the moral justifications for nuclear deterrence with leading members of the Anglican clergy and other British opinionmakers.[2] Meanwhile, Thompson

1

had just finished a lecture tour in the United States, where he had expanded on the arguments for nuclear disarmament already presented in his widely read essay "Letter to America" (1981).[3] He had finished his American tour in spring 1983 at the prestigious National Press Club in Washington D.C., speaking to a mixed audience of government officials, reporters, and policy-interested elites.[4]

The Weinberger-Thompson debate was a remarkable display of public diplomacy. It revealed the vitality of the special nuclear relationship between the United States and the United Kingdom as well as the centrality of nuclear issues in American and British society during the final decade of the Cold War. These dynamics characterized the period known as the nuclear 1980s and provided a foundation for the rise of public opinion as a major force in shaping international relations.

The nuclear 1980s began in 1979 with a dramatic increase in nuclear fear and a revival of the antinuclear movement. These shifts were a response to the partial meltdown of Pennsylvania's Three Mile Island nuclear power station and to the North Atlantic Treaty Organization's (NATO's) dual-track decision to deploy new nuclear missiles in Western Europe while pursuing arms control talks with the Soviet Union. Nuclear issues were particularly pervasive and volatile in 1983. In March, the Strategic Defense Initiative (SDI) was announced, and nuclear debates played a major role in that spring's British elections. Then, in September, the Soviets shot down Korean Airlines flight 007, not long before the public became aware of nuclear winter theory in late October. November was a fraught month, with a trio of events that included a nuclear war scare caused by NATO's Operation Able Archer exercise, the initial deployments of U.S. cruise and Pershing II missiles to Europe, and the widely watched television premiere of the nuclear disaster film *The Day After*. Finally, in December, the Soviets walked out of arms control talks. The high tensions of the nuclear 1980s began to ramp down as the political influence of the antinuclear movement diminished after 1984 and the decade came to a close with the bilateral summits that led to the Intermediate-Range Nuclear Forces (INF) Treaty in 1987 and a peaceful end to the Cold War.

Americans' and Britons' reaction to these events turned nuclear weapons into a symbol of the broader fissures in the Anglo-American world. Literature on nuclear weapons incorporated transnational debates about race, gender, the environment, and the realignment of politics. Other forms of nuclear culture—television programs, music, films, video games, fine art, fashion, and more—bonded nuclear themes to myriad concerns in Anglo-American society. Pronuclear attitudes became intertwined with the contentious transnational rise of neoliberalism as the prevailing political and economic order in the United States and the United Kingdom, under the leadership of President Reagan and Prime Minister Margaret Thatcher. Nuclear politics compelled both science and religion to reform their relationship with the state and the general public. More than any other single issue, nuclear anxiety motivated westerners to become politically active. The flashpoints of the nuclear 1980s were critical in stimulating a revolution in how diplomacy related to the public sphere. [5]

During the nuclear 1980s, the U.S. and British governments conceived of public diplomacy as a means to reconcile Cold War culture and Cold War strategy. In the spring of 1981, Kenneth Adelman, the deputy U.S. ambassador to the United Nations and eventually the director of the U.S. Arms Control and Disarmament Agency under Reagan, predicted in the journal *Foreign Affairs* that "public diplomacy . . . may become Washington's major growth industry in the coming years. . . . It has the makings of becoming a hallmark of the Reagan administration's foreign policy."[6] Adelman's words would appear prophetic, but the public diplomacy revolution that would come to pass was not preconceived or preordained by the president. Rather, the public diplomacy innovations of the U.S. and British governments were responses to the transatlantic peace movement that increasingly asserted the role of antinuclear opinions in international relations. By the time the West encountered the public celebrity of Mikhail Gorbachev and the reinvigorated Soviet peace offensive, the U.S. and British governments had spent five years refining the practice and theory of public diplomacy in competition with the peace movement.

How did public diplomacy change during that time, and should those developments be termed a reform, a revolution, or a return to earlier practices? At the most general level, scholars and practitioners consider public diplomacy to be any activity that seeks to influence the views, attitudes, and emotions of foreign people. Disassociating public diplomacy activities from the pejorative connotations of propaganda has posed an enduring challenge for public and cultural affairs officers and other agents of U.S. public diplomacy. President Harry S. Truman began to steer the U.S. government away from the term *propaganda* with the launch of the "campaign of truth," which combined overt and covert information practices to entrench the ideological dimensions of the Cold War.[7] The definitional inflection point for public diplomacy and propaganda came in 1965, when Edmund Gullion, a prominent diplomat and the dean of the Fletcher School of Law and Diplomacy, coined the term *public diplomacy* to replace *propaganda* as the preferred nomenclature for U.S. influence operations in foreign countries. According to Gullion, public diplomacy

> encompass[es] dimensions of international relations beyond traditional diplomacy; the cultivation by governments of public opinion in other countries; the interaction of private groups and interests in one country with another; the reporting of foreign affairs and its impact on policy; communication between those whose job is communication, as diplomats and foreign correspondents; and the process of intercultural communications.[8]

Those activities have variously been referred to as *cultural diplomacy, information operations,* and *propaganda.* Today, scholars' most rigorous construction of Cold War public diplomacy considers the feedback of foreign opinion in the creation of U.S. foreign policy; advocacy of U.S. government policies to foreign publics; cultural diplomacy; the reciprocal exchange of political leaders, students, and other peoples; and broadcast diplomacy.[9]

The idea of public diplomacy was not new in the 1960s but was an assemblage of public persuasion methods and theories that predated the Cold War. Public diplomacy advocates invoked the term to resonate with the period immediately following World War I, when advocates of new diplomacy and open covenants hoped to construct a model for international engagement that was different from the one that had led the world's industrial powers into the Great War. After the war the United States deconstructed its first large-scale propaganda apparatus, the Committee on Public Information (CPI), believing that its activities were a function of war, not peace. CPI's subtle censorship pressures, blunt nationalism, and one-way flow of information threatened the fundamentals of democracy; but many of its methods, such as speaker bureaus, pamphlets, motion pictures, and the drafting of American journalists and cultural elites into influence operations, would become central features of public diplomacy.[10]

Exchange and cultural diplomacy became fixtures of U.S. overseas influence operations in the 1930s, beginning with technological and educational missions to Latin America as part of President Franklin D. Roosevelt's Good Neighbor Policy.[11] The launch of Voice of America during World War II made international broadcasting the hallmark of U.S. foreign persuasion activities, as it continues to be today. After the war, President Truman's 1950 Campaign of Truth attempted to create an alternative to the term *propaganda* while also systematically integrating intelligence activities and psychological operations into the long-term U.S. mission to court international public opinion.

These developments presented important questions for public diplomacy throughout the twentieth century. Should the government sponsor the long-term cultivation of a favorable impression of America abroad, or should public diplomacy be a wartime exigency? Creating an infrastructure and a bureaucracy to sell the idea of a country unified behind a war effort represented a monumental task in its own right, but it paled in comparison to the challenge of fairly representing a pluralistic American democracy to foreign publics in perpetuity. Concerns about the sanctity of democracy at home—whether genuine or politically motivated—factored into frequent jurisdictional battles between the executive branch and Congress over the nation's information policy, which became more intense when both domestic and foreign audiences were involved. Government officials never reached a consensus during either of the world wars as to whether the president's policy should be the message carried by public diplomats to foreign publics around the world. That lack of agreement raised the question of how centralized or decentralized public diplomacy should be. Could the U.S. government trust elites accustomed to the critical standards of the journalistic profession to operate far-flung field offices with little oversight and produce an image of the United States that benefited its international ambitions? The degree of private sector involvement in public diplomacy—that is, preventing government's public diplomacy operations from infringing on the commercial aspirations of private media enterprises—emerged as still another point of contention.

These questions became live issues during the legislation of the Smith-Mundt Act in 1948, which for the first time in U.S. history entrenched public diplomacy as a peacetime instrument for the exercise of American power. Simultaneously, however, it created a de facto ban on the dissemination of U.S. propaganda materials, a prohibition that would become official law in 1972.[12] In practice the Smith-Mundt Act contributed to two shifts in the use and cultural impact of public diplomacy. First, the act drew on tools previously reserved for war to triumph in the Cold War ideological competition for hearts and minds. Public diplomacy initiatives that emerged from the act further blurred the boundaries of peace and war, to a point where Americans believed they were both the beneficiaries of a long peace and citizens of a state locked in permanent war.[13] Second, public officials and private citizens

who were committed to "selling" and "telling America's story to the world"
were continuously engaged in a struggle to "close the gap between how we
define ourselves—and how we actually act at home and abroad."[14] The sym-
bols, modes, and strategies involved in telling America's story to the world
and constructing an image of American democracy changed in relation to
public officials' and private citizens' view of the effects of racial strife, family
and gender norms, technological innovations, and capitalism's modes of con-
sumption and its discontents.[15]

U.S. public diplomacy was fundamental to the growth of the national security state and how the world perceived Washington's stewardship of atomic
power. With the 1953 formation of the U.S. Information Agency (USIA), 40
percent of the State Department's personnel moved into the newly established
agency, a clear demonstration of the value of public diplomacy within Washington's early Cold War mission.[16] Almost immediately after its formation,
USIA became fundamentally intertwined with the atomic age as it assumed
responsibility for publicizing President Dwight D. Eisenhower's Atoms for
Peace campaign to "help world opinion adapt psychologically to the presence
of nuclear weapons in their everyday lives."[17]

When the assumptions underpinning the purpose of nuclear weapons and
the national security state came under scrutiny with the onset of détente in
the 1970s, so did the mission of and support for U.S. public diplomacy.[18] The
recommendations of the Stanton Panel in 1975 to abolish USIA and separate
the dissemination of policy information and advocacy from exchange programs and general information about American society arose from the belief
that the Cold War should no longer dominate "the international expression
of American ideas."[19] Despite subsequent Carter-era reforms intended to
empower an independent U.S. public diplomacy agency, such initiatives were
never fully supported with increased budgets, technological improvements,
or presidential attention and were disconnected from short-term policy goals
and the long-term cultivation of goodwill toward the United States.[20]

By the beginning of Reagan's presidency, the U.S. Advisory Commission
on Public Diplomacy considered U.S. public diplomacy to be in crisis, arguing that it had failed to operate effectively in the space between domestic and
international audiences, given its relatively limited resources and the rise of
global civil society made possible by the communication advancements of
the information age.[21] Confronted with the idea that outreach to foreign pub-

lics could no longer be separated from domestic political communications, public diplomacy practitioners began to conceptualize their audience in transnational terms to account for the reorientation of political communities around information space rather than geographical place. All of the innovations in U.S. and British public diplomacy were developed to meet the new reality of a transnational public sphere and the increased influence of public opinion in international affairs.

There were four primary areas of transformation in public diplomacy: bureaucratic, technological, thematic, and the private sector. The first two were most evident in the Reagan years, when public diplomacy became an administration-wide responsibility. The USIA (known as the U.S. International Communications Agency from 1978 to 1982), the National Security Council, the Department of Defense, the State Department, the White House communication team, and the intelligence community all created either dedicated offices for public diplomacy or devoted significant staff resources to interagency groups working on public diplomacy issues. This rearrangement of bureaucratic responsibility reflected a philosophical shift, revealing how Reagan's view of public diplomacy differed from that of his 1970s-era predecessors. Under Reagan, public diplomacy became oriented toward the realization of immediate policy goals, such as the modernization of the U.S. nuclear arsenal, instead of the long-term cultivation of favorable foreign impressions of American society. Returning to the practices of the early Cold War, U.S. public diplomacy reincorporated the intelligence community and psychological operations into its apparatus. In addition, public diplomacy operations became more centralized in Washington and focused on the president himself.

Technological developments facilitated the centralization of public diplomacy in Washington, D.C., and lessened the operational independence of far-flung field offices. Technological improvements such as forays into satellite television broadcasting, upgrades to the Voice of America infrastructure, and increased reliance on computerized polling techniques were major line items for the USIA and justified the doubling of its budget from 1981 to 1987. These developments increased the clout of the agency's director, Charles Wick. In the history of USIA, Wick surpassed all other directors in terms of influence and direct connection to the president, including Edward Murrow, whose relationship with John F. Kennedy has been seen as the foundation of the first golden age of U.S. public diplomacy.[22]

. . .

The Weinberger-Thompson debate was both an exercise in public diplomacy for the Reagan administration and a real-time indictment by the peace movement. The rhetoric of Anglo-American moral exceptionalism was fundamental to the notion of peace through strength, which framed Reagan's and Thatcher's public nuclear diplomacy. For proponents, this meant marshaling moral fortitude and national will to support the modernization of NATO and the U.S. nuclear arsenal, with the goal of solidifying the western alliance's strategic superiority over the Soviet Union. The assertiveness of the peace through strength approach marked a sharp departure from the moral uncertainty that surrounded the Vietnam War and the Watergate scandal, both of which bedeviled U.S. public diplomacy in the 1970s. Reagan and Thatcher sought to craft memories of peace as a way to manage the social and cultural aspects of security and deterrence. They believed that intergenerational conflict was responsible for public antinuclear sentiment, that a younger generation of westerners was condemning the Reagan administration's nuclear policies because it had not witnessed the U.S.-led liberation and reconstruction of postwar Western Europe. Peace through strength was itself an allusion to the notion of "situations of strength," which held that U.S. nuclear superiority had been key to both its security relationship with the Soviet Union and the incorporation of Western Europe into the U.S. sphere of influence during the 1940s and 1950s. Paul Nitze, who had served in the upper echelons of the national security policy apparatus since the Truman administration, played a crucial role in the design and implementation of both ideas.[23]

In other words, pronuclear advocates justified their deterrence commitments with memories of decisive U.S. action during World War II and the early Cold War, when Washington policymakers had enjoyed indisputable nuclear superiority. In contrast, antinuclear activists recalled the excesses of the Cold War that had led to the Vietnam War and decried the escalating expense of the arms race in their arguments for disarmament. David Abshire, the U.S. ambassador to NATO and the founder of the Center for Strategic and International Studies, suggested that this split presented a "moral crossroads" for NATO leaders and their publics.[24] For him, the obvious choice was a program of peace through strength rooted in a particular Anglo-American moral tradition that had been refined over the course of two world wars and many decades of ideological competition with the Soviet Union.

Peace through strength rhetoric became a primary semantic battleground for the governments of the United States and the United Kingdom and the transatlantic antinuclear movement. The Anglo-American antinuclear movement and the nations' public diplomacy programs identified semantic corruption as a critical element in the Cold War battle of ideas. Each side accused the other of distorting the meaning of the English language so as to corrupt the moral and intellectual integrity of American and British society, leading either to belligerence or surrender, depending on one's point of view.

Private sector affiliates of Reagan's and Thatcher's peace through strength campaign were among the most influential public diplomacy operatives and fueled the dramatic growth of think tanks in Washington and London. At the same time, the campaign created a common cause for conservative journalists, fundraisers, and movement organizations, thus contributing to the rise of the transatlantic New Right. These groups accused antinuclear advocates of being Soviet stooges and peacemongers who distorted the meaning and morality of nuclear deterrence. Organizations such as the Heritage Foundation and the Coalition for Peace through Strength operated in both countries and were instructed by the same cohort of American and British defense experts. The proliferation of these advocacy groups remade the foreign policymaking machinery in both countries.

For the antinuclear movement, phrases such as "peace through strength," "the peacemaker" (MX missile), and "limited nuclear war" were forms of "nukespeak" designed to sell the merits of deterrence as an international security relationship and a domestic social contract. They considered this terminology to be a method for persuading citizens that their countries' nuclear policies did not infringe on public freedoms and that the benefits of deterrence outweighed its detrimental effects on government transparency, economic opportunity, and equal representation of all citizens in decisions about defense and democracy. Deterrence depended on secrecy, the veneration of specific forms of technical expertise, and therefore the exclusion of other forms of knowledge. A technical priesthood comprised of strategic analysts based at select think tanks, military engineers and experts, scientists at national laboratories, and high-ranking nuclear policymakers constructed deterrence by asserting control over how to define the problem of nuclear war and what processes and expertise could be employed to devise a solution for survival.[25] As the British scholar Michael MccGwire argued, "[the western construct of] deterrence dogma increased international tension by fueling the arms race and fostering a paranoid approach to arms control negotiations . . .

[which] encouraged exaggerated, moralistic rhetoric directed at domestic constituencies as well as opponents."[26]

Such criticisms circulated within the American and British antinuclear movement, driving peace activists to deconstruct deterrence language as a prerequisite for ending the Cold War. The Anglo-American peace movement understood the Cold War in the terms that George Orwell had first laid out in his October 1945 essay "You and the Atom Bomb," in which he presciently envisioned a future world dominated by a handful of superstates in possession of nuclear weapons. These world-ending arsenals would restrain global powers from major direct military encounters but nonetheless keep them locked in a "peace that is no peace."[27] In line with Orwell's prediction, the Cold War played out as an "imaginary war" of theoretical exchanges between the nuclear forces of the western and eastern blocs, which inhibited a direct military confrontation between the superpowers while sustaining geopolitical conflict and violence in the developing world.[28] Unlike traditional wars, whose ending is marked by the cessation of physical violence, the Cold War ended when nuclear war no longer dominated the public imagination and the official mind.

Because the debate between deterrence and disarmament centered on the English language, it also came to animate the special relationship between the United States and the United Kingdom. Courting the United States had been a "defining feature" of Britain's propaganda enterprise in the nuclear age, whether to combat American neutrality at the onset of the world wars or coordinate anticommunist propaganda initiatives in the early Cold War.[29] Public diplomacy was one of the few areas in which Britain's capabilities matched or exceeded those of the superpowers. U.S. officials considered the British Broadcasting Corporation's external services the gold standard of international broadcasting, and the BBC's audience share was on par with that of U.S. outlets, especially east of the Iron Curtain.[30] During World War II and in the early Cold War, British services midwifed the Voice of America and other public diplomacy initiatives, and by the 1970s Britain's long history of influential partnership operations with the United States had constructed a deep and unparalleled bond between both nations' public diplomacy enterprises and linked private sectors.[31] The British public diplomacy model had become so admired in the United States that it was held up as the solution for problems facing U.S. public diplomacy in those years.

While British organizational models did not ultimately become the basis for the public diplomacy revolution in the United States, the Anglo-American relationship did provide the impetus for Reagan- and Thatcher-era themes and strategies. Allusions to a distinct Anglo-American democratic and moral tradition became defining features of pronuclear public diplomacy—for instance, in Reagan's June 1982 address to the British Parliament, when the president promised to give people of the world "a voice in their own destiny."[32] The British government and Conservative Party organs were key to persuading his administration to take a transnational approach to its nuclear politics, and British officials provided the public diplomacy playbook for key presidential programs, notably for the Strategic Defense Initiative (SDI).

One reason that public nuclear diplomacy played such a dynamic role in the Anglo-American relationship is because of the unparalleled integration of both countries' nuclear establishments dating back to the Manhattan Project. Britain depended on the United States for nuclear testing facilities and for its primary deterrent force, which was composed of U.S.-supplied Polaris and Trident submarine-launched ballistic missiles (SLBMs). The United States relied on the United Kingdom for forward nuclear-basing facilities, both on the British Isles and around the world, and for diplomatic assistance on nuclear matters concerning NATO and the Soviet Union. Together they spearheaded nonproliferation efforts such as creation of the Nuclear Suppliers Group as well as joint working groups on technologies and intelligence methods to counter proliferation. Countless other areas of nuclear cooperation existed, including the trilateral comprehensive test ban talks in the 1970s. These points of cooperation were rooted in shared geostrategic and security interests defined by transnational social, cultural, linguistic, and intellectual affinities. Unlike most of their other NATO allies, American and British public diplomats and protestors did not have to contend with the loss of symbolic meaning that arose from the translation of phrases such as "peace through strength," or "protest and survive," and this shared linguistic clarity helped shape their publics' understandings of deterrence and disarmament.[33]

U.S. and British public diplomacy reconceptualized their audience in transnational terms because they responded to Anglo-American protestors who represented themselves as local, national, and transnational actors. Those actors accomplished this by reorienting communities around an ideational space—specifically, a progressive antinuclear space that assimilated environmental, feminist, racial, labor, moral, and scientific concerns into a critique of deterrence—rather than geographical place. The paradiplomatic activities of these antinuclear actors—whether they were from municipal Nuclear Weapon Free Zones (NWFZ), antinuclear religious congregations, or all-female protest encampments—detached them from their traditional hierarchical political geographies and realigned them into a horizontal trans-national antinuclear community.[34] Protestors established long-term durable relationships between elites and foreign publics through joint protest activities. They developed simple yet symbolic themes such as "nuclear freeze" and "protest and survive." They cooperated with foreign governments at the subnational level to advance their interests. Though disgust with deterrence served as a common principle for both the American and British antinuclear movement, distinct positions on disarmament limited the further integration and increased power of the Anglo-American antinuclear movement. The U.S.-based Freeze movement achieved widespread mainstream support and advocated for a halt in production and deployment of U.S. nuclear weapons and components, but it permitted existing nuclear weapons systems to remain in service until the Soviet Union responded in kind. The dominant British antinuclear group, the Campaign for Nuclear Disarmament (CND), achieved significant political power but ultimately was viewed as radical because its ambition was to bring about immediate, total, and unilateral disarmament of the United Kingdom's nuclear arsenal.

The nuclear 1980s also witnessed the public turn in science diplomacy. Science, diplomacy, and the nuclear arms race had co-evolved throughout the Cold War. The private exchange of views among scientists, government officials, military leaders, and other elites were critical to the prevention of nuclear war, most famously as the means by which the West broke through to persuade Gorbachev to radically alter the Soviet approach to arms control.[35] Less celebrated but equally important were scientists' embrace of mass movement politics and the integration of their expertise into the disarmament movement. In earlier periods of nuclear protests, the scientific community, though critical of the detrimental effects of nuclear weapons, had stood apart from the activist community, preferring to contemplate the morality of their own complicity in the nuclear arms race and directly lobby government officials for disarmament measures.

In contrast to the direct approach of private science diplomacy, public science diplomacy prioritized indirect influence, with the goal of informing public attitudes to then shape official policymaking. Using novel communication strategies, it leveraged scientists' technical authority to shape attitudes among both foreign and domestic stakeholders: for example, through scientific studies for local authorities on the effects of nuclear war; film consultations; teach-ins on college campuses; contributions to print, radio, and other forms of popular media; service on technical advisory boards for various grassroots antinuclear organizations; overseas speaking tours; and the establishment of specialized organizations to synthesize international scientific research on nuclear problems. Though their work was closely connected to transatlantic protest, these scientists saw their efforts as complementary to private diplomacy, a natural outgrowth of scientific internationalism, and descendant of a self-proclaimed science diplomacy tradition.

Public science diplomacy occurred at local, national, and transnational levels. At times, this was achieved by integrating local politics and scientific knowledge or by partnering with organizations with significant influence at the community level, such as the Catholic church. The British film *Threads* exemplified public science diplomacy. Released in 1984, it offered the first cinematic portrayal of the novel theory of nuclear winter and tapped the American scientists who had modeled the theory as expert advisors. Set it in Sheffield, a municipality whose NWFZ status was a political and social critique of the Thatcher government's nuclear posture, *Threads*'s visual depiction of nuclear winter provided a scientific vindication of domestic political opposition to Thatcher's neoliberal justifications for deterrence. This mixture of scientific knowledge, political activism, and cultural commentary made antinuclear ideas seem respectable in mainstream American and British society.

In the late 1980s, toward the end of the Cold War, participants in the competition between public diplomacy and protest reflected on their work. Shortly before his penultimate summit with Gorbachev, held in Washington, Reagan declared, "I believe that our public diplomacy represents a powerful force, perhaps *the most powerful force* at our disposal for shaping the history of the world."[36] His statement expressed his deep belief that the battle of ideas was the most important factor in winning the Cold War and achieving lasting nuclear peace. Thompson agreed but instead asserted the peace movement's importance, arguing that "[its] work was not only to oppose but also expose and to demystify the malodorous vocabulary of nuclear weapons, to disclose them not only as weapons but also symbolic rhetoric, for the suppression of politics. . . . The events of autumn 1989 . . . confirm our analysis."[37]

At the same time, new practices were affecting the creation of public diplomacy as an academic field. The terms that the U.S. Advisory Commission on

Public Diplomacy used in the 1980s in its oversight of the USIA and other governmental public diplomacy operations have since become the foundations for the theoretical study of public diplomacy.[38] In particular, Joseph Nye's influential description of public diplomacy practices as an exercise of soft power hewed closely to the advisory commission's categories. First, public diplomacy involves routine communications that explain the context of specific policy decisions to both the domestic and foreign press and to other elites known to be public opinion influencers. In addition, government and nongovernment actors should strategically communicate simple themes via symbolic events and speeches. Lastly, public diplomacy hinges on a "two-way flow" of information and influence between official and unofficial actors through educational exchanges, overseas conferences, political tours, and other activities.[39] This last element has proven especially important to scholars who advocate for a more encompassing definition of public diplomacy, one that goes beyond state-sponsored activities. They argue that public diplomacy is the process by which international publics and civil society groups form new meanings and vocabularies to help realize their policy ambitions.[40] Though the arguments in this book rest on the more limited definition of public diplomacy as a state-sponsored activity, I nonetheless agree that groups outside government can and do influence diplomacy, both public and private.

At the end of the Cold War, the most important battle of ideas was not between the western and eastern blocs but between western public diplomacy operations and the peace movement that made the Anglo-American nuclear experience an axis in the growth of the transnational public sphere. These developments changed American, British, and Soviet perceptions of the Cold War and created opportunities for world leaders to deescalate the conflict through superpower summits. The nuclear reduction agreements reached at those summits were a blend of disarmament and deterrence ideas that produced new ways of relating science and morality to political values. On the domestic front, nuclear debates became a proxy battle for the ideological conflict between conservatives and liberals and intensified the ongoing political and moral polarization of American and British society. Though the West triumphed in the Cold War ideological conflict, the fundamentals of American and British democracy were irrevocably altered by the nuclear debates of the 1980s.

CHAPTER ONE

THE WORLD REAGAN WANTED

A WEEK BEFORE THE 1980 presidential election, more than 80 million Americans tuned into to watch President Jimmy Carter debate candidate Ronald Reagan, making the event the most watched U.S. presidential debate of the twentieth century. Carter and Reagan had swapped leads in the polls throughout the year; but by mid-October, polling showed that the incumbent had a respectable advantage.[1] Early in the debate, the topic turned to the issue of war and peace. Reagan calmly described his vision of "peace through strength," framing it as a way to restore both America's "margin of safety" and its allies' confidence in U.S. leadership. Meanwhile, Carter stumbled, trying to explain his new thinking on the nuclear arms race within the context of a conversation with his eight-year-old daughter.[2] Closing the evening, Reagan pushed his advantage, asking, "Is America as respected throughout the world as it was? Do you feel that our security is as safe, that we're as strong as we were four years ago?"[3] A week later, in an election that was still very much up in the air, exit polls confirmed that Reagan's approach had been pivotal. A *New York Times* exit poll showed that a significant majority of voters desired a tougher stance toward the Soviet Union, and within that majority Reagan earned 70 percent of the votes. Carter, in contrast, won 64 percent of voters who did not approve of a hawkish approach to U.S.-Soviet relations.[4]

The key turning points in the presidential debate were linked to the unusually prominent role that foreign and defense policy played throughout the 1980 U.S. presidential election. One in three voters named national defense as the most important issue for Americans to consider at the polls.[5] Within that category, arms control and the expansion of the U.S. nuclear arsenal to confront the Soviet Union ranked at the top. Arms control and the nuclear arms buildup involved two major elements. The first concerned strategic arms: that is, nuclear weapons with intercontinental range that belonged to the superpowers. On the American side, these included weapons such as the MX intercontinental ballistic missile (MX ICBM), the Trident submarine-launched ballistic missile (SLBM), and heavy bombers such as the B-52 and B-2. On the Soviet side, they included SS-18 ICBMs as well as heavy bombers. The second involved theater nuclear forces, later renamed intermediate-range nuclear forces (INFs), which were primarily meant for use in Europe. NATO's INF forces included ground-launched cruise missiles (GLCMs) and Pershing II medium-range ballistic missiles (MRBMs). Responding to earlier deployments of Soviet SS-20 MRBMs in Eastern Europe, NATO had agreed on a dual-track decision to balance its INF deployments with an invitation to the Soviet Union to negotiate the reduction of nuclear weapons stationed on the European continent.

The 1980 election ushered in the nuclear 1980s, a decade in which nuclear issues preoccupied both the public imagination and the minds of government officials in the Anglo-American world. It signaled that public attitudes would play a larger role in shaping U.S. foreign relations and defense policy. The election revealed the importance of nuclear security and military superiority to Reagan's idealized vision of America, a vision that he had spent years refining but that became clearer in contrast to Carter's uncertainty and also more provocative to an emerging cohort of antinuclear activists. The tension between these two groups matured into a competition between public diplomacy operations and protest campaigns. Throughout this contest, Reagan drew on his campaign strategies for turning nuclear issues from a liability into an electoral asset to provide a roadmap for his administration's public diplomacy at home and abroad.

The election also foreshadowed the reprioritization of transatlantic ties and the NATO alliance, a system that had suffered under détente due to poor U.S. leadership and changing stakeholder priorities. Greater attention paid to NATO translated into an increase in the influence of the United Kingdom, the only other independent nuclear power fully committed to NATO and one governed by Prime Minister Margaret Thatcher's Conservative Party. With regards to public diplomacy and nuclear security, the Thatcher government proved especially important because it focused the Reagan administration's attention on transnational public opinion.

Peace through Strength

Nuclear weapons had a big part to play in Reagan's vision of a moral world order under the leadership of the United States. Many have argued that the abolition of nuclear weapons animated a grand strategy to win the Cold War that Reagan had clearly defined by the time he became president.[6] The evidence for this position is formidable on first sight. From March 1982 onward Reagan publicly insisted on the elimination of nuclear weapons more than 150 times, leading to the first-ever agreement to reduce nuclear weapons between the United States and the Soviet Union, signed in December 1987.[7] Reagan did indeed become committed to the abolition of nuclear weapons but only after a political and policy evolution that reflected what he had learned in office through his engagement with the defense bureaucracy, Congress, the antinuclear movement, European allies, and the Soviet Union. A year before Reagan's public commitment to abolish nuclear weapons, John Hinckley's assassination attempt inspired the president to proactively engage with the Soviet Union on the issue. In the month immediately before Reagan's first pledge to abolish nuclear weapons he received his first full briefing on U.S. nuclear warfighting plans, which estimated approximately 80 million American casualties. In that same period, the president witnessed a massive upswing in antinuclear organizing that led to a bipartisan-backed congressional resolution calling for a freeze on the production, testing, and deployment of U.S. nuclear forces.[8] It is likely that Reagan's turn to nuclear abolitionism was a result of these immediate developments rather than a long-term, deeper commitment to eliminating nuclear weapons, which he had yet to speak of during his decades of public life and has yet to be revealed in his extensive written record.

What did Reagan think about nuclear weapons and the value of nuclear deterrence before he became president? He did not detest deterrence, as some have claimed; rather, he had a clear preference for certain formulations of the concept. He and his neoconservative allies abhorred mutual assured destruction (MAD), which had become the deterrence paradigm of the United States during the period of détente. Reagan rejected MAD out of disdain for the vulnerability of the American homeland that accompanied U.S.-Soviet strategic parity codified by the nuclear arms control agreements of the 1970s. MAD accepted peaceful coexistence between the United States and the Soviet Union as a permanent feature of the international system. Reagan fundamentally did not accept such a premise: his view of the Cold War could be summed up by his famous statement "We win, they lose."[9]

Rather than nuclear abolition, strategic nuclear superiority as a means to contain and then roll back communism guided Reagan's policy toward the Soviet Union. As Republican primary voters headed to the polls in 1976, candidate Reagan made the failure of détente and the need to restore military superiority the central focus of his opposition to President Gerald Ford, noting in early March that "the truth is that this nation must trust less in the pre-emptive concessions we are granting the Soviet Union and more in the re-establishment of American military superiority."[10] In "To Restore America," perhaps the most important speech of his 1976 presidential campaign, Reagan asserted that "peace does not come from weakness or retreat. It comes from the restoration of American military superiority."[11]

Reagan's criticisms of Ford's détente policies pressured the sitting president to relent and authorize the creation of Team B, a controversial recommendation of the president's Foreign Intelligence Advisory Board. The team's objective was to produce an alternative to the assessment of the Soviet threat in the CIA's national intelligence estimates, which upheld the case for nurturing détente with the Soviet Union. Team B, which included experts such as Richard Pipes and Paul Nitze who would later fill prominent roles in the Reagan administration, charged that the U.S. intelligence community had fallen victim to the methodological flaw of "mirror imaging"—the tendency to operate under the assumption that Soviet leadership agreed with American interpretations and drew the same distinctions on the role of deterrence in regard to détente and confrontation, nuclear and conventional forces, strategic versus theater forces, and many other Cold War security concepts. More threatening still, Nitze and other team members agreed that Soviet adherence to Carl von Clausewitz's doctrine meant that Moscow saw deterrence as complementary to warfighting; war was not abnormal but simply politics by other means, and only an improper "correlation of forces" restrained the Soviet Union from launching an attack on the West. Nitze and those on Team B who advocated for Trident, B-1, the development and deployment of airborne early warning and control systems, and measures to even out civil-defense imbalances did so on the belief that the onset of strategic parity and the growth in Soviet defense budgets during the preceding ten years demonstrated the USSR's will to achieve the desired correlation of forces to destroy NATO.[12]

Though many of Team B's claims were later debunked, they provided momentum for the formation of the Committee on the Present Danger (CPD). The original version of this committee arose in the 1950s to advance the strategy of "massive retaliation," which Nitze developed in the NSC-68 policy paper for the Eisenhower administration. Now the reconstituted CPD objected to détente policies and arm control measures that kept the United States locked in state of nuclear parity with the Soviet Union. CPD proved to be consequential for Reagan because it mobilized a large network of intellectuals and experts who were disillusioned by détente into working for rearmament and the reassertion of America abroad. This group of nearly 150 former government officials, business leaders, prominent academics, military officers, and other elites—including Reagan—helped build the case for a return to nuclear superiority and spread it among both the general public and the nation's intellectuals, specifically in opposition to strategic arms limitation talks.

Reagan often featured CPD arguments in his daily radio segments. In May 1977, he emphasized that the question facing U.S. policymakers in 1950 were the same as the ones defining U.S. national security decisions in the late 1970s: "Can we accept military inferiority? Shall we settle for [nuclear] parity or superiority? Are alliances essential?" To restore U.S. security and win the Cold War, he recommended the strategy of nuclear superiority first put forward by Nitze in NSC-68 in 1950 and later embraced by the Eisenhower administration when it endorsed "massive retaliation" as the deterrence posture of the United States. "Only by mustering superiority, beginning with a superiority of spirit," he argued, "can we stop the thunder of hobnailed [Soviet] boots on their march to world empire."[13] As Carter neared a strategic arms limitation agreement (SALT II) with the Soviet Union, Reagan stepped up his calls for strategic superiority. In late summer 1978, he argued on air, "if a nation values anything more than freedom, it will lose its freedom. . . . we can have the strategic superiority we had in 1962 if we have the will, or . . . will our national leaders face the 1980s alone, with nothing but a broad smile and good intentions to protect us in our final days?"[14]

Reagan began to make foreign and defense policy a central part of his 1980 campaign shortly after he and Carter accepted their respective party nominations for president. He reintroduced peace through strength as his principal vision of the U.S. role in the world while accepting the endorsement from the U.S. Veterans of Foreign Wars at a Chicago convention hall.[15] Until that point, Carter still enjoyed an advantage among voters who were concerned about foreign policy, despite Soviet intervention in Afghanistan, the Iran hostage crisis and the subsequent botched U.S. rescue attempt, and the failed ratification of SALT II that the president had signed with the Soviet leader Leonid Brezhnev. After Reagan's rollout of peace through strength, a significant number of voters signaled their approval of this new foreign policy platform.[16]

Reagan promised that peace through strength meant a revival of U.S. economic, military, and strategic advantages to restore the country's margin of safety. On the campaign trail he claimed that Carter's weak-willed leadership, cuts to U.S. strategic capacity, and poor relations with allies diminished the country's prestige and invited assault on American interests in both the Third World and Europe.[17] Carter's own diagnosis of U.S. problems in the world, often derided as a "crisis of confidence," played into Reagan's use of rhetorical binaries to further align the New Right with American exceptionalism.[18] On the strategic front, Reagan deemed the deployment of the MX ICBM and the accelerated production of the Ohio-class submarine and Trident missile, the B-1 bomber, and the enhanced radiation warhead (neutron bomb) necessary for rebuilding American strength. He claimed that these advancements would also tighten alliance bonds and were thus essential prerequisites to the resumption of arms control with the Soviet Union on equal terms.[19]

In fact, the Carter administration had initiated or accelerated many of the weapons initiatives and programs that Reagan associated with peace through strength, but it had failed to link those programs to a more comprehensive, long-term vision for U.S. security.[20] While the administration had advanced counterforce targeting, the Trident weapons system, and the MX missile, it failed to win allies in Congress, and that disconnect reactivated the antinuclear movement in the western United States, which had the effect of suppressing the peace movement's support for the president.[21]

Détente and the appearance of progress in arms control negotiations had dampened antinuclear enthusiasm in the 1970s.[22] Now, with both of them jeopardized by Carter's policies and Reagan's rhetoric, an antinuclear impulse emerged in American society. In the years between the Vietnam protests (which had consumed the attention of the peace movement) and Reagan's election, antinuclear activity had generally arisen from regional environmental concerns or nuclear power issues.[23] At the national level, antinuclear activism could be broken down into four factions: (1) expert groups such as the Federation of American Scientists (FAS), the Council for a Livable

World (CLW), and the Union of Concerned Scientists (UCS), based at the Massachusetts Institute of Technology; (2) professional organizations such as Physicians for Social Responsibility (PSR), revived by Helen Caldicott; (3) pacifist associations such as the Quaker-oriented American Friends Service Committee, Clergy and Laity Concerned, the interfaith Fellowship of Reconciliation (FOR), and the Women's International League for Peace and Freedom (WILPF); and (4) a few groups such as the National Committee for a Sane Nuclear Policy (SANE) that were specifically devoted to nuclear disarmament.[24] While the segmented antinuclear activism of the 1970s produced few tangible results, deep roots in local communities across the United States and the sustained tradition of expert dissent provided the necessary institutional and intellectual foundations for the antinuclear wave of the 1980s.

These groups expressed limited support for Carter. His decision with NATO allies to deploy intermediate-range nuclear weapons in Europe and to upgrade U.S. strategic nuclear forces provided the impetus for defense expert Randall Forsberg to issue a "Call to Halt the Nuclear Arms Race," an address delivered to roughly six hundred activists at a December 1979 meeting hosted by the antinuclear alliance Mobilization for Survival. Forsberg had developed her expertise during the several years she spent working as a nuclear analyst with the Stockholm International Peace Research Institute, and she based her appeal on the notion of a nuclear freeze. The effectiveness of the freeze concept lay in its simplicity and the fact that it could be broadly applied to any part of global nuclear arsenals. The first plank of the freeze recommended a bilateral agreement to halt testing, production, and deployment of nuclear missiles and aircraft. A second, unverifiable plank, called for a halt in warhead manufacturing and production of fissile material. Forsberg argued that a freeze would lock in existing levels of nuclear parity and claimed that the United States and the Soviet Union would each save an estimated $100 billion, which could be invested in the economic conversion of the defense industry as a step to further deescalate the Cold War.[25]

Much early support for the freeze came from veterans of the Vietnam War protests and voters whom Carter had won over in 1976 by promising to recast American foreign policy in moral terms. Four years later, Carter no longer had the support of the peace electorate and had failed to replace it with those in favor of a more aggressive approach to U.S. security. According to Sean Wilentz, "at home, Carter's newfound bellicosity further alienated liberal Democrats. . . . Among conservatives and neoconservatives, Carter's foreign policy, no matter how hawkish, would always pale beside the robust cold war militancy proclaimed by Ronald Reagan and the Republican right."[26]

Carter's drift toward a hardline defense policy has been a major factor in the recent development of the Carter-Reagan continuity thesis, which supposes that world events led both presidents to pursue similar policies. Other issues, including Carter's and Reagan's Latin America policies, positions on abortion, relationship to the leadership of the Federal Reserve, shared view of the political importance of faith and evangelicals, and insistence on the moral dimension of America's role in the world, make the continuity thesis a compelling interpretive framework rooted in a historical approach that emphasizes structural causes over individual agency.[27] However, the public's reaction to Carter and Reagan at the polls suggests that whatever continuities may have existed in policy terms were not reflected in public attitudes toward each candidate's leadership styles. Americans came to accept an individual agency–based narrative that saw Carter as reactive and Reagan as proactive. While their sense of Carter as a reactive president undermined the notion that the United States controlled its own destiny and ultimately doomed his chance for a second term, they saw Reagan's stance on the Soviet Union and the threat of nuclear war as proactive, and this allowed him to capitalize on the political potency of American exceptionalism.

Peace through strength proved to be an effective political strategy for Reagan to highlight Carter's reactive foreign policy and undermine the public's approval of his leadership, but the election simultaneously raised doubts as to whether Reagan's premise of nuclear superiority enjoyed a popular mandate. Although Reagan and his allies' opposition to SALT II hinged on the idea that arms control eroded American strength vis-à-vis the Soviet Union, a November 1980 Harris poll recorded that 84 percent of the American public favored an agreement to limit the size of Soviet and American nuclear arsenals. A running poll conducted by NBC from January 1978 to October 1980 showed that support for a new arms control agreement had never dipped below 62 percent.[28]

Reagan's campaign rhetoric revived antinuclear sentiment as a potentially significant political force. A freeze on superpower nuclear arsenals had already been put forward as a grassroots organizing principle before the start of the 1980 election. In 1979, Senator Mark O. Hatfield, a Republican from Oregon, drew support from peace groups such as FOR, Pax Christi USA, and Sojourners for his proposed amendment to SALT II, which called for a freeze in strategic forces.[29] Hatfield's freeze amendment inspired Randy Kehler, a Harvard-educated schoolteacher turned peace activist, to bring the freeze to the ballot box in Massachusetts. In 1979, Kehler had founded the Traprock Peace Center, based in Deerfield, Massachusetts. From there he launched a nine-month campaign to put the bilateral freeze initiative on the ballot in three congressional districts and sixty-two towns in the western part of the state. The initiative carried all three districts and thirty of the thirty-three towns where Reagan won the popular vote.[30] Kehler's success in western Massachusetts demonstrated that the freeze had political potential and appealed to veterans of the peace movement. The simultaneous success of the freeze on local ballots and Reagan's election victory laid the groundwork for nuclear war to become a defining issue of his presidential politics. One organizer quipped that "every time Reagan opens his mouth, the Freeze campaign doubles in size."[31]

The challenge, then, for the incoming administration was to manage public expectations for arms control agreements that might hinder the restoration of U.S. nuclear superiority, which Reagan deemed critical for rolling back communism and winning the Cold War. For both practical and philosophical reasons, he responded to this challenge by privileging the battle of ideas and the channeling of emotions over nuclear policy specifics.[32] He had a view of the of the presidency as a primarily inspirational office. Raymond Garthoff argues that "Reagan conceived of the president's role as essentially that of an actor."[33] To accept Garthoff's view of Reagan as an actor in the role of president does not deny the authenticity or conviction of his approach to U.S.-Soviet relations, but it does prompt a reconsideration of how the president constructed policy. With a trained actor in the office of president, public diplomacy assumed a major role for the Reagan administration in its formulation of nuclear policy, and officials placed significant emphasis on how the president might communicate nuclear ideas to the public. This is apparent in the recollections of former speechwriters and cabinet members who recall Reagan's immersion in the speechwriting process as a way to set policy.[34] Indeed, Ford remarked that Reagan was "one of the few political leaders I have ever met whose public speeches revealed more than his private conversations."[35]

Reagan's key tactic in the battle of ideas was to reject the notion of moral equivalency between the superpowers. In so doing, he also rejected arms control premised on MAD. An early example of this approach came just nine days after he assumed office. During his first press conference as president, Reagan confirmed his administration's intention to back away from arms control altogether when, in an answer to White House correspondent Sam Donaldson, he claimed,

> [The Soviets] have openly and publicly declared that the only morality they recognize is what will further their cause, meaning they reserve unto themselves the right to commit any crime, to lie, to cheat, in order to attain that, and that is moral, not immoral, and we operate on a differ-ent set of standards. I think when you do business with them, even at a détente, you keep that in mind.[36]

Reagan's appointments to key communication and foreign policy posts reflected the importance he placed on public opinion and the battle of ideas in U.S. foreign policy. He named more than thirty members of the CPD to various positions in his administration. This committee provided him with a ready-made private-sector foundation for public diplomacy through its strong ties to the Atlantic Treaty Association, a confederation of private national organizations founded in the 1950s to maximize support for the fledgling Atlantic Alliance. The British Atlantic Committee, in particular, embraced and disseminated CPD arguments in the press, and it would become a key facilitator between the peace through strength campaign of the Reagan administration and the pro-deterrence campaign of the Thatcher government.[37] In leading the assault on the Carter administration's nuclear policies, CPD had developed new polling techniques, a comprehensive media strategy, and alliances between labor organizations and peace through strength conservatives. CPD also worked with Richard Viguerie and a host of conservative activists who had predominantly focused on domestic and economic issues to deploy a new computerized mailing system to launch a fundraising and persuasion operation in opposition to arms control.

Those operations informed the administration's public affairs initiative in foreign policy. Morton Blackwell, a special assistant to the president in the White House Office of Public Liaison, who had worked closely with CPD, had already outlined what such a strategy should look like: "Why don't we bring the lessons we learned in domestic politics to bear on our problems in foreign policy? . . . We have tacked too many liberal scalps to our barn doors. We have had too many successful media events. Trained too many bright activists. Any reporter who ignores us risks being called blind to reality." Blackwell and other communications operatives encouraged the setup of new advocacy organizations around foreign policy issues that could organize media briefings and training programs for allies, develop strategies for discrediting and taking legal action against opponents, and lead fundraising operations to support all of the above with the hope of integrating the administration's foreign policy into the broader ideology of the New Right. The same strategy had to be applied internationally.[38] State Department aides agreed, insisting on the urgent development of a political and information program to offset growing antinuclear sentiment in Western Europe, which they largely attributed to an effective Soviet peace offensive.[39]

The Heritage Foundation emerged as a key ally of the Reagan administration in advancing the type of political and information program envisioned by newly minted government officials. Founded by Capitol Hill veterans Paul Weyrich and Ed Feulner in 1973, Heritage represented a new type of conservative think tank. It prioritized issue advocacy rather than the scholarly enterprise that defined the efforts of older think tanks such as the Brookings Institution, the Carnegie Foundation, or the U.K.'s Chatham House. Heritage's mission in the 1970s had been to reinvent the policymaking apparatus of conservatism, and the organization's focus on limited government and domestic social and economic issues had been critical to the emergence of the New Right as a force in American politics.[40]

When Feulner became president in 1977 he set the not so modest objective of making Heritage a central post of conservatism, requiring the organization to become a clearinghouse for conservative people, ideas, information, and money. His interest in public diplomacy tied directly to this lofty goal. In his estimation, how the United States presented itself to the world inevitably influenced the determination of American values at home.[41] With Reagan basing his pitch for peace through strength on an assertion of American moral fortitude, Feulner directed Heritage's first systematic dive into the foreign policy arena. The foundation set out to organize new groups in both the United States and the United Kingdom, leading the private dimension of the Reagan administration's public diplomacy that would spur the proliferation of conservative think tanks devoted to advocating for the cause of peace through strength, which would eventually remake the policymaking environment in Washington and London.[42]

For practical reasons, Reagan privileged the battle of ideas because it provided space and time for his administration to transform its criticisms of Carter into a comprehensive set of policies to govern nuclear cooperation with NATO allies and nuclear competition with the Soviet Union. Emerging centers of bureaucratic power primarily debated two points: the degree to which arms control should be insulated from or interconnected to the broader range of U.S.-Soviet relations, and how much consideration should be given to public opinion in forming policy.[43] Some officials, especially those loyal to Defense Secretary Caspar Weinberger and his top aides, Assistant Secretary of Defense for Global Strategic Affairs Richard Perle and Undersecretary for Defense Policy Fred Iklé, fundamentally opposed arms control or any treaty that constrained U.S. military power and limited pathways to regain strategic superiority. Cautious arms control proponents included Secretary of State Alexander Haig and his deputies Richard Burt and Lawrence Eagleburger, who supported arms control in part because of its importance to NATO allies.[44] The eventual confirmation of Arms Control and Disarmament Agency (ACDA) officials further complicated matters. ACDA Director Eugene Rostow's appointment of CPD and arms control veteran Paul Nitze to lead INF negotiations satisfied neither Haig's State Department nor the anti–arms control contingent that took root in the Pentagon and the staff of the National Security Council. Nitze's initial opposition to the dual-track decision and then subsequent determination that the United States should adhere to the agreement to demonstrate its reliability to the alliance it professed to lead challenged the impulses of both sides of Reagan's foreign policy team.[45]

British Warnings about the INF Problem

The Reagan administration's response to the INF issue provided the first major indicator that public diplomacy considerations might play a larger role in foreign and defense policymaking. Reagan inherited a connection between the dual-track decision and strategic arms control that Carter had forged out of political necessity. At the beginning of Carter's term in office, NATO allies began voicing the concern that strategic arms control had unleashed a process of "decoupling" Western European security from that of the continental United States.[46] Without preponderant strategic nuclear capabilities and in a position of assumed conventional and theater nuclear inferiority on the European continent, would the United States be willing to risk its own safety to defend Western Europe from a Soviet invasion? In exchange for European support for SALT II, Carter agreed in December 1979 to the dual-track decision to deploy INF weapons and simultaneously begin negotiating the reduction of American and Soviet INF systems in Europe.[47] In theory, separating INF systems from strategic arms control and placing them in their own set of negotiations guaranteed that the United States would not sacrifice weapons designed for European deterrence in order to retain certain strategic advantages in a grand deal with the Soviet Union. With little time or political capital left, however, Carter left INF negotiations to be largely defined by Reagan's administration.

The rise of transnational civil society made Soviet active measures and authentic antinuclear protest linked to leftist politics an acute challenge for U.S. public diplomacy. Even before the prospect of Reagan's nuclear buildup stoked the anxieties of European publics, antinuclear opinion had begun to factor into the Thatcher government's calculations concerning alliance politics, nuclear modernization, and arms control. The British Campaign for Nuclear Disarmament (CND) had initially increased its activity and membership in response to NATO's neutron bomb political crisis in 1978, with the organization expanding to 102 local chapters and more than 3,000 members.[48] The neutron bomb controversy opened a new chapter in the nuclear arms race, in which well-financed Soviet active measures sought to create an advantage by exploiting the peace movement to mobilize western public opinion against deployments of new nuclear weapons. A U.S. intelligence assessment from 1980 pegged the cost of the Soviet campaign to undermine the neutron bomb at more than $100 million.[49]

The dual-track decision also provided an impetus for revival of public debate and led the veteran CND activist and prominent historian E. P. Thompson to launch the European Nuclear Disarmament movement (END). CND and END had jointly developed into a formidable organizing network for European antinuclear movements, one capable of mobilizing hundreds of thousands of demonstrators in coordinated protests in London and across Europe's major cities by the time Reagan took office.[50] END in particular, because it was an English-language coordinating body of transnational activism and was making the case for both western- and eastern-bloc disarmament, became a primary target for Soviet active measures.[51]

British officials found Reagan's transition from campaigner to commander-in-chief particularly trying. They were uneasy about the president's struggle to transform his hawkish election rhetoric, which had been crafted for a domestic audience, into statements of reassurance intended to build alliance solidarity around issues of nuclear modernization and arms control. Douglas

Hurd, Britain's minister of state for Europe, commented, "The danger about the rhetoric now coming out of Washington is not that it will upset the Russians but that it will upset our own opinion in Europe."[52] Throughout the summer of 1981, the U.K. delegation to NATO's Nuclear Planning Group produced a critical analysis of Europe's antinuclear movement and the Soviet peace offensive, which impressed upon the U.S. delegation the scope of public opposition to INF and the current U.S. approach to managing the dual-track process.[53]

Charles Z. Wick, Reagan's long-time friend from the film industry and a newly installed director of USIA, led the administration's initial response to the problem posed by European public opinion. Importantly for the U.K's influence, Wick's view of European publics filtered through his long-standing connections to Britain, which dated back to the 1950s, when he had served as Winston Churchill's literary agent for the U.S. market and had produced television programs for the BBC.[54] Wick was a former big-band leader and a friend of countless A-list celebrities. He brought a distinctly unorthodox style to USIA that created tension with career public diplomats, who chafed at their new boss's deep suspicion of federal bureaucracy and perceived shallow understanding of U.S. foreign affairs. What Wick lacked in knowledge and experience in government and foreign affairs he made up for with his personal relationship with Reagan. Wick and Reagan had been close friends and neighbors in California. Their families spent the Christmas holidays together and Reagan's son, Ron, Jr., had lived with the Wicks for a year so that he could finish high school while his father took up residence in the governor's mansion. Wick was also a prolific fundraiser, and he had chaired Reagan's inaugural committee and organized the grandest and most expensive set of inaugural celebrations in U.S. history at the time. His appointment to lead USIA brought bureaucratic clout to the agency, which for more than a decade had been marginalized through budget cuts and foreign policy turf wars with traditional diplomats in the State Department.[55] Not since the days of Edward Murrow and John F. Kennedy had the USIA director had such a direct line to the president.[56]

Wick's relationship with Reagan made USIA into a prioritized instrument for winning over European public opinion and triumphing in the Cold War. In autumn 1981, he launched Project Truth, an initiative to counter Soviet disinformation and restore the confidence of international publics in U.S. foreign policy.[57] Seeing Project Truth as critical to the battle of ideas, Reagan directed the State Department, the Defense Department, and the National Security Council (NSC) to fully cooperate with Wick's USIA on Project Truth. In effect, the initiative was both a cause and a consequence of the reintegration of covert psychological operations run by the intelligence community and the softer side of public diplomacy, such as cultural programs and radio broadcasts managed by USIA. The movement of career intelligence operatives into key public diplomacy posts across the U.S. government, especially Herb Romerstein to USIA, portended a cultural change in the agency.[58] For more than a decade USIA had avoided highly politicized issues and sought greater separation from the intelligence community, but these steps had made it less important to U.S. foreign policy. With the Reagan reforms and Charlie Wick in charge, USIA suddenly, according to John Lenczowski (at the time a State Department special advisor working on public diplomacy), went from "cowering in the shadows as a third class citizen in U.S. foreign policy to now being the tip of the spear."[59]

Heightened cooperation among public diplomats, the intelligence community, and the defense establishment produced defense information materials and unclassified assessments of the Soviet threat, which for months British and European officials had insisted were critical to making the public case for INF deployment.[60] The 1981 release of a report titled *Soviet Military Power* was especially successful. U.S. officials circulated this glossy, in-depth examination of Soviet defense infrastructure, capabilities, and aims to public-opinion makers, media, government officials, and diplomats in Europe to reinforce the case for the dual-track decision.[61] Under the auspices of Project Truth, a semi-regular Soviet propaganda alert was paired with the "wireless file," a computer-based network that increased the speed and amount of information flowing from USIA headquarters to public affairs officers posted in European embassies. By October 1981, this had created a rapid-response system that dramatically improved the U.S. government's ability to counter Soviet nuclear narratives.[62]

Reformed public diplomacy operations formed the vanguard of the Reagan administration's initiative on the emerging political crisis over INF, but considerations around European public opinion kept the thrust of the administration's INF policies in flux. A rapport had developed between British representatives and Secretary of State Haig, so they made him their primary channel to the Reagan White House on the INF issue.[63] Haig had grown sympathetic to Europe's decoupling fears during his time as NATO's supreme allied commander in Europe, a position he held from late 1974 to July 1979. His trust in these European partners lay behind his advocacy for early negotiations to alleviate public pressure on NATO governments as they prepared for INF deployments.

Secretary of Defense Weinberger, in contrast, opposed early negotiations on any class of nuclear weapons. He saw the withholding of arms control talks as the best way for the United States to put pressure on the Soviet Union's international behavior.[64] Weinberger's deputy, Richard Perle, even organized an internal campaign to dissolve U.S. commitment to the dual-track decision altogether.[65] INF negotiations conducted within the SALT framework initially had been promised to the Europeans to alleviate their concerns about the decoupling of their security from that of the United States. The compromise put in place between the administration's rivals made the relationship between INF and strategic arms as ambiguous as possible. Intelligence assessments suggested to policymakers that the administration could delay negotiations on strategic weapons by relying on INF talks as a favorable stand-in to satisfy the Soviet Union.[66] General Edward Rowny, who hoped to lead both strategic and European arms control negotiations after being passed over as ACDA director, forfeited the INF portfolio to Nitze after the decision to split talks.[67] By September 1981, Haig and Andrei Gromyko, the long-serving Soviet minister of foreign affairs, had committed their governments to INF negotiations. These were scheduled to begin in late November in Geneva.[68]

Ahead of the INF talks, Reagan announced that the administration had completed its comprehensive review of U.S. nuclear forces. The president's five-point modernization program introduced in early October included the construction and deployment of one hundred B-1 bombers and the deployment of cruise missiles on existing bombers; the development of the Trident D-5 SLBM and sea-launched cruise missiles; the completion of MX missiles, which would be deployed in an as-yet-to-be-determined basing mode; the improvement of command, communications, and control systems; and the revitalization of U.S. strategic and civil defense.[69] Reagan claimed that the $180 billion modernization package would restore a "margin of safety" and close the "window of vulnerability," problems that Reagan argued had emerged out of U.S. arms control efforts in the 1970s.[70] U.S. nuclear targeting posture articulated in National Security Decision Directive (NSDD) 13 had produced a second outcome that hindered INF negotiations. Though consistent with Carter's nuclear targeting directives, NSDD 13 reemphasized the targeting of Soviet leadership and military targets to prevail in the event of nuclear war, which appeared more threatening when considered alongside the Reagan administration's statements about a potential war.[71]

Public diplomacy gaffes from members of the Reagan administration continued to fuel the European antinuclear movement and reignited decoupling concerns across the Atlantic that played directly into the hands of the Soviet peace offensive. In late October, following the announcement of modernization plans and a targeting posture, the president had unintentionally suggested that nuclear war could be confined to the European theater.[72] A dispute between Haig and Weinberger over the validity of firing a "nuclear warning shot" over Europe in the event of Soviet aggression appeared, at best, to be another public relations blunder.[73]

These public missteps increased support for antinuclear campaigns in Europe, especially in the United Kingdom, where the CND's late October rally in central London caught Thatcher's government off guard. The composition of the protest provided further proof to Reagan and fellow NATO heads of state that the views of Europeans born in the postwar years accounted for the surge in antinuclear opinion that was threatening the political foundations of the dual-track decision. Their memories of the Cold War were not the same as Reagan's, who recalled the U.S. rebuilding of Europe in the 1950s as justification for a return to nuclear superiority. Instead, they recalled the horrors of American military hubris in Vietnam and the troubles befalling the United States in the 1970s. NATO officials framed the conversion of antinuclear generations into deterrence believers as an alliance security objective.[74] This recognition of Thatcher's political vulnerability hit both Whitehall and the U.S. State Department hard as U.S. officials had considered a Conservative Party government in Britain to be one of two key European pillars upholding the dual-track strategy.[75] Richard Allen warned Reagan, "We must make a greater effort to appeal to British and European public opinion. . . . Thatcher's domestic position. . . . is getting more vulnerable, and the possibility of a Tory defeat, with the present government replaced by a coalition government, cannot be discounted."[76]

U.S. arms control principals agreed on the fundamental premise that no conceivable INF deal could be reached by Washington and Moscow. Instead, U.S. officials set their sights on using negotiations to limit the effectiveness of Soviet peace propaganda in Europe. The real debate between the Defense

Department, on the one hand, and ACDA and the State Department, on the other, came down to a commitment to the "zero-option."[77] While the concept came from West German Chancellor Helmut Schmidt's suggestion of *Null-Lösung*, Perle took ownership of it within the administration, seeing it as a clever way to prevent an INF agreement without upsetting NATO allies, given its West German origins.[78] Under this framework, Reagan offered the Soviets nondeployment of all intermediate-range nuclear missiles in exchange for the complete dismantling of equivalent Soviet systems.[79]

Reagan initially questioned the validity of the zero-option on strategic grounds. He feared that it would leave NATO vulnerable to Soviet conventional superiority. The president came to favor the idea only after Haig assured him of the idea's German origins and Weinberger promised that it would "capture world opinion."[80] Haig, though, cautioned that an immediate turn to the zero-option without first advocating for some low and acceptable level of reductions could set a bad precedent for the future by possibly encouraging the Soviets to pursue the zero-option in the separate negotiations on strategic arms reduction talks (START), which might compromise the core deterrent force of the U.S. nuclear arsenal and prevent the Reagan administration from reestablishing strategic superiority.[81]

The final NSC meeting determining the administration's first-round INF proposal exemplified the internal discord in the administration over the purpose of arms control. Weinberger stood by his view that arms control existed solely for public diplomacy reasons. Rostow claimed that the "primary objective [of INF negotiations] is the unity of our Alliance, not getting an agreement," but rejected the idea that allies should have a voice in U.S. arms control policy; Weinberger loyalists agreed that European public opinion must not constrain U.S. nuclear policy.[82] Haig preferred to orient INF talks around robust European consultations. On this point he asserted his belief in the State Department's supremacy in foreign policy, snapping at fellow cabinet-level officials, "I have to decide how we conduct diplomacy with our allies."[83] Disagreement over the zero-option at the cabinet level revealed Haig's ferocity. His disregard for Reagan's attempts to reconcile the cabinet's attitudes on INF marked the beginning of his end as secretary of state.

For public diplomacy to be a successful component of nuclear policymaking, Reagan had to conceive of the public in transnational rather than national terms. This conceptual reworking made public diplomacy a form of political communication distinct from campaign rhetoric. Nonetheless, it also had to remain consistent with such rhetoric to avoid an impression of a disorganized and reactive administration. Acknowledging the direct link between U.S. statements on nuclear war and rising antinuclear sentiment among the British public, a rise that jeopardized Thatcher's political standing, was the first step to effecting change in how the administration conceived of the public when discussing nuclear politics. These considerations shaped the president's first major address on arms control, given at the National Press Club on November 18, 1981, in which he embedded his offer of the zero-option in visionary rhetoric to target a younger generation in Europe.[84] The speech was delivered at 2 p.m. Eastern Time so that it would reach European audiences in prime time.[85] Thatcher, who was in Bonn for talks with West German leaders, celebrated the speech as the most significant of the Reagan presidency.[86] For her, the president's offer of a zero-option demonstrated not a negotiating position but a serious commitment to the task of public diplomacy.

Even though the zero-option appeared to be a public diplomacy triumph, some Reagan officials argued that it could only be regarded as a temporary position. Richard Burt, the director of political-military affairs at the State Department, believed that the zero-option was "good for now, but in six months to a year . . . maybe we ought to have a plan B."[87] Burt realized, along with many in the State Department who kept close tabs on European politics, that the INF issue had come to represent a broader clash of politics and ideologies in Europe, especially in Britain. As that political struggle evolved, pressure mounted on the Reagan administration to adjust its public diplomacy in order to secure support for INF deployments.

CHAPTER TWO

BRITAIN'S CHOICE
Disarmament, Deterrence, and Democracy

[The Campaign for Nuclear Disarmament] is now supported right across the spectrum, by academics and trade unionists, Liberals and Labourites, ecologists and Welsh nationalists, Church men and women, feminists, and by the youth culture in the popular music world.
—E. P. Thompson, *Protest and Survive* (1980)

IN OCTOBER 1979, the famed English historian and longtime Campaign for Nuclear Disarmament (CND) member E. P. Thompson sat unsettled in his living room, having learned from the television news that American cruise missiles were coming to the United Kingdom.[1] He was not alone. A few months later, Ken Coates from the Bertrand Russell Peace Foundation phoned Thompson to propose that the two co-author an appeal for a nuclear-free Europe. Out of their collaboration—along with substantial input from Mary Kaldor, a science policy expert at the University of Sussex; CND leaders Bruce Kent and Dan Smith; and Dorothy Thompson, the preeminent historian of the Chartists and E.P.'s wife—came an "Appeal for European Nuclear Disarmament."[2] On April 28, 1980, the authors held a press conference in the House of Commons. Flanked by Tony Benn, a member of Parliament (MP) and a leading figure in the Labour Party, Thompson and Coates opened with the warning that "we are entering the most dangerous decade in human history." They condemned designs for limited nuclear war, proclaimed the moral bankruptcy of the superpowers, bewailed the bipolar framework of the Cold War, and argued for a nuclear-free zone stretching from "Poland to Portugal."[3] Even before the authors publicly released this appeal, more than sixty MPs, along with powerful union leaders such as Moss Evans of the Transport and General Workers Union and Arthur Scargill of the National Union of Mineworkers as well as an impressive list of academics, bishops, and artists, had declared their support and signaled the dramatic rise of antinuclear sentiment across the country.[4]

Three events had directly triggered the sharp increase in British nuclear fear, and keyed the revival of the antinuclear movement, headed by CND and the European Nuclear Disarmament campaign (END), which integrated professional organizations, church parishes, women's groups, producers of popular culture, the scientific community, and the Labour Party into a crusade for unilateral nuclear disarmament. First, British nuclear anxiety spiked with the Soviet deployment of SS-20 missiles in 1976, followed by NATO's December 1979 announcement of the dual-track decision that accepted the basing of nuclear armed cruise missiles on British soil as a response to Soviet actions. Second, the agreement to purchase Trident SLBMs from the United States to upgrade the British nuclear deterrent, revealed during a defense debate in January 1980 in the House of Commons, raised public concerns about the inertia of the arms race and the United Kingdom's involvement in it. Third, the public reveal of the civil defense pamphlet *Protect and Survive,* a ham-fisted attempt by the Home Office to convince British citizens that simple precautions could ensure their survival in the event of nuclear war, engendered criticism of the government's ability to truly grasp and manage the nuclear threat. In addition to these three events, U.S.-European disagreement over the neutron bomb, the collapse of the SALT II agreement, controversial developments in U.S. nuclear-targeting policy, and Ronald Reagan's anti-Soviet rhetoric validated peace movement claims that incremental progress in arms control had failed to produce a safer world.

In response to the antinuclear revival, the Thatcher government initially relied on organs of the Conservative Party and a transatlantic network of private think tanks to develop the pronuclear public diplomacy plan. British think tanks such as the Centre for Policy Studies and the Coalition for Peace through Security (CPS) readily adopted a new model for policy advocacy that had been pioneered in the United States by the Heritage Foundation. Thatcher's Conservatives believed they could exploit the Labour Party's adoption of unilateral disarmament for political gain by suggesting the opposition had been overtaken by leftist radicals. As the British deterrence debate became more entangled with developments in the United States, the Thatcher government's cooperation with the Reagan administration on combating the transnational antinuclear movement became a cornerstone of a broader revolution in U.S. public diplomacy in Europe and around the world.

From 1979 until the end of 1982, the disarmament debate intensified the contest in British society between Thatcher's "Victorian values," which appealed to a "strong current of moral traditionalism," and the shifting domestic values of the political left that had been infused with elements of radicalism as a result of Labour Party reforms and the revival of antinuclear activism.[5] Arguments over the semantics of peace and war animated the conflict between deterrence advocates and disarmament activists, as both groups accused the other of distorting language and logic to manipulate the public to accept their nuclear policies and ideological designs for British society. Leftwing firebrands such as Tony Benn were especially adept at using the nuclear debate to promote their vision of "moral democracy."[6] At its core, moral democracy demanded government transparency, the equal participation of an informed citizenry, and social solidarity through the empowerment of local government and constituencies. Success for both democracy reform and the disarmament agenda hinged on CND's ability to channel the efforts of scientists, Christian ethicists, radical women protestors, and trade unions into a cogent movement.

To Protest and Survive

Two months before Thompson and his allies announced their "Appeal," the press had exposed Home Office plans to release a revised version of the 1950s civil defense pamphlet *Protect and Survive*, drawing critical attention to the broader government approach to assuaging rising public fear of nuclear war.[7] This revelation followed an impassioned plea from the respected Oxford military historian Michael Howard in the January 30 edition of *the Times,* in which he begged the government to provide the public with more robust civil defense guidelines.[8]

Thompson and Howard were inverted images of one another. Thompson, the country's foremost disarmament intellectual and a prominent Marxist historian, was a veteran of CND and a leading voice of the transnational antinuclear movement. Howard, an archetypical defense intellectual and a pathbreaking military historian, had established the influential War Studies Department at King's College London and had cofounded the International Institute of Strategic Studies, a leading British think tank on defense and deterrence issues. Perhaps more importantly, Howard was a member of an elite group of academics who periodically advised the prime minister on foreign and defense issues at her country retreat at Chequers.

Thompson, who had been developing concepts of militarized and police states in his academic work, found civil defense planning to be a thinly veiled attempt to marginalize dissident voices.[9] Shortly after releasing "Appeal for European Nuclear Disarmament," he published the pamphlet *Protest and Survive* as both a critique of *Protect and Survive* and a direct challenge to Howard's nuclear warfighting assumptions that had called for increased expenditure on civil defense. According to Thompson, Howard deliberately employed the coded language of defense intellectuals, with the intent of persuading the public to accept the premise of nuclear war without thinking through the moral implications of NATO's nuclear posture.[10] Thompson concluded:

> The deformation of culture commences within language itself. It makes possible the disjunction between the rationality and moral sensibility of individual men and women and the effective political and military processes. A certain kind of "realist" and "technical" vocabulary effects a closure which seals out the imagination, and prevents the reason from following the most manifest sequence of cause and consequence. It habituates the mind to nuclear holocaust be reducing everything to a flat level of normality. By habituating us to certain expectations, it not only encourages resignation—it also beckons the event.[11]

Thompson reached his conclusion after evaluating the importance of cruise missiles, Polaris and Trident second-strike capabilities, and the strategic doctrines—such as limited nuclear war—that underpinned notions of deterrence. Similar to the straightforward freeze proposal animating American antinuclear activism, *Protest and Survive* demystified nuclear knowledge for ordinary Britons while offering a simple solution: a European nuclear-free zone.[12]

Howard published his riposte to Thompson in the well-known anticommunist literary magazine *Encounter*. The American conservative intellectual Irving Kristol had cofounded *Encounter* in the 1950s as a British corollary *Commentary* and the *Public Interest,* which appealed to American audiences. The CIA had also covertly funded *Encounter* in its early days, at a time when psychological operations and public diplomacy were seen as two sides of the same coin. Howard's article accused Thompson of hypocrisy, arguing that abandoning deterrence ideas and technical terms in favor of peace language was a perilous simplification of the debate and set up the false notion that a nuclear-free Europe was both less dangerous and morally superior to civil defense and cruise missile deployment. Howard also blamed Thompson for framing opposition to the antinuclear left as a uniformed and monolithic extension of the nuclear establishment intent on quashing the civil liberties of British citizens. In Howard's view, leftist paranoia overlooked the primary objective of nuclear deterrence: "to preserve independence of a political system in which it is possible for E. P. Thompson—unlike his opposite numbers in the Soviet Union—to Protest and Survive."[13]

Howard's and Thompson's row carried over into the prestigious Oxford Union debating society, and arguments there further revealed the scope of disagreement between disarmament intellectuals and deterrence thinkers. Howard articulated a vision of peace maintained by a closed world of inconspicuous bureaucrats, lawyers, diplomats, businessmen, and political leaders who understood nuclear weapons as a means of reconciling the differences between culturally and ideologically distinct societies. He and other likeminded defense intellectuals valued open civil society domestically but believed it to be a liability in conflict with authoritarian regimes because social factors constrained the West's ability to translate its technological supremacy into an operational deterrent. This view emphasized the barriers between national public spheres. In contrast, Thompson and an emerging network of disarmament intellectuals stressed the role of the transnational public sphere in producing a deeper understanding and expectation of the requirements for peace within and between the western and eastern blocs.[14]

Protest and Survive stimulated debate and revitalized CND and was the first of several other bestselling antinuclear pamphlets that condemned the pernicious effects of civil defense on multiple levels of society, from the family to local government. Technical misrepresentations by the Home Office spurred a political reawakening among scientific experts, one that revolved around protest against civil defense. Their ensuing anti–civil defense campaigns often pushed local governments to reflect on their own complicity in the nuclear status quo. Should they aid the central government in upholding its deterrence relationship with the Soviet bloc or respond to the moral demands of their constituencies by rejecting civil defense regulations in favor of alternative defense policies. Because civil defense was a highly visible and local manifestation of Britain's nuclear status that pervaded the entire country, these criticisms were devastating.

After World War II, civil defense responsibilities had devolved to local authorities, and in the 1980s this set the conditions for a showdown between Thatcher's central government and municipal Labour governments. The 1948

Civil Defense Act had laid out a planning structure in which the central government relied extensively on cooperation from local authorities to carry out required preparations.[15] During the détente years, funding cuts led to an increased emphasis on individual responsibility and a decreased reliance on scientific expertise. In 1973 the Home Office changed the term *civil defense* to *home defense* and promulgated a new definition that emphasized securing of the country from internal threats and subversives as well as the use of alternative machinery for the continuity of government.[16] In 1968 funding cuts led to the gradual elimination of the civilian-staffed Civil Defense Corps and then to the 1976 dissolution of the Standing Advisory Committee on Home Defense, which had been comprised of one hundred scientists who had provided much-needed technical analysis.[17] By the end of the 1970s the prohibitive prospective costs of a public shelter program had led to a policy of "shelter in place," which aligned with the ideology of New Right Conservatives, who touted the value of individualism and self-reliance and the public's need to break its dependence on the state.

War games demonstrated how these policy developments put central and local government into conflict. Operation Square Leg, a military and civil-preparedness exercise coordinated with the NATO war game Operation Crusader, laid bare how intensification of the arms race had exacerbated the political challenges and problems of physical infrastructure for emergency planners. The scenario began just after noon on Thursday, September 19, 1980, when more than 120 nuclear bombs, packing an explosive power of 200 megatons, hypothetically rained down on Britain. Wave 1 struck Britain's military infrastructure, the most densely packed in the world. U.S. cruise missile bases at Greenham Common in Newbury and Molesworth in Northampton were utterly destroyed. Monitoring and communications stations linked to the submersible second strike were annihilated. Bombs dropped on nearly every other target of strategic importance. Between 1 and 3 p.m., wave 2 detonated over Birmingham, Newcastle, Sheffield, Liverpool, Leeds, and other important urban-industrial centers. Oddly enough, the lightly targeted city of London survived, though like nearly every square mile of the country it was covered with radioactive fallout. Parliament had been suspended a week earlier under threat of nuclear war. In the aftermath of the attack, civil defense authorities struggled to maintain social control from twelve decrepit bunkers spread across the United Kingdom. In the name of maintaining "law and order," police rounded up CND activists and radical elements of the Labour Party who were deemed to be "Red Peace Trotskyists."[18]

The Square Leg target list and complete disrepair of civil defense bunkers and facilities came to public attention thanks to Duncan Campbell's October exposé in the *New Statesman*. That information vindicated public scrutiny of Home Office civil defense guidelines, which had been ongoing throughout 1980.[19] For instance, in March, the BBC documentary *If the Bomb Drops had* presented civil defense as a system to retain government legitimacy rather than a program to protect Britons from nuclear war.[20] Square Leg validated Thompson's criticisms of the targeting assumptions that had supposedly justified the survival recommendations in *Protect and Survive*.

CND's bestselling pamphlet, *Civil Defence: The Cruelest Confidence Trick*, released in 1980 and again in 1982, disclosed further shortcomings. The author, Philip Bolsover, argued that spending on civil defense demonstrated the Thatcher government's priorities, which he saw as a focus on undermining the political opposition rather than addressing pressing social problems such as the funding crises confronting the National Health Service, the education system, and the housing industry.[21] CND chair Joan Ruddock attributed the significant boost in the antinuclear movement's recruitment in 1980 to the revelations of Square Leg and to regular and persistent civil defense criticism.[22] The development of disarmament as a local political issue would become a determining factor in the Labour Party's electoral reforms at the end of the year.

CND's resurgence made nuclear politics a feature of the Labour's Party's civil war. In January 1980, the U.K.'s defense secretary, Francis Pym, revealed that former prime minister James Callaghan's government had pursued the procurement of Trident and had authorized the Chevaline project—a secret £1 billion modernization of the British deterrent—despite a public commitment to the 1974 Labour manifesto that renounced next-generation strategic weapons.[23] The nuclear modernization issue perfectly suited Tony Benn's advocacy for the democratization of the Labour Party, a way to make its officials more accountable to constituents, which accounted for his prominent role in publicizing Thompson's and Coates's "Appeal" in the House of Commons.[24] An early demonstration of CND's growing strength came in June during a conference held in London's Wembley Stadium, where 20,000 protestors derided Callaghan and his former foreign secretary, David Owen, for their speeches supporting Trident and cruise missiles. Benn, on the other hand, drew a standing ovation for his call for disarmament.[25]

Shortly before the Labour Party's annual conference at Blackpool in October 1980, CND organized an 80,000-person rally in Trafalgar Square. The demonstration was Britain's biggest in twenty years, and CND organizers recruited local groups across the United Kingdom to join its network.[26] CND's structure, which closely resembled that of a political party, allowed it to dominate the British antinuclear movement. Member-led specialist sections that reported to the national council organized lobbying activities with the major political parties, Christian churches, trade unions, environmentalists, young voters, international organizations, and entertainers. Full-time employees staffed committees devoted to projects and demonstrations, parliamentary elections, finance and fundraising, and organization membership. The relaunch of CND's monthly magazine, *Sanity,* gave the movement a publication of record and a tool for expanding its donor base. Thousands of semiautonomous local chapters expanded the CND donor network and created a grassroots infrastructure for influencing antinuclear sentiment in every corner of the British Isles.

Other groups also emerged, such as the Greenham Common Women (GCW), Scientists against Nuclear Arms (SANA), the Medical Campaign against Nuclear Weapons (MCANW), Clergy against Nuclear Arms, Teachers for Peace, and Journalists against Nuclear Extermination, but most had deep ties to CND via either an overlap in leadership or shared membership.[27] CND's demands for the unilateral cancelation of Trident, the elimination of the independent deterrent, eviction of U.S. nuclear forces from the British mainland, and coercion of NATO to adopt a non-nuclear defense policy dominated the disarmament movement.

While CND built its grassroots political strength by organizing large political rallies, Labour Party reforms empowered constituent Labour parties at the expense of trade unions and the parliamentary party. In effect, this weakened the Labour Party's pronuclear elements, which remained most influential in the parliamentary party, and strengthened antinuclear politicians, whose power base was rooted in local constituencies—many of which were being organized by CND. But neither Benn, the antinuclear advocate and party reformer, nor Denis Healey, the preferred pronuclear candidate of former prime minister Callaghan, were victorious in the January 1981 leadership contest. Instead, latecomer Michael Foot, a veteran of CND, won the leadership contest as a unity candidate—a surprising label, considering his reluctance to join previous Labour cabinets and his twenty-plus years of backbench antagonism toward party leadership.[28] Foot's highest rate of support came from MPs who favored unilateral disarmament; they accounted for 95 out of his 139 endorsements.[29] Mindful of his support among unilateralists and aware that election reforms gave more power to constituent Labour parties that were increasingly influenced by the growing number of local CND chapters, Foot made disarmament a top party priority. From his victory stump, he exhorted, "The dismantling of those weapons is essential for the survival of our world."[30]

Likewise, trade unions increasingly came to accept antinuclear ideas as the basis for their political and economic positions. CND renewed its courtship of trade unions in 1975 with the establishment of its trade union specialist section amid a resurgence of union power. Trade unions' growing strength in the 1970s came from rising membership as well as from Prime Minister Harold Wilson's implementation of the social contract policy.[31] Gaining union support had been a key aim of CND in the 1950s and 1960s, but widespread union endorsement of unilateralism had remained a difficult sell, given that the British defense industry was one of the largest sectors of employment for union labor. Industrial decline throughout the 1970s compelled union shop leaders to rethink their reliance on defense production. In 1976, shop stewards at Lucas Aerospace drew up designs to reorganize factories for industrial production to meet social needs instead of retaining redundant capacities that all but guaranteed layoffs in the defense and aviation industries. Lucas Plan proponents emphasized the social utility of goods rather than exchange value to create a more equitable and sustainable economy that freed industry from the detrimental effects of command management and design required by weapons production.[32] Similar plans appeared on shop floors throughout the U.K.'s defense industry, including in the factories of premier contractors such as Vickers and British Aerospace.[33]

During his tenure as secretary of state for industry, Tony Benn had promoted the Lucas Plan, and it subsequently inspired the creation of the Centre for Alternative Industry and Technological Systems. The Centre's work on conversion planning rapidly gained the attention of union representatives, notably the leaders of the Transport and General Workers Union (TGWU).[34] The center's emphasis on production for social utility and human needs at the expense of exchange value ran counter to Thatcher's free-market principles while aligning with the moral focus of many in the peace movement. By 1980, CND's trade union arm and END's trade union committee had joined

TGWU to promote the compatibility of defense conversion and unilateral disarmament.[35] Conversion councils were set up across the United Kingdom through coordinated efforts among universities, scientists, Nuclear Weapon Free Zone (NWFZ) authorities, CND, and trade unions. The most significant of these was the Conversion Council of London, with £75 million in funding. As its director, Bill Nevin, explained, conversion councils "provide[d] the bridge from the peace movement to labour."[36]

TGWU relied on the work of conversion councils and peace movement allies to help it push through a motion for unilateral disarmament at the 1981 Trade Union Congress's (TUC's) annual meeting. CND fringe meetings swamped regional and national conferences of unions and the Labour Party, and disarmament measures came to dominate the political agenda.[37] As the largest constituent representative of TUC's nearly 12.5 million members, TGWU brought along several other major unions, including the National Union of Public Employees, the National Union of Mineworkers, and the Civil and Public Services Association, to demand an unequivocal declaration on disarmament and economic conversion from the Labour Party.[38]

Foot's election and Labour's shift leftward on disarmament led to several high-profile defections from the party's leadership in 1981. David Owen, Roy Jenkins, Shirley Williams, and William Rodgers, known as the Gang of Four, cited unilateral disarmament as one of their primary motives for splitting from Labour to form the pro-multilateral disarmament Social Democratic Party (SDP).[39] Labour Party leaders who favored multilateral rather than unilateral disarmament had encountered multiple prongs of opposition within the party. While the secession of several of Labour's ex-cabinet ministers and more than twenty MPs put antinuclear activists in a stronger position to influence Labour Party policy and organization, it also complicated CND's long-term electoral strategy.

In Labour Party reforms and the split that resulted in the SDP, Thatcher's political advisors identified unilateral nuclear disarmament as one of the main weaknesses of Labour's incoming leadership to exploit.[40] The Conservative Research Department (CRD), which served as the conservatives' strategy arm and policy nursery, saw Foot's ascension to Labour leader as a hostile radical takeover of the Labour Party. In response, CRD undertook an anti-CND campaign, which had two goals: to prevent unilateral disarmament from becoming the policy of the United Kingdom, and to marginalize the Labour Party in Parliament by branding it as a group of radical unilateral disarmers. The Reagan administration came to share this mission, once the Labour Party formally adopted unilateral disarmament as its policy.[41]

Thatcher's government initially outsourced much of its anti-CND operation to a rapidly developing transatlantic network of think tanks. Initially, the British Atlantic Committee (BAC) seemed to be the perfect choice for coordinating the various components of the conservative counter-campaign.[42] Established in the 1950s to support NATO, the BAC operated as an umbrella organization for Atlantic and defense-minded groups in Britain and maintained connections to similarly styled committees abroad. The Thatcher government entrusted BAC with hidden government funds to organize the messaging of dozens of other pronuclear organizations, including Coalition for Peace through Security (CPS), Young Conservatives, and the Council on Arms Control, in conjunction with the Ministry of Defence's (MoD's) and the Foreign and Commonwealth Office's public affairs strategy.[43]

Conservative Party strategists quickly judged the BAC incapable of mounting a modern public diplomacy campaign against the antinuclear movement, only months after being entrusted with the mission by the Foreign and Commonwealth Office. It lacked the authority, staff, and expertise to dictate tactics or messaging to its peer groups. CRD found the group incapable of producing leaflets and audiovisual materials and unable to develop other strategies to reach local audiences and citizens who had not yet been radicalized by antinuclear sentiment. CRD summarized, "The BAC is old fashioned, too establishment, uninspiring and dreary and isolated."[44] Wedded to an outdated form of international diplomacy that focused on elites, BAC could not adapt to information-age public diplomacy, and this misstep hindered early stages of the anti-CND campaign.

CRD considered the antinuclear dilemma to be a generational struggle for British politics. It estimated that 50 percent of Young Conservatives—a training ground for party leaders—had joined the antinuclear movement because of the effectiveness of CND materials and cultural strategies.[45] To effectively deal with the generational problem, the anti-CND campaign needed to enlist and develop a new breed of think tanks that would adopt the political advocacy practices pioneered by the U.S.-based Heritage Foundation under the leadership of Ed Feulner. One of the most notable British institutions to reform its approach was the Centre for Policy Studies, the high temple of Thatcherism, but smaller upstart organizations formed the backbone of the transatlantic campaign against the antinuclear movement. At Heritage, and later as chair of the U.S. Advisory Commission on Public Diplomacy, Feulner had emphasized the importance of public diplomacy to U.S. foreign policy and western nuclear security. He had grown familiar with the British political and fundraising scene while completing his graduate studies in the United Kingdom, and he considered Britain to be Heritage's "eyes and ears for Europe" on nuclear and foreign policy matters.[46]

Both Feulner and the Reagan administration styled the Heritage Foundation as a private agent of U.S. public diplomacy. Heritage worked primarily with nongovernmental organizations that Thatcher had charged with defeating the antinuclear movement. It conducted joint studies with CRD to analyze the origins of disarmament arguments, bases of antinuclear support, and financial conditions of peace groups. These studies focused on the effects of new antinuclear protest tactics on public opinion, especially among youth and religious communities, to inform the development of a right-wing counter-campaign.[47] This manifested itself in new organizations such as the London-based Institute for European Defence and Strategic Studies (IEDSS), for which Feulner raised more than $500,000 in a year and served as chair. Picking up where Michael Howard had left off in his debates with E. P. Thompson, IEDSS reports such as *Protest and Perish* framed peace-studies curricula in schools as propaganda that distorted language to present the false choice of unilateral disarmament or nuclear holocaust.[48] Heritage went still further in its role as private agent of U.S. public nuclear diplomacy, funding programs to bring British and European personnel who opposed the antinuclear movement to the United States to participate in counter-campaign activities.[49]

Heritage focused on influencing Britain's print media, and IEDSS and similar organizations passed on Heritage ideas and briefings to inform sympathetic media outlets such as *Encounter* and the *Times*.[50] Winning the nuclear debate in the British print media had value for the Reagan administration beyond the United Kingdom. In terms of public diplomacy, Britain matched the superpowers, in particular because of the unrivaled reach and reputation of BBC's World Service, which, independent from government, broadcast a London-based view of the world by summarizing British print headlines and leading opinion pieces. Courtesy of the BBC, a favorable vision of the Reagan administration's nuclear policies, transmitted by Heritage's network of British think tanks and promoted by the British press, would echo east and west of the Iron Curtain and around the world.

Other British organizations also supported peace through strength, and they positioned themselves as private-sector conduits linking the Thatcher government to the Reagan administration and U.S.-based think tanks. Tony Kerpel, who had chaired Britain's Young Conservatives and later worked as a speechwriter for U.S. presidential candidate John Anderson in 1980, became a key figure in the Thatcher's government's campaign against CND. In early 1981 he advised the Conservative Party to use its own organizations to block CND from gathering influence in other spheres of public life, warning of damage not just to deterrence but to the entirety of the Thatcher vision.[51] To that end, in 1981 Kerpel founded the Coalition for Peace through Security (CPS), at times referred to as the Coalition for Peace through Strength, with Edward Leigh, a close former aide of Thatcher's and chair of the National Council for Civil Defence, and Francis Holihan, an American businessman living in the United Kingdom.[52]

Whitehall encouraged the Reagan administration and conservative contacts in Washington to support CPS in its mission to link local campaigns supporting nuclear deterrence with the national and international narrative coming from Whitehall, Washington, and NATO allies.[53] CPS set up a lobby operation on Capitol Hill to persuade the Reagan administration to invest more resources into shaping European nuclear attitudes for years to come. Among its most important associates in Washington were Heritage's cofounders Feulner and Weyrich. They introduced CPS leaders to White House officials and provided funds for the organization's Atlantic project, an initiative designed to obstruct increasing coordination between the American nuclear Freeze movement and Britain's antinuclear movement. Generational concerns in particular motivated these efforts. CPS had voiced concerns that CND had developed a robust college organizer and exchange program for the "exporting of unilateralism."[54] Working to offset the further development of a transatlantic youth campaign against deterrence, CPS established close ties with the U.S.-based College Republicans. The cooperation between the two organizations drew the White House's attention to the generational issues at play in public nuclear diplomacy.[55]

With offices in London and Dayton, Ohio, CPS emerged as an effective transatlantic influence operation, circulating pro-deterrence arguments and disarmament critiques between the British and American publics as well as between the Reagan administration and the Thatcher government.[56] Rather than develop the intellectual and moral arguments to make the case for deterrence itself, CPS's adoption of the Heritage advocacy model elevated the importance of the pro deterrence ideas coming out of other, more scholarly think tanks, such as Royal United Services Institute, the International Institute for Strategic Studies, and BAC.

The Heritage Foundation's major role in establishing and funding CPS, IEDSS, and other organizations in Britain gave the Reagan administration a private-sector infrastructure for public nuclear diplomacy. Just as the United Kingdom had come to serve as a forward base for U.S. nuclear weapons and the projection of military strength into Europe, so could it serve as a forward base for U.S. public diplomacy and the projection of soft power into the continent to combat the antinuclear movement and the Soviet peace offensive. More than that, British society became a laboratory for public diplomacy tactics and initiatives that could be employed in the United States by both public and private actors. These transatlantic public-private partnerships would become even more important in 1982, when Feulner assumed the chair of the U.S. Advisory Commission on Public Diplomacy and Reagan introduced a major overhaul of U.S. public diplomacy efforts worldwide from the hallowed halls of Westminster.

Morality, Science, and Anti-Americanism

In light of the Church of England's (CoE's) July 1979 decision to form a working party to explore the theological debate around disarmament, pronuclear advocates recognized early on that a moral case for deterrence should be a component of their public diplomacy campaign. The CoE's decision set off a broader discussion about the effects of nuclear weapons on the relationship between Christianity and democracy. John Austin Baker, who would be elevated to bishop of Salisbury by the time the working party published its findings, chaired what became known as the Salisbury group, which met eleven times between July 1980 and April 1982. Officials from the MoD, the Foreign and Commonwealth Office, the Home Office, and other government departments served as project consultants.[57] Government representatives drew on the arguments produced by Michael Quinlan's transatlantic network to promote the morality of their position.

Quinlan had begun dealing with nuclear matters when he entered the civil service in 1954, the same year that Britain had fielded its first operational nuclear weapon. By the 1980s, he had established himself as the "high priest of deterrence" among his colleagues.[58] He served in numerous positions within the defense establishment, serving as director for defense policy related to arms control, counselor to Britain's NATO delegation, deputy undersecretary for policy and programs in the MoD during NATO's drafting and acceptance of the dual-track decision, and ultimately permanent undersecretary of state at the MoD. Jesuit-educated, he also strongly identified as a Catholic.[59] In 1981 Quinlan wrote an essay for the government's *Statement on Defence* in which he defended Britain's commitment to NATO's nuclear policy against the peace movement's criticisms. After this, his moral views of deterrence effectively became Whitehall's policy.[60] The MoD and the CRD agreed that a resolution to the religious debate demanded a decisive moral argument.[61]

Antinuclear advocates framed unilateral nuclear disarmament as an essential component of a moral democracy, which they offered as an alternative to the Thatcher society.[62] In the context of the nuclear debate, moral democracy advocates argued that the proper role of experts was to inform the public in a way that increased their participation in civic and democratic functions. Thus, antinuclear demonstrations fueled by new developments in scientific knowledge about the consequences of nuclear war morally improved British democracy. A political reawakening of the scientific community seemed essential to bringing about a moral democracy. Over the course of the Cold War, Britain's scientific community had remained relatively silent on nuclear matters in public.[63] One commentator went so far as to declare British scientists "political eunuchs" on the issue of nuclear weapons.[64] This began to change when the CoE and other groups began looking for technical counsel to inform their moral deliberations. The Salisbury group, for instance, consulted with Pugwash, an international organization of prominent experts who held antinuclear views, as well as with David Owen, an SDP leader and a former foreign secretary, who advocated for disarmament.[65]

Martin Ryle, a Cambridge radio astronomer who had won the Nobel Prize in physics in 1974, stood out among his colleagues as one of the few British scientists working to bridge scientific and humanistic expertise by arguing for the codependent goals of disarmament and democracy.[66] Ryle argued that antinuclear morality could transcend traditional class divisions in British society, placing his ideas within broader discussions on the NWFZ movement and new thinking about the place of science in democracy. Tony Benn carried these themes forward in his arguments for a moral democracy. In his view, scientists had an essential role to play in the revitalization of British democracy by deconstructing the technical language that defense intellectuals had used to keep the general public from participating in discussions about nuclear strategy and deterrence. Benn maintained:

> [Scientists] must not mystify, for that establishes a new religion. They must not oversimplify, because that misleads and deceives. Their role is to clarify the choices for society. To offer leadership through education, but not to dominate through expertise or power. Decisions, in a democratic society, must ultimately be made by the people as a whole.[67]

The group Scientists against Nuclear Arms, established by Mike Pentz, a CND council member and the founding dean of sciences at the Open University, enacted Benn's ideas. By providing the underlying technical analysis for the campaign against Thatcher's civil defense plans, SANA was able to develop new methods for public science diplomacy. Pentz proposed the idea of SANA on December 6, 1980, at a meeting with nine scientists from Imperial College, Cambridge University, the University of London, Manchester University, and the Open University.[68] The group officially formed in January at the Friends House in London, with the backing of sixteen Royal Society fellows; in just over a year it had 250 active members.[69]

At first Pentz and his colleagues were wary of finding a place for SANA within the broader peace movement. As a communist from South Africa, he was committed to anti-elitist principles and did not wish to make the group another form of British Pugwash. That venerable body of scientific citizens, founded in 1957, had structured its efforts to combat the arms race largely around meetings between prominent scientists and high-ranking government officials.[70] Pentz also did not wish to attach the credibility of scientists to the complex politics of an organization such as CND. Rather than taking an official stance, SANA officers opted to be "toolmakers for the peace movement," acting as independent consultants for CND, END, and likeminded organizations. Though Pentz and other SANA members were deeply involved with CND and END, their choice to avoid an official stance allowed them to attract British scientists who wished to work on particular issues but not necessarily endorse the polarizing platform of unilateral disarmament. At their inaugural conference in March 1981, SANA scientists agreed to establish a series of working groups to provide technical assessments of the most common issues championed by the peace movement. Civil defense became a special focus.[71] CND immediately began encouraging local chapters that were coordinating NWFZ campaigns with municipal governments to rely on SANA's expertise.[72]

Those who argued that antinuclear activity was essential for moral democracy saw that it was fostering a vibrant and expanding public sphere, which they believed was a necessary if society were to hold the state accountable to democratic principles. Women, in particular, took advantage of the antinuclear moment to elevate their public voices. Since the 1960s, British women had become more independent from traditional expectations and were now better equipped, both legally and educationally, to challenge the nuclear status quo. The number of women with higher-level degrees had quintupled from 1960 to 1980, despite only modest increases in the total British population.[73] Though employment as a whole had declined during the late 1970s and early 1980s, women's employment steadily trended upward. At the same time, a series of legislative developments, including the 1970 Equal Pay Act, the 1975 Sex Discrimination Act, and the 1975 Employment Protection Act, addressed major gender inequities in British society.[74]

Despite these advances in equality between the sexes, the meaning of a women's-only camp and single-sex protest emerged as a major point of contention in the British peace movement. Inspired by the NWFZ movement, Ann Pettitt, a young mother from Carmarthenshire in Wales, organized the Greenham Common Women's occupation of land outside of the Royal Air Force's (RAF's) Greenham Common, which had served as a forward base of operations for the U.S. military throughout the Cold War and had been selected as the first deployment site for cruise missiles in Europe.[75] The women of GCW argued that feminist principles could set a new moral course for political progressives and British society as a whole.[76] But as they moved to the forefront of antinuclear media coverage, peace movement leaders bristled at their radical image. GCW protests embodied rhetoric, symbolic action, and nonviolent direct action. Even though the group contributed to the Labour Party's increasingly radical reputation, it also led to the evolution of British views of gender roles, family values, and collective morality.

Faced with this variety of antinuclear demonstrations, conservatives on both sides of the Atlantic recognized that nuclear issues had become intertwined with the fundamentals of British democracy and the broader ideological conflict between Thatcher's Conservative Party and the increasingly radicalized Labour Party. American involvement in the British nuclear debate—either by the Reagan administration or by civil society actors—amounted to an intervention in British democracy. Reagan's October 1981 announcement of the details of his nuclear arms buildup boosted turnout for CND's annual October rally in Hyde Park: 250,000 protesters appeared, triple the number of the previous year's participation.[77] In his analysis of the October rally, Peter Shipley, the CRD strategist in charge of the anti-CND campaign, advised, "The unilateralist case reaches a much wider audience than the political left. The disarmament movement also represents an emerging radical movement, the aims of which extend far beyond the immediate question of nuclear weapons. . . . it represents a cultural awakening against the establishment and in favor of democracy."[78]

The connection between Reagan's nuclear modernization and the October rally confirmed the soaring political importance of the antinuclear movement and also showed that CND appeared to feed off a strong current of anti-Americanism among the British public.[79] Reagan officials heeded warnings coming from Whitehall and the private anti-CND campaign, which claimed that the antinuclear movement represented a real threat to Thatcher's position. Reagan's national security advisor, Richard Allen, warned the president in late fall of 1981, "Thatcher's domestic position is getting more vulnerable, and the possibility of Tory defeat, with the present government replaced by a coalition government, cannot be discounted."[80] The question facing Reagan officials was whether the administration should step back and allow the Thatcher government to manage the debate, or whether it should increase its commitment to public diplomacy in Britain and bring attention to shared values, with the goal of demonstrating the good intentions underlying the modernization of U.S., U.K, and NATO nuclear forces.

The Reagan administration's public diplomacy plan for Europe revolved around the promotion of the zero-option proposal. The focus of U.S. public diplomacy on the European nuclear debate also helped USIA's director, Charles Wick, extract funds from Congress to modernize the agency's technological capabilities, which could then be used not just in Western Europe but in the broader American public diplomacy offensive against communism in Eastern Europe and Latin America. Reagan's zero-option speech on November 18, 1981, provided cause for the expansion of the "wireless file" and computer-based communications between USIA and its European field offices, which increased the visibility of the USIA's complementary efforts on arms control such as the broad dissemination and readout of its bulletin *Soviet Military Power.*[81]

Even during the initial formulation of the zero-option, State Department officials predicted that the position would be politically viable for only about six months.[82] Indeed, criticism of the zero-option as a reasonable approach to arms control contributed to the significant gains of the British antinuclear movement.[83] In December 1981, 70 percent of Europeans approved of the zero-option; but by March 1982, only 30 percent of them saw it as a serious attempt at arms control, and another 30 percent considered it to be simply a propaganda ploy.[84] Even more alarming, Wick reported a sharp decrease in support for U.S. security policies in Europe, a drop of 20 to 30 percent since the days of the Carter administration.[85] In Britain specifically, more than half of British citizens wanted U.S. nuclear bases removed from U.K. soil, and more than 60 percent believed that Reagan's foreign policy made nuclear war more likely.[86]

Among British protest groups, the GCW continued to be most effective at resisting U.S. nuclear presence in Britain. The all-women's protest had grown from a small group of activists located outside the main gate of the RAF base to a diversified and nonhierarchical peace camp positioned at all eight entry gates around the installation's nine-mile perimeter. Activists used the fence as a tool for symbolic action. On the inside military personnel preparing for war enjoyed the amenities of modern life. On the outside women were housed in small polyethylene makeshift tents with no access to running water; they likened their living conditions to trench warfare.[87] GCW viewed these conditions as a necessary part of the fight for peace, one that required a remaking of family and gender practices as well as the reconstruction of language that the nuclear patriarchy was using to entrench war as a permanent feature of society. One camp resident explained, "I've been accused of being cruel and hard-hearted for leaving my children behind, but it's exactly for my children that I'm doing this. In the past, men left home to go to war. Now women are leaving home for peace."[88]

GCW's very existence—out of the home and away from the children—emphasized the sharp ideological contrast between Thatcher's promotion of Victorian values and the feminist principles under debate at Greenham Common. By the late 1970s, the emergence of New Right rhetoric and its emphasis on Victorian values had altered the intersection of morality and nuclear politics. Thatcher infused the British New Right with pride in individualism when she took control of the Conservative Party. She heavily relied on moral rhetoric to condemn the permissiveness of the 1960s and the alleged cultural degeneration of the 1970s while offering the restoration of Victorian values as the solution to British social ills.[89] When Thatcher first accepted the term *Victorian values* as a metaphor to unify her core political themes of self-reliance, stability, God-fearing attitudes, thrift, pride in country, and the sanctity of family life under the banner of British traditionalism, she did so while also demeaning the values of British protestors, specifically the GCW. For the prime minister, nuclear weapons were thus both essential to protecting "our way of life" and part of her Victorian socioeconomic vision for Britain's future.[90]

American diplomats in London observed the rise in anti-Americanism in connection to the faltering zero-option and were concerned about how disquiet among the British public would affect the nature of Britain's relationship with the United States. They cautioned the White House, "The United States has not fared well in British public opinion over the last year. This is evident in the polls, in the rhetoric of the Labour Party, in the growth of the 'peace movement.' . . . there is a perceptible shift in thinking toward skepticism about the U.S. connection—a sense that the West has reached the end of an era."[91] CRD strategists and their counterparts in Western Europe attributed these developments to the fact that "U.S. propaganda and intelligence agencies were not matching up to the Soviet Union's."[92]

Wick agreed. In early April 1982, he wrote to Reagan that the decline of America's image in Europe as a result of poorly managed nuclear controversies would soon produce serious political difficulties at home. Illuminating the new realities of an emerging transnational public sphere, Wick pointed to the administration's failure to counter CND's sponsorship of student activists on American college campuses. He viewed this as an indication of how the piecemeal and reactive approach of U.S. public diplomacy was hindering the administration's ability to realize its objectives. Wick urged Reagan to emphasize values rather than policy specifics. He implored the president to carefully select a site at which he could deliver a dramatic televised speech with a "historic, ringing phrase that will stir hearts, and capture the minds, of men and women who yearn for freedom around the globe."[93] Such a speech could then serve as a springboard for a public diplomacy revolution in theme and operations.

The Reagan administration decided that a joint session of Parliament at Westminster would be the perfect place for such an initiative. A speech from Westminster would emphasize Britain's historic role as a cradle of democracy as well as the need to check the sharp rise of anti-Americanism among the British public.[94] Reagan and his public diplomacy advisors also believed that Thatcher's Victorian values were precisely the themes that would best support the president's defense of the dual-track decision and his broader ideological offensive against communism around the world. One USIA official noted, "He could've made the speech to the Bundestag or Paris, but it wouldn't have had the same meaning."[95] Importantly, speaking at Westminster also meant BBC coverage and thus significant access to a wide British and international audience. As it turned out, Reagan's address became one of the most watched television segments in British history.[96]

As Robert Rowland and Jonathan Jones have pointed out, the drafting of Reagan's Westminster address highlighted the conflict between hardline conservatives and pragmatists in his administration.[97] An unusually large number of people were involved in writing the address because administration officials had come to realize that shaping Reagan's major speeches was the best way to affect the direction of policy.[98] Hardliners in the administration wanted to let "Reagan be Reagan," encouraging his strident moral tone and his rhetoric of escalation. Yet Reagan did not have an intuitive grasp of European audiences that matched his sense of the American public. Public diplomacy officials beseeched him to alter his rhetoric for European audiences. In the United Kingdom specifically, Wick's staff insisted that the president discard his cowboy image.[99] Much of the content of the Westminster address came from the active-measures working group that was designed to combat Soviet disinformation and propaganda.[100] This group—comprised of intelligence community veterans, USIA representatives, and State Department officials— embodied Reagan's revolutionary changes to U.S. public diplomacy. In order to win the long-term battle of ideas as well as short-term public support for specific policies, he had united political warfare and psychological operations with the softer side of public diplomacy.[101]

On June 8, 1982, Reagan spent the morning riding horses with the queen around the grounds of Windsor Castle. Just after noon he took the floor of the Royal Gallery at Westminster to address a joint session of Parliament. This was his first state visit to the British Isles, his first public address to the British people, and the first time a sitting U.S. president had addressed the British Parliament. In his speech, Reagan contrasted the proud tradition of British democracy with the authoritarian philosophy of the Soviet Union, which he declared to be destined for the "ash heap of history." In essence, the president offered a British version of peace through strength. Before his parliamentary audience, Reagan refined the rhetoric that he would later offer in his famed evil-empire speech, given several months later and referred to throughout the 1982 U.S. midterm election season. He replaced allusions to the American moral tradition with references to Victorian virtues and a Churchillian sense of duty, which characterized Thatcher's own deterrence language. Reagan worded his key peace through strength appeals almost exactly as he would later do in his evil-empire speech: "Our military strength is a prerequisite to peace, but let it be clear we maintain this strength in the hope it will never be used, for the ultimate determinant in the struggle that's now going on in the world will not be bombs and rockets, but a test of wills and ideas, a trial of spiritual resolve, the values we hold."[102]

Reagan's parliamentary address created different reactions in the United States and the United Kingdom. American peace through strength advocates credited it as the impetus for the administration's move toward prioritizing public diplomacy, later outlined in NSDD 77 in January 1983. Carnes Lord, who led the drafting of NSDD 77 in his capacity as the NSC's director of international communications and information policy, wrote in *Commentary* that the Westminster address had announced the most "radical dimension" of the public diplomacy revolution and was a signal that "the elevation of public diplomacy to a position of major importance in American foreign policy reflects a fundamentally new attitude toward the role of opinion and ideas in international politics."[103] A leading neoconservative intellectual, Richard Pipes, later identified the speech as a turning point in the administration's moral framing of the Soviet and western systems.[104] The president's allies continued to cite the speech as a foundational rhetorical component of peace through strength well into the 1984 presidential election and in arms control debates throughout the remainder of the decade.[105]

In Britain, Reagan's emphasis on the resolute defense of a conservative vision of Anglo-American values played directly into Thatcher's own domestic politics. George Urban, a veteran of the U.S. and British public diplomacy broadcast agencies and a trusted member of the select group of experts from the Centre for Policy Studies that advised Thatcher on foreign affairs, asserted, "[By] announcing, in effect, the end of the West's retreat in the Cold War, the president undertook to confront Moscow's worldwide ideological offensive with an offensive of our own."[106] Thatcher commented that Reagan had "put freedom on the offensive where it belonged."[107] For the prime minister, such comments were directly attached to her own attempts to cultivate an image of a resolute wartime leader. Two months earlier, the military government of Argentina had invaded the Falkland Islands (the Malvinas), a British territory in the South Atlantic, an act that was seen as a direct challenge to Britain's prestige and potentially another sign of western decline. By the time of the Westminster address, Britain had turned the tide of the war, despite a lack of U.S. assistance. Reagan's celebration of decisive British action in his speech was a conciliation intended to heal the damage done to U.S.-U.K. relations by America's failure to provide more significant military or political support for the British war effort. Six days later, Argentinian forces surrendered in the South Atlantic.

Britain's victory thousands of miles away from home vindicated the prodefense mentalities of Thatcher's conservatives that underpinned support for the Anglo-American nuclear alliance. Research funded by the Conservative Party targeted the need for leadership with a strong moral drive as one of three fundamental beliefs held by British citizens. The Falklands affair provided a clear example of Thatcher filling that role.[108]

Reagan's June visit to the British Parliament also invigorated the antinuclear movement. In Britain, therefore, the net effect of the speech was an intensification of the deterrence debate rather than a turn of momentum in favor of pronuclear ideas. The Reagan administration had selected Britain as the place to go on the ideological peace offensive because of its status as a cradle of democracy, but in an odd twist American nuclear policies were generating profound discussions about the nature and fairness of British democracy. An overwhelming majority of Labour parliamentarians skipped the address because of the Thatcher government's failure to obtain the consent of the loyal opposition to invite a foreign head of state to speak at Westminster.[109] Reagan's visit also served as antinuclear organizing event: on the eve of the president's address, 250,000 protestors gathered in Hyde Park to protest the dual-track decision and the Trident program.[110] The makeup of the crowd suggested that antinuclear ideas were appealing to people outside of the radical wing of the Labour Party and that disarmament could potentially swing an election in favor of the party most committed to disarmament. As many as 65 percent of the protestors had no political affiliation.[111] At the same time, the number of British citizens attracted to disarmament ideas and simultaneously skeptical of the Labour Party created the possibility for discord in the Labour-CND alliance. The work of CND specialist sections with the new SDP Party, the Liberal Party, and even the Conservative Party heightened suspicions on both sides of the Labour-CND alliance.[112]

In October 1982, the publication of the CoE's reassessment of deterrence and the culmination of the civil defense protest known as the Hard Luck campaign, along with GCW's high-profile December demonstration, were offering an acute moral challenge to Thatcher's domestic, political, and geo-strategic aims. As Matthew Grimely has outlined, Thatcher viewed morality as inextricably linked to religion, and she frequently likened morality without religion to a flower detached from its roots.[113] The CoE represented a potential strategic asset for her nuclear agenda, not just because of its moral authority but because organized religion revolved around fundamental practices of public diplomacy. Sunday sermons, for example, were a trusted and routine communication for followers, and symbolic themes and events such as holiday celebrations were the foundation of religious worship. Historically close relations between the CoE and the Tories underpinned Thatcher's appeal to Christian morality, but the rise of the New Right had also coincided with the transformation of the Anglican clergy into a far more liberal body, a result of its declining recruitment from the upper middle class, where conservative mentalities reigned.[114] The potential alignment of unilateral nuclear disarmament with Anglican bishops, Catholic leaders, and parish councils across the United Kingdom robbed Thatcher of the moral mantle that she wanted to seize in support of New Right conservatism and denied her a valuable public diplomacy advantage.

Many important figures within the multifaith British Council of Churches —among them, Methodist leader Kenneth Greet and a number of respected CND contacts—were active in the antinuclear movement; and though Michael Quinlan's network promoted a moral case for deterrence, that argument appeared to be losing out to a climate that condemned nuclear weapons and deterrence.[115] In his May 1982 Pentecost sermon in Coventry, Pope John Paul II stated that "peace is not just the absence of war," and he urged British Catholics to reject deterrence as a form of peace and partake in a broader Christian and interfaith mission for finding peaceful means to eliminate the threat of nuclear war.[116] CND leadership relied on its largest specialist section, Christian CND, and its widespread network of aligned parishes to pressure the Salisbury group from the bottom up.

The widespread examination of nuclear morality took place in the context of the NWFZ movement that was overtaking much of municipal Britain. Scientists who were evaluating the technical merits of Whitehall's civil defense planning were able to influence acts of civil disobedience and opposition to civil defense, acts that CND used as a way to relate the antinuclear movement to other issues confronting British society. Thatcher's belief in monetarism had gone hand in hand with her desire for a strong central government, and this left the five county councils and the Greater London Council under siege by conservatives eager to reform the balance of power between municipal and central government. In rejecting civil defense exercises, local governments fought back against Thatcher's drive for centralization. The Lothian Regional Council's refusal to participate in the Square Leg exercise modeled a nuclear-free Europe on a local scale.

In the fall of 1981, CND and municipal governments had begun coordinating their opposition to the next civil defense drill, known as Hard Rock, planned for the fall of 1982.[117] Dozens of NWFZ representatives gathered in Manchester in late October to draft programs for public education and counter-exercises.[118] The important county seats of West Yorkshire and South Yorkshire along with local governments in Bradford, Manchester, Cleveland, Derbyshire, and dozens of others subsequently announced their refusal to participate in civil defense exercises.[119] By March 1982 the number of local authorities declaring themselves to be NWFZs had climbed to 125.[120] All five county councils, the primary bureaucracies for civil defense operations, declared NWFZ status by April and pledged participation in CND's counter-operation, Hard Luck.[121]

The Hard Luck campaign succeeded largely because SANA experts undercut the technical credibility of the Home Office. Mike Pentz and his SANA colleague Owen Greene joined CND's Hard Luck working group in the spring, and this led to the decision to have SANA guide all municipal governments and local chapters that were rebelling against the Hard Rock exercise.[122] Early in the campaign, SANA scientists observed major discrepancies between casualty-rate studies conducted by the U.S. Department of Defense and Office of Technological Assessment and the Square Leg casualty estimates produced by twelve scientists who staffed the Scientific Research and Development Branch of the Home Office.[123] The Home Office's lack of a clear methodology, and especially its odd calculations for blast effects, provoked SANA scientists to set their sights on building a transparent casualty model for all of the United Kingdom based on the targeting assumptions employed in Square Leg.

The London after the Bomb Working Group (LATB) provided the most devastating assault on Home Office casualty estimates. SANA's prediction of 5 million dead in the London area dwarfed the Home Office number of only

600,000.[124] LATB findings were immediately more credible than those of the twelve unnamed scientists working in the Home Office. Importantly, LATB relied on the U.S. Department of Defense and Office of Technological Assessment methodologies for calculating blast effects, which were based on data collected from the pre-1963 above-ground testing era and from damage surveys of Hiroshima and Nagasaki. Blast fatalities provided by the Home Office were 2.5 times less than those calculated by U.S. authorities and came with no explanation on method of computation.[125] LATB subjected shelter guidelines recommended in civil defense pamphlets to their projected blast effects. It also took account of the time, space, and financial constraints limiting the majority of Londoners from erecting suitable protection from the prolonged aftereffects of radiation, which the Home Office had deliberately overlooked.[126] The group's realistic assessment of electromagnetic pulse bursts and damage done to emergency services provided a more accurate assessment of fatalities suffered due to weakened immune systems and lack of medical care.[127]

The credibility of anti–civil defense reports such as the LATB study provided one of municipal Britain's last parting shots against the forces of centralization. The Greater London Council's leader, Ken Livingstone, known as Red Ken and the bane of Thatcherites in Whitehall, directed resources and guarded knowledge of civil defense plans to help LATB reach its conclusions. The Nobelist Maurice Wilkins, Pugwash's founder Joseph Rotblat, and SANA's vice president, Tom Kibble, known worldwide for his contributions to quantum field theory, were notable commentators on the project.[128] Several local governments, including those in Brighton, Bristol, Cheshire, Cumbria, Leeds, Manchester, Merseyside, Sheffield, and municipalities in the West Midlands, cooperated with teams conducting studies similar to the LATB report.[129] CND's publication *Sanity* released SANA's national figures, which had been compiled by a purpose-built computer program that analyzed nuclear attack variables and casualty rates for every ten-by-ten square kilometer of the United Kingdom. The projected casualty total for the whole of the United Kingdom reached nearly 39 million dead, with more than 4 million more severely injured.[130] Thanks to the liberal use of SANA studies by local governments involved in the Hard Luck campaign, twenty of the fifty-four government entities scheduled to participate in the Hard Rock exercise in September and October 1982 did not comply with civil defense measures, while seven more made only a token commitment.[131]

Instead of participating in civil defense planning and drills, dozens of municipalities hosted street art competitions, public vigils, and antinuclear theater and music performances. Sheffield City Council found a loophole to underwrite grants for peace groups with municipal funds. Local authorities in Bradford opened up civil defense bunkers to press and media in the name of public education. Leicester sponsored a Nuclear Free Festival during the days that Hard Rock had been scheduled to take place. The city of Manchester hosted an NWFZ conference that produced the Manchester Resolution, a commitment to challenging the power of civil defense authorities and to exploring what municipal governments could do with foreign contacts to lower the risk of nuclear war.[132] Within a week, 129 local authorities came out in support of the Manchester Resolution.[133] Labour's National Executive Committee encouraged such activity, imploring local authorities to expose civil defense as an exercise in "brainwashing."[134] The extent of noncompliance compelled the suspension of the Hard Rock exercise. Conservatives blamed Labour, which controlled all noncompliant governments, for politicizing the defense of British civilians.[135] Most members of the press, however, scored the suspension of Hard Rock as CND's biggest win yet.[136]

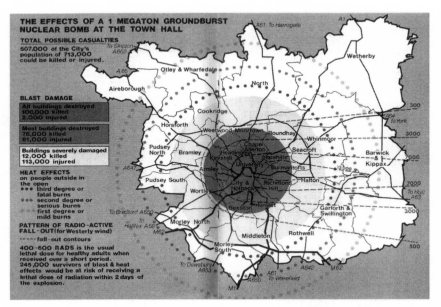

FIGURE 1. Depiction of blast and fallout effects from a one-megaton nuclear bomb, based on calculations from Scientists against Nuclear Arms. From Leeds City Council, Leeds and the Bomb, 2nd ed. (Leeds, UK: Leeds City Council, May 1983).

The NWFZ movement's influence over the Labour Party was made clear at the party's annual conference in October. A majority of delegates supported unilateral disarmament at the Labour Party conferences in 1980 and 1981, but the two-thirds majority needed to officially adopt the policy had not yet been reached. The combined efforts of the TUC, CND, END, and NWFZ activists flooding constituent Labour parties persuaded 72 percent of delegates at the 1982 annual meeting to support the inclusion of unambiguous language on unilateral disarmament, cuts to military expenditure, economic conversion, and the closure of U.S. nuclear bases in the 1983 general election manifesto.[137] Overall support for unilateral disarmament at the 1982 Labour conference increased by 222,000 more votes than the preceding year.[138]

This antinuclear climate of ideas influenced the report of the bishop of Salisbury's working group. *The Church and the Bomb*, released in October 1982, highlighted several elements of the nuclear establishment that ran counter to the spirit of Anglican morality and British democracy. The report argued that Parliament received nuclear decisions as a fait accompli and sanctioned the activities of the antinuclear movement in supporting "the place of moral legitimation in controlling what governments do, and the specific legitimation involved in seeking endorsement for their policies from the electorate."[139] The Salisbury group declared that "to accept in general that governments have fateful choices to make as part of their responsibilities does not entail the conclusion that they are the sole judge of the justice or wisdom of that choice."[140]

Once again the semantics of war and peace became a focus of debate. The Salisbury group took issue with government campaigns to mislead the public on nuclear developments. They labeled civil defense a "misnomer" because heightened publicity did not correspond to the real state of preparations. They also rejected the proposed zero-option position in INF talks as a non-negotiable proposal designed to soothe European opinion and do nothing more.[141]

As American Catholic bishops were working in their pastoral letter on war and peace, the Salisbury group grounded its theological discussion in an analysis of the applicability of just war theory to nuclear conflict. Its members concluded that nuclear war could never be considered just, given issues of proportionality and collateral harm, the unlikelihood of success, and an increased reliance on automated technology that could subvert states' decision-making processes.[142] Disenchanted by the lack of progress in multilateral initiatives to eliminate nuclear weapons, the Salisbury group advocated for unilateral disarmament; but by confirming the importance of NATO and non-nuclear defense, it stopped short of a totally pacifist platform.[143]

The success of the Hard Luck campaign and the release of *The Church and the Bomb* had come on the heels of Reagan's address to Parliament and the growing unpopularity of the zero-option. This situation led Thatcher's government to two conclusions. First, British officials judged Washington's public diplomacy insufficient because the Reagan administration struggled to reconcile the message it developed for domestic purposes with the message its disseminated to British and European publics. Second, cabinet members predicted that implementation of the broad Conservative Party agenda hinged on the government's ability to bring antinuclear opinion under control. In October 1982, Secretary of Defence John Nott warned Thatcher of the potential collateral political damage of rising antinuclear sentiment: "The experience of the last 3 years suggests to me that in our original decision we under-estimated the problem of possible public opposition. . . . we may find that public opinion runs away from us. If this happens we will lose our strategic deterrent—and much else."[144] As a result, Whitehall felt a new sense of urgency about scaling up the British pronuclear public diplomacy campaign.[145]

Before the Thatcher government could set a new direction for its pro-deterrence campaign, GCW brought further attention to the radical and transatlantic dimensions of the deterrence debate. On December 12 and 13, 1982, the third anniversary of the dual-track decision, 30,000 women participated in the Embrace the Base protest, which blockaded every point of the nine-mile perimeter of the Greenham Common RAF base. GCW replicated elements of the 1980 Women's Pentagon Action demonstration in Washington, D.C.—for instance, by rallying around feminist anthems written by Indigenous American women.[146] Activists brought down the barbed-wire fence in three places, resulting in encounters with police that led to dozens of arrests and injured a number of protestors. Confrontation with the mostly male police force had long been a tactic of GCW, a way of suggesting that the police's rough handling of women activists reflected the proclivities of male-dominated governments to use violence as a political tool.[147] But actions during the Embrace the Base demonstration—specifically, the destruction of the fence—also generated a conversation about the peace camp's commitment to nonviolent tactics, which fueled the semantic conflict between pro-deterrence advocates and unilateral disarmers over which side was truly creating conditions for a peaceful world. For its part, GCW argued "that whole fence and its purpose is violence. . . . If you are strongly arguing for respect and non-violence and uncompromisingly opposing nuclear weapons and male violence in the streets, you suddenly find people accusing you of violence."[148]

Much of the media coverage interpreted GCW's radical tactics as violent confrontation, and this publicity stoked tensions within the antinuclear movement. Responses to GCW protests showed that the nuclear debate had clearly become a proxy for the ideological competition between the political left and right and that it had the potential to produce a generational realignment in British politics. Between 1982 and 1983, CND national membership grew by almost 10,000 to reach nearly 60,000, and close to 300,000 members were affiliated with local CND chapters.[149] Yet the Labour Party and CND remained skeptical of one another. Labour leaders feared that their association with the radical tactics of unilateral nuclear disarmers might alienate the party from much of the voting public, while CND leadership and local chapters were divided over the sincerity of Labour's commitment to unilateral disarmament and the party's prospects for an electoral victory. Consequently, rather than endorsing the Labour Party and campaigning on its behalf, CND spread its organizing efforts thinly.[150] After the formation of CND's Parliamentary and Elections Committee, which was created to bring an antinuclear Parliament to power, the peace strategist Neville Pressley wrote to the national council, saying that "it would be rather stupid to base our hopes on an improbable Labour victory and an optimistic hope that a Labour government would deliver all its promises."[151]

Concerned about the government's agenda, Conservative Party cabinet officers lamented the "thousands of people coming into active politics for the first time through the peace movements."[152] Thatcher's chief press secretary, Bernard Ingham, commented that "the main problem remains divided responsibility and the lack of adequate campaigning resources. We have been—and to some extent still are—fiddling while Rome burns."[153] Yet the fragility of the Labour-CND alliance presented a unique opportunity for the Thatcher government to simultaneously consolidate its political power and defeat the disarmament movement. The press portrayal of GCW as violent agitators suggested that a counterattack strategy could revive the pronuclear public diplomacy campaign. On the day after the Embrace the Base demonstration,

Lord Max Beloff, an influential conservative historian and a political advisor associated with the Centre for Policy Studies, advised the prime minister to "abandon the kid-gloves approach" to taking down the antinuclear movement.[154] He considered CND a great moral threat and promised, "I shall not be content until it becomes as hazardous to wear a CND badge on the streets of London as it would be to sport a swastika in Tel Aviv."[155]

CHAPTER THREE
AN ANTINUCLEAR AWAKENING

A sleeping giant of public opinion had suddenly awakened, including not only
peace activists, but a broad new constituency reflecting America as a whole.
—U.S. senators Edward Kennedy (D-MA) and Mark Hatfield (R-OR), Freeze! How You Can Help
Prevent Nuclear War (1982)

A WAKENED BY CARTER'S turn to more hawkish nuclear policies and incited
to mass mobilization by Reagan's quest for nuclear superiority, the U.S.
antinuclear movement of the 1980s distinguished itself from its 1960s prede-
cessor by adopting different tactics for coalition building. Amid the collapse
of the New Deal order that had long organized the left and center of the U.S.
political spectrum, the antinuclear cause coalesced women's groups, civil
rights activists, and labor interests into a progressive movement.[1] The anti-
Vietnam War protests had taught these groups the limits of radicalism, and
they now recognized the benefits of criticizing Cold War militarism from
the mainstream.

The emergence of an alliance between the mass antinuclear movement
and the scientific community conferred a new degree of legitimacy to disarmament positions. In the 1970s, a convergence of innovations in scientific
practice, the marginalization of government science advising, and Vietnam
protests that brought the scientific community into closer contact with progressive political elements led to a public turn in science diplomacy in the
1980s. Its practitioners sought indirect influence over nuclear policy by mobilizing public opinion to their positions through a variety of educational campaigns, op-eds, and mass communication tactics and by providing underlying
scientific analysis for publicly touted disarmament concepts. They recognized
the value of using scientific knowledge to inform grassroots activism to effect
change on an international scale.

Women established themselves as tactical innovators in both protests and public science diplomacy. They sought to establish a transnational dimension to antinuclear protests by representing themselves as local, national, and global actors. William Moomaw has argued that science diplomacy is most effective when a synergy exists between scientists who act as diplomats (diplomat scientists) and diplomats who draw on scientific knowledge (scientist diplomats).[2] In the peace movement, women antinuclear leaders often modeled the scientist diplomat role while developing a critique of deterrence that transcended national boundaries.

As in the United Kingdom, organized religion—in particular, the Catholic church—gave antinuclear positions a moral legitimacy that enhanced their credibility within the political mainstream. U.S. Catholic bishops' moral condemnation of deterrence directly undermined Reagan's use of moral arguments to justify his nuclear buildup. The pairing of Catholicism's moral legitimacy with scientific knowledge created an especially potent argument in favor of the antinuclear movement and multiplied the effects of both public science diplomacy and the American Catholic church's reevaluation of its accommodation of Cold War militarism. The Freeze channeled these developments into an impressive level of financial, operational, and intellectual support for Democratic congressional candidates in the 1982 midterm elections. Success in that election solidified the place of antinuclear ideas in American politics; and proponents of these ideas emphasized the moral complexity of American society, using it to drive their conflict with the Reagan administration's efforts to highlight the moral exceptionalism of the United States within the international system.

The Reagan administration was initially ineffective in responding to the antinuclear movement and resigned itself to a congressional defeat in the 1982 elections. Nonetheless, that year the administration also laid the groundwork for an effective public diplomacy campaign that would emerge in 1983. Supplementing those efforts, private initiatives organized by the burgeoning political operations of the New Right and a fast-emerging network of conservative think tanks broadly disseminated Reagan's message of peace through strength.

Elements of the Nuclear Peace Movement

Looking back over the 1980s, Father Theodore Hesburgh, the president of the University of Notre Dame as well as a nuclear expert and a Catholic luminary, identified the emergence of "a wider moral consciousness" across American society rooted in the existential anxiety brought on by heightened nuclear fear.[3] The antinuclear movement fueled its emergence, and coalition-building efforts that challenged the rationality of nuclear deterrence made this moral consciousness a significant force in domestic and international politics. That process required the Freeze to clarify its broad moral authority as a step to establishing its political legitimacy while simultaneously channeling the enthusiasm generated by radical symbolic protest to create a climate of ideas that could restructure mainstream thinking about nuclear weapons.

Even before the Freeze became the primary antinuclear organizing concept in the United States, the Catholic church had become more involved in nuclear debates and less accommodating toward Cold War militarism. Between the 1950s and the 1970s, a series of political transformations had liberalized its clergy, putting them into a better position to leverage their moral authority in the nuclear debates of the 1980s.[4] By 1980, 25 percent of Americans identified as Catholics, and their political preferences more accurately reflected American public opinion than did those of any other major religious group.[5] They helped bring 142 Catholics into Congress in 1982, the largest representation of any religious denomination in U.S. history.[6]

As Judeo-Christian institutions considered nuclear war, new trends arose in church-state relations, and substantial interfaith dialogue helped revive morality as a feature of politics. The steady rise of Catholic political influence in the United States corresponded to the growing number of leading clergy who began publicly reacting to the moral predicament presented by nuclear deterrence. In Catholic thought, the menace of nuclear war not only represented the advent of more deadly technologies but also reflected a broader moral crisis in political culture.[7]

The first U.N. Special Session on Disarmament, held in May and June 1978, and the ratification fight over the SALT II treaty in the winter of 1979–80 awakened the U.S. Conference of Catholic Bishops to the need to integrate scientific and technical perspectives with moral considerations if they were to wield influence over nuclear policy.[8] The neutron bomb controversy further incited the bishops to speak out against the arms race. At its core, the moral debate came down to a question of means versus ends. Could the threat of indiscriminate killing itself be considered morally acceptable if it caused much of humankind to live in a constant state of terror? Even if this state of terror were seen as a necessary evil, could one expect deterrence to be a permanent and stabilizing force, or would it inevitably lead to a nuclear war that encroached on the divine's power to make and unmake civilization?

San Francisco's archbishop John Quinn, Denver's archbishop James Casey, and Jesuit theologian Francis Winters suggested that the unique capabilities of nuclear weapons precluded the application of just war theory, which had been the dominant Catholic teaching on violent conflict since the days of Thomas Aquinas.[9] Much of the Catholic criticism of deterrence centered on its inherent instability: because it narrowed the available choices to surrender or destruction, it obscured humanity's moral obligations to each other and the sanctity of life and thus limited the free will granted by the divine. Only the most conservative Catholic pronouncements accepted deterrence as a morally defensible position, but only on the condition that states move away from the strategy through political negotiation, not through technological end runs.[10]

In the 1970s the Catholic clergy had reluctantly supported arms control because it reinforced the principles of MAD, although they would have preferred to see the U.S.-Soviet security dynamic organized around something other than nuclear weapons. Cardinal John Krol of Philadelphia argued in his September 1979 testimony before the Senate Foreign Relations Committee that "it is impossible to regard [the SALT II] Treaty as a spectacular achievement in the field of arms control," reasoning that deterrence could not be considered a long-term moral solution because it guaranteed continued nuclear competition.[11] Speaking on behalf of the 350 American bishops who comprised the U.S. Catholic Conference, Krol suggested that the very existence of nuclear weapons actively harmed humanity, for their cost directly deprived the poor and hungry in America and around the world.

The progressive transformation of the American Catholic clergy coincided with changes in the women's movement, and these shifts allowed antinuclear ideas to become the foundation for cooperation between the groups, though in the past they had often opposed each other on key public-policy issues. At the onset of the nuclear 1980s, women's activism was directed into a range of collaborative causes and identities. Scholars of feminism who study this period now tend to view these activists as "women in movement[s]" rather than as members of "a women's movement."[12] Since its beginnings in the 1960s, second-wave feminism had centered around a radical protest of the systematic suppression of women, rooting its activism in a critique of the social, economic, environmental, intellectual, and governing structures that maintained the dominance of the white-male power elite. Because antinuclear women had long experience with this wide-ranging approach to protest, they were particularly effective coalition builders, able to incorporate various forms of radical pacifism and scientific knowledge into the larger project of constructing a disarmament language that exposed the flaws in deterrence thinking.

The physician Helen Caldicott came to embody the intersection of feminism, antinuclear ideas, and science. She staked the credibility of her antinuclear opposition on the three pillars of her identity: mother, pediatrician, and woman. As a former practicing doctor on the Harvard medical faculty, Caldicott had a strong claim to scientific expertise, especially when speaking to the public about the medical consequences of nuclear war. In 1978, she orchestrated the revival of Physicians for Social Responsibility (PSR), which had become moribund since its founding in 1961. PSR's revival came about in part because of Caldicott's belief that doctors, who were familiar and trusted by the general public, had a special role to play as experts and scientific communicators.

In her standard antinuclear stump speech, Caldicott treated the earth as her patient. She laid out the effects of the nuclear arms race on the earth's health as if this conversation were an exchange one would have with a family doctor. Such acts of scientific translation inspired other practitioners of public science diplomacy and were effective across local, national, and international contexts.[13] As a pediatrician and a mother, Caldicott appealed to the political mainstream and epitomized the nurturing, healing, and life-bearing qualities of women that cultural feminists celebrated. At the same time, radical feminists welcomed her public rhetoric, in which she contrasted women's inclination for peace with the male-dominated nuclear establishment. Reclaiming fear and expertise from the nuclear establishment, Caldicott turned them into grassroots recruitment tools for the antinuclear movement.

Together, women's groups and religious groups organized mainstream nuclear fear and pockets of radical antinuclear activity into a public influence operation, with the goal of remaking nuclear policy. The Freeze's interim steering committee was dominated by religious groups such as the American Friends Service Committee (AFSC), Clergy and Laity Concerned (CALC), the Fellowship of Reconciliation (FOR), Sojourners, the Presbyterian church, and the Riverside church, alongside women's groups such as Women's International League for Peace and Freedom (WILPF) and PSR under the direction of Caldicott. Their charge was to build a national movement around Randall Forsberg's 1979 call for a freeze and Randy Kehler's local success in putting the freeze on the ballot in the 1980 elections in western Massachusetts.[14]

Freeze strategists at the 1981 national conference mapped out a two- to five-year organizing plan aimed at people in the middle of the political spectrum. In phases 1 and 2, they sought local, regional, and national endorsements, targeting unions, religious institutions, minority groups, academics, students, businesses, and expert associations with specific messages that appealed to the core political concerns of each. Organizers planned to use these endorsements in local and statewide resolutions and referenda, thereby generating involvement at the grassroots level. In December 1981, they asked Randy Kehler to head the official Freeze campaign, hoping that the success of his referendum drive would guarantee a shift toward mainstream politics. Unlike many of the other peace movement veterans, who had learned their skills via the radical actions of the anti–Vietnam War movement, Kehler was experienced with electoral and legislative processes.[15]

In phases 3 and 4, strategists turned their attention to congressional politics, working to defeat MX ICBM legislation and block deployments of INF weapons, thereby linking the European and American peace movements. In early 1982, freeze legislation was introduced in Congress, a move that provided visibility to the issue in the months before the U.N.'s special session on disarmament, scheduled for June, as well as the congressional elections in November. In the final phase, Freeze strategists prioritized science diplomacy, calling on nongovernmental experts such as the Federation of American Scientists (FAS) and PSR to explore Soviet and international support for the Freeze while the national office of the Freeze campaign continued to work through Congress to legislate its positions into U.S. arms control proposals.[16]

Reagan's first-year budget, which prioritized military spending, played into the hands of Freeze messaging that aimed to make antinuclear ideas more universally appealing. Critiques of Cold War militarism came from radical voices within religious institutions, the scientific profession, organized labor, and minority communities; and they gained traction with the mainstream elements of those constituencies as the public learned that the pursuit of strategic superiority had budget priority over other urgent national needs. Reagan's administration argued that the high cost of his Cold War policies, which would be paid for by deficit defense spending, would also help abate U.S. economic decline. Defense Secretary Caspar Weinberger claimed that the defense budget was "the most important social welfare program," calling it "the second half of the Administration's program to revitalize America," with tax cuts being the first half.[17] Such claims reflected the widely held assumption that defense dollars produced economic benefits, a belief that dated back to World War II and the early Cold War, when military spending and the U.S. economy had grown hand in hand.

The National Committee for a Sane Nuclear Policy (SANE) was a legacy antinuclear organization established earlier in the Cold War. SANE's studies in the 1970s and early 1980s on the negative economic effects of defense spending gave antinuclear leaders the analysis and data they needed to challenge the welfare logic of Reagan's Keynesian military budgets.[18] In the 1970s, SANE had begun analyzing the economic burdens of the arms race as part of its campaign to lobby for a conversion from a defense economy to a peace economy. Seymour Melman, a professor of industrial engineering at Columbia University, became the organization's co-chair in 1970. He had made a name for himself in academia by analyzing the effects of the permanent war economy on society.[19] That expertise underpinned SANE's new focus on economic conversion, a shift in that made the organization the hinge in an emerging labor-peace alliance.

In 1975, SANE began airing its award-winning nationally syndicated radio program *Consider the Alternatives* and sponsored a major national conference, "The Arms Race and Economic Conversion." Speakers in both venues blamed military spending for runaway inflation. Two years later the same theme spawned SANE's bimonthly newsletter, *The Conversion Planner*, intended to be a union resource. Melman and his fellow SANE board member and Columbia colleague, Lloyd Dumas, even authored the Defense Economic Adjustment Act, introduced to Congress in 1978.[20] With SANE making the case for economic conversion, a peace phalanx expanded in organized labor as several major unions moved closer to the progressive movement. William Winpisinger, who was elected as president of the International Association of Machinists and Aerospace Workers in 1977, welcomed a platform of economic conversion and commissioned a study in 1978 which found that machinist employment was declining in direct proportion to increases in military spending. Winpisinger joined SANE as a co-chair in 1979 and initiated a peace movement among traditionally pro-defense labor leaders.[21]

When Reagan announced his first budget, the leaders of Freeze and SANE reached out to the African American community, stressing the connection between economic and social crises at home and increases in the military budget.[22] Some in the Black community who worked for disarmament felt neglected by the larger movement. Gary Johnson and Brenda Johnson, a husband and wife team who had founded Blacks against Nukes in 1981, rejected the common argument that Black Americans were too concerned about putting food on the table to worry about nuclear war. They argued that the largely white antinuclear movement made no effort to address nuclear issues from the Black perspective or to actually work within the Black community.[23] The dominant perception among Black activists was that the antinuclear cause was a "white issue," a messaging problem that stemmed from the obstinacy of dogmatists in the peace movement who valued purity of purpose over coalition building.[24] Qualifying his support for the Freeze movement, Barack Obama, then a young Columbia University student, said, "One is forced to wonder whether disarmament and arms control issues, severed from economic and political issues, might be another instance of focusing on the symptoms of the disease itself."[25]

Reagan's policies made the new emphasis on the economic dimension of antinuclear activism more consequential to the Black community. Impoverished urban African American neighborhoods were the hardest hit by Reagan's first term-budgets, which cut social programs by $140 billion to finance an increase in military spending by $181 billion.[26] Black jobless rates were nearly twice that of white Americans', and paring back the Comprehensive Employment and Training Act, which provided job training and placement assistance for the unemployed, exacerbated the crisis.[27] During the first twelve months of the Reagan administration, the real median income of Black families fell by more than 5 percent.[28]

Reagan's budget also appeared to vindicate the warnings of radical scientists, whose political voice, like that of Catholics, women, and minorities, grew louder during the late 1960s and 1970s. Along with opposition to the Vietnam War, rising fear on university campuses about the militarization of space had created an opening for Marxist and socialist critiques of science's role in U.S. foreign and defense policy.[29] Radical scientists were emboldened in their campaign against the military-industrial-academic complex by revelations in the Pentagon Papers, which revealed the influence of the JASONs, an elite group of nongovernmental scientists who had served as advisors on the use of military technologies in the Southeast Asian conflict as well on numerous other scientific and technological questions related to national security.[30] Scientists and Engineers for Social and Political Action, which later became Science for the People (SfP), published a condemnation of the JASONs in 1972 and used the ensuing controversy as a platform to nudge established institutions of science toward a more critical evaluation of U.S. defense policies and to engage in wider discussion with the general public.[31]

With Reagan's budget indicating an acceleration of the arms race, SfP emerged as an innovator in public science diplomacy. In the nuclear 1980s, its monthly magazine served as a routine source of disarmament ideas that structured a range of critiques into a transnational antinuclear community. Its avowedly Marxist outlook aligned it with historically marginalized voices on the left that were gaining political influence via their opposition to Reagan's nuclear policies and budgets. Ronald Dellums, a Democratic representative for California and a leader of the Congressional Black Caucus, was a prominent arms control advocate, and he highlighted the warnings about military control of research and development that SfP had published in the summer of 1981. SfP analysis centered on making science a tool for racial, gender, and economic equality. Going further than mainstream scientists' appeals for greater civilian research and development funds, SfP echoed SANE's call for the economic conversion of U.S. national laboratories, with a special emphasis on the nuclear weapons facilities at Lawrence Livermore and Los Alamos.[32]

In the early 1980s, mainstream scientists remained engaged in activities intended to directly influence government officials and senior policymakers, but they initially had only limited success. Their efforts became significantly more effective when paired with public approaches to science diplomacy, and they quickly recognized that indirect influence—that is, using their expertise to mobilize public opinion—had been an underappreciated strategy for halting the arms race. Richard Garwin proved to be especially adept at pairing public and private approaches to science diplomacy to advocate for a moderation of U.S. nuclear policies. As a defense consultant for national laboratories and the Pentagon, a senior scientist at IBM, and an Ivy League professor, Garwin was deeply immersed in the military-industrial-academic complex. Yet he argued that Reagan's budgets reflected the thinking of a "nuclear mafia" who viewed nuclear weapons as a panacea to the problems facing American power. This mafia, he said, sought to reassert monopoly control over nuclear knowledge and other technical defense information that had lured Americans into uncritically accepting deterrence.[33]

Garwin took issue with the nuclear mafia's vision that nuclear weapons could defeat the Soviet Union and simultaneously revive the economy. His primary concern was that defense funding would coerce academic scientists, and universities in general, to once again accept Cold War militarism.[34] Reagan's revised budget, submitted in the fall of 1981, lent credence to his fears. This budget mandated still more cuts for nonmilitary research in the national laboratories, suggesting that the administration planned to keep science subservient to the interests of national security and its regime of secrecy.[35]

The authority of scientific experts made them vital to the mainstreaming of antinuclear positions. In the critical early days of the Freeze campaign, a series of well-attended symposia in major U.S. cities examined the strategic, medical, and biological dimensions of nuclear war. They were organized by PSR and the Council for a Livable World (CLW), an organization of antinuclear experts formed in 1962 by the Hungarian-American physicist Leo Szilard, who in 1939, with Albert Einstein, had brought the possibility of an atomic bomb to the attention of President Franklin D. Roosevelt.[36] Henry Kendall, a physicist and future Nobel laureate affiliated with the Stanford Linear Accelerator Center, put the full weight of the Union of Concerned Scientists (UCS) and its 110,000 nationwide sponsors behind the Freeze. Kendall, with fellow physicist Kurt Gottfried, had cofounded UCS while at the Massachusetts Institute of Technology, conceiving of it as a response to the ABM treaty debates in the late 1960s and early 1970s.[37]

Expert-led education and awareness campaigns launched in opposition to Reagan's nuclear policies became an effective track for public science diplomacy. On Veterans Day in 1981, 100,000 students participated in teach-ins hosted by UCS, PSR, and FAS. These events, held on 150 college campuses across forty-two states, were led by five hundred experts who spoke about solutions to the arms race. The teach-ins inspired the formation of United Campuses to Prevent Nuclear War, which grew to five hundred college chapters, helped develop dozens of college courses on nuclear issues, and carried out annual actions for many years.[38]

Radical and mainstream public science diplomacy invited moral, cultural, and political authorities to participate in the scientific community's self-reflections on who bore responsibility for the past, present, and future of the arms race. Frank Barnaby, the director of the Stockholm International Peace Research Institute, blamed the professional ambition of defense scientists for the creation of the "military technological tail [that] wags the political dog."[39] The United Nations acknowledged in its comprehensive report on nuclear weapons that "it is widely believed that . . . technology on its own impetus often takes the lead over policy, creating weapons for which needs have to be invented and deployment theories readjusted."[40] Conversely, Wolfgang Panofsky, a past member of the Presidential Science Advisory Committee and the director of the Stanford Linear Accelerator Center, argued that the arms race continued unabated due to a failure of politicians to understand the technical aspects of strategic weapons rather than the inability of scientists to understand the political dimensions of nuclear weapons.[41]

The scientific community's public diplomacy benefited from cooperation with other institutions with international reach, especially the Catholic church. Pairing scientific knowledge with the moral authority of the clergy enhanced the legitimacy of antinuclear claims. During his visit to Hiroshima in 1981, Pope John Paul II offered a solution to the moral dilemma arising from the relationship among science, politics, and nuclear security. He said, "Science and technology are the most dynamic factors of the development of society today" but argued that only through a closer binding with other cultural institutions could science avoid three serious pitfalls: aimless, inequitable, or power-serving technological development. Science, he believed, must serve culture and culture serve science.[42]

The pontiff's remarks increased the effect of public science diplomacy by making it a focus of religious teaching at the community level and encouraging an environment of mutual respect between moral and technical authorities. In this way, scientific knowledge became a foundation for local actors who were formulating opinions about national and international issues.[43] By appealing to the scientific community for moral introspection, his approach also encouraged the American Catholic hierarchy to rely on scientific counsel as they drafted "The Challenge of Peace: God's Promise and Our Response," their pastoral letter on war and peace.

The Catholic church's recognition that nuclear deterrence presented a nexus of moral, social justice, and scientific problems elevated its involvement in public debate. Reagan's pronuclear and anti-Soviet rhetoric compelled the National Conference of Catholic Bishops (NCCB) to establish an ad hoc committee to compose their pastoral letter.[44] The disparities between defense spending and social spending in the Reagan administration's first budget offered further proof to church leaders of the necessity of intervention.[45] Forsberg, Kehler, and other Freeze leaders viewed religious involvement in deterrence debates as essential to developing a climate of antinuclear ideas, and they cultivated a relationship with the American Catholic church, viewing it as a source of authority that could confer mainstream political legitimacy on the antinuclear movement.[46]

Archbishop Joseph Bernardin of Cincinnati, widely respected for his skill in reconciling the views of conservative and progressive Catholics, chaired the committee. He brought a wide variety of voices into the group, selecting the progressive Thomas Gumbleton, the auxiliary bishop of Detroit and founding president of Pax Christi USA, as well as the conservative John O'Connor, an auxiliary bishop who served the military vicariate based out of New York. Between these extremes were Bishop Daniel Reilly of Norwich, Connecticut, and Auxiliary Bishop George Fulcher of Columbus, Ohio, who were key to establishing a middle ground.[47] Father J. Bryan Hehir, the author of Cardinal John Krol's 1979 congressional testimony and other treatises on ethics and foreign policy, served as the committee's chief staff writer.[48] Hehir had been with the U.S. Conference of Catholic Bishops since 1973, directing their Office of International Affairs after earning degrees from Saint John's Seminary and Harvard University.

The committee met fourteen times between July 1981 and July 1982, gathering input from former defense secretaries Harold Brown and James Schlesinger, former deputy director of the CIA Herbert Scoville, and Reagan administration officials including Secretary of Defense Weinberger, Arms Control and Disarmament Agency Director Eugene Rostow, and Under-secretary of State Lawrence Eagleburger.[49] They held additional meetings with European bishops and Vatican officials to coordinate the international Catholic response to the nuclear crisis.[50] The Bernardin committee spent two years (July 1981 to May 1983) consulting with experts and drafting its pastoral letter, and this level of engagement made it a primary player in the broader conflict between deterrence and disarmament ideas. The group set a new precedent for deliberating pastoral issues, expanding the consultation process beyond church circles to include scientists, government officials, and other experts as well as publishing drafts of the pastoral letter that made it more responsive to the wider public debate.[51]

Opposition to the arms race allowed Catholic leaders to distinguish their moral principles from those of Reagan's evangelical supporters, and they based this difference on a consistent approach to the sanctity and dignity of life. Reagan's nuclear rhetoric had been part of a concerted effort to frame the president as a defender of western Christian values and thus appeal to the 8 million members of the Moral Majority voting bloc.[52] In the late 1970s, growing Catholic political power had sparked the formation of the Moral Majority to organize predominately southern evangelical and conservative Christian voters into a political force. Their support for Reagan's nuclear policies prompted prominent Catholic leaders to charge both with moral hypocrisy due to their willingness to expand budgets for military hardware at the expense of social programs. Georgetown University's president Timothy Healy summed up the mood of many Catholic leaders when he accused Reagan and his Moral Majority allies of promoting the "rhetoric of condemnation" rather than supporting the well-being of American citizens.[53] At the November 1981 conference of American bishops in Washington, D.C., John Roach, the archbishop of Minneapolis–Saint Paul, became the first NCCB president to criticize evangelicals' use of morality in public policy discussions. By pointing out their inconsistent approach to the sanctity of life and other political issues, he reinforced the Bernardin committee's commitment to the importance of its pastoral letter, which they saw, in part, as a way to respond to the increased use of morality as a political tool.[54]

Nuclear Politics and the 1982 Midterm Election

Antinuclear ideas emerged as a focus of the 1982 midterm elections, demonstrating that the fight over nuclear modernization also reflected broad moral, technical, and political trends influencing the American electorate. By the beginning of the year, the antinuclear activities of the American Catholic hierarchy had started to alarm Reagan's political allies, who had been hoping to build on the gains that Republicans had made in the 1980 election. At that time, Reagan had won the national Catholic vote by an eleven-point margin over Carter, the first time a Republican candidate for president had outperformed a Democratic rival with the Catholic constituency since before the Civil War. Heading into the 1982 midterms, however, Reagan's advisors recognized that the president's morality politics had begun to cater too much to evangelicals and not enough to the increasingly important Catholic vote.[55]

Meanwhile, several new publications about nuclear war had been released, and they illustrated how a small band of defense intellectuals framed the problem. All of these treatises directly linked humanistic and moral developments in American society to changes in public science diplomacy. This integration of scientific expertise and nonscientific knowledge claims into a coherent and widely disseminated critique of deterrence made nuclear debates in the 1980s qualitatively different from those earlier in the Cold War. Consider, for instance, the gap between Herman Kahn's controversial *On Thermonuclear War* (1960) and Jonathan Schell's bestselling essay collection *The Fate of the Earth* (1982).[56] The prose in Kahn's massive volume reflects the cold culture of nuclear analysis, rooted in mathematical calculation and the physical sciences, and Kahn hoped it would galvanize society to think about the unthinkable—life on earth after a nuclear war. Yet his disinterested and statistical assessment of that future drew heavy criticism from readers who saw it as devoid of humanistic or moral substance.[57] To many, the work perfectly illustrated the disturbing trend illuminated by C. P. Snow in 1959: a widening gulf between literary and scientific cultures that produced incomprehension and hostility.[58] Kahn's *On Thermonuclear War* was the archetypal expression of the technical priesthood's limited approach to defining and resolving the problem of nuclear war and survival.

In contrast, Schell, a veteran columnist at the *New Yorker*, propelled the antinuclear movement forward by reconciling science and literary cultures in *The Fate of the Earth*. A bestseller in America, the book also sold 80,000 copies in Britain its first week of release.[59] Schell spent five years consulting with the scientific community and thoroughly studying recent reports on nuclear war from the Department of Defense, the Department of Energy, the Office of Technology Assessment, the National Academy of Sciences, and many other government offices and independent scientific institutions. In his book, he unreeled a broad range of scientific and humanistic rationales to argue that the unthinkable should also be the undoable. Schell explored nuclear war's transformation of the physical environment in conjunction with its effects on the cultural, emotional, and psychological realms of human society, providing numerous access points through which people could grapple with the consequences of the arms race and deterrence.

The Fate of the Earth, published only three weeks before the Freeze hosted its second annual conference in Denver in late February, dramatically increased the event's attendance and vibrancy.[60] Legislative staffers representing Congressman Edward Markey and Senator Edward Kennedy, both Democrats from Massachusetts, scouted the conference in preparation for an upcoming joint congressional resolution.[61] On March 10, 1982, following Markey's House resolution for a nuclear moratorium, Kennedy and Senator Mark Hatfield, a Republican from Oregon, introduced a Senate resolution for a nuclear freeze. The announcement at American University generated much fanfare.[62] Thanks to these political moves, Schell's bestseller, and the Freeze's measurable electoral impact in the Northeast, national media outlets began paying significant attention to the antinuclear movement.[63]

Schell's book had demonstrated the effectiveness of eloquently communicated scientific knowledge, especially in regard to the ecological effects of nuclear war, and soon the astronomer Carl Sagan also emerged as a pivotal figure on this front. After winning the Pulitzer for his book on the future of human intelligence, *Dragons of Eden (1977),* the Cornell professor began hosting the popular television series *Cosmos.* He quickly became the nation's premier science communicator and a Democratic darling in Washington. Along with Kennedy, Senator William Proxmire of Wisconsin, Senator Alan Cranston of California, and Congressman Al Gore of Tennessee relied heavily on Sagan's analysis of nuclear war and hailed his authority when they publicized the March 1982 freeze resolution.[64] Democratic lawmakers gradually encouraged Sagan to contextualize his scientific assessments of nuclear war within more political, social, and strategic arguments, thereby making him a leading practitioner of public science diplomacy.[65] Those lessons would shape the preparation and presentation of a study that Sagan was leading on the environmental and biological consequences of nuclear war.[66]

The public defection of scientists from the nuclear security establishment legitimized antinuclear arguments, attracted media attention, and accelerated the growth of the antinuclear movement.[67] Roger Molander's 1982 bestseller *Nuclear War: What's in It for You?* brought public attention to divisions among what he referred to as the "technical priesthood" of nuclear experts, the group that Garwin had earlier referred to as a "nuclear mafia."[68] Molander himself had been a member of this select group. After earning a PhD in nuclear engineering, he had joined the National Security Council, where he had worked on arms control issues for the Nixon, Ford, and Carter administrations. His criticism of the establishment to which he had once belonged was becoming a trend among defense scientists and technical elites, who were publicly challenging Reagan's justifications for an increase in nuclear armaments and, in the process, worrying administrative officials about the antinuclear movement's growing technical and scientific legitimacy.[69]

The Reagan administration's peace through strength rhetoric accelerated Molander's launch of a nuclear education program to stimulate informed public debate. Ground Zero, the organization he had founded with his wife Mary and a small band of experts late in 1980. Ground Zero Week, the program's signature event was scheduled for April 18–25, 1982, and planned to coincide with Easter. The goal was to keep the public focused on antinuclear sentiments as they headed into the summer. In June and July the U.N. Second Special Session on Disarmament (SSOD) would take place, followed by the fall midterm elections. Though Ground Zero organizers had early fundraising struggles, they received a significant boost from the antinuclear events of February and March. When Ground Zero Week arrived, nearly 1 million people participated in activities ranging from peace runs and bike rides to academic seminars, across 2,000 municipalities and 350 college campuses, an event that nearly emptied the tank of qualified speakers.[70]

Ground Zero Week motivated a significant innovation in public science diplomacy, one that would influence the deterrence debate for the remainder of the decade. Inspired by the event, numerous scientific organizations devoted to reversing the arms race decided to prioritize nuclear curriculum design for schoolchildren. This new focus created a point of cooperation between the scientific community and women activists. With the backing of the National Education Association, the American Association of University Women, and the National Council of Churches, among other groups, Ground Zero developed curricula for elementary and high school students, and FAS launched the Nuclear War Education Project to train teachers and experts on how to educate children about the complexities of the nuclear age.[71] Because women dominated the ranks of primary- and secondary-school teachers as well as the 5.3 million-member Parent Teacher Association, they were able to determine guidelines for teaching nuclear issues and could use nuclear curricula to structure conversations about civic life in ways that reflected the values of the peace movement.[72]

Anxieties regarding motherhood and child rearing in the nuclear age had shifted from earlier concerns about the effects of radioactive fallout on the physical development of children to the psychological trauma caused by the arms race, and this shift factored into educational concerns.[73] The psychiatrists John Mack of Harvard and Eric Chivian of the Massachusetts Institute of Technology had been deeply affected by Helen Caldicott's activism. In fact, Chivian had helped to reestablish PSR and was a leader of International Physicians for the Prevention of Nuclear War, which would win the Nobel Peace Prize in 1985. Mack and Chivian had worked with both American and Soviet children and had concluded that children's preoccupation with nuclear war could cause long-term psychological trauma.[74] They found that, compared to American children, Soviet children were more aware of nuclear weapons and less likely to believe they could survive a nuclear war. Soviet children were also more confident that the superpowers could avoid such a war. Mack, Chivian, and their Harvard-based team chalked up the differences in children's views to Soviet curricula that covered nuclear issues.[75]

Psychological assessments of children's nuclear fear contributed to the public turn in science diplomacy. Organizers seized on the Harvard study's findings to lobby for new school curricula that would meet the intellectual and emotional demands of the nuclear age. They were particularly motivated by the Reagan administration's perceived disregard for scientific knowledge about the consequences of nuclear war. In the United States, the Federal Emergency Management Agency's pilot program, Emergency Management Instruction, taught 80,000 students that nuclear war was survivable, while T. K. Jones, the deputy undersecretary of defense for strategic and theater nuclear forces, asserted that the best protection from nuclear war was a hole in the ground, a door to cover the hole, and two feet of dirt on top of the door. The press and the antinuclear movement widely disseminated Jones's ill-informed quip, "Everybody's going to make it if there are enough shovels to go around."[76] Responding to these developments and informed by ongoing research at Harvard, Roberta Snow and Tony Wagner launched Educators for Social Responsibility (ESR) in 1982, using the same model as PSR.[77] The group quickly grew to more than 10,000 members and supporters, with more than one hundred chapters in more than thirty states and Canada.[78]

Emphasizing U.S. moral superiority over the Soviet Union had been envisioned as a main component of the Reagan administration's nuclear public diplomacy plan, but White House officials now acknowledged the difficulties in selling an image of moral clarity in the face of public science diplomacy, growing Catholic opposition to deterrence, and the variety of social justice issues tied into the antinuclear movement.[79] In April 1982, top advisors who were outlining the public nuclear diplomacy campaign against the Freeze feared antagonizing and alerting antinuclear opponents. National Security Advisor William Clark wrote to his colleagues, "In no way do I wish to foster a 'we/they' syndrome, where in we become antagonists with Roger Molander of Ground Zero, or Billy Graham, or 40 Catholic Bishops, or the Mayor of Pella, Iowa."[80]

Alexander Haig set out to revamp the psychological, moral, and social justifications for nuclear superiority by providing a roadmap for the administration's public relations offensive. MAD represented an interest-based realist philosophy and rested on a bargain with the Soviet Union that supposedly compromised the moral values of the West. Strategic superiority, however, rested on the political will among western publics to build and deploy weapons that granted an advantage over the Soviet Union. In essence, Haig wanted the contract for deterrence to be between western governments and their publics rather than between the United States and the Soviet Union; he wanted to shift to strategic superiority and away from MAD.

In his speech to the Center for Strategic and International Studies at Georgetown University, which heavily informed the president's later address on arms control, Haig asserted that "deterrence . . . is the essential political bargain which binds together the Western coalition. . . . deterrence, is the only effective intellectual, political and moral response to nuclear weapons. . . . sustaining deterrence, we protect values of Western Civilization—democratic government, personal liberty, and religious freedom."[81] His reference to these principles as the foundation of western civilization, in the context of an alliance commitment to deterrence, reflected a pervasive view in the Reagan administration—one that stemmed from the opinions that Reagan had expressed in the 1970s—that the West's moral superiority should manifest itself in nuclear superiority. Quoting Reinhold Niebuhr, the high priest of Christian realism and a long-favored theologian of the American foreign policy community, Haig stated, "The highest possibilities are inextricably mingled with the most dire perils." He implied that human nature required that the most morally righteous of political systems—western democracy—inherently demanded the deadliest of weapons systems, nuclear arms, for its defense.[82]

Haig was far from alone in emphasizing a western moral imperative as both a public defense of deterrence and a rational basis for formulating nuclear policy. Top advisors frequently made similar arguments in their analysis of U.S.-Soviet relations, in part because the senior ranks of the administration were stocked with devoted Catholics.[83] As the veteran diplomat Tom Melady advised White House Chief of Staff James Baker, "our position is the moral one for a responsible major power in an imperfect world, where aggressive communists—atheist forces are out to destroy Judeo-Christian values."[84]

Whereas the Reagan administration emphasized Christian realist ideas to justify nuclear superiority, the drafts of the pastoral letter on war and peace remained focused on two Catholic traditions: just war theory and pacifism.

Several Catholic bishops had raised the national profile of nuclear pacifism through acts of civil disobedience. Archbishop Raymond Hunthausen of Seattle, who referred to Naval Base Kitsap, which harbored Ohio-class nuclear submarines, as the "Auschwitz of Puget Sound," had urged members of his diocese to withhold half of their income tax to protest military spending.[85] His antinuclear advocacy vexed one of the Senate's most hawkish members, Henry Jackson, a Democrat from Washington, in his own backyard and emboldened local organizers. In 1982, to elevate awareness of the nuclear dilemma, Hunthausen helped organize Target Seattle, which involved sixty-seven community organizations, two hundred churches, most of the city's public schools, and drew 25,000 people to the Kingdome for an antinuclear rally.[86] Hunthausen's activism inspired Amarillo's bishop, Leroy Matthiesen, to promote tax resistance and organize a protest of the nearby Pantex plant, the primary nuclear weapons assembly site in the United States.[87]

Versions 1 and 2 of the pastoral letter—completed in June 1982 and November 1982—bookended a period of heightened intensity in the deterrence debate, and they stirred public interest and triggered responses from both the Reagan administration and the Vatican. For the most part, American bishops—with some notable exceptions—called for an even stronger condemnation of Reagan's nuclear policies and an implicit endorsement of the principles of a nuclear freeze.[88] Bernardin's committee, however, had to avoid pushing too hard against Reagan's nuclear policies, for Pope John Paul II, an avowed anticommunist, was working closely with the White House on other Cold War problems.[89] Yet the drafts had an impact on the domestic debate and on foreign publics, so Reagan's public diplomacy operations focused intensely on rebutting the arguments of the peace bishops during the letter's draft stages.

Pro- and antinuclear activities were planned to coincide with the second U.N. SSOD, and the timing of that session, in summer 1982, ensured that the nuclear debate would become a major issue in the upcoming election. Momentum from Ground Zero Week carried into summer demonstrations, which set the backdrop for a series of critical votes in Congress on nuclear issues.[90] For nearly eighteen months Freeze leaders had prioritized organizing for their SSOD demonstration because they considered it to be an important component of their congressional strategy. They hoped to build on its momentum as they worked toward their goal of bringing disarmament-minded legislators to Capitol Hill.[91] On June 12, 1982, the antinuclear SSOD rally took place in New York City's Central Park, drawing a crowd of between

750,000 and 1 million people, the largest demonstration in American history up to that point. Cultural icons such as Bruce Springsteen, Pete Seeger, James Taylor, Harry Belafonte, and Orson Welles attracted the national media.[92] Yet even though the press captured an impressive show of progressive unity, it failed to cover the content of the antinuclear speeches, which offered an array of critical perspectives on U.S. power.

The Freeze campaign's SSOD rally appeared to jumpstart the administration's public diplomacy strategy. To do so, the government relied on an official line pushed from the White House, the State Department, the Pentagon, and, importantly, from private-sector initiatives that could expand upon the conservative moral case for nuclear superiority free from the burdens of officialdom. With Reagan in the Oval Office, an impressive network of think tanks had increased their influence, and televangelists and conservative activists at the peak of their power spearheaded the moral aspect of public nuclear diplomacy.[93]

In Herman Kahn, the provocative author of *On Thermonuclear War*, the Reagan administration found an ally willing to make the moral case for nuclear superiority from an expert's perspective.[94] His *New York Times* editorial, "Thinking about Nuclear Morality," published the day after the record-breaking Central Park antinuclear rally, sought to debunk the Freeze movement's strategic arguments in favor of disarmament. Kahn's mix of rhetoric, cultural imagery, expertise, and moral arguments encapsulated the goals of the Reagan administration's anti-Freeze campaign. He reclaimed the cowboy criticism of Reagan and turned it into a positive characteristic, framing the president not as an uninformed rogue but as a compassionate leader able to make the tough decisions required of an American president in a nuclear world: "'Reagan the cowboy,' really does seem to understand that skillful diplomacy and negotiation are as important as military defense."[95] Identifying himself as a futurist concerned with the well-being of all humanity, Kahn defined the president's peace through strength rhetoric as a visionary promise for world peace. He accepted the antinuclear movement's premise of a no-first-use policy, a position the president had rejected a month earlier, but argued that such a policy generated a moral imperative to enhance deterrence at both the conventional and nuclear levels. According to him, no-first-use did not imply disarmament but actually required the rearmament championed by the Reagan administration. Kahn conjectured, "Nowhere is it written that weakness is a virtue, *and* a nation which does not have high moral visions (a no-first-use policy)—accompanied by practical planning (an adequate war-fighting capability)—is weak. An appropriate national posture is to be strong both morally and military."[96]

Throughout the summer of 1982, the administration's allies hammered down on arguments about the morality of deterrence. George Will, an ascending national pundit, agreed with Kahn that the positions forward by the peace bishops and Bernardin's committee demonstrated not moral revelation but a bankrupt intellect. Ernest Lefever, a Christian ethicist who earlier had served the neoconservative cause with his cutting criticisms of the prestige press, now turned to organizing the moral case for rearmament around the premise of the apocalypse, a theme that the televangelists soon picked up.[97]

Fresh from her successful battle to block passage of the Equal Rights Amendment, the conservative activist Phyllis Schlafly announced in 1982 that she was taking on the Freeze movement as the focus of her next campaign. She saw the empowerment of progressive women's values through the antinuclear movement as a threat to all that she had achieved. During the 1970s, Schlafly had been a key voice in the neoconservative assault on the intellectual foreign policy elite. Her books, coauthored with the staunchly conservative Chester Ward, a retired rear admiral, had highly sensationalized then secretary of state Henry Kissinger's alleged betrayal of U.S. national security interests. In Schlafly's and Ward's view, every geopolitical challenge to U.S. hegemony could be blamed on Kissinger's arms control policies. Their best-known diatribe, *Kissinger on the Couch*, written in the style of a slanderous gossip column, featured "translations" of nuclear jargon into "non-intellectual American language" to show how elites were retreating in the face of growing Soviet nuclear power.[98] Now, in 1982, at an event at the Shoreham Hotel in Washington, D.C., Schlafly declared to her 50,000-member Eagle Forum: "The Atomic Bomb is a marvelous gift that was given to our country by a wise God."[99]

For his part, Reagan appealed directly to conservative Catholics, whose views of geopolitics and moral convictions seemed to align with his positions rather than those of the peace bishops. In an address to the Catholic-affiliated Knights of Columbus in August 1982, he applauded the 8,000-member fraternal organization for its consistent defense of deterrence. Reagan also reiterated his commitment to the alternative freeze resolution sponsored by his congressional allies, Washington's hawkish Senator Jackson and Senator John Warner, a Republican from Virginia, which endorsed a freeze only if the United States and the Soviet Union were to implement a sharp mutual

reduction in strategic weapons.[100] The resolution would not change negotiating positions or offer modernization plans that might bring on reductions
more rapidly. Though the American Catholic hierarchy had become more
progressive since Vatican II, Reagan's speech to the Knights of Columbus
sought to court the still-substantial conservative Catholic population that
had reacted against church reforms of previous decades.

The internal conflict between conservative and liberal Catholics became
a key component of the Reagan administration's broader public diplomacy
plan to roll back communism.[101] Developing the president's pronuclear
agenda lay behind the creation of several new organizations through which
conservative lay Catholics challenged the progressive hierarchy. For instance,
the American Catholic Committee and the Catholic Center for Renewal,
launched by the Heritage Foundation's director of studies, Philip Lawler,
sought to mitigate the influence of the bishops on lay Catholics, arguing that
the clergy should not involve themselves in foreign policymaking.[102] Reagan's
most prominent Catholic ally, Michael Novak, had, like the president, transformed himself from New Deal Democrat to conservative darling. During
his graduate studies at Harvard, under the mentorship of Reinhold Niebuhr,
Novak had begun examining the place of morality in international relations.
Now, as Reagan increasingly emphasized the extraordinary moral role of the
United States, Novak found himself aligned with the man he claimed to have
voted against in California gubernatorial contests.[103] A former seminarian, he
sought to establish a pastoral tradition for conservatives rooted in the Christian realist framework, an approach that put him in competition with the
progressive U.S Catholic clergy. By the early 1980s, Novak was the religious
editor of the *National Review* and had emerged as one of the most prominent
lay theologians in the United States. As conflict between the peace bishops
and the Reagan administration deepened, he became an important informal
advisor to USIA's director Charles Wick, influencing public diplomacy operations and the White House's public messaging on nuclear issues.[104]

As a resident scholar at the leading conservative think tank, the American
Enterprise Institute, Novak nearly single-handedly launched the public diplomacy campaign that supported conservative Catholic resistance to the peace
bishops. His pro-deterrence articles appeared in the pages of *Commentary, the
Wall Street Journal, the National Review, Time*, and several other high-profile
publications throughout 1982. Novak argued that the bishops' arguments
against deterrence lacked theological sophistication, which he blamed on

their eagerness to turn nuclear anxiety into a pastoral opportunity. He took issue with both their tactics and their supposed political goals. He reserved his most adversarial tone for his claim that the bishops had unethically marshaled their moral authority to support their actions as citizens and had thus opened divides within Catholicism that could only favor the Soviet Union's Cold War aims.[105]

Other conservative writers went further, seeking to discredit Freeze campaigners and transnational peace activists as agents of the Kremlin. Soon after the massive antinuclear rally in Central Park, the wife and husband team Rael Jean Isaac and Erich Isaac published their essay "The Counterfeit Peacemakers," in the *American Spectator.* The Isaacs contended that Soviet fronts in the form of the World Peace Council (WPC) and the U.S. Peace Council had taken hold of the peace movement during the terminal decline of pacifism in the United States. This, in turn, had produced an "adversary culture" that transformed public anxieties into a "weapon to prevent achievement of the Reagan administration's keystone effort: the restoration of U.S. defense capabilities."[106] John Barron's September 1982 *Reader's Digest* article, "The KGB's Magical War for Peace," escalated the assault.[107] At the time, *Reader's Digest* was the bestselling magazine in the United States, and Barron used that platform to argue that the Freeze and parallel antinuclear movements in Europe owed their existence and superior organization to the KGB.[108]

The press campaign to link the peace movement to the Kremlin was an ongoing task of the Reagan administration's interagency working group on active measures. The WPC was a particular focus.[109] In July 1982, the State Department released a report asserting that the council had strong connections to the antinuclear movement in the United States and Europe.[110] Much of the evidence for these claims relied on the testimony of Soviet dissidents such as the British-based Vladimir Bukovsky, who, in articles for the *Times* in December 1981 and *Commentary* in May 1982, had brought new attention to how the Soviet Union conducted active measures operations through the peace movement.[111] Even before launching his 1980 presidential campaign, Reagan had been captivated by Bukovsky's insights into Soviet propaganda and intelligence operations.[112] The Freeze movement, in fact, shared Reagan's concerns about Soviet active measures. Recalling the Kremlin's influence over 1970s peace campaigns, Freeze activists had, from the beginning, taken steps to distance themselves from front organizations to avoid rightwing accusations. In July testimony before the House Intelligence Committee, both CIA and FBI officials dismissed charges that Soviet active measures were having a significant influence on U.S. policymakers and the peace movement, and they doubted that Soviet operations had boosted turnout for the Central Park rally.[113]

Despite their efforts, peace through strength advocates did not make significant inroads in liberal states or establish a useful rapport with skeptical women, minorities, or most Catholics.[114] The administration and its allies simply could not marshal the expert speakers, moral paragons, and mix of sensationalist and astute media coverage to match the grassroots strength of the antinuclear movement. Late in the summer of 1982, Freeze activists were finally able to tally where incumbent legislators stood on the issue when a Freeze initiative in the House of Representatives failed on a tight vote of 204 to 202. (In the case of a tie, parliamentary procedures would have resulted in the bill's passage.) Now the Freeze campaign had a one-vote motto to brandish and list of representatives to challenge in the upcoming midterms.[115]

Scientists continued to add technical merit to the Freeze's political momentum. After the Stanford-trained mathematician Jeremy Stone became director of the Federation of American Scientists in 1970, the organization began aggressively advocating for arms control. Stone had been an early developer of the nuclear-freeze concept, first formulating the idea during a 1969 trip to Moscow. Under his leadership, FAS was the primary organization of experts pushing back against the neoconservative assault on SALT I and II during the years of détente. In the leadup to the 1982 elections, FAS conducted and publicized its own series of freeze hearings, repeating this process in 1983 to parallel those being held on Capitol Hill.[116] FAS was both a technical and a networking organization, able to work out the details of a freeze verification while bringing other defense experts into the fold. By the early 1980s it was comprised of some 5,000 scientists, including dozens of distinguished defense experts and at least fifty Nobel laureates.

FAS's commitment to the idea of a freeze aligned many influential American scientists with the progressive antinuclear coalition, and they, too, became involved in supporting midterm challenges to pronuclear conservatives. Several scientists served as conduits between the antinuclear movement and congressional Democrats. Al Gore, for instance, used Carl Sagan as a resource for challenging Reagan's deterrence claims, while Sagan saw Gore as a powerful ally in making new scientific knowledge the basis for political and behavioral solutions to the arms race. In September 1982, Gore led a hearing of the House Committee on Science and Technology on the consequences of nuclear war for the global environment.[117] His goal was to link the emotional, political, and sociocultural elements of antinuclear sentiment to a scientific and technical case for constraining Reagan's nuclear expansion. Jonathan Schell's *The Fate of the Earth* had foreshadowed this connection, in part because his work had been informed by the preliminary research from nuclear-winter experts that was also feeding Gore's nuclear politics. Based on the findings of the House hearing and his knowledge of preliminary work supporting what would become nuclear winter theory, Gore eventually tabled a congressional resolution calling for a year of international research on the environmental effects of nuclear war: "What [scientists] seem to be saying is that not only might life after a nuclear war be ominously difficult, but that nature, itself, could conceivably wither under a major nuclear attack."[118] This focus on the ecological effects of nuclear explosions naturally intensified the environmental movement's opposition to nuclear weapons.[119]

As more and more scientists became involved in the antinuclear movement, members of the technical priesthood intensified their lobbying of the Reagan administration. They wanted an increased focus on technological fixes to the political problems posed by the Freeze and petitioned the president to prioritize ballistic missile defense (BMD). Between 1980 and 1983, a group of conservative defense intellectuals operating out of the Heritage Foundation made the most of their close ties to the White House's science advisor and Reagan's inner circle of political advisors and donors. Among the experts on the Heritage committee, Edward Teller was the most prestigious. A member of the team that had developed the first hydrogen bomb and a well-known Cold War hawk, he had captured Reagan's imagination in 1967, discussing the concept of strategic defense while the future president toured Lawrence Livermore National Laboratories.[120]

Nearly two decades later, in a one-on-one meeting with Reagan on September 14, 1982, Teller pulled together the various strategic and technical arguments for BMD into a political framework that he believed could alleviate the president's problems with Congress and the antinuclear movement. The High Frontier Project, an ally of the Heritage committee's venture on strategic defense, directed by retired general and Committee on the Present Danger member Daniel Graham, had already shown how technical advances in BMD could improve area, or "point," defense of MX deployments in existing ICBM silos. The MX issue had dogged Reagan's broader modernization program in Congress and had been the focus of opposition for many antinuclear organizations, notably SANE. Now Teller focused specifically on how strategic defense could rebut the antinuclear movement and the threat it posed to national security by shifting the terms of the deterrence debate.[121] Earlier that year he had proposed to Reagan that strategic defense constituted "a uniquely effective reply to those advocating the dangerous inferiority implied by a 'nuclear freeze.'"[122] He was correct: Teller's and the Heritage Foundation's lobbying and consulting activities had indeed grabbed the attention of the antinuclear movement. Organizers' fears that "High Frontier would turn the grass-roots nuclear Freeze movement inside out" validated Teller's political instincts.[123]

Admiral James D. Watkins was also sympathetic to Teller's ideas about strategic defense. Watkins was a devout practicing Catholic, and he began publicly touting a moral framework for deterrence soon after he became chief of naval operations, with the goal of combating the influence of the disarmament movement in the Navy. After watching Teller's skillful advocacy for BMD development on a June 1982 episode of the television public affairs show *Firing Line*, Watkins commissioned a study on strategic defense.[124] That summer's developments suggest that the political and moral implications of BMD were becoming more important to the Reagan administration than the technical and strategic aspects were. Nonetheless, the numerous technical complications associated with the prospect of launching a major strategic defense program remained significant enough to prevent the administration from using the idea to counter the Freeze movement's political momentum heading into the midterms. Even in the National Security Council, home of the strongest advocates for BMD, officials did not consider a major research and deployment program to be a realistic option. In August, NSC aide Sydell Gold recommended, "At this time, the knowledge base is not sufficiently developed, and the applications are not clearly enough defined, to support a decision to go all out on the explosively driven x-ray laser."[125] National Security Advisor William Clark told Reagan in mid-September, "Although some scientists believe the class of technologies that Dr. Teller is endorsing holds great promise, a number of studies indicate that applications are now too ill-defined and there remain too many technical uncertainties to justify any crash program."[126]

By the end of summer, Reagan officials had resigned themselves to a Freeze victory in November.[127] In August, forty-eight states and more than 315 congressional districts reported varying levels of Freeze activity.[128] Following the

long antinuclear summer of 1982 that began with Ground Zero Week, peaked
with the Central Park rally, and concluded with a final national demonstration
in October, 56 percent of voters said that they would vote against a congressional candidate who favored an escalation in the arms race, even if they agreed
on all other issues.[129]

The electoral activities of antinuclear organizations played a significant
role in the Democratic Party's 1982 congressional comeback and established a blueprint for the 1984 presidential elections. Much of this activity
had focused on preparing for the hundreds of freeze referenda at the state,
county, and municipal levels, which Freeze's national office had been coordinating throughout the summer. In total, nearly a third of the country's
electorate voted on a freeze referendum—perhaps the closest the United
States had come to a national plebiscite on a single issue in the twentieth century.[130] The Freeze campaign enlarged its national staff to include minority
and labor coordinators, and the national committee opted to include more
representatives at the state and municipal levels to better reflect the nation's
mood on disarmament.[131] These organizers were key to successful voter and
petition drives that propelled Freeze allies to victory. Midterm voter turnout
increased for the first time since the 1960s and shifted in favor of the Democrats, who added 6.1 million votes compared to an additional 3 million for the
Republican Party.[132]

Results of the midterms illuminated the political power of the Freeze.
Eight of the nine states with the issue on the ballot, as well as Washington,
D.C., voted in favor of the freeze, thirty-four of thirty-seven counties passed
the freeze, and the hundreds of municipal elections that had included a freeze
referendum passed it by a three-to-two margin. Pro-Freeze candidates won
in thirty-eight of the forty-seven races where nuclear issues were of concern,
according to Congressman Markey's calculations. Against the *Congressional
Quarterly*'s predictions, antinuclear efforts led to four upsets, swung six of
eleven undecided contests for Freeze candidates, wiped out the company of
hawks on the House Armed Services Committee, and moderated the effects
of redistricting that moved seventeen seats from the liberal Frostbelt to the
conservative Sunbelt.[133]

CHAPTER FOUR

DETERMINED TO DETER

History shows that peace movements only bring on war.
—Phyllis Schlafly (1982)

O N A SATURDAY evening in late April 1983, Walter Cronkite, "the most trusted man in America," returned to prime time two years after retiring as anchor of *CBS Evening News* to host "The Great Nuclear Arms Debate." This unprecedented satellite broadcast event appeared on television screens in the United States, the United Kingdom, and Europe. Cronkite, who was seemingly sympathetic to the nuclear freeze, moderated the debate between a pro-deterrence pair—Henry Kissinger, a former U.S. secretary of state, and Michael Heseltine, recently appointed as British defence secretary—and an antinuclear duo: Paul Warnke, who had been the chief arms controller for the Carter administration, and Egon Bahr of West Germany's Bundestag, a prominent leader of the opposition to INF deployments. Heseltine was the only debate participant who was actively serving in a government that was preparing for nuclear deployments; and, as such, he persuasively argued a historical case for why the Soviet Union only respected strength at the bargaining table. The peace movement, Heseltine claimed, weakened the West's negotiating position by undermining the public will to maintain that strength.[1]

Heseltine's steady debate performance was just one example of the Reagan and Thatcher governments' major push to reorganize their public diplomacy in preparation for critical legislative and electoral challenges in 1983. In Britain, the outcome of the general election would determine if the country would accept U.S. cruise missiles later in the year. American and British officials considered a Conservative Party victory vital to maintaining the credibility of both extended deterrence for European security and NATO's INF negotiating strategy in talks with the Soviet Union. Conservatives' public diplomacy exploited emerging tensions within the peace movement and in the Campaign for Nuclear Disarmament–Labour Party alliance. The Thatcher government's efforts also mattered for its allies in the United States. The Reagan administration valued Heseltine's performance and others like it because they showed American audiences that U.S. allies believed the president's approach to be an effective strategy for reducing the possibility of nuclear war.

In the United States, Reagan's public diplomacy developed an even stronger moral dimension with the introduction of the Strategic Defense Initiative (SDI), which disrupted the antinuclear campaign against Reagan's nuclear agenda. The moral case for deterrence and Reagan's dealings with congressional Democrats staved off cancelation of the MX missile, which the administration considered key to reestablishing strategic superiority so that the United States could negotiate from a position of strength in arms control talks with the Soviet Union.

Though the British and American antinuclear movements failed on both the electoral and legislative fronts, progress in coalition building and the further refinement of tactics for engaging the general public primed both to prioritize their transatlantic connection. Their efforts made antinuclear ideas fundamental to an emergent global civil society and would condition nuclear diplomacy between the superpowers.

The Deterrence Debate and the 1983 British General Election

Heseltine began his term as defence secretary in January 1983 after Thatcher's cabinet was reshuffled in anticipation of the general elections later in the year. In a meeting that month with her relevant cabinet ministers, Thatcher placed him in charge of the government committee to garner support for its nuclear policies and counter CND's activities.[2] Heseltine's operation subsumed the existing government steering group run by Douglas Hurd, Peter Blaker, and Patrick Mayhew that had coordinated the activities of the Ministry of Defence, the Foreign and Commonwealth Office, the Conservative Research Department, and pro-deterrence pressure groups.[3]

With Heseltine in charge, the public diplomacy contest in the months before the general election became a battle over authority in the public sphere. The pronuclear campaign noted some internal fractures within the antinuclear movement that could be exploited for the Thatcher government's gain, especially the persistent fragility of the Labour-CND alliance and unease over radicalism. In 1983, the Thatcher government's public diplomacy suggested that the public sphere, pervaded by antinuclear themes, did not accurately represent the views of the British people. Heseltine devised a strategy that framed antinuclear advocates as interlopers in British public life and foreign affairs, which he suggested were properly the reserve of elected officials. He refocused the government campaign on abstract strategic concepts and the doctrine of deterrence rather than on defending concrete systems such as Trident and cruise missiles. This approach dovetailed with efforts to structure the broader defense debate around patriotic themes that capitalized on the public's positive impression of Thatcher's leadership during the Falklands affair.

To implement the new public diplomacy approach, the British cabinet focused on women. The Greenham Common Women had threatened not just Thatcher's policy of deterrence but the Victorian values around which she had organized the entire political philosophy of the British New Right.[4] The pronuclear campaign invested heavily in reestablishing traditional gender roles in an effort to put antinuclear radicalism on trial. By January 1983 more than half of British respondents to a MORI poll stated that GCW had made them think more seriously about nuclear disarmament, yet only 8 percent of CND supporters felt comfortable with the GCW's radical protest tactics.[5]

The GCW Embrace the Base demonstration had generated significant anxiety among Thatcher's public relations staff on how to combat the effects of antinuclear women on broader public opinion, especially with other women.[6] Because polling data showed that women and mothers tended to be more receptive to unilateral disarmament arguments, advisors recommended that Thatcher issue a call to support deterrence in either a popular women's magazine or via an address at a major women's conference.[7]

In a highly anticipated live broadcast interview on January 16, 1983, with the prominent British journalist and former Labour MP Brian Walden, Thatcher incorporated pro-deterrence logic into a broader program for restoring Victorian values. Her interview struck at the defining features of the GCW peace camp. She defined Victorian values as a respect for private property, which contrasted with the women's communal living on publicly owned land. She framed protests as fundamentally selfish acts that placed undue burden on British ratepayers and limited true equality of opportunity for those in the "silent majority," another defining feature of Thatcher's Victorian values. She spoke to the same public dimension of deterrence that Michael Quinlan had recognized as the source of arms control asymmetries between East and West: "I do wish people who brought pressure on Greenham Common and everywhere else would understand there's no public opinion in the Soviet Union. . . . If they truly hated nuclear weapons as much as I do . . . they'd want them down in the world as a whole. . . . I am the *true disarmer*. I keep the peace and freedom and justice with it."[8]

Thatcher's focus on GCW as the most effective method for branding antinuclear advocates as extremists pitted the views of womanhood held by Thatcher's New Right against those promulgated by the radicals who were expanding their influence over the Labour Party. Thatcher made a habit of rejecting feminism, once stating that "the battle for women's rights has been largely won. The days when they were demanded and discussed in strident tones should be gone forever. . . . I hated those strident tones that you still hear from some Women's Libbers."[9] Accusations of hysteria leveled against the antinuclear feminists of Greenham Common replicated Victorian-era logic that undermined the moral and intellectual authority of women in the public sphere. In contrast, Thatcher regularly identified herself first and foremost as a mother and a housewife, a strategy to connect with the ordinary woman voter.[10] Her appeals were aimed at the 40 percent of the British population who believed that it was impossible for women to maintain a career and a family.[11]

British officials and their allies also began organizing their public diplomacy campaign to influence the Reagan administration's revitalization of its public diplomacy efforts in Europe and to support NATO allies that were confronting their own domestic opposition to nuclear weapons. On January 14, 1983, Reagan signed NSDD 77, "Management of Public Diplomacy Relevant to National Security," in anticipation of general elections throughout Europe and heightened opposition in NATO basing countries to American INF deployments scheduled for later in the year. The directive highlighted the importance of international opinion to the administration's foreign policy aims, putting more emphasis on winning public support for short-term security goals than on the abstract objective of generating long-term international goodwill toward the United States.

NSDD 77 put a specific focus on international information at the same time that Thatcher was asking Hugh Thomas and his colleagues Leopold Labedz and Melvin Lasky at the Centre for Policy Studies to review Whitehall's lackadaisical information campaign on nuclear issues. Labedz and Lasky were the editors of two of Britain's leading anticommunist publications, *Survey* and

Encounter, and their writings pushed U.S. officials for more substantial investment in the private-sector public diplomacy campaign. Nongovernment campaigns, they argued, had a broader impact in the war of ideas. They worked
through Walter Raymond, an influential National Security Council staffer in
charge of much of the Reagan administration's interagency public diplomacy
efforts emerging from NSDD 77. Raymond had years of experience in the CIA
and had likely been involved in the U.S. government's covert establishment of
Encounter and *Survey* earlier in the Cold War. Labedz and Lasky praised those
involved in USIA's Project Truth for recognizing that ideas were "the most
powerful weapon of them all" but cautioned that Soviet propaganda had effectively undermined public will to support INF deployments, claiming that "the
intellectual disorientation has never been deeper and more widespread." They
recommended that the administration channel funds through U.S.-based
think tanks to launch a vigorous information program run by private citizens and organizations in London, where an "American-European nucleus"
already existed that could "restore the moral dignity of anti-communist ideas"
that upheld justifications for INF deployments.[12]

Anglo-American peace through strength advocates were particularly
motivated to establish a stronger moral case for deterrence in response to the
Church of England General Synod debate in February 1983 and the expected
release of the final draft of the American bishops' pastoral letter in the spring
or summer. Britain's Catholic bishops also grappled internally over whether
to issue a pastoral letter on nuclear weapons similar to the one being drafted
by their American counterparts. In meetings with FCO civil servants and
cabinet officers in January, British Catholic bishops had shared their concerns
regarding the influence of the CoE's General Synod debate on the Salisbury
report.[13] David Goodall, the deputy secretary of the cabinet, stressed to colleagues who were making the public case for deterrence that "the arguments
to concentrate on in dealing with the Roman Catholic Bishops are the ones
repeatedly emphasized by Michael Quinlan."[14]

The Pembroke Group, an association of British Christian strategic experts
founded by the chaplain of the HMS *Pembroke* earlier in the decade, became
a proving ground for Quinlan's moral arguments for deterrence. Goodall,
Quinlan, and other Pembroke thinkers who formulated the moral arguments
for Whitehall's campaign for deterrence did so in conversation with peers
across the Atlantic. In particular, Quinlan's correspondence with the influential
American nuclear strategist Albert Wohlstetter and the prominent Jesuit theo-

logian Francis Winters at Georgetown University anchored the moral thinking of the Pembroke Group. Through his exchanges with Winters, a key figure in shaping the American Catholic church's teachings on nuclear war, Quinlan hoped to influence the U.S. peace bishops' thinking on deterrence and contain their effect on the debate among British Catholics and in the CoE.[15]

Quinlan's anxiety over the moral dimensions of the transatlantic debate peaked when he learned that Winters had contacted the Bernardin committee and had categorically recommended condemning nuclear weapons and deterrence in their pastoral letter, in hopes that this move would shape concurrent debates in European church hierarchies.[16] In response, Quinlan and Wohlstetter together crafted a response to Winters's recommendations and to the drafts coming out of the Bernardin committee. Their defense of deterrence ultimately gave the Thatcher government a persuasive argument to feed its allies in the Catholic church and the CoE ahead of the General Synod debate.[17]

What arguments did Quinlan and his Pembroke Group associates share with Whitehall and religious leaders to defend Britain's deterrence stance? In a 1984 essay sent to Thatcher, Quinlan summarized the moral arguments that had guided the British pronuclear campaign earlier in the decade. He framed the stability of deterrence as a matter of practical ethics and criticized the U.S. peace bishops' arguments about proportionality, their flawed acceptance of the concept of no first use, and the logic of pacifism. Quinlan dismissed accusations that Whitehall had accepted the possibility of 100 million fatalities—megadeath—as an outcome of a retaliatory strike. Instead, he argued, the totalitarian adversaries who embraced countervalue strategy read their own assumptions onto those of the U.K. defense establishment; this was due to the government's ambiguous targeting doctrine, which thus provided a deterrent bonus that was not actually reflected in British nuclear war plans. In other words, Quinlan claimed that Britain's nuclear ambiguity had lured Soviet strategic planners into the trap of mirror imaging. Most importantly, he insinuated that the peace bishops themselves were acting immorally by undermining the stability of deterrence. By condemning it, he said, the bishops recognized that their "views on these matters inevitably have an importance reaching out beyond their country." This, he believed, created further asymmetries in the deterrence relationship between the West and the Soviet Union, for the "security policies [of democracies], to be dependably effective, must command a certain level of general public assent." That is, while the Soviet Union needed only to contemplate deterrence in technological terms (the functionality of the weapons) and psychological terms (the mental capacity of leaders to manage a nuclear conflict), the West had to grapple with a social dimension: civil society's will to accept the premise of deterrence. Opposition from religious leaders thus undermined the will of the West.[18]

In combination with this moral case for deterrence, British officials promoted an adjustment to the zero-option position around which the United States could organize its public diplomacy campaign in Europe. The proposed adjustment helped the Thatcher government domestically but also allowed it to reinforce allied resolve in Europe about the dual-track decision. In 1983, the Conservative Party was contending with more than just the radical unilateral disarmament advocated by the Labour Party. Mass defectors from Labour's right wing and a few stray moderate conservatives had joined to form the Liberal–Social Democratic Party alliance, which advocated neither unilateral disarmament nor the inevitability of INF deployments portended by the zero-option. It also touted serious defense credentials—among them, Roy Jenkins, a former chancellor of the exchequer, and David Owen, a former foreign secretary. Together, they crafted a detailed plan for multilateral disarmament as the alliance's policy platform.[19] In a parliamentary session on January 18, 1983, Jenkins pressed Thatcher to create realistic paths for arms control. She responded, "In the absence of the zero-option, we must have balanced numbers. The place to get balanced numbers is at the negotiating table at Geneva."[20]

As the Thatcher government revitalized its domestic campaign in favor of deterrence, British diplomats lobbied their U.S. counterparts to develop a new public diplomacy track, one that was mindful of European opinion.[21] The prime minister's emphasis on "balanced numbers" reflected ongoing coordination with West German officials who were advocating for an "interim solution" for INF with officials in Washington.[22] In December 1982, the USSR's new general secretary, Yuri Andropov, had proposed reducing the number of Soviet missiles in Europe to the combined numbers of British and French ground-launched nuclear forces. His proposal registered positively among Britons and Europeans who were not quite in favor of unilateral disarmament but were committed to reducing nuclear arsenals. For Thatcher and West Germany's new chancellor, Helmut Kohl, the interim solution seemed to be a middle ground that could appease public opinion before their countries' upcoming elections but leave open the goal of a zero-option.[23]

By February 1983, it seemed that Anglo-American pronuclear public diplomacy had at last arrested the momentum of the U.K.'s antinuclear movement. In late January and early February, Vice President George H. W. Bush visited the prospective INF-basing countries, a tour that was the first major U.S.-U.K. joint initiative on nuclear issues since their governments had decided to revitalize public diplomacy. Crucially, the visit preceded the General Synod's highly anticipated debate on the Salisbury report later in February. In a subsequent debriefing, British diplomats assessed Bush's visit to be the deciding factor in how Reagan might manage the dual-track strategy in the critical months ahead of winter deployments.[24] Now U.S. officials resolved to demonstrate a greater degree of flexibility on INF, specifically to give Thatcher and European allies more room to maneuver in their pronuclear campaigns.[25]

Bush opened his trip on January 30 with a dinner in West Berlin, where he read aloud Reagan's open letter to Europe, which included an invitation to Andropov to engage in a bilateral summit. Whitehall saw Reagan's offer as a cunning political move designed to swing public opinion back in favor of the dual-track decision. Throughout the trip, Bush pleased Thatcher and Kohl by frequently mentioning Washington's willingness to consider interim solutions and alternative INF negotiating positions.[26] British officials also noted the weight Bush placed on moral arguments for deployment and deterrence, which appeared to reflect the thinking of Quinlan's transatlantic network.[27]

Following Bush's visit, consultations continued between Whitehall and Washington on the nature and timing of a new announcement on a U.S. INF proposal.[28] The State Department, in particular, pressed the British line on balanced numbers and an interim solution.[29] On February 22, Reagan delivered a speech to the American Legion that had been crafted to reflect British and West German thinking.[30] He spoke warmly of a deep sense of values and political community shared by the NATO alliance and of the importance of Bush's recent tour in reaffirming these bonds. However, he rejected Andropov's proposal to include British and French forces in negotiations and insisted on a global deal. To indicate a new flexibility in the U.S. position, he also noted he had directed his administration's chief INF negotiator, Paul Nitze, to explore all possibilities that would be consistent with NATO's principles.[31]

The Reagan administration's new flexibility on INF appeared to validate Thatcher's arms control program, and Michael Heseltine took this opportunity to play up a frighteningly radical image of the antinuclear movement. On February 7 he had visited Greenham Common, where gate blockades had stalled his entrance. At the same time women activists were cutting down large portions of the fence in order to wind woven snakes into the base itself. Peace activists and government officials disagree on the actual events of that morning, but press coverage depicted a mob of angry women dragging the defence secretary into the mud. In their articles, the press used Heseltine's nickname, Tarzan, earned from his mace-wielding antics in Parliament, to frame the visit as masculinity under assault by aggressive feminism. On February 8, the *Daily Mirror* labeled the confrontation, "Tarzan's War."[32] The political cartoon that appeared in the *Sun* two days later captured much of the angst in the peace movement, with Heseltine and the police depicted as victims of burly women who were attacking them under the banner of CND.

The sensational nature of GCW press coverage complicated the relationship between the women's camp and the broader peace movement. Reporters had difficulty covering GCW because its structure and tactics did not conform to standard media narratives.[33] They could not interview leaders and spokeswomen because there was no camp hierarchy. Various subcultures across gates

FIGURE 2. Stanley Franklin, "For God's Sake Let Me In, Willie!," *Sun*, February 9, 1983. The Sun / News Licensing.

and the transient nature of the activists themselves made it difficult to construct a narrative, and the women often refused to cooperate with reporters, whom they viewed as tools of the nuclear patriarchy. As a result, the press regularly mocked the theatrical tactics of GCW and paid attention to their deviation from social norms rather than the alternatives they proposed.

The Heseltine incident incited many within the peace movement to question whether GCW's polarizing image was helping or hurting the antinuclear cause. Was GCW a distraction that diverted attention from the nuclear dilemma onto feminists who were seeking to radically restructure British family life and sexual politics? Or was it successfully bringing more citizens to think deeply about the moral legitimacy of the state's monopoly on violence, the situation that made nuclear weapons an issue of social, political, and moral consequence for the entire United Kingdom?

By the time the CoE's General Synod came together to debate the conclusions of the Salisbury group's report, *The Church and the Bomb,* in late February, Heseltine's public diplomacy campaign had dramatically shifted public perceptions of deterrence. In the end, Quinlan's morality-based arguments proved to be decisive in the General Synod debate.[34] As the Thatcher government had hoped, Quinlan's network wielded significant influence over a number of important religious figures, and this faction was able to successfully outmaneuver the Salisbury group in the debate.[35] Using Quinlan's arguments, the archbishop of Canterbury and the bishop of Birmingham were able to lead and carry the motion to defeat the unilateralism proposed by the report.

Another Thatcher ally, Graham Leonard, the archbishop of London, bridged the practical ethics of deterrence with the Christian realist logic that pervaded the pronuclear moral rhetoric coming out of the United States.[36] During the debate, he spearheaded the argument against the Salisbury group's unilateralist recommendations. In rejecting the pacifism of the Salisbury report, Leonard's position echoed Quinlan's arguments. He anchored his pronuclear advocacy in the view that nuclear weapons could not be uninvented, which meant that deterrence was the only morally logical position in a fallen world. Leonard argued that, while pacifism called for a rejection of force as a moral good, it could not be applied to a government body with the responsibility for collective defense. Neither could deterrence and pacifism be considered moral opposites. Rather than being the use of force, then, deterrence represented, in Leonard's view, the "control of force." While the rejection of force could be considered a moral right and the use of force a moral wrong, the control of force could be interpreted as morally permissive.[37]

Robert Runcie, the bishop of Birmingham, put forward a compromise that accepted the general principle of deterrence, and the synod agreed to it, disappointing antinuclear activists. His first motion declared that "it is not the task of the Church to determine defense strategy but rather to give a moral lead to the nation." It sanctioned deterrence and NATO's defensive posture but also rejected the first use of nuclear weapons that underpinned the strategic doctrine of the Atlantic Alliance. His second motion instructed CoE dioceses to further study the nuclear dilemma in order to offer informed moral and theological contributions to the debate.[38] Based on the televised portions of the debate, CND activists judged Runcie—who, they hoped, would prosecute the moral case against deterrence—to be most concerned with "mending broken fences to Downing Street."[39]

Thatcher's government believed that the General Synod debate and resolution played an essential role in enhancing the public's acceptance of deterrence.[40] The Catholic hierarchy in England and Wales, unlike those in the United States and Europe, had backed away from issuing a unified statement on deterrence because of the persuasiveness of Quinlan's ethical interpretations.[41] Later in 1983, Cardinal Basil Hume, the archbishop of Westminster, went so far as to reproduce Quinlan's arguments in his *Times* op-ed, "Towards a Nuclear Morality," while reprimanding his ecclesiastical subordinate, CND leader Bruce Kent, for his antinuclear activities.[42]

Setting the CoE's moral sanctioning of deterrence alongside increasing public unease about GCW radicalism, the Thatcher government moved assertively toward ostracizing disarmament ideas in public discourse. In March, Heseltine established Defence Secretariat 19 (DS-19), a low-profile, seven-person unit tasked with centralizing management of the government's public nuclear diplomacy. The unit's secrecy engendered controversy when a former British intelligence agent went public, accusing it of illegally monitoring CND activists.[43] Yet Heseltine's group continued its work, determining, via a network of Conservative Party organs and pro-deterrence groups, that the CND-Labour alliance was at best tenuous heading into the general elections.

These suspicions were confirmed in March when a Labour Party draft manifesto was leaked to the press. The draft contained no specifics on unilateral disarmament. CND had belatedly recognized that the obstinacy of MPs in favor of multilateralism was preventing disarmament from becoming the focus of the campaign.[44] By the time of the leak, CND's work with trade unions, Labour leaders' use of unilateralism as a tool to move the party further to the left, and Thatcher's campaign to depict the party as a group of antinuclear radicals had tied their fates together. Disagreement over disarmament as a political priority prevented them from building a coherent campaign that linked the peace movement's radical energy and social critiques with Labour's broader populist policies. Fundamentalists within CND quixotically believed unilateralism to be significant enough of an issue to determine voter behavior on its own. A number of that group's strategists considered running independent candidates in Britain's parliamentary elections.[45] Those devoted to the single cause of disarmament feuded with those loyal to Labour leader Michael Foot.[46] This discord led to CND's greatest tactical failure, the decision not to endorse the party, on the basis that this alignment might lead to a decline in membership, smaller demonstrations, and thus less political clout overall.[47]

Disjointed CND and Labour Party efforts squandered opportunities that might have reestablished antinuclear momentum ahead of the general elections. The press had rallied around a new report on the effects of nuclear war, released in the spring of 1983 and produced by the prestigious and nonaligned British Medical Association (BMA).[48] In yet another rejection of Home Office assumptions by external experts, the BMA estimated that up to 38.5 million people would die in a nuclear attack, compared to official estimates of 20.5 million. Though the report came out under the BMA's aegis and was endorsed by the British medical community, roughly half of it—including sections dealing with the direct effects of nuclear explosions—had been secretly written by SANA scientist Philip Steadman.[49] Conservative officials found the BMA report so damning that they conceded to rebellious local authorities and permanently put Hard Rock to rest, hoping this move would help them avoid any political consequences for the upcoming general elections in June.[50] CND and Labour, however, failed to use the report to reestablish unity and respectability for the disarmament movement; instead, they allowed the radical image of antinuclear activism created by Heseltine's campaign to persist in the public mind.

With the Labour-CND alliance in disarray, the Thatcher government and its allies implemented a deterrence double-speak strategy to further confuse the case against nuclear weapons. Alun Chalfont, a favorite British proxy of the Reagan administration, was an influential crossbench member of Parliament who had left Labour in the 1970s to support Thatcher after the party's leftward shift. Now he put forward a comprehensive case against the peace movement's adoption of Orwellian "Newspeak." Inspired by the 1982 arguments of American peace through strength advocates in *Reader's Digest*, he published his own version, "The Great Unilateralist Illusion," in *Encounter*. Chalfont asserted that the peace movement's connections to Soviet front organizations had corrupted their morality and underpinned their "semantic vandalism" of the English language. In his view, the movement had "no right to monopolize the word *peace*." In fact, he argued, it had corrupted the word to generate anti-Americanism and had raised moral equivalence into a political virtue that would lead to the neutralization of Western Europe. Taking direct aim at antinuclear leaders such as E. P. Thompson, Chalfont's broadside revealed that the moral divergence between peace through strength advocates and antinuclear activists had evolved into a battle to control the English language itself.[51]

Conservative politicians' success in the battle for control of the English language translated into political victory. Throughout the spring of 1983, Heseltine repeatedly claimed that the antinuclear movement and its Labour Party allies had "hijacked" the term "peace movement." He argued that, because successive British governments, beginning with Clement Attlee's, had endorsed deterrence, Whitehall represented the "peace movement, the real peacekeepers, the people upon [whom] peace depends."[52] Thatcher also consistently referred to the British government as the "true peace movement," and Whitehall assailed CND and GCW as "peacemongers" who were intent on using disarmament as a vehicle for other political ends.[53] Heseltine capitalized on GCW's alleged February assault to challenge the credentials of the peace movement and substantiate the logic of Thatcher's criticisms of antinuclear feminism. The sensationalized assault also gave him a pretense for dodging invitations from CND chairwoman Joan Ruddock to publicly debate Euromissile deployments.[54]

Heseltine's view of the debate controversy exposed a deeper division in 1980s Britain over the relationship between the government and the public sphere. Comments from Thatcher, Heseltine, and the rest of the government confirmed their rejection of protest as a legitimate form of political power and their insistence on maintaining the public consensus upon which deterrence stood. Heseltine explained away his campaign against CND, END, and their supporters: "The task of the politician is merely to remind people of what people strongly believe." Remarking on the proposed debate with Ruddock, Heseltine recalled with disdain, "The idea was preposterous. The idea that the British secretary of state, a member of the British cabinet, a representative of the British government was going to be *matched evenly* with a group of people who represented nobody, a mob on the street, was *unthinkable.*"[55]

By early April, transatlantic pronuclear public diplomacy was effective and coordinated while internal tensions had considerably undercut the peace movement. Thatcher's influence over Reagan was particularly clear on the issue of the zero-zero precondition and on the timing of the new INF announcement.[56] She believed that the more flexible INF negotiating positions should be announced before Good Friday so that the European press could publicize the news ahead of the traditional Easter antinuclear demonstrations. In response, the president moved up the date of his planned press conference with NATO officials, when he would be introducing new U.S. arms control principles.[57] Reflecting Whitehall's preferences, the revised INF negotiating principles issued in NSDD 86 stated that zero-zero continued to be the most optimal outcome, that without an acceptable agreement U.S. deployments would continue on schedule, that an interim agreement could be reached based on equal levels, that any agreement must be global in scope. However, NSDD 86 also allowed the United States to negotiate an interim agreement without the precondition of a final zero-zero outcome.[58] Reagan administration officials acknowledged that Whitehall's input on the latest INF position had given them concrete ideas for politically managing the nuclear debate in the United States and Europe.[59]

Anglo-American diplomacy maintained its edge through Easter weekend, a prime time for antinuclear protests, and this proved to Conservative Party strategists that they had persuaded the public to accept the government's nuclear policies. There were positive public reactions to Heseltine's visit to the Berlin Wall during the weekend, when he reiterated peace through strength logic, and Thatcher's subsequent statements on deterrence confirmed to Conservative leadership that it now controlled the nuclear narrative.[60] As the month progressed, the number of antinuclear petitions that constituents sent to the government fell by half compared to January's totals, and they continued to drop as the June election neared.[61] Though the strategists had taken three years to refine the moral arguments for deterrence and construct a New Right network of pronuclear organizations, that work was paying off as they escalated their efforts to take advantage of the troubled alliance between the Labour Party and the antinuclear movement.

Two demonstrations on Easter weekend—one near the Scottish home base of Britain's nuclear submarines, the other close to the Berkshire base that housed Britain's initial deployments of cruise missiles—received substantial media coverage.[62] In addition, the press took note of a fourteen-mile-long human chain connecting the blockade around the Greenham Common RAF base to demonstrations at the Aldermaston Weapons Research Establishment and the nuclear ordnance factory in Burghfield. CND claimed that 80,000 people participated in these demonstrations, but police placed the number at 40,000.[63] Though the actions had been intended to inspire unity within the fracturing antinuclear campaign, they instead triggered more internal strife over appropriate roles within the movement. One GCW activist complained, "The worst day I ever had was the Easter hand-linking. I think that might have put off more women than any other day. . . . I arrived and see all these men. . . . Haven't they heard that this is a women's action?"[64]

As the antinuclear movement struggled internally, pronuclear groups emerged in direct response to GCW, organizing around a commitment to peace through deterrence and using family values as a guiding principle. Lady Olga Maitland founded Women for Defence, later known as Women and Families for Defence (WFD), in opposition to GCW's 1983 springtime activities, and it quickly gained an international profile. In contrast to the Greenham Common peace camp, which had voted to exclude men from permanent residence, WFD deliberately included men.[65] The group primarily focused on organizing counter-protests and counter-vigils to demonstrate the passion for defense within Britain's so-called silent majority.[66] These counter-demonstrations provided opportunities for local pronuclear activists to join the larger New Right political network of think tanks and pressure groups. The group Ratepayers against the Greenham Encampments (RAGE) emerged out of counter-protests organized by WFD members. RAGE's particular issue, GCW's alleged sexual deviance, drew support from not only the pro-deterrence campaign but also a variety of pressure groups concerned with restricting homosexual influences in primary schools and other family settings—another feature of Thatcher's New Right social agenda.[67]

The rhetoric and tactics of the pro-deterrence lobby in Britain were similar to the methods employed by the moral crusaders enlisted in the U.S. pronuclear campaign, due in large part to the proliferation of contacts between the American and British New Right. Maitland, for instance, fostered extensive contacts with the Reagan administration and the peace through strength lobby in the United States. She became a darling of conservatives on both sides of the Atlantic, attending dinners and cocktail parties with Phyllis Schlafly; with John Tower, the Republican chairman of the House Armed Services Committee; and with countless members of the American New Right. Maitland saw her regular trips to the United States and her interactions with the New Right lobby as a necessary way to support her cash-strapped organization.[68] Thatcher's government also worked with U.S. public relations firms on the messaging for its pronuclear campaigns.[69] Reagan's administration directed its public diplomacy staff and think tank allies such as the Heritage Foundation to focus specifically on creating transatlantic links with churches, scientists, women's organizations, student movements, and other influential groups "to help activate the silent majority" in Britain.[70] Funded by USIA, the conservative intellectual Ernest Lefever (see chapter 3) ran a series of seminars in the United Kingdom and Europe to build support among moral leaders and religious communities for U.S. nuclear policies.[71]

Heseltine later recollected that it only took six weeks to turn the nuclear issue around in favor of deterrence.[72] On May 10, 1983, after the Conservative Party believed this turnaround was complete, Thatcher issued a call for general elections, which would be in held June, eleven months before the end of her five-year term. Party officials believed that the division within the Labour Party and the SDP-Liberal alliance over the nuclear issue became directly responsible for returning Conservative parliamentary majorities and Thatcher to No. 10 Downing Street.[73] According to CRD, "the truth is that Labour's so-called defense policy was not devised as a rational policy for the British people. It was devised as a cloak to cover the rampant and rancorous divisions in the Labour Party."[74]

CND leaders accused their Labour allies of "strategic misjudgment . . . compounded by fudging and betrayal."[75] Though nearly 30 percent of Foot's speeches during the 1983 election season had focused on disarmament, most Labour MP candidates were poorly versed on unilateralism. The party failed to articulate a clear connection between the moral imperatives of disarmament and issues such as economic recovery, women's equality, and municipal democracy that had been championed by CND, the major unions, GCW, and diplomat scientists dedicated to the NWFZ cause. Labour MP candidates' poor performance on disarmament reflected continued disunity among party leaders. At the same time, CND had undervalued its alliance with the Labour Party, with its leadership stubbornly holding on to the idea that people might decide their votes solely on the issue of disarmament."[76]

Labour's precipitous collapse in the polls in the second half of the 1983 election campaign coincided with the frontbench fallout on the issue of disarmament. The political analyst W. L. Miller's view rings true: the election did not so much show that unilateralism was unpopular but that Labour had no single unified defense policy.[77] Foot's history as a divisive backbench critic had made him ill-suited to unify the party, and his leftwing credentials had taken a beating, thanks to his mismanaged position on the Falklands and his handling of Tony Benn's failed run for deputy leader. Leading MPs Robin Cook and Neil Kinnock had joined Foot in continued support for unilateral disarmament.[78] The right of the Labour Party remained committed to James Callaghan and Deputy Leader Denis Healey, who continued to repudiate unilateralism.

By exploiting such divisions among its rivals, Thatcher's government was able to check the power of the CND. The success of Heseltine's anti-CND campaign rested on persuading the organization's political opponents to downplay the disarmament issue and cede the narrative to the peace through strength lobby. Labour's ineptitude on the nuclear issue was a major element; but the SDP-Liberal alliance, which had cut deeply into Labour's vote margins, also failed to present a unified stance on multilateral disarmament. SDP leader, David Owen, had held fast to the notion that the Polaris nuclear submarine would be a feasible deterrent into the twenty-first century. His statements contradicted Liberal Party leader David Steel's commitment to remove Polaris from the country in the first year of an alliance government. Only the Conservative Party presented voters with a unified position on deterrence and disarmament.[79]

With only 27.6 percent of the vote share in 1983, Foot oversaw Labour's worst defeat in the postwar period. The party barely beat out the Liberal-SDP alliance, which secured 25.4 percent of the vote.[80] Polling evidence initially suggested that Labour's nuclear policies were broadly responsible for the desertion of its voters.[81] Given, however, that the Liberal-SDP alliance had advocated for NWFZ and the cancelation of Trident, it seems that at least 53 percent of voters had hoped that disarmament would play some part in the policy of the next government. What the election did expose was Labour leadership's fear of the antinuclear movement's radicalism. By relinquishing the defense narrative to Thatcher's government, they had allowed the Conservative Party to win higher approval on this position than on any other top issue, a clear political miscalculation, considering that exit polls showed

defense to be the second-most-important matter facing the British electorate (38 percent of voters ranked it a top-two issue).[82] Moreover, the election
totals reflected voters' disillusionment with disunified leadership rather than
revealing their general principles and values. A BBC/Gallup survey taken
shortly after the election showed that 38 percent of the electorate generally
identified as Labour supporters, compared to 16 percent for the alliance that
had chipped away at Labour's vote totals.[83] While Labour had produced several contradictory defense policies, Thatcher had successfully integrated her
pronuclear position into the broader set of policies underpinning the New
Right morality project.

Labour and CND did some deep soul searching immediately after the
general election. Foot quickly resigned as Labour leader and was replaced
by the avowed unilateralist Neil Kinnock. Under Kinnock, Labour united
behind unilateralism and pursued the development of a credible non-nuclear
defense policy. With Healey remaining as deputy leader, the party reached
a compromise of sorts, agreeing to commit fully to unilateral disarmament
one last time to see if it could in fact be a successful electoral strategy. Though
political observers and many historians have suggested that the 1983 election
triggered the downslide of CND's appeal among British voters, that was not
the case. Instead, the election results persuaded the group to shift toward an
international and cultural perspective. CND voluntarily distanced itself from
the Labour Party and pursued a new strategy focused on creating a British
cultural affinity for disarmament, one that was linked to the broader international peace movement.

The 1983 general election results were not a popular mandate for nuclear
rearmament. Conservatives won a smaller percentage of the vote in 1983
(42.4 percent) than they had in 1979, though they increased their number
of seats in Parliament by fifty-eight, reaching a majority total of 397 due to a
strong third-party showing from the Liberal-SDP alliance. Two days before
the election, only 36 percent of voters said that they approved of cruise missiles, while 50 percent remained opposed; public opinion on Trident was
evenly divided. Adam Roberts, a distinguished Oxford University professor
of international relations, later observed, "Beneath the superficial appearance of a landslide result for Mrs. Thatcher, evidence of public unease about
nuclear weapons remains. It deserves a better articulation from our political
leaders."[84] Considering the handwringing from Labour's leadership over
the potential negative impact of peace-movement radicalism on the party's

electability, it is worth noting that the Conservative Party's traditional advantage with women voters shrank in 1983. This happened even though Labour lost a tremendous share of its vote and women were the primary audience for GCW, the movement's most radical element. By the next general election, the gender gap would disappear entirely.[85] Unilateral nuclear disarmament may have failed to match the popularity of deterrence at the polls, but some version of British nuclear disarmament remained politically viable.

Moral Combat and U.S. Nuclear Politics

With a pro-freeze House of Representatives and a less hostile Senate, many antinuclear leaders felt confident about pursuing a disarmament agenda in Congress. To buttress its congressional strategy, the antinuclear movement expanded its political operations, attempting to use disarmament ideas to organize a broader progressive coalition for the 1984 election. Electoral fortunes clearly favored the freeze, but questions persisted. Did pro-freeze leanings indicate pervasive antinuclear sentiment? Were those leanings linked to a broader range of anti-Reagan issues? And would a more freeze-friendly Congress yield legislative victories?[86]

Immediately after the 1982 midterms, the Freeze movement seemed to be poised for a significant victory in Congress. Reagan had promoted the deployment of MX missiles as critical to restoring a margin of safety for the United States, but by the end of the year the issue had become an albatross. The president's proposed interim solution of converting existing Minuteman and Titan missile silos into housing for a hundred MX missiles proved to be a nonstarter, and Congress demanded recommendations for a more viable permanent basing by December.[87] Weinberger likened the task to "asking NIH to come up with a cancer cure by December 1."[88]

In mid-December, the administration endorsed dense-pack, or closely-spaced basing, which relied on the concept of nuclear fratricide.[89] Theoretically, spacing MX missiles in super-hardened silos 1,800 feet apart would be a problem for Soviet planners as the blasts created by the first round of warheads would destroy late-arriving missiles. Dense-pack proponents argued that a small target area would channel Soviet missile trajectories into a narrow corridor susceptible to improved missile defense systems, a claim that foreshadowed the desirability of a future deployment of area missile defense systems to increase survivability.[90] But criticisms of dense-pack had been circulating for years. Several defense scientists, notably Richard Garwin, had already laid out ways in which the Soviet Union could easily overcome densely packed hardened silos.[91] Critics suggested that the strategic implications were destabilizing and cited launch-under-attack as the only option for MX survivability, which they argued would be an incentive for the Soviets to launch a preemptive strike of their own.[92] On this basis, congressional opponents swiftly rejected the December dense-pack proposal, marking a second victory for the Freeze.[93]

These successes in the midterms and in Congress validated the antinuclear movement's organizing abilities and legislative clout, and it became a sought-after partner in efforts to draw attention to other progressive issues. Having observed the movement's voter drives and the launch of its Black Participation Project, civil rights leaders were among those who hoped to align their causes with the Freeze campaign. In late 1982 and early 1983, they invited peace movement partners to help organize the twentieth-anniversary events commemorating the 1963 March on Washington for Jobs and Freedom, to be held in the summer. Writing on behalf of Coretta Scott King, Jesse Jackson, Joseph Lowery, Benjamin Hooks, John Jacobs, and Stevie Wonder, Congressmen Walter Fauntroy, a Democrat representing Washington, D.C., framed their appeal as a "Call to the Nation," one that emphasized jobs, peace, and freedom: "three critical conditions in our society—insufferable unemployment, an escalating arms race, and the denial of basic rights and programs which ensure freedom."[94] Civil rights leaders organizing for the march wanted to reimagine the public sphere around a "New Coalition of Conscience" built from the five core nonviolent movements of social change: civil rights, peace, women, labor, and religion.[95] Its purpose would be to resurrect Martin Luther King, Jr.'s, argument that "all humans are caught in an inescapable network of mutuality. . . . whatever affects one indirectly affects us all."[96] Antinuclear leaders responded positively. Randy Kehler of the Freeze, Leslie Cagan of Mobilization for Survival, and William Sloane Coffin of Riverside Church agreed to serve on the national planning council for the anniversary march, and preparations for the event guided the peace movement's public relations efforts to convince the Black community to accept nuclear issues as a core political concern.[97]

In January 1983, the Freeze movement set out to define the political debate for the coming two years. It expanded its fundraising and field organizing operations, hoping that this would convince a Democratic Party desperately

short on manpower and money to embrace the freeze.[98] The Freeze strategy
task force began work on Project '84, which evolved into Freeze Voter '84
(FV '84) and became the political arm of the movement. FV '84 outlined an
ambitious set of goals covering virtually every dimension of electoral politics.[99] The Democratic Party took notice. Observing the rapid expansion of
the Freeze movement's operations, its leaders agreed with Senate Minority
Leader Robert Byrd, who regarded the movement as the party's most substantial stock of "political muscle."[100]

The Reagan administration also took notice. As it considered its midterm
defeats, the growing political operations of the antinuclear movement, and
a potentially more hostile legislative environment, it recalibrated its public
diplomacy around technological solutions that could enhance its moral
arguments. Edward Teller had already convinced Reagan of a way to politically frame ballistic missile defense, proposing in the summer of 1982 that
strategic defense constituted "a uniquely effective reply to those advocating
the dangerous inferiority implied by a 'nuclear freeze.'"[101] Now, after the rejection of dense-pack had placed the administration's strategic modernization
plan on life support, Deputy National Security Advisor Robert McFarlane
began developing a two-pronged public affairs approach that could improve
the president's negotiating position with Congress. First, McFarlane took
charge of forming a commission of defense luminaries from previous administrations to broker a solution that would be both technologically robust
and politically feasible.[102] On January 3, 1983, the first day in session for the
supposedly freeze-friendly Ninety-eighth Congress, Reagan established the
President's Commission on Strategic Forces under the direction of Brent
Scowcroft, a retired general and a former national security advisor. The
bipartisan commission included previous secretaries of state Henry Kissinger
and Alexander Haig and former secretaries of defense Melvin Laird, James
Schlesinger, Donald Rumsfeld, and Harold Brown. Former CIA directors and
other high-ranking officials rounded out the group.

The MX controversy had not gone over well in the administration's recent
public events, so McFarlane also began formulating better ways to publicly
present a program for strategic defense. He told Reagan that he thought
some of the concepts touted by Teller and the Heritage committee could
be used to outflank the peace movement.[103] Reagan directed him to speed
up work on the issue, so in January 1983 McFarlane assigned several NSC
aides—Admiral John Poindexter, Major General Richard Boverie, Colonel

Bob Linhard, and Al Keel—to dedicate themselves to the Strategic Defense Initiative (SDI).[104]

Between January and March, the team focused on the potential of SDI to disrupt moral arguments against the administration's quest for strategic superiority. Admiral James D. Watkins, the chief of naval operations, was instrumental on this front. According to the White House's science advisor, George Keyworth, Watkins possessed no clear understanding of the technical concepts but liked "the ethical and moral implications of SDI."[105] The admiral later declared, "You have to think in terms of what American people think, and basically we are founded on a Judeo-Christian ethic in this country. . . . it's very important that you think in those terms, too, about your decisions, because that is the political reality. . . . And we had to find an alternative rather than going down the tubes on unilateral disarmament."[106] He linked his views on morality to the asymmetry of the social component of deterrence vis-à-vis the Soviet Union: "[Public opinion] doesn't exist in the Soviet Union. They just turn the button and squash that whenever they want to. So, they don't have those kinds of obstacles."[107] Watkins agreed with McFarlane that the nation's moral values were incompatible with MAD and necessitated a shift to assured survival. As McFarlane explained, "For our president to have no other option than to destroy society and to expect our own would also be destroyed is not credible for a Western Judeo-Christian leader."[108]

Watkins became the key advocate for SDI among the joint chiefs of staff (JCS), who were split on the issue. In a February JCS meeting with the president, Watkins was particularly persuasive in his advocacy; and the chair, General John Vessey, Jr., joined the admiral in recommending a new strategic vision. Sources disagree, but either Vessey or Watkins asked, "Wouldn't it be better to protect the American people rather than avenge them?" The phrase triggered Reagan's rhetorical instincts; he replied, "Don't lose those words."[109] After the meeting, the president directed McFarlane to incorporate the rhetorical question into plans for the public presentation of the new initiative.[110]

The Reagan administration's moral and technological adjustments to its nuclear modernization project corresponded to developments in its reinvigorated public diplomacy campaign. Conservative activists had interpreted midterm defeats and obstacles to MX deployment as signs that the president's public diplomacy needed to be better coordinated with perspectives from the religious right in order to mount an effective defense of peace through strength. The Heritage Foundation collated past

proclamations from religious leaders to advocate for deterrence and suggested that the peace bishops' understanding of MAD as U.S. policy had
invalidated their teachings. Reagan's modernization programs, Heritage
claimed, promoted counterforce strategy, which prioritized military targets and thus kept civilian populations safe from nuclear annihilation.[111]
Phyllis Schlafly, a Roman Catholic, also expressed her concerns to the
White House about the moral consequences of the peace bishops' activities. She underscored that the lack of coordination among religious communities had benefited the peace movement in the midterms.[112]

Michael Novak responded to the midterm defeats by issuing his sharpest
attack on Catholic arguments against deterrence. In early March 1983, he
expanded upon his earlier theological and secular arguments against the
peace bishops in a two-part article, "Moral Clarity in a Nuclear Age," published in his magazine *Crisis,* which he had founded with Ralph McInerny in
response to what they saw as a civil war in the Catholic church. Editors at the
National Review found Novak's article so compelling that they reprinted it as
a dedicated issue in April. The piece became the preeminent argument for
framing deterrence as the will of God on earth and thus upholding America's
moral leadership of the world. Apocalyptic scenarios, wrote Novak, featured
regularly in biblical exegeses around just war theory. Stressing these apocalyptic continuities, he suggested that nuclear war did not alter the Christian
obligation to defense but in fact only strengthened it.[113]

Reagan's "evil empire" speech to the National Evangelical Association on
March 8, 1983, integrated peace through strength rhetoric into the broader
vision of the United States as a Christian nation that was compelled to act
in a fallen world. The administration approached the president's speech as a
public diplomacy operation in support of arms control negotiators abroad.
Only a day before Reagan delivered it, General Edward Rowny, the chief
U.S. negotiator in the Strategic Arms Reduction Talks (START), had cabled
Washington from Geneva, noting that "negotiations on reducing strategic
arms will be made immensely more difficult, if not impossible, by passage
of a freeze resolution."[114] Through references to the nation's founding fathers
and early observers of U.S. democracy, the president linked faith in God to
American exceptionalism. He cast the freeze concept as a "dangerous fraud"
and the movement as an ally of the Soviet cause because it dared to suggest
a moral equivalency between the two superpowers. Reagan argued instead
"that we must find peace through strength." He urged Americans to "speak

out against those who would place the United States in a position of military and moral inferiority" and concluded that "the struggle now going on for the world will never be decided by bombs, rockets, and armies or military might. The real crisis we face today is a spiritual one; at root, it is a test of moral will and faith."[115]

Antinuclear advocates, especially those involved in minority outreach, pointed out that Reagan was preaching an exclusively white Judeo-Christian morality to defend his administration's nuclear programs. In contrast, as the Freeze's minority outreach coordinator, Patricia Williams, observed about her campaign, "No other peace group in history has had the advantage of working for an issue that can potentially unite us all."[116] Her optimism reflected the growing alliance between the antinuclear movement and the civil rights movement under the banner of the New Coalition of Conscience, which increasingly made nuclear issues a focus within the traditional centers of Black moral contemplation and political power.[117]

Churches and ministries spotlighted the subject of Black economic displacement, which was exacerbated by the expanding costs of nuclear deterrence. In early 1983, the Black Participation Project, launched by Judy Pennington and Larry Bailey the year before, flooded Black radio stations with antinuclear advertisements, programs, and guest speakers. The project was a cost-effective means for reaching a wide audience in Black urban communities, and Pennington and Bailey selected Detroit as their test case for using ministry and radio tactics to alert Black Americans to the ill-effects of the nuclear economy. That city, with its large Black, blue-collar population, seemed to be the perfect place to make nuclear disarmament synonymous with jobs and racial justice.[118]

For his part, Reagan did not choose to court support from an unlikely demographic. Instead, he used his focus on morality to help his influential religious allies make their own case for a nuclear arms buildup. In his 1980 campaign, he had drawn on evangelical support by professing a common belief that social justice issues should be informed by religious beliefs.[119] Now his televangelist allies stressed the president's role in preparation for the apocalypse. For evangelicals, this brand of morality politics prepared the nation's soul for the second coming of Christ and prefigured His thousand-year reign on earth, known as the millennial kingdom, though victory in that apocalyptic battle was far from preordained. Reverend Jerry Falwell, a cofounder of the Moral Majority, was notably adept at merging apocalyptic rhetoric with policies fed to him by the administration. White House officials valued Falwell's support so much that they not only enlisted him in the fight against the Freeze but also reportedly gave him classified nuclear briefings in the Oval Office in early 1983.[120] In response, Falwell launched an eighteen-month-long anti-Freeze campaign across his platforms of influence. Much of this campaign took place on his television show *The Old Time Gospel Hour*, a syndicated series of sermons that, at its peak in the mid-1980s, was carried by nearly four hundred stations and attracted more than 2 million donors, taking in close to $100 million in its highest-grossing years.[121]

Falwell's sermon "Nuclear War and the Second Coming of Jesus Christ," which aired on *The Old Time Gospel Hour* on March 20, 1983, generated the highest donor response yet. In this sermon, he, like other televangelists, such as Pat Robertson on the Christian Broadcasting Network, interpreted the Book of Ezekiel as a prophecy of Soviet aggression. Denouncing the social dynamics associated with the rise of the antinuclear left, these pronuclear ministers argued that universities' increased focus on liberalism and humanism and the creeping influence of secularism on world institutions (represented by developments such as the Second Vatican Council) invited the Soviet Union to launch and win a nuclear war.[122] Falwell saw the anti-Freeze campaign as his top moral priority, even more so than his anti-abortion and school-prayer campaigns.[123] He explicitly depicted antinuclear advocates as moral agents of the Kremlin, labeling them "freezeniks" in full-page attack ads in the *Washington Post,* the *New York Times,* and seventy other newspapers, in addition to his regular denunciations in *The Moral Majority Report.*[124]

Neoconservatives, conservative Catholics, and evangelicals found a measure of common ground in their defense of deterrence. Neoconservatism and conservative Catholicism both relied on Novak's moral arguments to defend the administration's nuclear buildup, and Reagan's rhetoric created continuity between Novak's perspective and the prophecies preached by the president's televangelist allies. The March uptick in moral arguments supporting nuclear weapons corresponded directly to the resumption of arms control talks and imminent deadlines for votes on the funding of the MX missile. Yet, on the whole, neither the public nor congressional opinion were moved by these tactics. Nor were they convinced by questionable reporting around accusations of contact between the Freeze movement and the KGB. If anything, Reagan's rhetoric had only further convinced those outside of the New Right bloc that the president intended to sabotage arms control.[125]

On March 23, Reagan sought to reverse the negative momentum of his administration's public nuclear diplomacy operations in a televised prime-time address to the nation. In addition to reiterating his moral rhetoric and peace through strength commitments, his speech presented a new formulation of deterrence: the possibility of assured survival rooted in advanced ballistic missile defense. In calling for the accelerated development of such defense systems, Reagan claimed that the requirements for deterrence no longer needed to be based on the threat of nuclear annihilation. He called upon the nation's scientific and technical talent to bring about advances in ballistic missile defense that would make "nuclear weapons impotent and obsolete." He urged the country to marshal its industrial strength in the cause of national security. Then he followed up his argument that a freeze would make nuclear war more likely with the question posed to him by the JCS: "Wouldn't it be better to save lives than to avenge them?"[126] Keyworth later stressed the president's leading role in drafting the speech: "SDI definitely [drew] . . . from the President's views of morality and views of long-term, endurable history."[127]

Congressional reaction to Reagan's speech demonstrated the widening ideological divide between liberal Democrats and conservative Republicans on nuclear matters. Reagan's opponents derisively nicknamed the initiative "Star Wars."[128] Among the Democrats, presidential candidate Walter Mondale, hoping to court freeze voters, condemned Reagan for making nuclear issues a public diplomacy exercise.[129] Les AuCoin, a congressman from Oregon and a leading member of the House Appropriations Committee, disparaged the president's "fixation on doomsday weapons and military spending."[130] Congressman Tom Downey of New York condemned SDI as "appalling and ridiculous."[131] William Proxmire, a veteran senator from Wisconsin, was slightly kinder, saying, "This is an appealing proposal, but it actually could be a dangerous development."[132] In contrast, conservative Republicans hailed the president as a visionary who was compelling science and statesmanship to follow his moral lead. Congressman Ken Kramer of Colorado called Reagan's plan "the greatest hope for mankind."[133] Senator Jesse Helms of North Carolina, a leading voice of the New Right, claimed that the president had "turned a historic page . . . away from the incongruous doctrine known as MAD."[134]

Scientists likewise split along ideological lines. In attempt to court that community, Reagan had invited a small group of scientists who had made outstanding contributions to U.S. national security to dine with him at the White House on the evening he announced the new priority for defensive systems.[135] They offered a mix of views, though the majority warned against the development of SDI. Teller, the most hawkish among the group, praised the president for providing the "needed basis for a stable, lasting peace."[136] But Jerome Weisner, the former chairman of the President's Science Advisory Committee and president emeritus of the Massachusetts Institute of Technology, referred to the speech as a "declaration of a new arms race."[137] Likewise, Cornell University professor Hans Bethe, a Nobel Prize winner and long-time government consultant on nuclear and national security issues, predicted that the impractical proposal would greatly increase the difficulty in reaching new arms control agreements and impede the prospect of nuclear peace.[138]

In his televised speech, Reagan repeatedly asked Americans to make the sacrifices that a wartime economy demanded, but activists in the peace movement were unmoved by those appeals. All along they had argued that one of the most sinister aspects of the arms race was its constantly evolving requirements, which had permanently militarized the U.S. economy and thus robbed minorities and working-class Americans of the opportunities for social mobility that could be found in a peace economy. This stance further consolidated the emerging alliance between the antinuclear and civil rights movements and created new prospects for transatlantic cooperation with the British disarmament movement.

Spotlighting the arms race as a source of economic inequality also helped cement an alliance between the antinuclear movement and racial justice activism at the municipal level. Local Freeze chapters worked extensively with the Jobs with Peace (JWP) campaign on economic conversion, municipal budget reforms, civilian job-creation strategies, and municipal antinuclear referendums, especially in Black and Latino communities.[139] In the view of Manning Marable, a member of the National Coordinating Committee and director of the Race Relations Institute at Fisk University, a central mission of JWP was to connect the socioeconomic analyses and moral views of Black elites to the grassroots of the unemployed: "Simply winning [the support of] Coretta Scott King, Joe Lowry, Jesse Jackson, doesn't mean we'll really get local SCLC leaders to throw their forces behind our [peace] motion."[140]

Focusing on peace and jobs within the municipal context enabled the New Coalition of Conscience to ally with powerful Black mayors whose support

could be tapped for mass demonstrations and potential voters.[141] Various
state conferences of Black mayors as well as the National Conference of Black
Mayors were early supporters of the Freeze campaign and were influential in
persuading other Black civic organizations to cofound Citizens against Nuclear
War, a collection of groups with non-nuclear primary missions that were nonetheless concerned about the issue.[142] To strengthen their own coalitions, many
African American mayors seized on the connection between economic injus-
tice, which registered with minority voters, and nuclear adventurism, which
concerned white middle-class voters. Robert Arrington, Jr., was an early pro-
ponent of this strategy, having crafted the freeze call into a proclamation after
he was elected mayor of Birmingham, Alabama, in 1979.[143] Harold Washington,
who became Chicago's first Black mayor in April 1983, urged Black voters to
recognize that domestic stability was being sacrificed to finance the production
of "Armageddon devices."[144] During that spring, leaders of the Freeze's Black
Participation Project worked with the Congressional Black Caucus, the Martin
Luther King, Jr. Center for Social Change, the National Association of Black
State Legislators, the National Urban Coalition, and several other organizations to develop a strategy for convincing Black elites that they should create
a stronger intellectual basis for linking the needs of jobs, peace, and freedom
ahead of the twentieth-anniversary march on Washington.[145]

The suggestion that a peace economy could create more jobs than a defense
economy compelled many labor leaders to rethink their traditional support
of Cold War policies. A significant challenge for antinuclear activists had
been to avoid disrupting the more established alliance between organized
labor and the civil rights movement, both of which the peace movement
hoped to enlist in the fight for disarmament. Lane Kirkland, the president
of the American Federation of Labor and Congress of Industrial Organizations (AFL-CIO), had been a founding member of the Committee on Present
Danger and remained firm in his orthodox view that more defense spending equaled more jobs. Kirkland pressured AFL-CIO affiliates and allies to
suppress antinuclear positions, even threatening to revoke charters of local
affiliates that sympathized with the Freeze.[146] As a result of such pressures,
the A. Philip Randolph Institute, which, in cooperation with the Coalition of
Black Trade Unionists, was the authority on Black labor issues, initially lobbied against the twentieth-anniversary march, but eventually it did commit
to the event.[147]

Even Kirkland's influence had its limits, however. Outside of civil rights leaders, organized labor leaders dominated the list of conveners for the march. They included William Winpisinger of the International Association of Machinists and Aerospace Workers, Murray Finley of the Amalgamated Clothing and Textiles Workers Union, Mary Futrell of the National Education Association, and Addie Wyatt of the United Food and Commercial Workers. Freeze activists had prioritized establishing contacts with these unions and labor groups during their planning for the march.[148] Pushing their message of economic conversion, they touted the estimated savings from a freeze—$100 billion over five years and roughly $380 billion by the year 2000—as a key source of funds for job-creation programs.[149] According to the Congressional Budgetary Office, $10 billion invested directly into the civilian economy could create 250,000 jobs, compared to 210,000 jobs if the same amount were spent on defense.[150] The three largest defense contractors, which accounted for 40 percent of Pentagon purchases, created fewer jobs per dollar than the average industrial manufacturer did.[151] When compared to civilian investment, military spending also created more high-skilled technical jobs and fewer blue-collar union jobs.[152]

The economic justice message thus doubled as outreach to both the Black community and organized labor. Planning for the twentieth-anniversary march brought a wave of labor support, notably from United Auto Workers, which lobbied Congress for a freeze. The American Federation of State, County, and Municipal Employees also spoke out in support of the freeze, while the American Federation of Teachers and the Communications Workers for America voted to endorse the freeze despite opposition from their presidents.[153] The combination of growing antinuclear sentiment among unions and a desire to remain close to the Black community eventually compelled the AFL-CIO to overrule Kirkland's objections, support the march, and endorse the freeze.[154]

Arms Control, Public Diplomacy, and Congressional Bargaining

Reagan's March 23 proposal that ballistic missile defense would usher in an age of assured survival tied directly to the release of the Scowcroft commission's recommendations two weeks later. Many experts and activists questioned whether ballistic missile defenses would shield American citizens or facilitate nuclear warfighting by protecting the deployment of MX missiles. Reagan's correspondence from the period indicates that he did not have a clear view of what SDI would become. Writing to friends in California, he said, "Frankly, I have no idea what the nature of such a defense might be. I simply asked our scientists to explore the possibility of developing such a defense."[155]

Released on April 6, the Scowcroft commission's report stressed the need for political unity. Noting the geopolitical consequences of partisanship, which complicated arms control and modernization, it reaffirmed that "our task as a nation cannot be understood from a position of moral neutrality toward the differences between liberty and nationalism."[156] In this regard, the commission accepted Reagan's diagnosis that ensuring the moral mission of the United States required nuclear superiority. However, it also recognized the impropriety of casting antinuclear proponents as Soviet sympathizers. Its solution for MX was the interim deployment of one hundred missiles in existing silos and continued research on hardened silos and mobile systems, which would be readied for development by 1987. On ballistic missile defense, the report commented, "Applications of current technology offer no real promise of being able to defend the United States against massive nuclear attack in this century. An easier task is to provide ABM [antiballistic missile] defense for fixed hardened targets, such as ICBM silos."[157] Scowcroft's report signaled to MX skeptics in Congress that the ballistic missile defenses touted by Reagan could improve the survivability of MX silos. At the same time, the commission offered an olive branch to members of Congress who were in close contact with antinuclear leaders: an unequivocal endorsement of genuine arms control efforts rather than anti-freeze rhetoric.[158]

According to Stephen Kane, the Scowcroft report and the arms control developments that emerged from it demonstrate that Reagan's public diplomacy was less effective than his congressional bargaining strategy was at enacting his nuclear policy agenda.[159] In fact, given that the president preempted the report's release with the announcement of SDI and that his administration later sold the developments that came out of the report to court public opinion, he likely understood congressional bargaining and public diplomacy to be part of a single political maneuver. Victories and defeats in one arena determined Reagan's leverage in the other. Shortly after the report's release but before critical legislative voting on the administration's nuclear programs, the NSC's special planning group on public diplomacy pushed for the "defense budget, MX, strategic defense . . . [to] be considered as a package."[160] John Kelly, a State Department official working on public affairs strategies, confirmed that Congress, the American public, and European publics—in relation to each other and in that order—were the audiences that needed to be persuaded on the connected issues of MX and SDI.[161]

In early May, however, the antinuclear movement appeared to turn the tide in the public diplomacy battle. On May 3, U.S. bishops approved the final draft of "The Challenge of Peace: God's Promise and Our Response," their pastoral letter on war and peace. Reagan's March 23 argument that deterrence still worked as a permanent strategy had contradicted Pope John Paul's previous statements on the acceptability of deterrence as a temporary solution, which pronuclear advocates had relied upon to make the moral case for peace through strength. Seizing on this point, the peace bishops condemned deterrence as the most dangerous dimension of the arms race: "Good ends . . . cannot justify immoral means."[162] The pope's delegates in Washington applauded the bishops' leadership on the question of nuclear deterrence, and Bernardin's committee informed the Vatican's own study about the issue.[163]

The bishops argued that the concept of comparative justice means that no state should act with the conviction of absolute justice in a world where sovereign states recognize no single moral authority and that states must realize the limits of their just cause.[164] Reagan's public diplomacy messaging claimed the exact opposite. He asserted that his administration's nuclear-arms buildup served a just cause because he believed that the United States was a uniquely moral nation and the Soviet Union a distinctly immoral one. Moreover, the bishops were convinced that the notions of probability of success and proportionality made nuclear weapons incompatible with just war theory. Under that theory, only winnable wars or those that had a reasonable chance of success could be considered morally acceptable. Reagan himself acknowledged the incompatibility of preparations for nuclear war and just war, repeatedly stating that he considered nuclear war to be unwinnable.[165] In regard to proportionality, the stark reality that any nuclear attack would result in massive civilian casualties invalidated the morality of deterrence.[166]

Stepping assertively into the political realm, the pastoral letter prescribed Catholic morality as the foundation for civic responsibility and the antidote to a general moral crisis in the United States. The bishops stated that they had "two purposes: to help Catholics form their consciences and to contribute to the public policy debate"; and they directed their guidance toward a "wider civil community, a more pluralistic audience" comprised of all faiths.[167] Though they did not explicitly call for civil disobedience, the bishops essentially gave their sanction to the pacifist tradition that had inspired religious activists' nonviolent direct actions against the state, referring to the moral examples set by Saint Francis of Assisi, Dorothy Day, and Martin Luther King, Jr.[168] Political observers interpreted this final version of the pastoral letter as a tacit endorsement of the Freeze and a rebuke of Reagan allies who had claimed that earlier drafts supported the administration's nuclear policies.[169] By gesturing to the Freeze and to pacifists engaged in civil disobedience, the American Catholic hierarchy seemed to have shifted from its earlier nationalism to a more nuanced view of state militarism.[170] An article in *Rolling Stone* went so far as to call the writing of the letter a process of reinventing what it meant to be an American Catholic.[171]

On May 4, the day after the letter's final version was approved, the Democrat-controlled House passed a nonbinding freeze resolution by a vote of 278 to 149. Though Freeze advocates and congressional allies lamented that the legislative process had undermined the force of the resolution, its passage was nevertheless a clear sign that the antinuclear campaign's congressional strategy could triumph over the Reagan nuclear agenda.[172] Several weeks passed between the vote on the freeze resolution and the vote on MX planned for May 26. In that interim, Reagan used the Scowcroft commission's report as the basis for negotiations with key Democrats and moderate Republicans in Congress. The report recommended the deployment of one hundred MX missiles in Minuteman silos as well as the deployment of a much greater number of Midgetman missiles. The recommendations around these smaller, highly mobile, single-warhead missiles were more palatable to centrist Democrats such as Les Aspin of Wisconsin, Al Gore of Tennessee, and Norman Dicks of Washington because reducing the number of warheads on each ICBM missile would supposedly enhance strategic stability by removing the first-strike incentive for both superpowers.[173] As a result, these key members of the House were persuaded to vote for MX, and a number of senators—notably William Cohen, a Republican from Maine; Sam Nunn, a Democrat from Georgia; and Charles Percy, a Republican from Illinois—backed a commitment to the builddown concept, which proposed that a greater number of warheads on strategic-delivery vehicles be retired when warheads on modernized vehicles entered service. Build-down all but guaranteed that the MX would not be the future of the U.S. ICBM force, merely an interim solution. Still, these House members and senators, nicknamed the Gang of Six, had a caveat: they expressed a total lack of trust in START negotiator General Rowny and demanded that Congress have its own arms control monitor to ensure that build-down would receive proper treatment in negotiations.[174]

Victory on the MX vote negated the Reagan administration's disappoint-
ment over the freeze resolution that the House had approved earlier in
May. The congressional Democrats who voted for MX did so because they
believed that the Gang of Six had established a partnership with the Reagan
administration on arms control.[175] By creating a wedge between Democrats
in Washington and supporters of the freeze, Reagan's administration had
weakened the opposition and earned cover for his policies. SANE's executive director, David Cortright, whose organization had aggressively targeted
MX, excoriated the Democratic Party for "revert[ing] to its old ways and
betray[ing] the Freeze movement."[176] Randall Forsberg later said that the
vote for MX "tore up the Freeze movement" by demonstrating the shallow
nature of Washington politics.[177] In the end, while the MX vote did not defeat
the antinuclear movement as a public force, it did fatally weaken the Freeze's
agenda in Congress.

The Scowcroft report and bipartisan developments in Washington gave
NATO allies confidence that the Reagan administration could manage both
strategic nuclear issues and the INF portfolio. R. James Woolsey, Jr., who
served on the Scowcroft commission and later became the congressional
representative on the U.S. arms control delegation, said, "If we [had] can-
celled our only on-going ICBM program unilaterally that would [have]
deal[t] a blow to NATO and to the notion of the American nuclear deterrent
as part of NATO. . . . How in the world could we have asked the Europeans
to deploy Pershing IIs and ground launch cruise missiles?"[178] Instead, success
on the MX issue showed that the Reagan administration understood that the
increasing engagement between American and European publics had created
a transnational public sphere. This would ultimately determine if the president could implement a peace through strength program. Walter Raymond,
a member of the administration's Public Affairs Committee, which dealt with
the MX, the freeze, and other nuclear issues, noted that "the inclusion of
USIA factors in a foreign dimension [was key] to the development of effective [domestic] strategies."[179]

Under Charles Wick, innovations at USIA had now positioned the once-
marginalized agency to assume an important role in publicly communicating
the administration's nuclear policies at home and abroad. For years, foreign-
public-opinion polling and attitudinal research had lagged far behind the
sophisticated domestic operations run by the White House and political
campaigns. The priority given to public diplomacy by NSDD 77 encouraged

USIA to revamp its polling and research capabilities. Stanton Burnett, who led much of the effort, believed this would give its senior officials unique information and thus clout in the interagency meetings that determined the administration's public diplomacy.[180]

In the spring of 1983, USIA brought in Richard Wirthlin, Reagan's chief campaign pollster, to consult on the INF issue. He and the agency arranged to use the powerful polling computers at the Roper Center for Public Opinion Research to enhance the administration's ability to judge the effectiveness of its public diplomacy in Europe while laying the foundation for better coordination with domestic political campaigns. USIA's enhanced research and polling capabilities informed Peter Daley's working group on INF public diplomacy, notably in the decision that U.S. allies needed to clearly make the case for INF to their own publics and that senior administration officials such as Vice President Bush and Secretary of State Shultz should be on the frontlines of U.S. public diplomacy in Western Europe, where opposition to Reagan seemed to be driving broader anti-American sentiment.[181]

Developments at USIA contributed to the success of Reagan's next significant public diplomacy action on the INF issue. In May 1983, the Soviet Union formally proposed that its SS-20 launchers in Europe should equal the number of British and French nuclear systems. The timing of this proposal was intended to preempt discussions at the Group of Seven (G7) summit, scheduled to be held in Williamsburg, Virginia, later in the month.[182] The summit would be comprised of representatives from the United States, the United Kingdom, Italy, France, West Germany, Canada, Japan, and the European Union, but participants had initially been hesitant to consider arms control issues, afraid of alienating the NATO-basing countries that would not be present and thus of enflaming European public opinion.[183] Nonetheless, as summit host, the Reagan administration felt compelled to take the opportunity to make a unified statement on INF negotiations to bolster its ongoing public diplomacy efforts.

Mindful that some participants would be reluctant to participate in a joint statement on INF, American officials asked Thatcher to guide a dinner discussion on INF. They hoped that this and other discussions would produce agreement on a public statement to be issued at the close of the conference.[184] In preparing for this event, British officials focused on two dangers that could arise from the lack of visible progress on arms control. First, they feared a "renewal of impetus for the CND cause . . . [and] second, a temptation particularly among the less stalwart allies, to put the US under pressure to make further negotiating concessions for agreement at almost any cost."[185] These concerns were particularly acute in the United Kingdom, given the attention that NATO and nuclear politics were receiving in publicity surrounding the upcoming British general election, scheduled for June.

In advance of her dinner discussion on arms control, Thatcher held bilateral meetings with the West German delegation and the Japanese delegation to ensure their agreement on global limits. She agreed with Chancellor Kohl that acceptance of global limits (rather than simply European limits) required, in exchange, more favorable trade practices with Japan.[186] Prime Minister Yasuhiro Nakasone appreciated the western imperative to pursue a "collective peace offensive" and was willing to consider linking trade policy to allied unity on arms control.[187]

At her May 28 dinner discussion, Thatcher asserted Britain's privileged role in western dialogue on arms control during these bilateral meetings and discussions. In her view, global limits on INF were sources of potential pressure on the U.S. negotiating posture, and these issues could be uniquely addressed in the G7 forum. The Reagan administration had stressed the need for global limits on INF deployments, arguing that SS-20 missiles were mobile systems that could be moved from the Asian theater to the European theater relatively quickly. Washington could not afford to accept the export of the INF threat to the Asian theater, which would create problems for U.S. allies in the Pacific. Thatcher encouraged NATO leaders to take a cohesive approach to public diplomacy, advocating for positions on deployment that considered not just domestic opinion but also the attitudes of a transnational public. She pushed for a joint statement on INF to demonstrate a "steadiness of nerve" as NATO progressed toward deployments.[188] Reagan later remarked on the prime minister's firm approach in her dealings with the French and the Canadians: "I thought at one point Margaret was going to order Pierre [Trudeau] to go stand in the corner."[189] Thatcher also pressed Kohl: "I'm in the middle of an election. I bent over backwards for your election. Now it's your turn. I have taken a strong position, and I want a strong position here."[190]

At a press conference on May 29, Secretary of State Shultz read the joint statement that had come out of the dinner discussion. It emphasized G7 unity about the exclusion of British and French nuclear forces from INF negotiations and about the global dimensions of arms control talks. Shultz said that the agreement on global limits was important because they "identified Japan with the security system of the West, not just through the bilateral strategic partnership with the United States."[191] The statement castigated the Soviet Union for attempting to influence public opinion in INF-basing countries, and NATO would reiterate this position in its final communiqué from its early June ministerial meetings.[192] Reagan considered Thatcher's leadership on INF and her subsequent election victory as a welcome "shot in the arm to the Western alliance."[193] For her part, the prime minister viewed the summit as a valuable political tool for showing British voters that her policies enabled Britain to play a leading role in world affairs.[194]

Developing and disseminating a unified nuclear message at the Williamsburg summit was also important because the conference was the first test of USIA's new strategy for managing the European media. For the nearly five hundred foreign correspondents in Washington, D.C., access to news-gathering events had been a long-standing problem because administrations and politicians tended to prioritize contacts with domestic journalists. Unequal access had spawned the "borrowed news" phenomenon, in which foreign correspondents relied on news from secondhand sources and the domestic press—commonly the *New York Times* and the *Washington Post*—rather than independently reporting on direct engagements with U.S. officials.[195] This practice was problematic for Reagan's peace through strength agenda, given that the president and his allies blamed such prestige-press outlets for the erosion of U.S. moral and military superiority. Public diplomacy officials believed that filtering Reagan's foreign policy through the domestic press distorted U.S. nuclear security aims throughout Europe. As a consequence, USIA determined that it should reduce the number of intermediaries between the public and the presidency. Before and during the summit, through USIA's foreign press centers, George Shultz, Kenneth Adelman, Edward Rowny, Kenneth Dam, Richard Perle, and other high-ranking officials spoke directly to foreign journalists. The success of these direct briefings, especially in Washington, D.C., demonstrated their value as an instrument of the Reagan administration's foreign policy. The president got in on the act as well, giving direct interviews to major European outlets, such as Britain's *Financial Times*.[196]

Alvin Snyder, who served as USIA's television and film director under Reagan, considered Williamsburg a seminal moment for technological development in U.S. public diplomacy because it marked the first instance in which the agency directly fed live television and print coverage to Europe. This not only provided cable access across the Atlantic but also allowed

U.S. public diplomacy staffers and foreign delegates to instantly monitor and respond to how European television news agencies were covering the events. These approaches set a new pattern of operations that would be further developed for summits between Reagan and Gorbachev.[197] In addition, they allowed U.S. officials and western allies to regain momentum in their own peace offensive during the spring and summer round of INF negotiations. At home, Reagan's team reaped significant political capital from the summit's results. The *Washington Post* declared, "The president will take political credit for his performance, and he has every right to."[198] According to Shultz, Thatcher and other G7 leaders left Williamsburg far more confident in Reagan's understanding of the key arms control issues than they had been before their arrival.[199] Key American allies in the Atlantic and Pacific regions had agreed on the need for global restraints. Most importantly for Whitehall, the exclusion of British and French strategic deterrents remained a firm NATO position. Washington's demonstrated flexibility on negotiating positions, which had already aided the victory of Kohl's Christian Democrats in the March Bundestag elections in West Germany, now helped Thatcher's Conservatives in the June British general elections. Both successes were prerequisites for maintaining political consensus for the dual-track decision.

The British and Western German elections were not the only ones framing the outcome of the summit. By mid-1983, questions about Reagan's electoral future and the emergence of Democratic challengers for the 1984 presidential race had begun to shape the president's presentation of his foreign policies. Williamsburg had given him the opportunity to burnish his credentials as a world leader and a responsible manager of arms control, areas in which he had polled least favorably with the American electorate. Just before the summit, the *Washington Post* had published an editor's op-ed, "Go Ahead, Suckers, Bet on Reagan's Reelection"; a Harris Poll taken shortly after the summit projected the 1984 election to be a "cliffhanger."[200] Both sources found that a majority of the public opposed a second Reagan term on account of his handling of foreign affairs and his record-setting defense spending. Combined with the predicted return of white Catholics, Blacks, Latinos, and union workers to the Democratic fold in 1984, Reagan's electoral prospects in mid-1983 looked very different than the electoral landslide that would actually come to pass.

The New Coalition of Conscience represented precisely the amalgamation of ideas and groups that appeared to be the biggest obstacle to Reagan's reelection. Planning for the twentieth-anniversary march to commemorate the 1963 March on Washington had generated the connective tissue that now linked the antinuclear campaign, the civil rights movement, organized labor, and other progressive causes. Far surpassing the projections of cautiously optimistic organizers, between 250,000 and 400,000 demonstrators sweated out 90-degree temperatures to march for jobs, peace, and freedom on August 27, 1983. The march verified the durability of antinuclear ideas.[201]

After Williamsburg and the summer's protests, tensions between antinuclear protestors and the president's nuclear policies appeared likely to define the race for president in 1984. According to Richard Wirthlin, 51 percent of voters anticipated that a Reagan reelection would produce negative results in foreign affairs, with nearly 40 percent expressing concerns that the president would lead the United States into nuclear war. Moreover, the arms race registered higher than any other single issue among those that would lead Americans to vote against a candidate.[202] The Soviet peace offensive took advantage of this divide, focusing on making a nuclear freeze of both strategic and INF weapons a decisive issue in the election and stepping up criticisms of Reagan while refraining from attacking Democratic rivals.[203]

The fact that public opinion changed so rapidly and that such a change had an immediate impact on political leaders throughout NATO was a sign that the nuclear debate still required careful tending until the deployment of INF weapons in late 1983. Nitze and the U.S. delegation in Geneva concluded at the end of the spring-summer negotiating round that the Soviets now preferred no agreement at all to any agreement that sanctioned any deployments of U.S. nuclear forces in Europe.[204] In preparation for a looming collapse in negotiations, Reagan nominated David Abshire to serve as the U.S. ambassador to NATO. This selection confirmed that the administration increasingly understood congressional bargaining, the management of public opinion at home and abroad, confidence building with allied leaders, and electoral politics as a unified public diplomacy process.

In the late 1960s, Abshire had cofounded and modeled the Center for Strategic and International Studies (CSIS) on the London-based Institute for Strategic Studies. Building on his experience as assistant secretary of state for congressional relations in the Nixon administration, he had turned CSIS into a respected think tank with broad bipartisan participation from legislators on nuclear issues as well as extensive international contacts, especially in the United Kingdom. Abshire played a major role in the efforts to reform U.S. public diplomacy in the 1970s by hosting the Stanton panel at CSIS, which set the terms of the debate and argued that policy advocacy should be conducted in conjunction with cultural diplomacy and educational exchange.[205] His appointment was well received by foreign policy observers, with one expert saluting him for possessing "the political equivalent of perfect pitch," and another later hailing the move as the "master stroke of the INF campaign."[206] Given CSIS's extensive European programming and network and Abshire's relationships to the transatlantic peace movement, his selection demonstrated the increasing prominence of the think tank sector in foreign policy-making as well as the importance of the private dimension and two-way flow of public diplomacy.[207] Bolstered by Abshire, U.S. public diplomacy officials felt confident that they could generate a boost for the president among the American electorate and in European publics, in the likely event of a Soviet walkout from arms control negotiations.

CHAPTER FIVE

ARMS CONTROL UNDONE

If the U.S. is the first to have both offense and defense, we could put the nuclear genie back in the bottle.

—Ronald Reagan (1983)

I N 1983, REAGAN'S and Thatcher's public diplomacy plans had, on the whole, been successful. Reagan's introduction of SDI had added a defensive dimension to the U.S. nuclear buildup, which enriched the moral element of his public diplomacy. The revival of moral themes in his public diplomacy also benefited from the Soviet shootdown of a Korean airliner, which had allowed the president and the prime minister to emphasize the moral contrast between the western world and the Soviet Union. At the same time, by agreeing to congressional oversight of arms control, Reagan had astutely deflated the criticisms of his Democratic presidential rivals.

But at the beginning of 1984, intermediate-range and strategic nuclear arms control efforts were in peril, with negotiations suspended indefinitely. Scientific critiques of SDI had affected public opinion, as had the competing views of SDI held among Reagan's senior aides that complicated the program's public presentation. The debate that unfolded between SDI critics and Reagan's scientific allies illuminated a divergence in their philosophical perspectives on the relationship between science and the state. Critics articulated an ideal in which scientists informed the public and applied their scientific knowledge to advance political solutions and international compromise. SDI proponents, however, perpetuated notions of American technological exceptionalism, claiming that scientists had a civic obligation to help realize the security priorities determined by elected leaders.

SDI also presented a series of problems for Thatcher, compelling her government to decide if its nuclear priorities would remain aligned with the Reagan administration's. SDI appeared to undercut the arms control negotiations and the deterrence status quo that had maintained the effectiveness of Britain's nuclear arsenal. Moreover, opposition to SDI was reinvigorating the British antinuclear movement, especially after the issue became entangled with the politics of nuclear winter. This convergence of the public and private dimensions of scientific activism challenged the legitimacy of the Thatcher government's management of expertise and objectives in world affairs.

The Myth of Moral Equivalency

Shortly after the G7 summit in Williamsburg and Thatcher's electoral victory, the prime minister hosted Vice President George Bush at 10 Downing Street. Bush congratulated her on successfully managing the nuclear debate during her election, noting its importance for President Reagan's 1984 campaign. Thatcher told Bush that she no longer considered the antinuclear movement much of a threat, declaring that the Greenham Common women "had become an eccentricity." She nevertheless anticipated a renewal in antinuclear activity linked to the cruise missile deployments scheduled for the end of the year.[1]

The peace movement responded to its 1983 electoral and legislative disappointments by devoting more attention to the transatlantic dimensions of nuclear politics. Antinuclear women were key to this connection because they simultaneously represented themselves as local, national, and transnational actors. In a demonstration lasting from July 4 through Labor Day, the Women's Encampment for a Future of Peace and Justice occupied a fifty-one-acre plot adjacent to an army depot in Seneca Falls, New York, the storage site for intermediate-range nuclear missiles bound for Europe. Because Seneca County had been the birthplace of the modern women's rights movement in the United States, the location of the protest enhanced its symbolic effect. Moreover, the Seneca encampment was deliberately patterned on the GCW occupation of land surrounding the Greenham Common RAF base in the south of England, the first site for U.S. INF deployments in all of Europe, and it became was the most visible of the nine "twinned" peace camps in the United States that were established with the help of GCW activists.[2] After Seneca, the most important of these camps was at Puget Sound.

As a group, these camps occupied multiple stages of the INF life cycle: Puget Sound, production; Seneca Falls, storage and shipment, Greenham Common, deployment.[3] In both thought and action, British and American

FIGURE 3. Martin Angles, "Americans for British Independence from Nuclear Arms Race,"
Guardian, July 4, 1983. Copyright Guardian News & Media Ltd 2022.

antinuclear feminism exerted a mutual influence.[4] For instance, during interactions at American peace camps, GCW activists became familiar with the
nation's antinuclear debates as well as American culture and the U.S. legal
system. This primed them for their own direct action against the Reagan
administration.

Cooperation between American and British antinuclear feminists revived
the argument that that no qualitative moral difference existed between the
United States and the Soviet Union. Many British citizens who expressed
sympathy for the peace movement believed that extensive U.S. military
infrastructure in the United Kingdom amounted to an unwanted occupation
of Britain. The last round of INF negotiations was quickly approaching in
advance of November 1983 deployments of Pershing II intermediate-range
ballistic missiles and Tomahawk cruise missiles to NATO basing countries,
and U.S. and British officials were increasingly concerned that the peace
movement had reestablished the moral case against Reagan's and Thatcher's
approach to deterrence and arms control.

On September 1, after the Soviets downed Korean Air Lines 007, a pas-
senger flight from New York to Seoul, Reagan and Thatcher seized on the

incident as a clear example of the moral contrast between the western world and the Soviet Union, one they hoped to use to rebut the peace movement's moral equivalency thesis.[5] The incident killed the crew and all 269 passengers on board, including Congressman Larry McDonald, a Republican from Georgia and the influential head of the virulently anticommunist John Birch Society.[6] Quickly, USIA featured the Korean Air Lines flight 007 tragedy and Reagan's response in a series of specialized public diplomacy materials and broadcast spots, releasing selectively edited information to fuel the public perception of a moral dichotomy in the behavior of the two superpowers.[7] According to Raymond Garthoff, Reagan "seemed to enjoy again being liberated as a crusader against the evil empire" because it allowed him to revive his critique of Soviet morality in connection with his pursuit of U.S. strategic superiority.[8]

To persuade NATO leaders of the sincerity of U.S. disarmament efforts, Reagan and Thatcher petitioned the United Nations to censure the Soviet Union for the Korean Ari Lines flight 007 tragedy while also insisting that arms control must press forward.[9] On September 26 the president introduced the revised U.S. INF approach to the U.N. General Assembly. The *New York Times* observed that his focus on moral themes, presented in this highly symbolic space for a massive international broadcast audience, epitomized the administration's "new public diplomacy," an exercise of soft power judged in the moment to be more effective for altering the balance of power than any category of military equipment.[10] Citing the Kremlin's responses to KAL 007 as a "timely reminder of just how different the Soviets' concept of truth and international cooperation is from that of the rest of the world," Reagan emphasized U.S. initiatives on arms control in an effort to achieve equal reductions, consistent with the consensus that the G7 allies had reached at Williamsburg.[11]

Thatcher's office was in the midst of preparing for a critical conference on Anglo-Soviet relations at the prime minister's Chequers country retreat when Korean Air Lines flight 007 went down. Quickly, she recruited outside academics to inform a new policy direction for Britain in international affairs. The most influential members of this group, Hugh Thomas, Robert Conquest, and George Urban, were already deeply involved in the Centre for Policy Studies and the Hoover Institution, think tanks at the forefront of the Anglo-American public diplomacy campaign.[12] At Chequers, British leaders approved new efforts to elevate Britain's profile in East-West relations so as to gradually incorporate the Soviet Union into an Anglo-American world order, even if that meant little internal change in the Soviet system.[13] The United Kingdom's role in arms control topped the agenda. Officials especially focused on Thatcher's response to Soviet president Yuri Andropov's public letter of August 27, 1983, which insisted that Britain include its nuclear forces in INF talks.[14]

In her reply to Andropov, Thatcher asserted Britain's role in Cold War politics and staked out its position as powerbroker among the United States, NATO, and the Soviet Union. British officials hoped to curb the Soviet propaganda edge, suspecting that the Kremlin might publish the exchange of letters. In drafting the reply, they consulted widely with allies at the NATO working and ministerial levels to reinforce western resolve, particularly in light of Greece's recent disassociation from the dual-track strategy. West Germany's foreign minister Hans-Dietrich Genscher and Chancellor Helmut Kohl agreed with their British counterparts that Thatcher's reply to Andropov should defend Britain's nuclear sovereignty and the exclusion of its independent deterrent from INF talks. West German officials reasoned that a show of nuclear independence in these exchanges could ease the pressure in the Bundestag debate by demonstrating Europe's influence in arms control negotiations.[15]

British diplomats delivered Thatcher's reply to the Kremlin on September 27, one day after Reagan's announcement of new U.S. positions on INF negotiations. In the letter, Thatcher argued that intermediate-range forces should remain the subject of negotiations, but noted Britain's willingness to join arms control talks only after the Soviet Union and United States drastically reduced the size of their strategic arsenals. Britain's response appealed both to Washington's preference for "deep reductions" and to West German and Dutch audiences who wanted Europe's nuclear powers to consider the inclusion of their own forces.[16]

Intent on playing a larger role in East-West affairs, Thatcher followed her response to Andropov with a trip to the United States.[17] The prime minister lectured congressional leaders on nuclear issues and asserted herself on other matters related to economic warfare and the Cold War in the global south.[18] Her address at the Winston Churchill Foundation Award dinner in front of Washington's political elite continued the line that Reagan had employed throughout September. Thatcher warned, "We must not fall into the trap of projecting our own morality onto Soviet leaders. They do not share our aspirations: they are not constrained by our ethics. . . . their power is sustained by myth."[19] The echoes of Reagan in Thatcher's speech were deliberate, a result of George Urban's prominent role in writing it. Hungarian-born and educated in London, Urban had been involved in British and U.S. public diplomacy in the 1960s as a broadcaster for BBC's external services and Radio Free Europe, when the latter was still a front operation in Munich covertly funded by the CIA and USIA for broadcast across the Iron Curtain. In the 1970s, he had worked with the Centre for Policy Studies, which led to his involvement in the Chequers seminar on East-West relations. Urban would return to Radio Free Europe later in 1983 as its director. Uniquely familiar with the core moral themes and apparatus of U.S. and British public diplomacy, Urban gladly accepted Thatcher's invitation to help write her Churchill Foundation address.[20]

Urban and Thatcher viewed the speech as her version of Reagan's Westminster address: an opportunity to publicly advance the ideological counteroffensive against both the Soviet Union and the antinuclear left. An American audience offered something that the British public did not, a receptiveness to overtly moral arguments. Urban drew upon two sources of inspiration for the Churchill Foundation speech: Thatcher's interview with Brian Walden, in which she introduced the notion of Victorian values; and Reagan's Westminster speech. Her reaffirmation of the Anglo-American bond as a source of moral superiority in the fight against Soviet propaganda validated Reagan's public diplomacy at home and abroad. In coverage of the speech the *Washington Post* declared Thatcher "in her prime," while the *Daily Telegraph* headline read, "Thatcher spurs the West to win the Battle of Ideas."[21]

Public diplomacy coordination between Reagan and Thatcher worked to counter both Soviet propaganda and the increasing cooperation between the American and British antinuclear movements. On November 9, thirteen GCW activists, including U.S. citizen Deborah Law, joined U.S. Democratic congressmen Ronald Dellums of California and Ted Weiss of New York in a lawsuit demanding that President Reagan recall ground-launched cruise missiles from the United Kingdom. GCW plaintiffs argued that the cruise missiles violated the Fifth and Ninth amendments by making nuclear war inevitable, and Dellums and Weiss claimed that deployment of cruise missiles violated the right of Congress to declare war and provide for the defense of the United States.[22] The filing of the suit coincided with a massive campaign led by GCW to blockade all 102 U.S. military installations in the United Kingdom on the same day. The U.S. Southern District Court eventually dismissed the lawsuit on the grounds that it sought judgment over a political question, but the episode demonstrated the interconnections between the American and British antinuclear movements.[23] GCW's establishment of new channels for transatlantic nuclear dissent in foreign courts and the replication of its peace camps abroad exemplified how antinuclear activists sought to reimagine political community through ideas rather than geography.

Despite the flurry of antinuclear activity, cruise missile deployments for Europe arrived in the United Kingdom on November 14. The first battery of Pershing II missiles came to West Germany less than twenty-four hours after the Bundestag vote on November 22.[24] That same day, Soviet negotiators walked out of INF talks with no proposals to resume negotiations in the future.[25] Their walkout fit into the U.S. public diplomacy plan, and Paul Nitze played the star role in a press conference from Geneva. Public affairs officers had tutored him on how to position the U.S. delegation to dramatize the Soviet walkout in photographs that would appear in western newspapers. Heeding their counsel, Nitze had already begun cultivating beneficial relationships with the lead correspondents from the BBC, the *London Times*, the *Guardian*, and other European media operations in Geneva. Those established connections influenced a favorable media narrative about who bore responsibility for the suspension of arms control talks.[26]

In support of Nitze, Richard Burt, the assistant secretary of state for European and Canadian affairs, headlined the cast of U.S. officials who began appearing on the recently launched WORLDNET satellite television service, which featured leading journalists in direct conversations with senior U.S. policymakers.[27] Over the next five years, Charlie Wick made WORLDNET the primary technological instrument of U.S. public diplomacy. Launch of the service was a watershed moment in the technological modernization of USIA and public diplomacy; U.S. officials touted it as "truly the world's first global television service."[28] In fact, WORLDNET was both a cause and consequence of three public diplomacy imperatives. First, Wick convinced Congress that the broadcast service was an indication of USIA's influence and vision, a claim that increased controversy but also increased the agency's budget. Second, it played a part in centralizing U.S. public diplomacy around the president. Third, it was tasked with providing an alternative source of credible information to counter the unfavorable portrayal of U.S. Cold War policies in European media.[29]

The administration's response to the Soviet walkout highlighted some of these same trends in U.S. public diplomacy, notably a focus on the person

of the president and on technological innovations that reprioritized operations in Washington rather than in far-flung field offices. Arms Control and
Disarmament Agency (ACDA) director Kenneth Adelman briefed nearly
fifty foreign correspondents at the Washington Foreign Press Center. Reagan
capped the briefing with an expression of confidence that the Soviets would
return to the negotiating table.[30] European observers noted these early preparations for framing and blaming the Soviets for the suspension of arms control talks, and one foreign ministry official remarked, "There's never been an
arms negotiation where the real substance is more often public relations than
missiles, and this round goes to the Americans."[31]

For more than a year, Soviet officials had warned that the deployment of
cruise and Pershing missiles would invalidate any progress on START and
lead to the cancelation of talks.[32] Thus, on December 8, 1983, Viktor Karpov,
the veteran diplomat heading up the Soviets' START delegation in Geneva,
concluded the fifth round of negotiations by declaring, "In view of the deployment of new U.S. missiles in Europe, which has already begun, changes in the
global strategic situation make it necessary for the Soviet side to review all
problems under discussion."[33] Talks concerning intermediate and strategic
nuclear weapons were not the only negotiations in jeopardy. Discussing the
development of SDI in late November, George Shultz had reluctantly told
Reagan, "We will have to violate or renegotiate the ABM [anti-ballistic mis-
sile] and other treaties. We will need to consider new measures to assure a
smooth transition to a strategic balance relying more on defensive systems."[34]
The Pentagon Defensive Technology Study, known as the Fletcher report,
and the two-part Future Security Strategy Study underpinned Shultz's assessment of SDI in relation to the ABM treaty.[35] Those studies concluded that the
technical feasibility of ballistic missile defense should be reassessed, that the
Soviets were using arms control to "pursue competitive military advantage,"
and that defensive technologies could protect offensive nuclear assets of the
United States and thereby "enhance deterrence"—that is, allow America to
reclaim strategic superiority by lowering Soviet confidence in the effectiveness of its own nuclear arsenal.[36]

Science as Politics

Now the fragile compromise on nuclear policy between the White House
and Congress appeared to be in jeopardy. The Scowcroft report had been

the basis for the compromise between centrist Democrats and the Reagan administration.[37] By late 1983, however, Congressman Gore doubted that the domestic political balance and allied unity could withstand the collapse of arms control talks and recommended a return to the SALT II framework. Commenting on the state of arms control and nuclear anxiety, he told national security advisor Robert McFarland, "You do not have enough political capital to risk weathering this storm by standing pat. The question is how to maneuver without wasting precious assets."[38] As evidence of the elevated influence of the nuclear Freeze movement in American culture, politics, and life, he pointed to the 100 million Americans who had tuned in to watch ABC's graphic nuclear war drama *The Day After* in November.

Gore felt he had gained a new edge in negotiations with the Reagan administration on arms control. In late October and early November, Gore's political ally Carl Sagan had introduced nuclear winter theory as a new dimension in the deterrence debate, one that undercut many of the assumptions guiding Reagan's nuclear buildup and arms control strategy. Developed by R. P. Turco, Owen Toon, Todd Ackerman, J. B. Pollack, and Carl Sagan (the team was known by the acronym TTAPS), the theory held that, in the aftermath of multiple nuclear explosions totaling between 100 and 5,000 megatons, fine dust from ground bursts and smoke and soot from city and forest fires would rise into the atmosphere. Within one or two weeks, these particulates would reduce the amount of sunlight reaching the surface to a small percentage of what had formerly been normal. As a result, land temperatures would plummet to as low as negative 15 to negative 25 degrees Centigrade and have a catastrophic effect on ecological and biological processes. Such temperatures would likely persist for several months.[39]

To publicize nuclear winter theory, the TTAPS team organized "The World after Nuclear War: The Conference on Long-Term Worldwide Biological Consequences of Nuclear War," scheduled to take place in Washington, D.C., over Halloween weekend. One day before it began, Sagan published a brief article in the magazine *Parade* explaining the theory's key conclusions, which reached some 20 million American households.[40] More than five hundred participants from more than twenty countries attended the conference, including scientists, public officials, religious leaders, environmentalists, members of the defense establishment, antinuclear organizers, and educators.[41] Sagan's *Parade* article was one element of a major public relations strategy, a campaign managed by the conference's executive director,

Chaplin Barnes, and the marketing firm Porter, Novelli.[42] They organized newspaper placements in dozens of major and medium-sized media markets and secured special segments on CNN's *Crossfire*, ABC's *World News Tonight*, and NBC's *Today*.[43] Gore offered the conference the full support of his office and partnered with Republican senators Mark O. Hatfield of Oregon and Charles Mathias, Jr., of Maryland to urge members of Congress to attend a special briefing by Sagan and the biologist Paul Ehrlich on the morning of October 31.[44]

In an issue of *Foreign Affairs* that appeared in early December, Sagan advanced nuclear winter as the basis for policymaking, and the TTAPS study was featured in *Science* later in the month. In his *Foreign Affairs* article, Sagan made the case for the immediate reduction of global nuclear arsenals below the number that would trigger a climatic catastrophe in a full-scale nuclear war, a number that was estimated at between 500 and 2,000 nuclear warheads. He argued that the prospect of nuclear winter invalidated the strategic logic of ballistic missile defense, build-down proposals, technological improvements to missile accuracy, and related modernization trends as well as several other administration plans to establish U.S. strategic superiority.[45]

Reagan responded to these revelations by doubling down on SDI. On January 6, 1984, he authorized the formation of the Strategic Defense Initiative Organization (SDIO) to see through the recommendations of the Fletcher study and the aspects of the Future Security Strategy study overseen by Fred Hoffman.[46] The SDIO reported directly to the secretary of defense and operated separately from the bureaucracies of the various armed services. Though the study panels had officially offered an optimistic picture of SDI technologies, the White House's science advisor George Keyworth conducted his own consultations with the study teams and concluded that no single technology deserved exclusive development.[47] Therefore, multiple technologies were to be pursued in competition with each other.

The creation of SDIO advanced the integration of public diplomacy, domestic politics, and psychological operations. Existing missile defense programs pursued by the air force and the army now came under SDIO's control, which facilitated the public demonstration of intercept capabilities. Such demonstrations had two purposes: psychological warfare against the Soviet Union, and the generation of public enthusiasm to pressure Congress to finance SDI.[48] The most notable example of this intent took place a few months after SDIO's formation, when a rigged homing overlay experiment allowed the army to successfully intercept a test ICBM, suggesting major progress in ballistic missile defense capabilities.[49]

SDI, nuclear winter theory, and the Soviet suspension of arms control all suggested (albeit from very different points of view) that deterrence as a rational framework for the prevention of nuclear war was doomed to fail, either by politics or by other means. But Reagan did not seek to discard deterrence; rather, he wanted to reform it. Continued monetary and media investment in SDI tied directly to his argument that the United States had finally achieved "credible deterrence." Critics wondered how Reagan could make such a claim, given that the armaments that he had promised would shift the balance of strategic power back in America's favor—including the MX missile, the Trident weapon system, and the B-1 bomber—had not yet been produced and deployed.

Reagan's optimism about deterrence and the future of peace between the superpowers stemmed from his sense that the psychological and social dimensions of the arms race favored the United States and its allies, now that they had met the challenge of INF deployment, MX authorization, and the creation of SDIO. On January 16, Reagan delivered a major speech on East-West relations from the East Room of the White House to a global audience of more than 130 million viewers. In it, he asserted that American's renewed "strength of spirit" had restored credible deterrence.[50] Nonetheless, SDI had created a distinct set of public diplomacy challenges for the Reagan administration's broader nuclear narrative, especially in the context of an election year. In contrast to the Soviets, Reagan declared his willingness to resume arms control talks, making that clear in both his January 16 speech and his subsequent State of the Union address, and his attitude registered favorably among western publics.[51] His opponents, however, charged that his administration's increasing commitments to SDI not only undermined the ABM treaty, the last remaining bilateral strategic arms control treaty in force, but also the prospects for arms control agreements in general.

Foreseeing this line of attack, Reagan and his advisors developed a message around Soviet noncompliance with that treaty, hoping to persuade Congress to fund SDI.[52] As late as October 1982, the intelligence community had asserted that Soviet ABM activities were complying with arms control agreements.[53] Nonetheless, Reagan directed the Defense Department, the State Department, and the CIA to consider the Soviet ballistic missile defense program in the "context of overall Soviet efforts to possess a comprehensive strategic defensive capability."[54] The resulting interagency study found seven potential areas of noncompliance to publicly emphasize.[55] Only one of those possible violations—the Krasnoyarsk radar complex under construction—ran afoul of the ABM treaty.[56] Still, after announcing the formation of SDIO, the White House introduced its seven compliance concerns to Congress and the public.[57] This was seen as problematic, for under the terms of the ABM treaty a special consultative commission would litigate potential treaty violations in private. Gerard Smith, the lead ABM negotiator, claimed that, in an effort to gain a public diplomacy edge and to corner Congress, the administration had violated the spirit of the original agreement.[58]

The Reagan administration's report on Soviet violations did little to quell congressional opposition to SDI. In addition, disagreement among the president's top officials over SDI's purpose and value plagued its presentation to the public, allies, Congress, and the scientific community. Most of the senior national security officials who might normally have taken charge of a major defense initiative had already exhausted their political capital on other elements of the president's modernization program. The administration wanted Congress to allocate $26 billion to fund the first five years of SDI research and development, but officials' pursuit of competing objectives for the initiative undercut the administration's case.

Reagan turned to Keyworth to reverse SDI's political fortunes, largely because of his advisor's unrivaled ability to explain its technical dimensions. Keyworth found that the disjointed rollout of SDI engendered difficulties with the two groups most essential to realizing the president's vision: Congress and the scientific community. Though the administration's moral pronouncements had been intended to curry public and congressional favor, NSC staff observed, "We are seeing a catch-22 developing as our efforts to avoid adverse political consequences begin to cost the SDI support in DoD and the scientific community."[59] Keyworth complained to Defense Secretary Caspar Weinberger that the JASONs, those external scientists who advised on the technical dimensions of national security, "were faced with salesmen who were themselves not—too—sure of what they were selling," which left the group with severe reservations.[60] According to Keyworth, the president did not believe that SDI's endgame would be a perfect population defense; but because the administration's briefers had sold this idea to key stakeholders, even the program's supporters were confused about its objective.

Weinberger's insistence on pairing SDI with offensive modernization while deprioritizing arms control typified the hardline belief that U.S. security should be achieved through the nation's superior technological means rather than by compromising American values in negotiations with an immoral adversary.[61] In his memoirs, Weinberger blamed the ABM treaty for establishing MAD as the West's preferred deterrence paradigm. He contended that MAD was inherently unstable because it depended on "an assumption as to how a little-understood enemy, governed by men whose values, attitudes and standards are utterly different from ours, would act. . . . Perhaps the greatest assumption of all was that the Soviets also subscribed to MAD."[62] Weinberger's deputies, Richard Perle and Fred Iklé, also viewed SDI as an opportunity to break out of the ABM treaty and usher in an end to the arms control era. They promoted Weinberger's contention that "what we want to try to get is a system that will develop a defense that is thoroughly reliable and total." The defense secretary declared, "I don't see any reason why it can't be done."[63]

Managing allied reception of SDI fell to Secretary of State George Shultz, which proved to be a tough assignment for the skeptical elder statesman. Shultz had opposed SDI both on technical grounds and because of its implications for alliance unity.[64] Now that it had become a defining presidential initiative, however, he privately endorsed the program as a potential concession to win a favorable arms control settlement and aimed to keep the president committed to traditional concepts of deterrence.[65] The search for strategic superiority via defensive means meant violating the most successful arms control treaty in force and required a tightly controlled SDI narrative that stressed the moral promise of assured survival and Soviet bad intentions. Yet in March 1984, Shultz reopened arms control talks with the Soviets on U.S. terms and served as the primary public spokesmen on the process.[66] He saw SDI as an arms control bargaining chip in a broader set of umbrella talks that dealt with limitations on offensive and defensive forces.[67]

Without unity among top administration officials, support from the scientific community, or the buy-in of defense experts, SDI's fortunes looked bleak on Capitol Hill. Even Reagan's staunch congressional allies chafed at the poor-quality briefings and military leaders' faint praise.[68] General James Abrahamson, the newly appointed SDIO director, was thrust immediately into congressional hearings, where he implied that SDIO was striving for a 99.9-percent-effective five-layer defense, a position at odds with the more cautious statements from Keyworth's office.[69] After the administration's witnesses failed, during open testimony, to blunt technical and strategic criticisms from Democratic members of the Senate Foreign Relations Committee, Keyworth recognized that the program was in serious jeopardy. He implored the president, "Your leadership is necessary to re-establish our basic objective."[70]

Public reactions to nuclear winter theory were also generating skepticism about SDI. People grew concerned that the program would lead to an increase in the superpowers' stockpile of nuclear weapons and thus raise the possibility that nuclear war would end in climatic catastrophe. Sagan widely disseminated the theory among his peace movement contacts, a move that reinvigorated opposition to Reagan's nuclear agenda throughout 1984, both domestically and internationally.[71] Reacting to public interest in the theory, Democrats called on Sagan to play a larger role in defining the party's security policies and image. In 1984, he participated in meetings of the Democratic National Committee on party effectiveness, served on party platform-writing committees, and advised several presidential candidates on nuclear issues.[72] Meanwhile, Senator Ted Kennedy had invited Soviet participants in the Halloween conference to testify at the Kennedy-Hatfield forum on the climatic effects of nuclear war. Afterward he remarked, "So the debate changes. . . . The message of this panel is that the stakes are higher than we ever thought possible—what has been created is a doomsday machine."[73] Two members of the Soviet delegation—E. P. Velikhov, the vice president of the Soviet Academy of Sciences, and Sergei Kapitza, a famous physicist and popularizer of science—even appeared on the *Today Show* to make the case for nuclear winter theory.[74]

But Reagan still had effective allies on Capitol Hill. Congressman Newt Gingrich, a Republican from Georgia, sought to manage the scientific debate before Congress, seeing an opportunity to raise support for SDI and simultaneously discredit nuclear winter theory, which had quickly become a potent criticism of the Reagan administration's nuclear posture. In mid-May 1984 Gingrich and Congressman Tim Wirth, a Democrat from Colorado, invited Sagan and Edward Teller to debate nuclear winter theory and SDI on Capitol Hill in front of roughly fifty lawmakers.[75] As their debate unfolded, a frustrated Sagan asked, "Why are the standards of evidence so slack in assuring us there was nothing to worry about, but now, when it looks like there is something to worry about, we are told: let's not worry about policy implications until all the facts are in hand. All the facts will never be in hand."[76] Teller based his opposition to the theory on the work of scientists at Livermore Laboratory.[77] Though the lab's research on nuclear winter had been funded because of the TTAPS team's publicity campaign and had, for the most part, confirmed their findings, Teller distorted those findings to suggest that the theory was founded on incorrect assumptions that had been ideologically conditioned.[78] He argued that the dozen or so confirmatory studies of nuclear winter had relied on the same assumptions and had thus produced similarly flawed conclusions. Teller had the support of one of his protégés, Lowell Wood, who was leading SDI work at Livermore. Wood criticized Sagan on nuclear winter, stating, "It was an excellent first cut which you have advertised as the last cut."[79]

Wood's intervention in the nuclear winter debate shifted the discussion to SDI, exemplifying the ways in which pro- and antinuclear proponents viewed the proper relationship among science, the state, and society. The debate now touched upon the long-running question as to whether scientists should be "on top, or on tap." That is, should they be responsible to the global public and consider themselves public diplomats who operate independently of government so as to mold politics in a way that encourages international cooperation? Or should they defer to the political directives of national governments as the embodiment of society's will? Sagan's anti-SDI stance and his promotion of nuclear winter theory spoke to a broader belief that science should inform the public and create a way of thinking that encourages people to find diplomatic solutions to pressing social and political problems. In contrast, Teller, Wood, and their colleagues argued that science should create technologies that resolve social and political problems and thus provide the United States with an upper hand in the management of foreign relations, especially in dealings with illiberal societies. In this formulation, nuclear winter theory served not as catalyst for arms control concessions but as further justification for the development of SDI. Gingrich pinpointed the root of the difference: "Both the right and left do almost exactly the same thing psychologically. . . . the right tends to take nuclear war for granted . . . that we'll somehow deter. . . . On the other hand, I would say the whole reaction to the BMD [that is, to SDI] . . . are set piece arguments against it that fit exactly a certain model of thought."[80]

Two authoritative reports based on classified knowledge damned the technical arguments for ballistic missile defense in 1984. One came from the Congressional Office of Technological Assessment (OTA), the other from the Union of Concerned Scientists (UCS). The task of rebutting the Fletcher report findings fell to Ashton Carter, an Oxford-trained physicist and research fellow at the Massachusetts Institute of Technology, who was contracted by OTA to evaluate the claims of the studies commissioned by the administration. Carter submitted his report, "Directed Energy Missile Defense in Space," shortly before the Senate Foreign Relations Committee hearing in April.[81] Democrats seized on his findings to dispel the notion of a near-perfect defense that Abrahamson had promoted. Carter bluntly concluded that "the strategic goal of President Reagan's Strategic Defense Initiative calling for emphasized BMD research—perfect, near perfect, or less-than-perfect defense against ballistic missiles—remains unclear," further highlighting the administration's disjointed rollout.[82] He clarified several unknowns in building devices needed for space-based BMD and cast doubt on potential survivability. He also noted the prohibitive cost of the nearly 1,000 space-based battle stations required to fend off a Soviet launch of 2,800 missiles equipped with known countermeasures.[83]

Abrahamson organized a press conference to highlight technical errors in Carter's report. Concerned by what he perceived as intimidation, Carter wrote to Sagan and other allies in the scientific community, telling them that the Department of Defense had warned him that any public refutation of the alleged technical errors would violate his security clearance agreement. After the report drew technical criticisms from the Defense Department and a core of conservative scientists, an official review panel comprised of Charles Townes, a Nobelist and laser inventor; the widely respected General Glenn Kent; and William Perry, a former undersecretary of defense for research and engineering, confirmed Carter's conclusions.[84]

The Heritage Foundation also became involved in the questioning of Carter's report. Seeking to cast doubt on OTA's impartiality, Heritage did not focus on the technical merits of Carter's work but on his political motivations. Representatives of the think tank argued that Senator Kennedy, a liberal champion, exercised a commanding influence over the board, despite its equal number of Democrats and Republicans. Moreover, they claimed that the OTA study on BMD originated from a seminar headed by critic McGeorge Bundy, which had included only one pro-SDI participant.[85] By connecting the Freeze and Kennedy's antinuclear motivations to Carter's study, the Heritage Foundation suggested that partisanship—not science— explained the opposition to SDI.

Heritage cited Carter's connection to UCS and Sagan as further evidence of the OTA report's ideological bent.[86] Hans Bethe and Richard Garwin, who had spearheaded the UCS response to SDI, had established themselves as critics of ballistic missile defense in the late 1960s.[87] Both had prestigious reputations. Garwin became influential in the defense science community after helping to design the first hydrogen bomb, while Bethe won a Nobel Prize in 1967. Other experts on the UCS panels on BMD and the related discussion on antisatellite weapons included the renowned Cornell University scientists Kurt Gottfried, Frank Long, and Carl Sagan; the CIA's scholar-in-residence Richard Ned Lebow; the retired National Security Agency director Admiral Noel Gayler; the former CIA deputy director Herbert Scoville, Jr.; and the distinguished Massachusetts Institute of Technology physicists Henry Kendall and Victor Weisskopf. UCS's testimony on antisatellite weapons (ASAT) in May 1983 and the release of their report on space-based missile defense in March 1984 became touchstones of the SDI debate.

UCS compiled the ASAT testimony, the SDI assessment, and a historical overview of BMD into a booklet, *The Fallacy of Star Wars*, which quickly sold more than 50,000 copies after it appeared in stores in October 1984.[88] That same month Bethe, Garwin, Gottfried, and Kendall restated their case against space-based BMD in an article in *Scientific American*. Their analysis supported the OTA study, but a minor calculation error provided an opening for a group of conservative scientists.[89]

This small coterie worked to create a picture of a scientific community that was evenly divided on SDI. It included Robert Jastrow, the founding director of NASA's Goddard Institute for Space Studies; William Nierenberg, the former director of the Scripps Institution for Oceanography; and Frederick Seitz, the former president of the National Academy of Sciences. In September 1984 this group of retired scientists would form the George C. Marshall Institute as a home for conservative science critics, one that operated in league with the cohort of defense scientists at Livermore and Los Alamos who had established themselves under the tutelage of Teller.[90] They all sought to discredit Carter's testimony and the UCS report. Seitz and Nierenberg had become familiar with the Livermore BMD lobby when they served, alongside Teller, on candidate Reagan's Science and Technology Task Force in the fall of 1980.[91] In fact, Seitz had been Teller's first recommendation for White House Science advisor before he endorsed Keyworth.[92]

To thwart SDI critics on the other side of the scientific divide, Jastrow, Seitz, and Nierenberg wrote to Senator John Warner, a Republican from Virginia and a former secretary of the navy under Nixon, to point out discrepancies in the report's listing of the number of battle stations required for effective BMD.[93] Lowell Wood and Gregory Canavan, leaders of the anti-Soviet bloc based, respectively, at Livermore and Los Alamos, supplied them with additional technical criticisms.[94] In response, Garwin and other UCS members corrected their discrepancies in later testimonies to Congress, updated reports, and wrote appeals to Warner and other members of Congress on relevant committees.[95] Nonetheless, the attack line stuck, becoming the foundation for a broader criticism of sloppy and politically motivated science.

The conservative scientists' defense of SDI did not equate to a belief in population defense but showed their commitment to strategic superiority as a moral imperative. The neoconservative argument, which blamed liberal intellectuals for U.S. strategic vulnerability during the trials over SALT II ratification, increased Jastrow's interest in nuclear politics. In March 1983, shortly before the announcement of SDI, he took to the pages of *Commentary* to trumpet the necessity of strategic superiority.[96] Jastrow accelerated his *Commentary* campaign against scientific critics in 1984, endorsing BMD as a functional means to strategic superiority. In his eyes, American technology could succeed where diplomacy failed.

The emerging technical debate, which intensified in the coming years, presented problems for administration officials who had little faith in SDI but recognized its potential importance to international diplomacy and domestic politics. Though the administration claimed that the public highly approved of SDI, the popularity of BMD had significantly decreased after it became the subject of public scientific debate.[97] The plausibility of SDI needed to be maintained so as to leverage the program in East-West relations, either as a pressure point in arms control or as a new avenue for economic warfare. First, however, the administration needed to persuade its allies of SDI's technical validity before it had any hope of resolving their strategic, diplomatic, and economic qualms. By the summer of 1984, the Reagan administration had accepted Shultz's push for umbrella talks around some combination of INF, START, SDI, and space issues in 1985. These eventually became known as the Nuclear and Space Talks (NST). The Soviets accepted the idea during a plenary meeting in late November. This put INF back on the table but now also included defensive systems. As in the ABM and SALT I negotiations, separate delegations would conduct INF, START, and space talks in parallel, with an understanding that all three were interrelated.

The Cold Warrior in the 1984 Election

How was it that Reagan could both embrace Shultz's push for umbrella talks and trumpet SDI, which appeared to threaten what little confidence the Soviet Union and NATO allies had in Washington? Ironically, the public demanded both. Stabilizing arms control agreements remained stubbornly popular throughout the 1970s and the Reagan years. The administration's lack of clarity regarding its goals for SDI reflected not only internal disagreement but also a deliberate policy of ambiguity. Public approval of SDI was tied directly to the notion that it could offer an impenetrable shield for the civilian population rather than intermediate defenses of silos.[98]

During his first term, Reagan had become increasingly interested in crafting his presidential legacy around the reversal of the arms race and the abolition of nuclear weapons. His frequent referrals to his time in Hollywood, to stories of his boyhood, and to anecdotes of western history's most revered leaders indicate how legacy crafting dominated his thinking. Several events further motivated Reagan's movement toward nuclear abolition in these years. Surviving an assassin's bullet in 1981 had added a sense of urgency to his mission of reducing nuclear weapons.[99] This was reflected in an increased emphasis on public diplomacy, beginning in spring 1982. Briefings on the single integrated operational plans for nuclear war impressed upon him the true scale and consequences of such a conflict, as did graphic imagery in the film *The Day After*.[100] The Korean Air Lines 007 incident and the nuclear war scare connected with NATO's Able-Archer exercise in autumn 1983 helped the president comprehend the precarity of nuclear peace, as he took more seriously the notion that the Soviet Union might be arming itself out of fear of the United States rather than in preparation for preemptive nuclear war with the West.[101] By the 1984 election season, Reagan had come to accept nuclear winter as a serious policy consideration.[102] Progress on his modernization and deployment plans also validated his view that strength must come before peace.

For presidents seeking to secure their legacy, winning a second term is vital. While Reagan was polling very favorably on economic matters, nuclear issues had emerged as his biggest political vulnerability. At the start of the presidential campaign season in January, 35 percent of Americans considered international issues to be the nation's biggest problem, more than 50 percent disapproved of the president's handling of foreign affairs, and 20 percent listed the possibility of nuclear war as the number one problem facing the United States.[103] Reagan, like any politician in his position, found himself searching for ways to overcome his liabilities.[104] He came to realize that the effect of his communicative powers at home increased when he spoke simultaneously to a domestic and an international audience. In his January address in which he reaffirmed the importance of credible deterrence, he also introduced a new dimension to his Soviet rhetoric: common narrative building. Imagining a chance encounter between a Russian couple, Ivan and Anya, and an American couple, Jim and Sally, Reagan stressed that the commonalities of the human condition could help bridge the East-West divide and reduce the threat of nuclear war.[105] In earlier speeches, he had sought to help western audiences make the distinction between the Soviet government and that nation's dissidents, cultures, and peoples; but by speaking about the shared humanity of Ivan, Anya, Jim, and Sally, Reagan discovered the value of conceptualizing his audience in transnational rather than national terms.

The global broadcast of the "Ivan and Anya" speech via WORLDNET and Voice of America demonstrated that, when it came to the president's role as a communicator, no distinction existed between domestic politics and public diplomacy. This became true of the 1984 election more generally. In the spring of 1984, Carnes Lord, who had just stepped down as director of international communications and information in the NSC, took to the pages of *Commentary* to respond to criticisms that U.S. public diplomacy had taken on a more ideological bent reflective of conservative politics rather than the entirety of American society. He countered that, "because it has involved the doings and words of high officials, public diplomacy has inevitably tended to extend itself into the domestic arena."[106] ACDA's director, Kenneth Adelman, recalled that in terms of messaging on nuclear issues, domestic and overseas communication were one and the same.[107]

During the election season, Reagan's messaging on arms control relied on nuclear themes to shore up his base, identified as politically conservative, middle-aged, lower- to middle-income, no college education, living in southern and rural areas.[108] Various campaigns and political groups kept up the peace through strength rhetoric throughout the season. Reagan declared a National Peace through Strength Week in the fall to recognize the support that organizations such as the Coalition of Peace through Strength and the American Security Council had lent to his campaign.[109] Keyworth and other administration officials encouraged congressional candidates to stump for SDI.[110] The

Reagan campaign's famous "Bear in the Woods" commercial illustrated the administration's public diplomacy rationales for nuclear modernization.[111]

Nuclear politics generated acute moments of pressure during the election, perhaps most famously after Reagan's approval ratings plummeted following a hot mic incident in which the president joked, "We begin bombing in five minutes."[112] The election challenge for the president was to maintain his reputation as a Cold Warrior to keep the support of his political base, but also to "change the image of the Cold Warrior in U.S. culture" to a form that drew moderate support and deflected leftwing criticism.[113]

Yet the 1984 elections showed that Reagan's charisma would not be enough to win a strong mandate for his nuclear agenda.[114] His willingness to link SDI more closely to arms reductions during his campaign was not so much a veiled reference to a still undefined economic strategy but an acknowledgment of the domestic political realities that were determining his bargaining leverage with Congress. The nuclear issue may not have been the major theme of the 1984 presidential contest, but its importance has been understated. Antinuclear ideas proved to be especially important in maintaining the gender gap, which Democrats hoped would help them defeat Reagan and his congressional allies. For the primary election, Walter Mondale drew support from the antinuclear movement due to his lead in polling and his outreach to women. The Freeze movement and Mondale both prioritized women voters, hoping to learn a lesson from the 1980 election results, where Reagan had outperformed Carter by 1 to 2 percent with women compared to 17 percent with men.[115] In 1982, 4 million more women voted than men; and by 1984, women accounted for 60 percent of registered voters.[116]

Progressives and Democrats became obsessed with the gender gap, viewing it as the key to a presidential victory. Mondale selected Geraldine Ferraro to run as the first female vice presidential candidate from either major party, primarily as a strategy to capture women's votes. Women's leadership inside the antinuclear movement identified peace and reproductive rights as the core components of the gender gap.[117] In large-scale volunteer field operations and voter registration efforts, groups such as Gender Gap Action Campaign, the Women's Trust, and Women's Action for Nuclear Disarmament (WAND) worked closely with FV '84 and other antinuclear groups to make disarmament a major election issue.[118] WAND was especially active, launching its Millions of Moms Vote for Survival '84 campaign as well as a Women Vote for Survival '84 campaign that specialized in registering women

in impoverished communities.[119] WAND formed a political action committee ahead of the 1984 elections and used it to support Ferraro and forty
congressional candidates that the organization saw as allies on women's and
nuclear issues.[120] The group also set up a speakers' training course for women
on nuclear issues and launched a national poster campaign with the slogan
"Children ask the world of Us."[121]

As stakeholders paid increased attention to the possibility that antinuclear
issues could sway women to vote Democratic, they also began focusing on
the role of expert women in nuclear policymaking. One of those women was
Carol Cohn, who later published a groundbreaking analysis of the nuclear
situation, based on the time she spent with the overwhelmingly male elite
strategic community in the summer and fall of 1984. Cohn's 1987 article, "Sex
and Death in the Rational World of Defense Intellectuals," emphasized the
importance of setting a new paradigm for nuclear diplomacy. She wrote, "The
activity of trying to out-reason defense intellectuals in their own games gets you
thinking inside their rules, tacitly accepting all the unspoken assumptions of
their paradigms. You become subject to the tyranny of concepts. The language
shapes your categories of thought."[122] Her arguments echoed E. P. Thompson's
earlier claims about the nuclear establishment's deformation of language and
the ongoing Anglo-American peace movement critiques of "nukespeak": the
Orwellian vocabulary that governments used to rationalize nuclear weapons' relationship to peace.[123] Cohn believed that the peace movement, and
feminists in particular, needed to deconstruct the technostrategic discourse
that had allowed "militarized masculinity" to become the dominant voice
of rationality. She also argued that feminists faced a reconstructive project
that required them to develop and recognize new conceptions of rationality
drawn from diverse voices so as to create "compelling alternative visions of
possible futures."[124]

These ideas were the focus of the first National Women's Conference to
Prevent Nuclear War, held in the Cannon Caucus Room of the House of
Representatives in September 1984. Conference luminaries highlighted
how antinuclear aims and women's empowerment went hand in hand.
Ellen Goodman, a Pulitzer Prize–winning *Boston Globe* columnist, argued
that "our concern for peace is intricately related with the second half of this
movement for equality. . . . It is our time to make our policy, hold on to our
values."[125] Former first lady Rosalynn Carter and the veteran women's activist
Mildred Scott Olmsted, who had helped found SANE, echoed Goodman's

urgency. Other conference speakers emphasized that women merited inclusion in nuclear policy debates because they were experts, not just because of their role as moral stewards of the family. Randall Forsberg observed that only 50 percent of the nuclear-issues conferences included women presenters and that rejecting women speakers for not being well known perpetuated a "super-star syndrome" that reinforced inequality within the peace movement.[126] Forsberg and a number of other formidable experts broke down the technical dimensions of the Reagan administration's nuclear policy, among them Ruth Adams, the editor of the *Bulletin of the Atomic Scientists*; Vera Kistiakowsky, a physics professor at the Massachusetts Institute of Technology; Condoleezza Rice, a Stanford University professor of political science and a future secretary of state; and, of course, Helen Caldicott.[127]

Because these and other expert women had been excluded from elite forums for the discussion of nuclear policy, they had channeled their analyses of deterrence into the public sphere. This made them both influential political surrogates during the election season and catalysts for a public turn in science activism. Women educators, in particular, argued for the link between nuclear literacy and civic literacy, and they disparaged defense intellectuals for perpetuating a "Strangelove legacy" that had brought the United States to the brink of both a nuclear crisis and a crisis in government trust.[128] Women educational experts and scientific experts worked together to design nuclear-related curricula for the 1984 election season and beyond. For example, the League of Women Voters and the National Education Association partnered with Educators for Social Responsibility to produce curricula such as *Learning Peace, Decision Making in a Nuclear Age, Choices, Perspectives,* and *Participation*, all of which focused on raising awareness about nuclear issues, conflict resolution, peace studies, and civic action.[129] They also made an obvious political move with the curriculum *Elections*, designed to teach junior high and high school students about electoral politics.[130]

As it turned out, Mondale won a majority in only two categories: voters concerned with foreign policy and nuclear arms control, and those who based their votes on concerns for the poor.[131] Both were linked to the gender gap, for it was women who saw nuclear peace and the alleviation of poverty as top priorities.[132] Antinuclear campaigns featured more prominently in congressional elections, which helped down-ballot Democrats overcome the spillover effect of Reagan's landslide victory over Mondale. Though they could not match Republican fundraising efforts, antinuclear groups poured cash into Democratic campaigns.[133] FV '84 raised the second-largest amount of money of any Democrat political action committee, $3.4 million, most of which put two hundred paid organizers into the field to help manage nearly 25,000 campaign volunteers.[134] In many areas, FV '84 dwarfed the Mondale campaign; it was the backbone of volunteer operations in ten states.[135] Freeze field operations helped offset the massive gap in campaign spending, as the GOP's $225 million fundraising haul was quadruple that of the Democratic Party's. In his victory speech, John Kerry, the newly elected Democratic senator from Massachusetts, who had been outspent by his Republican opponent for the seat vacated by Paul Tsongas, declared, "I'm going to Washington to end the nuclear arms race," offering a thank you to the critical support provided by 3,000 Freeze volunteers in the field.[136] Paul Simon, the new Democratic senator from Illinois, relied on 50,000 Freeze voters in a narrowly decided contest with Republican Charles Percy, the powerful chair of the Senate Foreign Relations Committee and one of the stubbornest Freeze opponents on Capitol Hill.[137]

Despite his landslide, the 1984 election made Reagan more attuned to the value and limitations of his administration's approach to public diplomacy in the United States. Congressional candidates supported by the Freeze campaign won 70 percent of their races, and FV '84 estimated that 1 million voters had cast ballots based on the freeze.[138] Antinuclear organizing efforts had helped to win two Senate seats for Democrats and had moderated the gains made by Republicans in the House. These outcomes proved to be critical because they allowed Democrats in Congress to influence Reagan's approach to arms control during his second term.

A Return to Arms Control

Even before voters cast their ballots, national security officials had begun to consider what effect the 1984 elections might have on Reagan's modernization program and arms control strategy. In a mid-September meeting of the National Security Planning Group (NSPG), Shultz alone advocated for leveraging SDI in arms control discussions, arguing, "We have more difficulty with the politics of modernization than they do. Reductions are to our advantage. . . . The idea of holding simultaneous discussion of offensive and defensive systems is good. They are worried about our SDI program."[139] Defense Secretary Weinberger, CIA Director Casey, ACDA Director Adelman, and the joint chiefs of staff aligned against Shultz. Most opposed reconvening arms control talks, and they attempted to persuade the president that resuming them might trap the United States into a more extensive agreement that would limit SDI options.[140]

In four meetings, beginning on November 30 and running through mid-December, the NSPG articulated a possible role for SDI in arms control. CIA briefer David George brought Reagan's attention to SDI's impact on East-West economic competition. Although the Soviet Union had a large military-industrial base, expanding American high-tech supremacy via SDI could increase pressure during arms control negotiations and would dovetail nicely with hardliners' preference for using economic warfare to condition Soviet behavior.[141] Weinberger reasoned that SDI provided the best opportunity to mobilize the U.S. economy in support of national security objectives.[142] Reagan weighed arguments for Shultz's position versus the hardliners' and then shocked both groups by suggesting that the United States might share defensive technologies with the Soviet Union.[143] In the end, the NSPG principals did come to an agreement on two points: first, that SDI and the success of modernization would bring the Soviet Union back to the negotiating table; second, that the Kremlin would revive its peace offensive to exploit the impulse of the political left to halt western nuclear programs.[144]

Upcoming talks in Geneva would be the first real test of the administration's public diplomacy for SDI. Robert McFarlane organized the final preparatory meeting for those talks around the question of "how to sustain SDI, especially with the public."[145] It was one thing to sell the idea of SDI as a moral imperative while not involved in arms control negotiations but quite another to publicly defend the program if SDI turned out to be the one issue holding up meaningful discussions. "Geneva is going to be a public event," Shultz reminded his colleagues.[146] U.S. officials needed specific strategic, technical, and diplomatic justifications to defend SDI rather than vague promises of a world set free from nuclear terror. In anticipation, McFarlane ordered the NSC to develop an SDI Bible to serve as the administration's public diplomacy action plan.

During its compilation, Bob Linhard of the NSC Arms Control Directorate wrote to McFarlane in frustration: "One of the most difficult problems we face with respect to SDI is to get all the various players singing from the same piece of policy music."[147] Authors of the SDI Bible recognized this discord in the administration but ultimately put forward an NSC position. Intermediate defense, as endorsed by the Hoffman panel, was to be framed as a step along the way to a "complete SDI system." Contrary to State Department views, the NSC staff insisted that "SDI is not a bargaining chip for current arms negotiations." For public diplomacy purposes, the authors of the SDI Bible recommended emphasizing non-nuclear systems as a way to obscure public interest in research on several nuclear-powered concepts being conducted under SDIO, such as Teller's X-ray laser project, Excalibur.[148] Alongside this strategy, the NSC encouraged the administration to put out a special appeal for technical talent, with promises of substantial innovation funding that could overcome widespread skepticism in the scientific community.

The authors of the SDI Bible sought to nurture a theme of American technological exceptionalism to mitigate the effect of criticisms from the scientific community on public opinion.[149] Experts who considered SDI a technological realization of America's moral superiority often referred to the moon landing and the Wright brothers' aviation achievements before noting examples of famously invalidated predictions from scientific doubters, such as Einstein's skepticism about nuclear energy.[150] In *The Case for Space Defense* Daniel Graham made similar appeals to American technological exceptionalism, memorably depicting an astronaut in Davy Crockett's famous coonskin cap.[151]

Scientific critics of SDI fought back, arguing that references to American technological exceptionalism distorted the challenge at hand. Jack Ruina and George Rathjens, both nuclear experts from the Massachusetts Institute of Technology who had served in and outside of government, wrote, "SDI involves competing against a determined and resourceful adversary *as well as* unlocking nature's secrets and harnessing technology."[152] Sidney Drell, the director of the Stanford Linear Accelerator and a long-time JASON, said, "I never doubted that we would put a man on the moon. Here in the ABM battle, we're not talking about man against nature, which is a technological challenge. We're talking about man against man."[153] In their winter 1984 article in *Foreign Affairs*, four respected U.S. statesmen, McGeorge Bundy, George Kennan, Robert McNamara, and Gerard Smith, also debunked analogies to past technological achievements: "The effort to get to the moon was not complicated by the presence of an adversary. A platoon of hostile moon-men with axes could have made it a disaster."[154]

The Federation of American Scientists saw the debate between proponents of technological exceptionalism and SDI's scientific critics as an encapsulation of competing views about the obligations of science to domestic and international society. For Teller and his allies, the arms race was a scientific contest that could be won with a technological solution. They believed in general that advances in technology could resolve the nation's most pressing social and moral problems and help consolidate its hegemony abroad. For critics, the technical feasibility of SDI was, in part, linked to the twofold problem of humans against nature and humans against humans. By objecting to Reagan's nuclear policies, they were implicitly arguing that science should be the foundation for public reason.[155]

In the December 17 NSPG meeting, both Shultz and Paul Nitze challenged the recommendations in the SDI Bible, specifically the assertions from Weinberger, Adelman, and the NSC that SDI relied exclusively on non-nuclear systems. Shultz, who harbored serious technical concerns about the program's feasibility, believed that its value rested in its bargaining leverage rather than as a deployed system. Declaring that the balance of nuclear forces had changed in favor of the United States in 1983–84, State Department representatives were now searching for new approaches to reducing offensive weapons. In contrast, NSPG participants who were convinced of SDI's non-nuclear purity wanted to provoke another Soviet walkout and position the United States to earn the ensuing public diplomacy benefits.[156] Reagan remained committed to SDI, not because it provided bargaining leverage or public diplomacy value but because he still saw it as a viable avenue to strategic superiority. He told his advisors, "We must be resolved among ourselves that SDI is not the price for reductions."[157]

A British View of SDI and Nuclear Winter Theory

The NSC authors of the SDI Bible considered the British, among U.S. allies, to be the bluntest and most articulate critics of SDI.[158] U.S. officials had begun to claim allied support of SDI as an element of the administration's public diplomacy plan, but many NATO member states—significantly Britain—harbored serious concerns. The criticisms that British officials offered about SDI derived from their own long history of managing an independent deterrent and from frequent exchanges with Shultz and Nitze.[159]

Since Reagan's March 1983 speech announcing SDI, doubts about the technical feasibility of BMD had pervaded Thatcher's government. The release of the Hoffman and Fletcher reports in October left the FCO with more questions than answers.[160] The continued effectiveness of the Trident ballistic submarine, recently purchased from the United States, and SDI's potential impact on the existing ABM treaty topped the list of their anxieties.[161] The U.S. Department of Defense had emphasized that the ABM treaty permitted BMD research so long as development and deployment did not follow, but the State Department's more reserved assessment of the treaty had created confusion among Thatcher's officials.[162] No one in Washington had answers to queries about the complexities of battle-management software, the vulnerability of space-based defense systems, power sources for directed-energy weapons, the geography of deployment, and many other technical issues.[163]

FCO officials found the technical evidence to support SDI so underwhelming that they dismissed the Hoffman and Fletcher reports as mere propaganda.[164] In contrast, the Scowcroft report and Carter's OTA study, in tandem with the critique released by UCS, thoroughly convinced the MoD and the FCO of the technical futility of SDI.[165] Moreover, British intelligence had debunked the Reagan administration's claims about the advanced state of Soviet BMD research and ABM treaty infractions, both of which had been used to justify SDI.[166]

Thatcher, an Oxford-trained research chemist, had enormous confidence in her own scientific abilities, and her prior exposure to BMD concepts offset the negative assessments offered by the FCO and the MoD. In Britain, scientific advisors had little direct access to government, and those embedded in the civil service were often isolated from policymakers. After Thatcher's civil service reforms shrank the size of the bureaucracy, scientists' influence diminished even more, especially in nuclear controversies.[167] Thatcher preferred briefings from high-ranking U.S. personnel such as Shultz and General James Abrahamson and relied on technical assessments from the specialist press, most regularly from *Aviation and Space Weekly*.[168] Major General John Keegan, the chief of U.S. Air Force Intelligence, and Daniel Graham, in his previous capacity as director of the U.S. Defense Intelligence Agency, had briefed her on the "death-beam gap" several times during her tenure as opposition leader.[169] Now the prime minister drew on her own scientific background to question officials' valid technical concerns about SDI. She later claimed that "laid back generalists from the Foreign Office—let alone the ministerial muddlers in charge of them—could not be relied upon. By contrast I was in my element."[170]

Despite these internal disagreements, Thatcher's government unanimously viewed SDI as a potential public diplomacy crisis rather than a visionary program for mutual survival.[171] Implementing the program risked reviving the British peace movement, in part because the issue had become entangled with the politics of nuclear winter theory, which had quickly become a top priority for antinuclear activists. SANA and Pugwash, representing, respectively, the public and private dimensions of science diplomacy, identified both SDI and nuclear winter as obvious causes for scientists. By merging these two tracks of science diplomacy, the organizations presented a formidable antinuclear challenge to the Thatcher government. SANA and Pugwash sought to illuminate contradictions in the Thatcher government's approach to science and to reform the relationship between expertise and the state.[172] They overlapped effectively as Pugwash members plugged a transatlantic network of scientists into a public diplomacy campaign that was managed, for the most part, by SANA.

At first, Pugwash held fast to its traditional emphasis: using its prestigious members to privately persuade national and international elites. Since its founding in 1957, it had developed from a suspected Communist front into the world's most influential body of diplomat scientists.[173] Pugwash was structured as a confederation of autonomous national membership organizations, with the goal of drawing balanced participation from the Soviet bloc, the West, and nonaligned nations. Private Pugwash diplomacy had produced positive results in discussions around the Partial Test Ban Treaty, the Nuclear Nonproliferation Treaty, and the Biological Weapons Convention. However, its limited success on the INF problem in 1981–83 signaled the waning significance of its private diplomatic reach.[174]

Lord Solly Zuckerman, who had transitioned from a career as an influential civil servant to a conduit for international science activism, exemplified the Pugwash approach to science diplomacy. Zuckerman's long government service began in World War II and peaked in 1966, when he became the chief scientific advisor to Her Majesty's Government amid the "white heat" of Prime Minister Harold Wilson's aspirational technological revolution. His accomplishments earned him a lifetime peerage after his retirement in 1971.[175] Zuckerman's credentials made him an unimpeachable authority on the relationship between science and politics. He participated extensively in Pugwash activities, eventually becoming a trustee of the British chapter.[176] By leveraging his reputation and impressive list of scientific and political contacts in support of nuclear winter research, he served as the British node in an international network of technical experts who were grappling with the issue.

Opposition to SDI and concern about nuclear winter theory tightened the relationship between public and private approaches to anti-SDI science diplomacy. The American scientist Richard Garwin, who had become close friends with Zuckerman through Pugwash and previous government-related projects, wrote to him in August 1984 to gauge the level of SDI opposition in Britain and the rest of Europe. Zuckerman noted that the initial response from the scientific community seemed to be hostility to this new technological twist in the arms race. However, he could not identify any government official or influential public figure who was currently willing to stand up to U.S. technological ambitions. To alter this situation, and with the aid of Garwin's expertise, Zuckerman orchestrated a covert campaign to persuade government officials to oppose SDI and "moderate the crazy technological battle between the USA and the USSR."[177] Beginning with overtures to NATO's secretary general, Peter Carrington, and to members of the FCO and the MoD, Zuckerman's campaign reinforced the technological suspicions of SDI that were animating conflict in Whitehall.[178]

Zuckerman had served on technical and advisory boards for Sagan's nuclear winter conferences, and now he began bringing attention to the issue in Britain. The U.K. branch of Pugwash saw nuclear winter concerns as an opportunity to reassert itself in world affairs. Whitehall had dismissed the theory, an action that Zuckerman took to be yet another example of the Thatcher government's anti-science attitude, and he started working feverishly to prevent this view from becoming entrenched in the civil service and the public conscience. He decided to publicize nuclear winter as part of a broader effort to promote the use of scientific expertise in government decision making. In pursuit of these efforts he joined the scientific advisory board of the newly formed Centre on the Consequences of Nuclear War.[179] His mission was to market a study on the environmental effects of nuclear war released by the Scientific Committee on Problems of the Environment. Known as SCOPE-ENUWAR, the study was an objective, comprehensive assessment of nuclear winter theory. At the same time, Zuckerman used his fundraising talents to channel funds to the Royal Society of London, which had sponsored SCOPE-ENUWAR, where they were earmarked for further research on nuclear winter theory.[180]

The authoritativeness of SCOPE-ENUWAR helped resolve the scientific controversy around nuclear winter—though not its political issues. The study had taken place under the chairmanship of the British scientist Sir Frederick

Warner, was administered by the University of Essex, and was made possible by an initial grant from the Royal Society.[181] It was a thorough synthesis of studies done in the United States, the United Kingdom, Canada, Australia, Japan, the Soviet Union, and dozens of countries in Eastern and Western Europe and the developing world.[182] Warner had relied on Zuckerman to help him recruit experts throughout the world and in the United Kingdom, especially scientists from within government.[183] Zuckerman's endorsement of nuclear winter research in parliamentary debates and in private correspondence to Thatcher's cabinet secretary, Sir Robert Armstrong, lent credibility to the theory within official circles—a credibility that SANA alone could not provide.[184] It also allowed Denis Healey, the deputy Labour leader, to critique the Thatcher government's nuclear winter position as an illustration of its anti-science attitudes and, in so doing, capture antinuclear support for his party and marshal the scientific community to the side of Labour.[185]

Zuckerman's engagement with the politics of nuclear winter had a transformative effect on British science activism. In 1981 he had turned down an invitation from SANA's founder Mike Pentz to join that organization, basing his decision on his belief that nuclear weapons had a small, if important, role to play in international security.[186] But dissemination of nuclear winter theory could be a shared goal for moderate opponents of the arms race, such as Zuckerman, and the outspoken unilateral disarmers of SANA. Their combined activism helped override some of the initial concerns among Pugwash leadership that SANA might go too far in politicizing science.[187] In turn, Zuckerman's offer to headline SANA's speaking engagements about the theory was a sign that Britain's older scientific elite had become willing to involve themselves in mass politics and that they and other organizations shared concerns about the poor state of science advising in government.[188] If SANA now had access to the international networks of experts and officials maintained by Pugwash, then Pugwash, too, benefited, with new forums for engaging the British public.

CND leaders identified nuclear winter theory as "a very powerful campaigning tool."[189] Many of the scientists who had lent their expertise to the NWFZ movement now became nongovernmental public diplomats, trumpeting the issue of nuclear winter in service of British antinuclear protest. Since the success of SANA's Hard Luck campaign, the Home Office had endeavored to control what scientific advice was available to local civil defense authorities. Now, by pressuring Parliament from the bottom up,

SANA was spearheading the peace movement campaign to raise local awareness of nuclear winter, capitalizing on activist networks that they had established during the anti-civil defense campaign and the spread of the NWFZ
phenomenon.

By the end of 1984, nuclear winter theory and opposition to Britain's involvement in SDI were sustaining SANA's growth and authority with the NWFZ
movement.[190] Pentz produced a film on nuclear winter and disseminated it
widely among his peace movement contacts, local governments, and European antinuclear groups, encouraging them to use it as a tutorial on the issue.[191]
The film and a corresponding conference attracted funding from the Greater
London Council, the West Midlands Council, the Sheffield City Council, and
the Strathclyde Council, money that allowed the American nuclear winter
experts Richard Turco and Paul Ehrlich to lead SANA scientists on a ten-day
"Britain after Nuclear War" briefing tour in early November.[192] Presenters
visited twelve cities around the United Kingdom, and the events attracted
thousands of attendees throughout the United Kingdom. It included eight
university seminars, nine public meetings, a day-long scientific symposium
at Oxford featuring more than sixty experts, parliamentary briefings for forty
MPs, a consultation with the Greater London Council, and a colloquium on
the moral dimensions of nuclear winter held in Westminster's Central Hall
for representatives of Britain's Christian, Muslim, and Jewish communities.[193]
The tour illustrated SANA's efforts to make science central to the transatlantic
disarmament debate but also key to local formulations of nuclear policies,
especially in matters of civil defense.

Nuclear winter theory revitalized the cultural strategy of the British antinuclear movement. This was particularly notable in the development of British
nuclear cinema. During the 1983 Halloween conference, Sagan and Ehrlich
had asked Norman Myers, a well-known British expert in biodiversity, to
work up plans for publicizing nuclear winter theory in the United Kingdom.
He responded, "Television producers clamour for graphic materials they can
use on camera to illustrate the points made during discussion/confrontation
with government officials, notably defense and civil defense people."[194] Soon
Myers, Sagan, and Turco, along with other participating scientists, became
advisors for the BBC production *Threads,* the world's first onscreen portrayal
of nuclear winter, released in September 1984. After *Threads* came *On the
Eighth Day,* a companion documentary on the origins of nuclear winter the-

ory. Ehrlich and every member of TTAPS (with the exception of Pollock) appeared in the documentary.[195]

Threads highlights the infusion of transatlantic expertise into the peace movement. Experts such as Stanford-based Soviet specialist David Holloway, SANA scientist Philip Steadman, and investigative journalist Duncan Campbell offered advice about the outbreak of war and civil defense.[196] Eric Chivian and Robert Lifton, the American doctors who pioneered work on the psychological consequences of nuclear war, consulted with the filmmakers on the mental states the actors should inhabit. Pugwash's co-founder Joseph Rotblat and Bernard Feld, a professor at the Massachusetts Institute of Technology and the editor of the *Bulletin of the Atomic Scientists,* offered general guidance. The film's portrayal of the effects of a nuclear holocaust in Sheffield so brilliantly captured the variety of concerns underpinning British antinuclear angst that it became a defining artifact of the decade's mass movement politics. Though the overriding message of *Threads* is a condemnation of the pro-deterrence policies that could drive Britain into a post-nuclear apocalyptic world, the social and economic hardships in pre-apocalyptic Sheffield are depicted as consequences of Thatcher's broader neoliberal program for society, the policy that was, the film implies, leading the United Kingdom into nuclear danger in the first place. In this way, *Threads* became emblematic of the local-to-global nature of the peace movement's public science diplomacy.

The Home Office's failure to study the nuclear winter issue for itself gave members of the SANA-informed parliamentary opposition an opportunity to attack the government. In a winter 1984–85 debate, after antinuclear MPs challenged Thatcher officials to explain why they had failed to update recommendations in the government pamphlet *Civil Defence and the Farmer,* Home Office representatives simply stated that nuclear winter was an unproven theory and that policy should not be made on such uncertain predictions. When pressed to identify members of the scientific community who doubted the validity of the theory, the officials carelessly listed the TTAPS authors and their ally Myers.[197]

The government's monopoly on nuclear knowledge had clearly been broken by internal and external opposition to SDI and concerns about nuclear winter. This meant that Thatcher's goal of raising Britain's profile in East-West affairs would require a different set of calculations. If the United States were to maintain the upper hand in arms control negotiations by claiming allied unity on SDI, the program's public presentation would need substantial reworking, and that revision would need to be mindful of the distinct lines of scientific opposition developing in the United Kingdom and the rest of Europe. Fortunately for the Thatcher government, two meetings with the superpowers in December 1984 would give the prime minister precisely the opportunity she needed to assert Britain's leading role in world affairs and quell antinuclear dissent at home.

CHAPTER SIX
SUMMITS

A T A SUMMIT in Washington, D.C., in December 1987, the United States and the Soviet Union agreed to the terms of an intermediate nuclear forces treaty. Soon afterward, a USIA study led by the Heritage Foundation's president Edwin Feulner, Jr., considered what can be learned from the preparations for superpower summits: "How summits are perceived fundamentally shapes these outcomes. . . . public diplomacy should be treated as a primary strategic part of summit statecraft. It is, after all, the public component that makes summits unique and distinguishes them from other forms of diplomatic dialogue."[1]

A series of summits between Ronald Reagan and Soviet premier Mikhail Gorbachev signaled the coming end of the nuclear 1980s. Gorbachev's ascension to the Kremlin's top job opened a new and more effective phase in the Soviet peace offensive to exploit western antinuclear opinion. Recognizing his potential as both a leader who could reform the Soviet Union and a statesman who might disarm western public support for peace through strength, Margaret Thatcher and her allies sought to stage-manage the new premier's rise.

Reagan, Thatcher, Gorbachev, the peace movement, and the scientific community all recognized that progress in the summits would turn on the SDI issue. That initiative had simultaneously been the impetus for a return to arms control negotiations and an impasse to productive talks, generating first disagreement and then collaboration between Washington's and Whitehall's public diplomacy strategists. Opposition to SDI sustained antinuclear politics while also connecting Soviet leaders, the scientific community, and public opinion. Because SDI spawned so much interest, Reagan and Gorbachev's eventual agreement to dramatically reduce nuclear arms remade public perceptions of the Cold War.

Britain and the Breakthrough in Superpower Relations

On December 22, 1984, five days after the final National Security Planning Group (NSPG) preparatory meeting for the Geneva talks, Thatcher visited Camp David to discuss arms control and SDI. She had more influence over Reagan's position on arms control than anyone else outside of the administration, perhaps more than many within. Officials such as Secretary of State George Shultz, who hoped to persuade the president to support his view of the situation, recognized her sway. In the months leading up to this meeting, Shultz had appealed directly to British cabinet officials and the prime minister to garner support for his vision of SDI and arms control.[2]

At the Camp David meeting Thatcher made it clear that she wanted to protect several British nuclear arms control objectives during the Geneva talks: progress on INF negotiations, restrictions on antisatellite (ASAT) weapons, and the integrity of the 1972 ABM treaty and the overall arms control framework. Regarding INF, British officials believed that SDI might create unmanageable links between strategic and INF negotiations.[3] On ASAT, Whitehall pushed for limitations because American and British intelligence relied more heavily on satellite information than their Soviet counterparts did.[4] In addition, Thatcher's government had a vested stake in maintaining the integrity of the nuclear arms control framework. The ABM treaty remained critical for the U.K.'s policy of minimum deterrence and was the most effective nuclear arms control treaty in force.[5] The resulting joint statement from Reagan and Thatcher, which linked SDI to arms control and reductions, reflected Shultz's effort to influence the already robust deliberations in Whitehall regarding Britain's role in Reagan's BMD plan. On the eve of the Geneva negotiations, which were set to begin in January 1985, Reagan's viewpoint at last appeared to be swinging toward that of Shultz, Paul Nitze, and other moderates in the administration.

British objectives for increasing bilateral contacts between the United Kingdom and the Soviet Union centered on influencing the overall course of arms control.[6] In July 1984, Geoffrey Howe became the first British foreign secretary to visit Moscow in more than a decade; by then the FCO had identified Mikhail Gorbachev as one of two likely successors to a clearly infirm Konstantin Chernenko.[7] Gorbachev's biography impressed British officials. With his training at Moscow University and his degrees in law and agronomy, he was better educated than most of the aging bureaucrats at the apex of the Soviet political system. Whitehall had watched Gorbachev's rise through the challenging ranks of agricultural management in the Soviet Union, noting his ability to curry favor with Leonid Brezhnev, Yuri Andropov, and Chernenko even as he clearly signaled his desire for economic reforms. While they saw this behavior as a mark of his political acumen and believed that his reform impulses might serve western interests, they also understood that the Soviet old guard's acceptance reflected his commitment to the Soviet system. Gorbachev's interest in economic reforms was linked to his commitment to the long-term viability of the Soviet project, and this lay behind his support for a new era of détente.[8] His goal of reducing Soviet military expenditure helped Whitehall persuade the Politburo to participate in the Geneva talks.[9]

In December 1984 Gorbachev visited the United Kingdom, his first trip to the West as Chernenko's likely successor. That visit was a critical step for the future of East-West relations. Both superpowers saw his meeting with Thatcher as a preliminary reengagement, and it affected the prime minister's Camp David meetings with Reagan later in the month and Shultz and Andrei Gromyko's opening of the Geneva plenaries in January.[10] Whitehall expected Gorbachev to use the trip to raise his international profile and thus aid his case in the competition for Soviet leadership. Because British officials preferred him to the alternatives and wanted to protect him from potential publicity traps in his first major exposure to the western press, they orchestrated a public diplomacy plan that would give Washington a favorable impression while safeguarding him from critics in Moscow.[11]

On December 16, Thatcher hosted Gorbachev at the prime minister's retreat at Chequers. In their discussions she framed Whitehall as an essential conduit in East-West relations, emphasizing the United Kingdom's unique relations with the United States and its status as a nuclear power. She noted that Britain had greater influence in NATO than any other member except for the United States. Yet, she explained, the nation was not simply an appendage of U.S. foreign policy. Unlike other countries' representatives, British officials could frankly and freely raise issues and objections with their American counterparts. Thatcher shared insights about Reagan, framing him as a man of moral purpose who could now pursue arms control more productively after having won reelection and consolidated his domestic base of support.[12] Gorbachev, in turn, displayed intellect and charm as he engaged with Thatcher's pragmatic yet bullish style of diplomacy.[13]

"I like Mr. Gorbachev. We can do business together," Thatcher declared the day after their meeting.[14] Her praise was a bit of preconceived public diplomacy, and it produced the desired effect in Washington and the western press. For most of the following week, coverage of the Thatcher-Gorbachev visit ran on the front pages of major American daily newspapers, and it universally promoted Whitehall's view that the meeting had been a crucial confidence-building measure for restoring a climate conducive to arms control.[15] During her subsequent visit to Camp David, Thatcher summarized Gorbachev's visit for Reagan. She admitted, "I actually rather liked him," even though "he was using me as a stalking horse for you."[16] Thatcher had noted Gorbachev's emphasis on SDI and the ABM treaty, which she believed hinted at a genuine fear of American technological supremacy. However, she did not say what she thought the Soviets might exchange for SDI or whether that exchange might effect a positive change in the balance of power.[17]

Thatcher pushed her assessment of Gorbachev and Soviet nuclear anxiety in hopes of persuading Reagan to agree with her SDI platform. From her conversations with Gorbachev, she had ascertained that the Soviets would come to Geneva with serious proposals and the intention to target SDI as a linchpin in negotiations. With SDI set to become a central focus of arms control, she needed the Reagan administration to consider orienting its public diplomacy for the initiative with an eye toward Europe. The campaign in the United States that had emphasized the morality of assured survival, but the possibility of a non-nuclear world raised problems for European allies—most of all Thatcher—who had spent significant political capital on claims that INF deployment was reinforcing nuclear deterrence.[18]

On December 22, Thatcher pledged British support for SDI, declaring the nation's commitment to alliance unity and arms control.[19] However, British support came with four conditions. First, the U.S. would commit to preserving the East-West strategic balance in view of Soviet developments and not strive for superiority. Second, SDI deployment would be negotiated in observance of treaty obligations. Third, SDI must aim to enhance deterrence. Finally, East-West negotiations should strive to achieve security by reducing offensive weapons on both sides.[20] In addition, Thatcher stressed to Reagan that the research component, rather than moral appeals, must be the public message. The four-point proposal became the foundation for alliance solidarity in the upcoming negotiations and eventually became the Reagan administration's official policy on the public presentation of SDI.[21]

Thatcher's insistence on eliminating the moral component reflected the

needs of European diplomacy and the surprising durability of the antinuclear movement. By 1985, CND had become the second-largest political
organization in the United Kingdom, trailing only the Conservative Party in
membership and leading the Labour Party and the Social Democratic Party–
Liberal alliance in size.[22] Morality, as framed in the SDI and nuclear winter
debates, was what was sustaining the vitality of the movement. Embracing
their role as public diplomat scientists, Pugwash's president, Dorothy Hodgkin, and highly respected SANA member Maurice Wilkins joined the
famed Irish international lawyer Sean MacBride and the American political
scientist Richard Falk in adjudicating the January 1985 London Nuclear Warfare Tribunal. Inspired by GCW's legal challenge in the U.S. judicial system,
the tribunal explored the legality of nuclear deterrence within the context of
international law. Nuclear winter and SDI were prominently featured issues.
Drawing on the expertise of SANA scientists and nuclear winter theorists,
American nuclear strategists, religious authorities, and lawyers from around
the Anglophone world, the tribunal reimagined international law as an
expression of global civil society's shared moral values. Its organizers hoped
to replace "deterrence with a system of international security responsive to
law and morality."[23]

The tribunal pursued three innovations that demonstrated how disarmament advocates were staking a claim in the arena of international diplomacy.
First, it sought to establish a normative practice in which international law
could serve as a source of moral legitimization for activists and transnational
organizations. Second, it advanced an alternative logic for international security built upon a summation of moral, scientific, legal, and social arguments
made by disarmament intellectuals who spoke to a set of interests not ade-
quately represented in deterrence. Third, it encouraged scientists to continue
to engage in public science diplomacy as a means of reversing the arms race.

Thatcher battled against this moral barrage. When she traveled to Washington in February 1985, she again stressed that the moral and strategic implications of SDI posed significant problems for British interests. Instead, she
argued, its technological ambitions could be spun as an innovation opportunity for the United Kingdom.[24] She emphasized the research aspects of SDI
in her address to a joint session of Congress on February 20, when she also
expressed her desire to see British scientists share in the technical work.[25]

Shortly after that visit, the Reagan administration agreed that Britain's
four-point program should become the foundation for SDI public diplomacy

in Europe.[26] The agreement became even more important for East-West relations after the death of Chernenko on March 10 and the elevation of Gorbachev to general secretary. In March, Thatcher arrived in Moscow for Chernenko's state funeral, the most prominent western leader to attend. Reagan dispatched Vice President Bush in his stead, and he and Shultz confirmed to Thatcher that the president had adopted the four-point agreement as the line to take with allies and Soviet representatives. They encouraged Thatcher to urge Gorbachev to do the same.[27] In a side meeting with the new premier, she asserted the centrality of the four-point program, and Gorbachev, in turn, made it clear that he wanted to expand contact between the Soviet Union and the United Kingdom to build confidence between the superpowers.[28]

In their early meetings, a diplomatic trade of sorts occurred between Thatcher and Gorbachev. In stating that she could do business with him, Thatcher accepted the reality of Soviet communism and acknowledged a willingness to expand East-West contacts that could help revive the Soviet economy under Gorbachev's reform-oriented leadership. Her credentials as one of the most anticommunist leaders in NATO made her endorsement all the more valuable as the general secretary appealed to western public opinion. In return, Gorbachev recognized the special relationship between the United States and the United Kingdom, which the Thatcher government identified as the greatest source of British diplomatic influence.

Though Thatcher had hatched a diplomatic plan for endorsing SDI to the international community, contention over the terms of British participation persisted because the Reagan administration had yet to develop a consistent message for allies on the technical, strategic, and political implications of the program.[29] The FCO in particular remained skeptical, unsure that Washington was taking Britain's strategic priorities to heart. In a March speech at the Royal United Services Institute, Britain's foreign secretary, Geoffrey Howe, put the FCO's view on public record. He conveyed its approval of SDI research and the four-point agreement but called for the implementation of the so-called Nitze criteria, which stated that any deployed system should be both survivable and cost-effective.[30] Howe also strongly cautioned against abandoning the thirty-five-year old deterrence doctrine: "Science may not be able to provide a safer solution to the nuclear dilemma of the past 40 years than we have found already."[31] The press widely interpreted his speech as proof of dissension in Whitehall, and it generated varying levels of disapproval in Washington.[32] The administration's most vocal hawk, Richard

Perle, strongly rebuked Howe's naïveté. Shultz privately indicated his distress to Howe regarding doubts raised in the media about the U.K. government's uncritical support for SDI.[33]

The Howe speech attuned the Reagan administration to disagreement over SDI in Whitehall, and American officials became more mindful of the political importance of drawing both support and participation in Europe. The administration launched a science diplomacy campaign to persuade skeptics in the Conservative Party of the value of British participation. George Keyworth's promotion of SDI found a welcome audience in the party, thanks to his friendship with Lord Chalfont. Chalfont's standing as chair of the House of Lords Defense Group made him an ideal proxy for SDI. He enjoyed significant political clout through his membership in the Monday Club, an influential pressure group that advocated for hard-right policy positions on matters of economy and defense. Chalfont had also previously served as the minister of disarmament. In 1985, he put together a speaking circuit so that Keyworth could convince policymakers and think tanks about the value of SDI participation and its contribution to deterrence. Chalfont hosted private dinners so that Keyworth could persuade uneasy party leaders, notably Michael Heseltine. In return, Keyworth provided the technical information and strategic and political arguments that appeared in Chalfont's pro-SDI publications, distributed by the Monday Club.[34] In addition, Chalfont relied on Keyworth to help him prepare for parliamentary debates on SDI.[35]

Keyworth's science diplomacy went far beyond Chalfont. By supplying several other influential Conservative officials and politicians with cleverly crafted technical arguments, he planted pro-SDI information both publicly and privately. He sought to establish a direct rapport with the British press, convincing the influential science editor of the *Financial Times* to come out in favor of SDI.[36] Keyworth and U.S. intelligence operatives cultivated David Hart, a Conservative Party activist, to persuade Thatcher of SDI's popularity with the British public. A Gallup poll that Hart commissioned and presented to Thatcher as an argument in favor of SDI participation appeared to be crafted by Reagan administration officials.[37] Hart hosted Keyworth during his frequent trips to the United Kingdom in service of SDI's European aims and facilitated meetings with key nuclear policymakers.[38]

The Reagan administration also inserted its scientific supporters into the public diplomacy apparatus it had developed during earlier debates on INF deployment. Edward Teller and Senator Malcolm Wallop, a Republican of

Wyoming, served as advisors for a key British government report on the future of high-energy physics in the United Kingdom, which considered the importance of SDI research.[39] Conservative MPs attended pro-SDI conferences headlined by speakers from groups such as High Frontier, the Heritage Foundation, and the Moral Majority.[40] The interest of British royals in SDI also received special attention from the administration.[41]

In addition, the Reagan administration sought to persuade the Thatcher government to act as its surrogate on SDI diplomacy in Europe. Now that Reagan and Gorbachev had acknowledged that the United Kingdom would serve as the third-party broker of superpower relations, the Thatcher government and the U.S. State Department were relying on Whitehall's four-point SDI program to be the key to generating NATO support for the Geneva talks, currently underway. Shultz confirmed to Howe in June 1985 that the Camp David agreement was "a strong and coherent allied position on which everyone could unite."[42] Yet even though U.S. and British officials sensed that the emergence of Gorbachev could be a productive opening for arms control, they also recognized that his charm and cosmopolitan demeanor made him a greater public diplomacy challenge and thus a greater threat to alliance solidarity than his predecessors had been. These concerns became especially acute when they considered that the current signature nuclear issue, SDI, had arisen not from an agreed-upon alliance policy such as the dual-track decision but from the president's faith in American technological exceptionalism.[43]

Progress in Geneva

Soviet concessions before the talks in Geneva meant that SDI was now the main obstacle to attaining a far-reaching arms control agreement. In July the White House and the Kremlin announced a superpower summit to be held in November 1985, and at the same time Gorbachev unveiled plans for an October visit to Paris—the opening salvo in what became a competitive round of pre-summit diplomacy.[44] The influential French daily newspaper *Le Monde* termed Gorbachev's visit "Operation Seduction."[45] The primary component of that seduction was the declaration of a new Soviet arms control initiative for the Geneva talks, which Gorbachev offered in a western-style press conference. Gone were the days when Soviet officials stuck to prepared scripts in front of international reporters. Now, following Gorbachev's example, they bantered with the western press and fielded questions from investigative journalists. USIA reported, "Gorbachev has scored an impressive public relations triumph with his new style, . . . making him a formidable opponent of President Reagan and putting Washington on the defensive."[46]

In fact, many of Gorbachev's announcements were arising from the ongoing Geneva process; he simply publicized them in an attempt to seize the spotlight.[47] He called for a 50 percent reduction in strategic forces and a separation of the INF and strategic issues while seeking a joint Franco-Soviet communiqué condemning SDI.[48] He also dropped demands for the inclusion of British and French nuclear forces in arms control talks, thus removing a key unifying point for London, Paris, and Washington.[49]

Isolating SDI as the lone impediment to nuclear peace played to the primary issue sustaining the transatlantic antinuclear movement; and Garwin, Zuckerman, Pugwash, SANA, and the British Royal Society led the scientific opposition to SDI among that public. Garwin appeared on the British television show *You the Jury* to debate Keyworth's ally Lord Chalfont.[50] SANA and British Pugwash cohosted anti-SDI conferences with scientifically oriented U.S. antinuclear organizations such as Council for a Livable World.[51] Zuckerman's close friendship with Garwin helped secure key figures from the American debate on SDI such as Ashton Carter, John Holdren, and George Rathjens to address the scientific community in the United Kingdom.[52]

The rapid advance of British scientific activism convinced antinuclear leaders to adopt the arguments of the scientific community in opposing SDI. In its search for new strategies, CND concluded in August 1985 that arguments about SDI's negative impact on Britain's technical base should be a new point of emphasis.[53] With SDI in focus, the antinuclear movement still proved capable of shaping public opinion. A late September Gallup poll indicated that 46 percent of Britons rejected a defense policy based on nuclear weapons and deterrence. In October, more than 100,000 demonstrators again flooded into London's Hyde Park to call for an end to the arms race.[54] This protest spotlighted the successor generation problem that had concerned the Reagan administration's public diplomacy strategists in Europe. That month, USIA resumed Voice of America's (VOA) English-language broadcasting in Western Europe, with the goal of targeting a younger generation that had no memories of World War II and thus presumably less appreciation for the importance of American security guarantees. VOA broadcasts amplified events such as Reagan's radio address to the nation on October 12, in which he called attention to Soviet treaty violations and situated strategic defense projects within a broader campaign to assert the moral and political differences between the West and the Soviet Union. The president's address, his other foreign policy speeches, and a regular lineup of commentaries from top-level officials became the core content of VOA and WORLDNET satellite broadcasts in Europe.[55]

Hidden in the pre-summit public diplomacy blitz was an opportunity for progress in East-West relations. Thatcher used her influence to give a "fresh impetus" to moving talks forward.[56] In his conversations with Thatcher, Reagan agreed with her view, and Shultz's, that Gorbachev appeared to be sincere in his interest in arms control, no matter the underlying motivation. The prime minister pressed Reagan to consider the psychological impact of SDI on the Soviet leadership.[57] Her assessment contributed to Reagan's view, as did his briefings with Shultz, which revealed the president's heightened sympathy for the nuclear anxieties of young people.[58]

But what might be achieved at Geneva? Gorbachev's charm campaign did not stop at public diplomacy. When speaking to others, he structured his personal diplomacy around a clear acknowledgment of his interlocutor's sense of place in world affairs. His style masked Soviet intentions but also engendered reciprocation and thus met the Soviet Union's traditional goal of having its interests and political system recognized as legitimate by the West. Upon his confirmation as general secretary, Gorbachev had received a memo from his close advisor, Aleksander Yakovlev, that evaluated Reagan's approach to international affairs. The pair recognized that the president wanted most to be remembered as a grand peacemaker, in the belief that this would solidify his legacy as one of history's great leaders.[59] As a result, Gorbachev tailored his tone and his diplomatic approach in his correspondence with Reagan. Even earlier in his presidency, Reagan had sought to establish a regular correspondence with Soviet leadership. He liked personal letters and informal communication because they reinforced his self-image as a man of laidback charisma.[60] Now Gorbachev became an enthusiastic pen pal, and their letters reveal that they were building a tacit, constructive understanding about negotiations.[61]

In addition to making personal connections with Reagan, Gorbachev sought to reset U.S.-Soviet relations via the two arms control advocates who, in his opinion, wielded the most influence with the president: Thatcher and Shultz. To do this, he made changes in his own government. Gorbachev shocked the Politburo when he replaced long-entrenched foreign minister Andrei Gromyko with Eduard Shevardnadze, a politician with a public style similar to Gorbachev's—a personal, unscripted diplomacy that appealed to western audiences.[62] Unlike Gromyko, Shevardnadze presented himself to Shultz as a friendly sparring partner.[63] He was precisely what Shultz had anticipated with Gorbachev's ascendency to Soviet leadership: a younger statesman of provincial origin, whose firsthand experience with the state's failure on the periphery would motivate him toward more dynamic East-West engagement as part of a broader effort for generational reform.[64]

Gorbachev's personal interactions with world leaders and his makeover of the Soviet foreign affairs establishment were intended to publicly frame him as a reasonable, peace-driven man. As British diplomat Roderic Lyne observed, "Mr. Gorbachev . . . impressed his personal style on a global audience."[65] In the premier's pre-summit interview with *Time* and in meetings with U.S. senators shortly thereafter, he dazzled the western press.[66] Yet Gorbachev's growing celebrity generated concern in the Reagan administration and among its allies, who worried that the Soviet Union might be gaining the upper hand in shaping the summit agenda. The journal *Human Events*, a favorite of Reagan's because of its unabashed anticommunist position, even accused the western media of "setting up Reagan on the summit."[67]

Not to be outdone, Reagan decided to speak directly to the Soviet people. On November 9, 1985, in a speech broadcast via WORLDNET to a global audience of roughly 120 million people, the president recalled his origins in small-town America, his Hollywood career, and his leadership of a labor union. He spoke of shared struggle in World War II and shared cultural respect. He reiterated his belief that nuclear war could not be won. Reagan laced his appeal for nuclear reductions with a call for an enhanced exchange of people and information, which he said was the key to superpower peace.[68] Reagan's speech reinforced his new pattern in public diplomacy, in which he presented a participatory moment for action not just to Americans but to people across the world.

Reagan and Gorbachev came to Geneva in mid-November with modest expectations. This would be the first Soviet-American summit in seven years, and Reagan was cautious, concerned about allied thinking as well as Gorbachev's talents as a public diplomat. Shevardnadze's and Shultz's preparatory visits to Washington and Moscow had set a constructive tone but also made it clear that little actual progress should be expected.[69] Reagan had

FIGURE 4. President Reagan delivers an address regarding the upcoming Geneva summit, November 9, 1985. Reagan White House Photographs, 1/20/1981–1/20/1989, White House Photographic Collection, 1/20/1981–1/20/1989, National Archives.

refused Moscow's request for a premade, agreed-upon statement; instead, in a personal memo, he stated, "Let us agree this is the first of meetings to follow. That in itself will give an aura of success."[70] Reagan's memo reveals that he wished to slow-play the summit so as not to run afoul of the hardliners in his own administration.

The "Spirit of Geneva" widely touted in the press and subsequently in scholarship as giving a fresh impetus to arms control emerged from a joint recognition of the similarities between Soviet and American society.[71] At a November 19 dinner hosted by the Gorbachevs at the Soviet mission, the general secretary structured his conversation with Reagan around a shared approval of conservative family values, references to ice cream parlors and coffee shops, and a review of the Moscow production of Edward Albee's play *Who's Afraid of Virginia Woolf?* He capped his gambit by including a biblical citation in his dinner toast. Reagan responded with his own biblical citation, a line from the Acts of the Apostles: "We are all of one blood regardless of where we live on the Earth."[72] Gorbachev's references to God made a very positive impression on the president. Immediately after the summit, he mentioned those allusions to NATO leaders at a special session of the North Atlantic Council.[73] And on his return to Washington, he confided in White House aide Michael Deaver, "I honestly think he [Gorbachev] believes in a higher power."[74]

As predicted, the Geneva talks were cordial but unfruitful. Though NATO leaders praised Reagan's statesmanship, Thatcher pointed out to Shultz that Geneva had dramatically raised the stakes for future summits.[75] If the next meeting were to produce only pleasantries, it would be widely construed as a step backward for East-West relations. The most promising agreements in Geneva were the guarantees that Reagan and Gorbachev had made to host and attend summits in Washington and Moscow.[76] The president's administration interpreted Gorbachev's openness to an interim INF agreement as a concession to detach the INF process from SDI politics.[77] The job of putting together a mutually acceptable INF agreement became a primary task for the Soviet and American Nuclear and Space Talks delegations that had been negotiating in Geneva since January. Positive steps toward INF and a more concerted approach to NATO consultations had created allied goodwill and undoubtedly helped the United States persuade several European partners to participate in SDI, beginning with the United Kingdom in December and followed by West Germany in March 1986 and Italy in September.[78] With Gorbachev targeting SDI as the cause of stalled progress in negotiations on strategic force reductions, allied participation in the program gave Reagan an important line of public defense.

Less than a month after the Geneva talks, the Federation of American Scientists (FAS) published an open letter to Gorbachev, asking him to become the key figure in arms control and to use his unique diplomatic gifts to break Reagan away from American hardliners' influence.[79] The letter perfectly fit into Gorbachev's plans. Shortly before the U.S. and Soviet delegations were set to reconvene in Geneva, he circulated a bold new public announcement to the western press. In it he called for the complete elimination of all nuclear weapons on earth by 1999.[80] Gorbachev's expansive proposal included a temporary moratorium on testing, an apparent olive branch to western scientific activists. In fact, the Kremlin had long hoped to exploit western scientific opposition to SDI, with former premier Yuri Andropov "appeal[ing] to all the scientists of the world" to reject an arms race in space as early as 1983.[81] That attempt had not gained much traction, but Gorbachev proved to be far more adept than his predecessors were at courting the western scientific community. Frank Von Hippel, the chair of FAS, later speculated that he saw the organization's interactions with the Freeze movement and antinuclear politics as an appealing way to capture public opinion in the West.[82] The FAS letter allowed Gorbachev to gain legitimacy from western science and use that connection to disrupt Reagan's public diplomacy on SDI.

The State Department saw interactions between Soviet and western scientists as a particularly effective Soviet active measure, reporting that "Moscow has used its own scientists and scientific institutions, including those not directly associated with space research, as a means of insinuating Soviet views into Western scientific and political forums."[83] Gorbachev later recalled that "the activism of scientists . . . [was] essential in overcoming the Cold War, primarily by pointing up the real dangers of East-West conflict and creating a spiritual climate for policies of détente, reconciliation, and retreat from confrontation."[84] For their part, British officials sensed that Gorbachev had seized the initiative on both substance and public diplomacy and in so doing was pressing the president to live up to his nuclear-free world rhetoric.[85] U.S. officials agreed that Gorbachev had made the proposal in order to portray himself as the man with the greater vision for peace. However, they were content to cede that image to him if it meant he was moving closer to U.S. positions.[86]

American officials saw Gorbachev's apparent public diplomacy edge as strategically significant, given what they perceived to be an accelerating transformation of international relations. The Geneva summit had elevated public diplomacy from a secondary feature of competition in East-West affairs to the primary instrument of statecraft, one that was advancing the revolution in diplomatic practice. As the U.S. Advisory Commission on Public Diplomacy reported,

> Public diplomacy is part of a worldwide transformation in the conduct of international affairs. Traditional secret government-to-government communications have become less important as world leaders compete directly for the support of citizens in other countries. . . . The Geneva Summit was as much a public diplomacy event as it as a bilateral encounter between two governments. No summit has been so extensively covered by the press, nor have the leaders and governments of both nations ben so solicitous of the media—and world public opinion—in shaping their agendas.[87]

Balancing public diplomacy and the substance of private negotiations became the crucial challenge for both Reagan and Gorbachev as the United States and the Soviet Union prepared for their next big meeting.

Regression at Reykjavik?

How serious was Gorbachev? This question confounded U.S. national security principals, British officials, and other NATO allies. Soviet sources in fact suggest that by the beginning of January 1986 he really did embrace nuclear abolition.[88] Nonetheless, the interagency review of Gorbachev's proposals for a nuclear-free world produced the usual stalemate between the State Department and Department of Defense.[89] Shultz took the position that, in spite of the propaganda elements of the Soviet proposal, Reagan should "see this as an opportunity to transform Gorbachev's concept so that it matches your own vision for achieving a non-nuclear world" and adjust U.S. positions on INF, START, and space talks to take advantage of the new substance in the premier's proposal.[90] In contrast, Weinberger argued, "Gorbachev's proposal is a rather transparent attempt to divert the energy imparted to the Nuclear and Space Talks by your joint statement at Geneva."[91] Kenneth Adelman, chief of the Arms Control and Disarmament Agency (ACDA), contended that "Gorbachev's plan is largely propaganda, using your vision of a nuclear-free world as bait to stop SDI."[92] Still, Gorbachev's proposals for a nuclear-free world produced a notable shift in public opinion. Europeans, for instance, trended toward viewing the superpowers as morally equivalent and grew increasingly skeptical of SDI.

In early March, the NSC and USIA called all public affairs officers stationed in Europe to a conference in London to lay out new public diplomacy guidelines for the next summit, to be held in Reykjavik. Though other NATO governments and Moscow were focusing on talks that would produce agreements, U.S. officials wanted to "redefine summitry so the lack of specific agreements will not be seen as failure."[93] To alleviate public pressure to reach an agreement that did not satisfy the administration's strategic goals or moral purpose, Washington argued that dialogue represented stability in and of itself.

Jack Matlock, chief of the European and Soviet affairs directorate at the NSC, later recalled the USIA conference as essential for the future success of U.S summit diplomacy. Public affairs officers left London with a more nuanced understanding of the administration's nuclear posture, which enabled them to proactively engage with European media rather than simply respond to Gorbachev's démarche on nuclear issues. Matlock, however, stayed on in the city to brief public opinionmakers, British government officials, and members of European parliaments as well as the editors of *Encounter*, the *Financial Times*, and *the Observer*, key academics at Chatham House and the Institute of International Studies, and practically anyone else willing to receive his message that the administration's posture represented a genuine commitment to peace.[94]

Guidance for these new public diplomacy initiatives focused on the president's statements and public engagements; in essence, they amounted to a bet that Reagan could outduel Gorbachev in the public arena. Reagan's skill at creating participatory moments through statements, movements, and public interactions made him the most important piece of the administration's public diplomacy. By the summit years, his oratory reflected the steady transnationalization of U.S. public diplomacy, moving beyond appeals to Americans and increasingly calling on citizens of the world, from East and West, to be agents of peaceful change.

Reagan's aides recognized that the success of public diplomacy in support of SDI would shape U.S. deterrence policy in the short term and the president's historical legacy in the long term. In the National Security Planning Group meeting that determined Reagan's reply to Gorbachev, Attorney General Ed Meese asserted that "SDI should become a moral imperative for future presidents."[95] Fred Hoffman, who led one of the original exploratory studies of SDI's strategic impact, indicated in a memo to the NSC that public diplomacy must be considered a component of U.S. nuclear strategy and doctrine in long-term competition with the Soviet Union. He cited "inadequate U.S. effectiveness in translating technological superiority into politically viable, usable, and affordable military power," noting that "these problems clearly transcend military strategy but pose important tasks for that strategy."[96]

Reagan declared to the public and in Congress that SDI had brought the Soviets back to negotiations. In his view, to undercut the program domestically would hamstring his authority in arms control talks.[97] But a glance at summitry through the lens of the Soviet peace offensive shows a different picture. By 1986, Soviet political leaders no longer considered SDI a major strategic threat. Gorbachev had even said to other Soviet officials, "Maybe we shouldn't be so afraid of SDI."[98] Though the Soviet defense industry played up SDI's threat to the strategic balance as way to press for exorbitant spending on military priorities, the nation's scientific community considered the initiative to be technologically infeasible, arguing that it could be easily defeated by countermeasures, in part because of widespread scientific opposition in the West.[99] SDI did not terrify Soviet political leaders into resuming arms control talks but presented another opportunity to exploit western public opinion to achieve a favorable settlement.

Soviet opportunities for exploiting western public opposition to SDI paralleled the western scientific community's increasing influence over the antinuclear movement. At an END strategy meeting in February 1986, E. P. Thompson said, "The peace movement has tended primarily to moral and political aspects and has been somewhat divorced from the scientific community. . . . [It] must not be too pushy, [and] must now listen to the scientific community and expert groups."[100] Much of this increasing influence emanated from Pugwash; and because the organization was centered in London, developments in British science activism had a significant international influence on science diplomacy more generally. As Pugwash, SANA, and the peace movement co-managed the opposition to SDI, Pugwash implemented organizational reforms that it had begun considering after the INF debates, when its influence had weakened. It eagerness for reform was stimulated by the success of SANA's tactics and the public activities of Sagan, Garwin, and others. The breadth of the SDI project allowed Pugwash to diversify its membership to include scientists outside the field of physics and to make new appeals to women experts. In addition to its traditional private forums, the organization made inroads into other arenas, including schools, museums, radio, and television. Its media relations improved, as did its support for young scientists through branches such as Student Pugwash. All of these changes became tools for mobilizing public opinion to indirectly influence nuclear policy.[101] Eventually, they would also make Pugwash activities in the Soviet Union more effective.

Public science diplomacy significantly strengthened the bonds between antinuclear activism in the United States and the United Kingdom. The NWFZ phenomenon, which had originally based its legitimacy on the U.K. government's mismanagement of nuclear expertise, became the foundation of the movement's "semantics of thinking globally, acting locally."[102] NWFZs in Britain inspired Hawaii County, Hawaii, and Garrett Park, Maryland, to become the first U.S. municipalities to declare themselves NWFZs in the 1980s, setting off a wave of similar municipal declarations.[103] Maryland then became the first state to reject civil defense funding from the Federal Emergency Management Agency.[104] To generate increased enthusiasm for municipal internationalism, CND's international committee conducted consultations on NWFZs with interested parties in the United States.[105] By 1990, the American NWFZ movement included 165 municipalities and 170 campaigns—important symbolic opportunities for American antinuclear advocates to refresh public opposition to Reagan's nuclear agenda.[106]

Municipal internationalism threatened the U.S. and British governments' ability to reinforce support for their arms control postures. By late 1985 dozens of American metropolitan areas were contemplating NWFZ declarations, including New York City, Boston, Chicago, Los Angeles, and San Francisco as well as the states of California and Oregon. Many of these communities had incorporated scientist- and ESR-designed antinuclear curricula into their school systems and had rejected pronuclear materials from the federal government.[107] In March 1986 Mayor Harold Washington, who had made nuclear opposition central to his political coalition, signed a bill turning Chicago into the largest NWFZ in the United States. The signing ceremony made specific reference to London and other major nuclear-free cities across the world. Though some state government officials criticized the mayor's decision, those references drew an explicit connection between Chicago's municipal concerns and the international tide of antinuclear sentiment.[108] The State Department's active measures working group was troubled by this domestic trend—but was even more disturbed because it recognized that the NWFZ movement was giving Gorbachev a public diplomacy advantage in Europe and the developing world.[109]

Rejection of the militarization of science became part of the broad transatlantic scientific debate on SDI. British Pugwash, for example, replicated the highly successful anti-SDI work pledge that had circulated among U.S. universities and drew signatures from 56 percent of the top 14 physics departments and a total 3,700 hundred academic scientists by November 1985. The British version that circulated in March and April 1986 enjoyed similar success, drawing wide support from the relevant departments at Oxford, Cambridge, the University of London, Imperial College London, and thirty other major institutions of higher learning.[110] The Greater London Council cultivated scientific experts to lead opposition to SDI, hosting John Pike from FAS as well as other U.S. scientists who spoke about the political dangers of American's faith in technology.[111]

In late April 1986 the Soviet Union's Chernobyl nuclear power plant suffered a reactor meltdown, a disaster that appeared to vindicate arguments about the dangers of overreliance on technology. Scientists' briefings to Parliament inspired Labour leader Neil Kinnock to launch the Coalition against Star Wars in June.[112] Composed of nearly two dozen technologically focused organizations, the new coalition focused on fears of a British brain drain, the danger of overrelying on technologies and automation, and the importance of recommitting to arms control.[113] With the help of representatives from Pugwash, SANA, and Engineers for Nuclear Disarmament, the group European Nuclear Disarmament (END) led the formation of Spacewatch, another coalition of antinuclear organizations devoted to advancing scientific arguments against SDI.[114] Its founding statement read, "We believe that Star Wars expresses the inadequacy of technological fixes to deep-rooted political and social problems," reproducing the arguments of American experts who believed that Reagan's confidence in American technological exceptionalism was misguided.[115]

The Chernobyl meltdown showed just how important public diplomacy had become to U.S.-Soviet relations and summit outcomes. Thatcher pressed Reagan to take advantage of the opportunity to achieve favorable results, noting that before the accident Gorbachev had been a "public relations star" but now appeared eager for progress on arms control.[116] In a meeting of the National Security Planning Group Reagan remarked, "Chernobyl has altered Gorbachev's outlook on the dangers of nuclear war. The time is right for something dramatic."[117] Convinced that he might make progress in private discussions with Gorbachev, Reagan directed the U.S. arms control delegation in Geneva to respond positively to Soviet proposals and rejected the advice of those in his administration who wanted to ruthlessly exploit the disaster for public diplomacy purposes.[118]

Both Reagan and Gorbachev now believed that the other leader genuinely preferred total disarmament, and this sustained U.S.-Soviet engagement even when events threatened to undo constructive relations. Domestically, Reagan yielded to conservatives in Congress and at the Pentagon, who pressured him to stop abiding by the limits of the nonratified SALT II agreement.[119] Then, on September 2, 1986, Moscow police arrested Nicholas Daniloff, a correspondent for *U.S. News and World Report*, an action that many interpreted as retribution for the U.S. arrest of a Soviet U.N. employee accused of stealing information related to military technologies. As a result of these events as well the administration's hesitation to respond positively to Gorbachev's January proposal, preparations for a 1986 Washington, D.C., meeting nearly came to a total standstill.

Hoping to break the impasse, Gorbachev wrote to Reagan in mid-September, warning him that arms control "will lead nowhere unless you and I intervene personally. . . . in the very near future and setting aside all other matters, we [should] have a quick one-on-one meeting, let us say in Iceland or in London, maybe just for one day, to engage in a strictly confidential, private and frank discussion."[120] Reagan accepted the invitation, pending the resolution of the Daniloff affair.

Since April, Gorbachev had been seeking Thatcher's assistance in arranging a Washington summit because he viewed Britain as a stabilizing agent in East-West relations. Throughout the year her arms control exchanges with Reagan had centered on sustaining U.S. commitment to SALT II, endorsing a summit meeting, and rebutting the influence of the Department of Defense. All were efforts to support Shultz's more conciliatory positions.[121] British diplomats in Washington were also increasingly in league with the U.S. State Department. Reporting on a September meeting between Foreign Secretary Howe and Defense Secretary Weinberger, they called it "a standard OSD [Office of the Secretary of Defense] performance, . . . disturbing insight into right-wing attitudes on arms control, . . . a vivid illustration of the problems Shultz faces in maintaining a constructive U.S. arms control negotiating position."[122] Shortly before the Reykjavik meeting, Thatcher's comments to Reagan placed great emphasis on the State Department approach and endorsed INF as the area most conducive to agreement.[123]

The meeting in Reykjavik was intended to be a private conference in which Reagan and Gorbachev could make progress toward formal talks at the still-stalled Washington summit. However, the public quickly began treating it as a summit in its own right. Despite plans for a press blackout, the meeting became a worldwide media phenomenon. Major telecommunications firms and American news networks completely modernized Reykjavik's information infrastructure to capture the drama. CNN launched twenty-four-hour live coverage, and more than 3,000 journalists descended on the city, including the star news anchors Dan Rather (CBS), Tom Brokaw (NBC), and Peter Jennings (ABC).[124] The media hordes so overwhelmed Iceland's capital that the Reagan administration arranged for correspondents to stay on boats docked in the city's harbors.

On the evening before the meeting, Reagan reached an agreement with House Speaker Tip O'Neil that would allow the president to follow through on his decision not to adhere to SALT II or accept a testing moratorium and provide $3.5 billion in SDI funding for the coming year. The last-minute deal boosted Reagan's confidence that he could manage Democrats' opposition to his nuclear agenda.[125] But he was also faced with conservative ire. Hardliners believed that, by arranging the Reykjavik talks on the heels of the Daniloff affair, the president was betraying the moral promise of his peace through strength policies and his emphasis on human rights. In addition to increasing opposition from his own Defense Department, Reagan was drawing criticism from pundits such as George Will, Charles Krauthammer, and William F. Buckley, Jr., all of whom had previously supported his nuclear politics as an expression of conservative worldviews.[126]

Gorbachev and Reagan opened Reykjavik with different ambitions. Reagan, juggling Democratic compromise and conservatives' temper, simply hoped that he and the premier could improve their mutual understanding. Gorbachev, however, began by taking a highly technical approach to negotiations; he wanted to secure an agreement and noted in their first session that failure to reach one would be scandalous.[127] He outlined a series of Soviet concessions. The Soviets would agree to the U.S. proposal of a 50 percent reduction in strategic forces rather than adhere to their earlier position of a 50 percent reduction in nuclear weapons capable of reaching each other's territory. In effect, this delinked INF issues from strategic arms control. Gorbachev also committed to excluding British and French forces from an INF agreement and to an equal cap in Europe. On the key issue of defense in space, the Soviets offered a ten-year guaranteed commitment to the ABM treaty with a subsequent three- to five-year negotiating period to redefine its terms. The Soviet interpretation now permitted research and testing in laboratories only.

For Reagan, specific terms mattered, but the person making the offer mattered more. To illustrate his nuclear philosophy, he stymied Gorbachev's technical approach by turning to parable-based diplomacy.[128] Gorbachev then changed tactics. Rather than attempt to express Soviet good faith through concessions on actual systems, he acknowledged Soviet insecurities as they specifically related to the economic power imbalance vis-à-vis the United States. This confession meshed better with Reagan's style; the president preferred to reach a shared understanding on philosophy, morality, and interpersonal communication and leave the details to the technical experts.[129]

At the start of their third session, Gorbachev referred to the creation story in Genesis in hopes of appealing to the president's visionary impulses. This was astute, for Reagan had come to see Gorbachev as a moral break in the historical trajectory of Kremlin leadership. He observed, "The only morality [in Marxist ideology] was that which advanced socialism. And it was a fact that every leader but Gorbachev . . . had endorsed in speeches to Soviet Party Congresses [with] the objective of establishing a world communist state."[130] Gorbachev responded in kind, stating he believed that he and Reagan could develop a "man-to-man relationship." Whenever technical details stalled the Reykjavik dialogue, a return to a discussion of personal philosophies and morality revived the conversation. At the end of the third session, Shultz and Shevardnadze departed with instructions from their superiors to clarify points of mutual understanding on INF, strategic weapons, nuclear testing, and the ABM treaty.[131]

By the final session, an agreement seemed to be within reach. Reagan no longer considered Soviet leadership to be irredeemable, intransigent, and morally bankrupt; rather, he blamed hardliners for blocking progress. The president spoke warmly of a future in which he and Gorbachev would meet to eliminate the final nuclear missile on earth. Moving quickly from phased reductions of specific strategic and INF weapons, the two leaders reached a preliminary decision to have the Geneva delegation draft an agreement to eliminate all nuclear weapons on earth. The president agreed to a ten-year nonwithdrawal on the ABM treaty but refused to go further. Appealing to Gorbachev as a politician, he explained that rightwing pundits were "kicking his brains out" over his alleged appeasement of the Soviet Union.[132] In reality, however, he relied on rightwing cover to excuse his own attachment to SDI, which reflected his deep confidence in the pioneering American spirit as the ideal means to any end.

Even in his nuclear abolitionism, Reagan expressed a preference for elimi-nating the threat of nuclear war through American technological innovation. Throughout the meetings he had attempted to persuade Gorbachev that the United States would share SDI technology; and according to his closest advisers, the president truly believed that the provision of SDI to the Soviet Union would abolish the nuclear threat.[133] Nonetheless, on this point, the administration's missteps on technological cooperation with Britain and other allies undermined his credibility.[134] The chance for total disarmament emerged and crumbled in the closing moments of the Reykjavik meeting when Reagan insisted on a liberal interpretation of the ABM treaty that preserved the U.S. right to test SDI components in space.[135] Reagan and Gorbachev, Shultz and Shevardnadze, Nitze and Sergey Akhromeyev (the chief architect of the Soviet positions) all expressed a mix of regret and anger, as well as hope for the future, as the talks came to a close without an agreement.[136]

Reagan's apparent willingness to abolish all nuclear weapons at Reykjavik upset the expectations of allies and adversaries alike. U.S. military leaders largely opposed the idea of a global zero-option for all nuclear weapons.[137] Members of Congress, U.S. diplomats, and NATO officials wondered if Reagan had walked into a propaganda trap, for now Gorbachev could show the world that only SDI stood in the way of global nuclear disarmament.[138] Political leaders' reaction to the Reykjavik news seemed likely to upturn the administration's public diplomacy plan in the United States and in Europe. Thatcher's private secretary told the prime minister, "One is tempted to say thank God for the Russians for having turned the proposal down."[139] The *Chicago Tribune,* the *Los Angeles Times,* the *Washington Post,* and *Foreign Affairs* all ran stories that blamed SDI for the stallout at Reykjavik.[140] Summing up this widespread criticism, a *Rolling Stone* editorial labeled Reagan the "Christopher Columbus of arms control, the man who found a whole new world when he was looking for something else."[141]

Yet Gorbachev's dismissal of Reagan's offer to share SDI proved to be a public diplomacy error in its own right. Had he accepted Reagan's proposal, the president would have faced the enormous challenge of persuading a skeptical Congress to greenlight an SDI sharing scheme. The task of implementing such a plan would have been equally burdensome, given the near universal hostility to the idea within his administration and the conservative outrage constraining his negotiating impulses.[142]

In fact, the president appeared to have a better grasp of the relationship between SDI, summitry, and public opinion than most pundits and politicians did. Contrary to some claims in the press, Gorbachev's media blitz on SDI did not blindside Reagan; his administration had previously published a new report detailing Soviet propaganda techniques used to undermine the initiative.[143] A poll conducted by CBS and the *New York Times* showed that 44 percent of Americans blamed Gorbachev for the summit's failure, compared to just 17 percent who held Reagan responsible. Better still, 68 percent of Americans sided with Reagan's position on SDI at Reykjavik. Overall, American public approval of Reagan's handling of East-West relations improved after the meetings in Iceland.[144]

Preparations for Geneva and Reykjavik had pushed public diplomatists to reflect on the innovations in their field that were dramatically reshaping the conduct of international relations. Shortly after Reykjavik, USIA sponsored a conference for American and European academics and public diplomacy professionals at the Hoover Institution, and those sessions provided a window into how the concept of public diplomacy was evolving in theory and practice.[145] A number of conference participants noted that Reagan's administration had broken down the distinction between foreign and domestic audiences that had characterized U.S. public diplomacy since the 1940s. For instance, Bernard Roshco, a State Department public diplomat, pointed out that the administration "directs what it defines as public diplomacy to the domestic public *and* foreign publics."[146] Likewise, Gifford Malone, a former State Department official remarked that Reagan had transformed public diplomacy from a USIA responsibility to an administration-wide task that "blurred the distinction between domestic public affairs and foreign-oriented information programs."[147]

By transforming U.S. public diplomacy into a fully transnational practice, the Reagan administration had reimagined the relationship between state and society in its pursuit of foreign policy objectives. Conference participants pointed out the necessity of such a transformation in the emerging information age, which was increasing America's vulnerability to Soviet disinformation. Moreover, as Kathleen Bailey, USIA's former deputy director of research, insisted, "United States public diplomacy efforts in Western Europe and other industrialized countries must now be integrated with its public diplomacy strategy in the Third World."[148] Bailey's remarks were a response to the Soviet propaganda push to make SDI the focus of anti-American sentiment in developing countries. Notably, Gorbachev had called for a "Star Peace" initiative while touring India shortly after the Reykjavik meetings, proposing that resources invested in SDI should instead be geared toward increasing scientific research and development capacities in developing nations.[149] Soviet active measures were also seeking to elevate anti-SDI public opinion by exploiting the spread of NWFZs between the West and the developing world.[150]

To counter the global spread of Soviet disinformation, U.S. public diplomacy needed to discard prior constraints. Stanton Burnett, USIA's highest-ranking career official, argued that President Carter's commitment to ideological neutrality had undercut the effectiveness of U.S. public diplomacy by separating public affairs field officers from significant policy developments in Washington. In contrast, by creating more avenues for cooperation with foreign governments and the private sector, the Reagan administration had pushed U.S. public diplomacy away from the doctrine of ideological neutrality toward a focus on policy advocacy. Speaking of the SDI debate, Mark Blitz, a former USIA director of private initiatives, noted that the involvement of private-sector partners and ordinary citizens centered on civic education.[151] From this perspective, public diplomacy no longer appeared to be a threat to American democracy, as Congress had viewed it in the early Cold War. Rather, it was enhancing public trust in government through private-sector support for civic participation and education.

The Reykjavik meetings had a different effect on stakeholders on the other side of the Atlantic. With a general election approaching in the United Kingdom, Thatcher feared a resurgence of the nuclear debate, given that Reagan's position now appeared to be closer to the non-nuclear defense policy promoted by the Labour Party. In a private call the day after the Reykjavik meetings ended, she warned him that the elimination of all nuclear weapons "is the sort of thing that [Labour leader] Neil Kinnock advocates. This would be tantamount to surrender." The prime minister reasserted the United Kingdom's intention to maintain its independent deterrent indefinitely as a hedge against Soviet conventional military might.[152]

Thatcher saw the Reykjavik sessions as a Soviet propaganda trap, one intended to isolate SDI as the single obstacle to nuclear peace and renew Western Europe's anxieties about decoupling its security from the United States.[153] To shore up NATO unity, Shultz briefed the allies immediately after the meetings, also emphasizing that the president was ready to live up to the implications of a world without nuclear weapons no matter what the allied response might be.[154] For their part, the NATO allies supported the progress made on INF but not in the context of a nuclear-free world. According to some NATO officials, the elimination of strategic weapons and INF forces would create an environment in which the Warsaw Pact would retain massive advantages in chemical weapons and conventional ground forces on the European continent, yet no U.S. nuclear umbrella would be available to protect Western European allies from a Soviet invasion.

Given these concerns, Thatcher stepped up her involvement in superpower diplomacy with the aim of refocusing Western Europe, the Reagan administration, and Kremlin leadership on the issue of INF.[155] Meanwhile, Gorbachev appealed to her to open a backchannel with Reagan after conversations in Vienna between Shultz and Shevardnadze fell flat in early November.[156]

Shevardnadze had left those talks asking, "If we were not to be guided by the agreement to eliminate all nuclear arsenals . . . what then would be the result of Reykjavik?"[157] Thatcher relayed Gorbachev's thoughts on arms control to the president but also expanded diplomatic contacts between the United Kingdom and the Soviet Union in attempt to exert a moderating influence. At a Camp David meeting with Reagan in mid-November and in subsequent correspondence with Gorbachev, she pressed both leaders to progress toward attainable steps—specifically, the signing of an INF agreement that would be separate from strategic and space issues.[158]

FIGURE 5. Margaret Thatcher and Ronald Reagan discuss the outcome of the Reykjavik meetings, Camp David, November 1986. Courtesy Ronald Reagan Library.

Promise in Washington

British diplomacy was responsible for removing much of the uncertainty around a possible U.S.-Soviet summit in Washington in 1987. In February Gorbachev had offered to separate INF from other nuclear issues. In response, Thatcher traveled to the Soviet Union in late March—the first official state visit of a British prime minister to the Soviet Union in more than ten years. Her trip validated the authenticity of the premier's offer; and while there, Thatcher appeared to convince him, despite opposition from the Soviet military, to move toward an INF agreement that would also eliminate short-range nuclear forces, a sticking point for NATO allies in Europe.[159]

Thatcher's public diplomacy was even more successful. She sat for a fifty-minute interview with three prestigious members of Soviet state media, and the program was broadcast to millions of screens throughout the country via state television. Though Thatcher shocked Soviet citizens with western perspectives on the East-West balance of nuclear weapons, her interview also demonstrated the Kremlin's commitment to *glasnost*, a set of reforms intended to make the Soviet Union a more open civil society. In the West, Thatcher's interview persuaded the public and political leaders that glasnost and other reforms would be part of a fundamental transformation of the Soviet regime. Her television appearance provided the most striking example yet that engagement with the Soviet public could offer real benefits for western nuclear diplomacy.[160]

Gorbachev saw improved British-Soviet relations as a prerequisite to progress in superpower summitry. In a review of Thatcher's visit, he told to the Politburo, "It is in our interest to raise the British role in international affairs. . . . Two things played a role here. Great Britain seems to be a side-kick to the United States. But Thatcher sees that Reagan is getting old, that Mitterrand is in opposition with Chirac, and that Kohl is in a sticky situation. So it is her chance to stand out."[161] Western media hailed Thatcher's visit as a "remarkable diplomatic event" that had generated a new impetus for the superpowers to meet.[162]

Between April 1987 and the Washington summit scheduled for December, Shultz and Shevardnadze engaged in shuttle diplomacy to sustain progress toward an agreement. Shultz introduced the idea of global zero, the removal of all INF weapons around the world and not just in Europe. His argument hinged on verification: the mobility of INF weapons made it difficult to verify proper numbers in specific regions, and global zero solved this problem. Though the United States continued to attempt to extract additional INF concessions from the Soviet Union, Shultz managed to persuade Shevardnadze and Gorbachev of the sincerity of Reagan's interest in an agreement. Gorbachev told the Politburo that "Shultz is a special figure," a crucial aid in helping the Soviet Union and the United States make progress by identifying their broad shared interests.[163]

U.S. officials supplemented the Shultz-Shevardnadze dialogue with intensive public diplomacy efforts. They wanted to keep Gorbachev from gaining a public approval advantage over Reagan that he could use to shape the summit agenda or coerce the United States into INF concessions. A February 1987 USIA survey had shown that, for the first time in thirty years of polling, the British public was expressing a higher degree of confidence in Soviet leadership.[164] In May, USIA gauged that public opinion in Britain, France, and West Germany was giving more credit to Gorbachev than to Reagan for recent progress in arms control. People in these countries feared that Reagan would agree to an INF agreement that would decouple U.S. and European security.[165] Thus, Charles Wick and National Security Advisor Frank Carlucci moved to institutionalize public diplomacy as a primary feature of summit planning. Carlucci funneled additional talent and resources into those efforts.[166] Meanwhile, USIA stepped up INF programming on WORLDNET and EURONET and renewed its focus on cultivating elite and public understanding of what an INF agreement would mean in the broader context of U.S.-Soviet relations.[167]

By 1987, mass antinuclear demonstrations in the United States and the United Kingdom had largely subsided. Nonetheless, Reagan officials saw that antinuclear scientists had become an increasingly effective source of public opposition. That spring, SANA began organizing media workshops to train scientists to advocate for antinuclear positions, coaching them to use their specialist knowledge as a means to break through what SANA believed was a media blackout of the peace movement. The organization forged new partnerships with the group Journalists against Nuclear Extermination to help expand scientists' presence in British dailies such as *the Guardian* and *the Independent* and to seize on more local media opportunities. These activities were coordinated with the American scientific community, which continued to pressure Reagan on core parts of his nuclear agenda at home while pursuing new scientific and political contacts in the Soviet Union.[168]

Western scientific activism served as an effective public diplomacy channel for Gorbachev. Much of his new thinking in foreign policy reflected
the Pugwash creed, and the organization's influence in the Soviet Union
expanded when the Soviet delegation added several figures who had been
prominent in international discussions on nuclear winter.[169] In an attempt
to humanize the Soviet Union in the eyes of the West, Gorbachev pardoned
exiled Soviet dissident scientist Andrei Sakharov in 1986 and greenlit a
Moscow forum for scientists in 1987. He even invited international scientific
personnel and congressional representatives to examine the Krasnoyarsk
radar complex under construction.[170] Assessing the impact of Soviet public
diplomacy, Gorbachev's leading national security advisor, Anatoly Chernyaev,
wrote in his diary, "[Gorbachev] has already laid the foundation for a new era
in international relations. . . . Gorbachev has surpassed Reagan as the 'ruler'
of the political atmosphere in Europe."[171]

Gorbachev's foreign popularity likely helped to consolidate his power over
nuclear policy at home, given that approval abroad could be used to support
his positions in the increasingly open information environment in the Soviet
Union. His acceptance of global zero for INF, which he announced over the
summer, reflected a dramatic change in the direction of Soviet foreign policy.
Overcoming the objections of a powerful cohort of Soviet officials, including
Yegor Ligachev, Anatoly Dobrynin, and Andrei Gromyko, who wanted to go
backward on INF, Gorbachev insisted that Soviet foreign policy objectives
should not center on using the military threat to divide NATO but on creating a business-friendly atmosphere with Western Europe and developing
a "conception of economic relations with the United States."[172] Eliminating
INF weapons on U.S. terms, he reasoned, would remove the "residue from
our relations."[173]

Gorbachev's eagerness to remove the confrontational component from
U.S.-Soviet negotiations motivated his speedy concessions on INF in 1987.[174]
He continued the pattern of using Soviet-British dialogue as a precursor to
summit activity. He kept Thatcher closely informed on Soviet nuclear thinking throughout the year; and en route to the Washington summit, he stopped
over in the United Kingdom to speak with her personally. In the meantime,
the U.S. hardline right had been weakened by its culpability in the Iran-
Contra scandal, and Shultz executed a power play by refusing to discuss his
negotiating strategy with the National Security Planning Group. This move
effectively cut Weinberger and his allies out of the arms control policymaking

process and reduced the players to Reagan, Shultz, and the Geneva delegations.[175] Moreover, because Richard Perle had left the administration in early
June, prominent conservative journalists such as George Will and Michael
Novak, who had helped established the moral and intellectual substance of
peace through strength and had held Reagan accountable to hardline nuclear
diplomacy, lost access to their main source of insider information.[176]

The Kremlin concluded that, rather than await the election of a new
president, talks with Reagan's administration would be their best chance to
reach arms control agreements acceptable to Congress.[177] During September
meetings with Shultz, Shevardnadze urged his counterpart to speed up work
on INF and other arms control agreements.[178] These meetings confirmed an
agreement on the major principles of INF; details on reduction processes and
shorter-range weapons would be ironed out during Shultz's trip to the Soviet
Union in late October. The secretary of state arrived in Moscow that month
with orders to finalize treaty details.[179] Rapid progress on INF benefited from
Gorbachev's growing impatience with economic reforms, which were premised on a reduction in military spending through arms control, and from
the overwhelming popularity of nuclear disarmament in Soviet society, a
fact of growing significance in Soviet foreign policy, thanks to the glasnost
reforms that had expanded civil discourse.[180]

The success of the Washington summit was linked to political urgency,
moral understanding, and a convergence of public diplomacy goals. Reagan's trust in Gorbachev's ideological softening and moral perspective
explain why the president felt comfortable disregarding rightwing criticism
of arms control and CIA claims that Gorbachev intended to revive Soviet
abuses of détente.[181] When the summit opened in Washington, Reagan gave
Gorbachev a pair of cufflinks depicting swords being hammered into plow-
shares, an allusion to a passage in the Book of Isaiah. This was another significant example of how the basis for summitry rested on the president's belief
that he had come to a moral understanding with the general secretary.[182]

The primary outcome of the summit was the INF treaty, which banned all
conventional and ground-launched cruise and ballistic missiles with a range
between 500 and 5,500 kilometers. In addition to being the first agreement
to reduce—rather than limit—nuclear weapons, the treaty also introduced
a comprehensive verification protocol that included onsite inspections of
missile sites and production facilities. Negotiators envisioned the verification
protocol as the model for a future agreement on strategic forces. Alongside

the INF agreement, Gorbachev pushed for greater reductions in conventional forces. The rapid pace of concessions spooked U.S. negotiators, who insisted that NATO allies must be involved in reduction talks. The Washington summit even spurred movement on the difficult issues of strategic arms reductions and defensive weapons in space. START negotiations progressed due to a remarkable string of concessions from Gorbachev, including an agreement to include missile throw weight as a category for reductions and a bomber counting rule that favored the United States. Shultz conveyed to the North Atlantic Council that "we can now see the shape of an agreement. . . . it is now clearly possible to achieve."[183]

The INF treaty is the premier example of how public diplomacy actually shaped and secured arms control outcomes.[184] Shultz claimed on December 2 that the INF agreement was "an illustration . . . of the tremendous impact and importance of public diplomacy."[185] The zero-option policy eventually codified by the treaty had been formulated explicitly to soothe European public opinion but had also been designed with the expectation that it would not form the basis for actual progress on arms control negotiations. Moreover, the interim solutions for an INF agreement developed in early 1983 by Thatcher and Kohl ensured enough public support for the deployment of cruise and Pershing missiles on Western European soil. In the end, it was the Reagan administration's moderates, such as Secretary of State George Shultz, with aid from Thatcher's government, who crafted the approach that led to the treaty.

American, Soviet, and British public diplomacy made the Washington summit one of the most anticipated diplomatic events of the Cold War. Its careful preparation epitomized the Reagan administration's prioritization of policy advocacy. USIA distributed 3,000 press credentials to foreign journalists and 7,000 total, creating a bustling atmosphere at the purpose-built summit press center, where Nitze and other senior arms control officials led specialized briefings. Virtually every senior official from the State and Defense departments as well as the NSC took turns leading interactive discussions with U.S. allies via WORLDNET or sat for interviews with VOA. The BBC provided the heaviest coverage of any network, broadcasting in North America, Europe, and around the world. U.S. officials prioritized appearances on the British network, seeing it as the most important foreign supplement to the U.S. government's foreign broadcast capabilities. Shultz and Adelman headlined a group of current and former U.S. officials who gave interviews for a November 30 episode of *Panorama*, BBC's premier investigative news program, which was broadcast around the world.[186] For its part, the Soviet Union adopted a full-scale western media strategy, with Gorbachev charming the American public in interviews with NBC and other news outlets.

This media bonanza represented an unprecedented commitment to inform the public about high-stakes diplomacy in real time, and it gave Reagan an important measure of defense against the ideological right wing, who complained that his attempt to revitalize his presidency through super-power diplomacy amounted to a wholesale abandonment of hardline values. Their onslaught on Reagan's summit diplomacy had begun much earlier in the year, with erstwhile peace through strength allies lining up against a potential INF deal. Throughout 1987 and 1988 Reagan wrote repeatedly to William F. Buckley, Jr., asking him to restrain his criticism of summitry. But Buckley continued to critique the president's arms control policy, reaching a new level of intensity with a spring 1987 article in the *National Review*. Titled "Reagan's Suicide Pact," it featured commentary by Richard Nixon and Henry Kissinger, speaking out jointly for the first time since leaving office.[187]

The powerful conservative fundraiser Richard Viguerie commented, "[Conservatives are] concerned about abortion, pornography, busing, and economic issues, but at the core of the criticism is anti-communism. Across the board he [Reagan] seems to be deserting his anti-communist position."[188] Pressure from the right intensified after Reagan signed the INF treaty. Senator Wallop warned, "The Soviets have broken most every treaty they have signed."[189] Senator Helms, who had lauded Reagan's first-term arms buildup, now grumbled, "The President doesn't need to discard the people who brought him to the dance."[190] Helms lined up testimony from Kissinger, Haig, and former NATO supreme commander General Bernard Rogers to oppose treaty ratification. Republican senators Dan Quayle of Indiana and Steve Symms of Idaho, who had frequently equated arms control to appeasement, praised Rogers's criticisms of the treaty.[191] The Conservative Caucus, one of the New Right fundraising groups that had grown rapidly during the Reagan years, also picked up on the appeasement theme. It sponsored advertisements in conservative publications such as the *Washington Times*, comparing Reagan to former British prime minister Neville Chamberlain, infamous for his appeasement of Hitler.[192] Senate Minority Leader Robert Dole, a Republican from Kansas, hedged his bets, declaring that treaty ratification might require amendments or qualifications, apparently seeing this approach as a strategy to curb progress on the next round of strategic arms control talks. Preparing his own run for the GOP presidential nomination in 1988, Dole was seeking a position that would be acceptable to both mainstream Republican voters and the right wing of a party that cherished nuclear superiority.[193]

A Moscow Epilogue

Through the final moments of Reagan's presidency, Gorbachev sought to maximize his investment in their relationship.[194] A dramatic revision of Soviet foreign and defense policy undercut the arguments of rightwing critics of the INF agreement, and in April 1988 Shultz and Shevardnadze signed an understanding regarding the withdrawal of Soviet forces from Afghanistan.[195] Nonetheless, a small but persistent opposition to the INF treaty held up ratification until late May 1988, just hours before Reagan met with Gorbachev in Moscow for their last formal summit, held from May 29 to June 3.

As Reagan administration officials prepared for the meeting, their focus changed from reaching an agreement to managing expectations for superpower relations, with the goal of ensuring that Reagan's successor would be politically capable of following a constructive course. In early spring Shultz and Shevardnadze had resumed their regular meetings, with an eye toward progress on a START deal and an agreement on defense and space issues.[196] However, their conversations made it clear that the United States and the Soviet Union remained too far apart on critical issues to reach a START agreement before the end of Reagan's term.[197] The administration now suggested that the signing of the INF treaty had proven that the countries' relations had matured into a new stage. In lieu of strategic arms control, negotiators could allow their focus to move to other aspects on their diplomatic agenda: human rights, regional conflict, and bilateral issues.[198] This shift allowed the parties to take a more comprehensive approach to resolving the non-nuclear issues perpetuating the Cold War.

A week before the Moscow summit, an article in the *New York Times* raised the possibility that the talks could lead to the end of the Cold War. It quoted Stephen F. Cohen, a Russian historian at Princeton University: "The most important aspect of the trip is that the most right-wing president in our lifetime goes to Moscow, enjoys it, has a good time, makes something of it and completes the coronation of the idea that the Cold War has to end. . . . It strips the Cold War of a lot of its ideological rationality."[199] Though the

Moscow summit lacked the high drama of Washington's, it did result in a series of minor agreements that demonstrated the growing normalization of U.S.-Soviet relations and suggested that the Cold War would soon come to an end. Reagan's attachment to SDI remained the obstacle to reaching an agreement on strategic reductions, but further arrangements were made for joint verification experiments and test-launch verification protocols. Both sides agreed to greatly expand their cooperation in cultural, scientific, and economic spheres.[200] A friendly optimism characterized the exchanges between Gorbachev and Reagan, in contrast to the earlier summits, all of which had included moments of intense ideological display from both leaders.

The tone of public diplomacy in Moscow revealed a crucial change in Reagan's and Gorbachev's view of the Cold War. American, Soviet, and European citizens were the primary targets for both leaders' cooperative public diplomacy. During a televised stroll with Gorbachev through Moscow's Red Square, Reagan responded to a Soviet citizen who asked if he still believed the Soviet Union to be an evil empire: "No, . . . I was talking about another time, another era."[201] The president's answer showed that memories of the early Cold War no longer dominated his approach to U.S.-Soviet relations. The summit also gave Gorbachev an opportunity to achieve his foreign policy objective of creating a favorable impression of his political and market-economic reforms known as *perestroika* by opening up Soviet society to foreign observation. In reviewing the summit's outcomes for the Politburo, he argued that Reagan's willingness to correct his previously objectionable perspective of the Soviet Union and the coverage of Soviet life on American television had vindicated the premier's emphasis on the human factor in diplomacy.[202]

On his way back from the Moscow summit, Reagan stopped in London, a visit that, along with his earlier Westminster speech, came to serve as a bookend to his public diplomacy campaign. In an early afternoon speech at the famed Guildhall, Reagan reflected on his celebrated peace through strength manifesto, delivered before Parliament in June 1982, in which he had called on the West to muster the moral fortitude to overcome Soviet nuclear expansion. Morality, memory, and technology had been essential foundations of Reagan's pursuit of nuclear modernization, but now these components were being rearranged to promote the idea that the Cold War was fast coming to an end. Returning to the moral themes in his earlier address, Reagan claimed victory and pronounced, "We are entering a new era in history, a time of lasting change in the Soviet Union."[203]

It is difficult to assess the effect of specific developments in U.S.-Soviet relations on the end of the Cold War because multiple events are often conflated with that moment.[204] Before the revolutions that swept communism out of Eastern Europe in 1989 and the dissolution of the Soviet Union in 1991, American and British attitudes had already begun to change as a result of the Reagan-Gorbachev summits in 1987 and 1988. This shift suggests that many in the West were ready to accept that the Cold War was coming to an end. Leading voices did not shy away from saying so. In a November 1988 interview with the *Washington Post* and *Newsweek*, Margaret Thatcher herself declared, "The Cold War is already at an end."[205] American pollster Daniel Yankelovich and political scientist Richard Smoke observed in the fall of 1988 that "the American public is willing to experiment with winding down the Cold War," speculating that the INF treaty had produced a spirit of cooperation and a general acceptance that verification was an essential component to bilateral agreements.[206] Even when measured against the optimism of détente, these new attitudes were very different from those held by the American public at any other time during the Cold War, for they embraced the idea that the Soviet Union was open to making fundamental changes in its society and in its relations with the United States.[207]

Scholars have largely overlooked the transformation of public diplomacy as a cause of Americans' and Britons' cautious acceptance of the end of the Cold War. This may be, in part, because a different story was established. Ignoring the importance of the public diplomacy interactions among the peace movement, the U.S. and U.K. governments, and the Soviet Union, contemporary hardliners instead constructed a narrative around an ideological and strategic coherence in Reagan's grand strategy that they claimed had predated his presidency and culminated in the fall of communism.[208] The historian Jay Winik set about crafting this victory thesis in a 1988 issue of *Foreign Policy*: "If the neoconservative heyday of the Reagan administration's first 6 years is studied, the conclusion can be drawn that the sensible course for neoconservatives is to declare victory—victory in the sense that the logic of their views has largely been confirmed by the course of events."[209]

This oft-repeated thesis does a disservice to the president's foreign policy legacy.[210] It shows Reagan to be overly rigid and less dynamic in his response to world events than he actually was. The transformation of his public diplomacy in his second term—especially the way in which he revised his use of morality and memory to achieve specific arms control objectives—reveals that his overall foreign policy was flexible and receptive to public opinion. The U.S. Public Diplomacy Advisory Commission argued in its 1988 report that this transformation was enormously important, given that "since 1985 public perceptions have done much to change the bilateral relationship between the two superpowers."[211] The president's consideration of public diplomacy requirements in response to the antinuclear movement, the scientific community, and Thatcher's government made him a more empathetic negotiating partner for Gorbachev.[212] While hardliners claim that Reagan was a principled, rather than a pragmatic, conservative, the reality is that he was principled in his values—with the security of the American people foremost among them— but pragmatic in his choice of partners to manifest those values.

The public diplomacy revolution of the nuclear 1980s had effects beyond its role in ending the Cold War. When the Reagan and Thatcher governments, the Soviet Union under Gorbachev, the transnational peace movement, and the scientific community embraced public diplomacy, they altered the institution of diplomacy itself. Diplomacy no longer could be considered the exclusive jurisdiction of government officials, and government officials could no longer expect geopolitical matters to be settled independently of world opinion. As Kenneth Adelman wrote in his reflections on the summits:

> [Reagan] altered the process—with the primary emphasis going from private to public diplomacy. He somehow sensed that, in the new information age . . . what was said boldly in local speeches, town hall meetings, and intellectual salons counted more than anything said behind the closed doors of foreign ministries. . . . Reagan's new style of diplomacy was adopted and expanded years later.[213]

The first round of official government studies on the U.S.-Soviet nuclear negotiations and summits during the nuclear 1980s presaged Adelman's thoughts, concluding that diplomacy had increasingly been conducted in public and with the public.[214]

CONCLUSION

SURVIVING THE COLD WAR

TEN DAYS AFTER George H. W. Bush won the 1988 presidential election, Ronald Reagan and Charles Wick kicked off the "first of the really great parties" to commemorate the Reagan era and revel in the transformation of U.S. public diplomacy.[1] Reagan and Wick toasted their hosts, USIA's private-sector committees, which Wick had established at the start of his tenure as chief of the agency. The committees' sponsorship of the party highlighted one dimension of the public diplomacy revolution under Reagan: the incorporation of the private sector into the U.S. government's apparatus for disseminating the administration's values and policies around the world and reinforcing them at home.

Reagan's speech honoring Wick emphasized other public diplomacy innovations of the 1980s. The former president spoke of USIA's "technological sophistication" in establishing WORLDNET and making advancements in radio broadcast. He noted Wick's role in developing the moral and thematic aspects of U.S. public diplomacy during crises such as the KAL 007 shootdown. He praised Wick for helping to making public diplomacy an administration-wide task through his engagement with the broader U.S. foreign policy establishment. Within the administration, Wick's close friendship with Reagan propelled the bureaucratic refashioning of U.S. public diplomacy, which not only put international information policy at the center of U.S. foreign relations but also reintegrated psychological warfare into public diplomacy after that connection had been weakened during the 1960s and 1970s.

These developments had created a revolution in public diplomacy. Yet hindsight shows that the revolution was limited. Reagan did not transform public diplomacy's raison d'être; if anything, he coupled public diplomacy more tightly to Cold War imperatives by focusing U.S. influence operations abroad

on short-term policy initiatives and anti-Soviet objectives rather than invest-
ing in a long-term vision for USIA and cultivating foreign publics. U.S. public
diplomacy became a relic of the Cold War. When the superpower conflict
finally came to an end, USIA began a rapid march to irrelevance. The agency's
functions would be subsumed into the State Department's a decade later.

Nonetheless, the Reagan administration's reforms did generate enduring
change in how U.S. public diplomatists conceived of their audiences. Thematic, technological, bureaucratic, and private-sector changes emerged to
meet the new realities of a global civil society. The onset of the information
age had combined with the ubiquity of nuclear fear, regardless of race, gender, class, education, nationality, location, or any other identifier. Within this
transnational public sphere, what was communicated to foreign publics produced a direct impact on politics at home. The opposite held true as well: what
was said at home shaped public opinion abroad.

Two forces helped awaken the Reagan administration to the need to recon-
ceptualize its public diplomacy audience in transnational terms: the Thatcher
government and the transatlantic antinuclear movement. Though unable
to match U.S. and Soviet economic and military might, Britain remained
every bit a public diplomacy superpower. Not only did the United States
value Britain's public diplomacy capabilities, but the Reagan administration
wanted to preserve the countries' wide-ranging nuclear partnership and the
shared commitment to conservative principles that underpinned the premise
of peace through strength. On both INF and SDI, the Thatcher government
provided a transatlantic perspective and much of the public diplomacy
playbook that helped reconcile the subtle but significant differences in the
disarmament and deterrence attitudes of Americans, Britons, and Europeans. Britain served as a vanguard for U.S. nuclear ambitions geographically
and technologically (via their cooperation on Trident and SDI development)
but even more so diplomatically and in the realm of public opinion. This
dynamic became apparent during the rise of Gorbachev. The premier's close
relationship with Thatcher enabled her to play superpower mediator and
facilitate the direct engagement of western leaders with the Soviet people and
of western publics with Soviet leaders.

The nuclear 1980s were both the environment and the impetus for public
diplomacy reforms. Public diplomacy was the means through which U.S. and
British officials squared nuclear strategy with nuclear culture. The cultural,
moral, and scientific arguments produced by the peace movement proved

to be the major inhibiting factor to Reagan's dreams of strategic superiority vis-à-vis the Soviet Union through a massive buildup of the allies' nuclear arsenal. The very development of the transatlantic public sphere represented the most important innovation of antinuclear protest. Britain played an especially important role, serving as both the organizing hub for disarmament organizations throughout Europe and a unique source of inspiration to the American antinuclear movement because it shared a language and a moral tradition with the United States.

The English language itself became a particularly contested battleground for controlling the nuclear imagination and parameters of political thought. Disarmament intellectuals infused their critiques of deterrence language with alternative logics rooted in gender, race, labor, and class as well as a different sense of moral community, obligation, and governance. Peace through strength proponents leveled claims of semantic distortion against the peace movement and their alleged Soviet backers. Though the fight over the nuclear politics of the English language superficially centered on questions of disarmament and deterrence, the conflict more generally represented a moral divergence between left and right that intensified the political polarization of American and British society. For conservatives, an emergent group of transatlantic think tanks, political operatives, and journalists became the lead combatants in the semantic battle, while CND and the Freeze movement organized nuclear discourse that influenced the distribution of power on the left.

Science, religion, and women were keys to the circulation of disarmament ideas in the Anglo-American world. Antinuclear women proved to be particularly important in realigning the political community around ideas rather than geography. The tactics of GCW and other radical legal and site-occupation methods developed by American and British women activists brought significant attention to the disarmament cause, in part because they were a direct moral challenge to the societies envisioned by the Anglo-American New Right. To peace through strength conservatives, this moral challenge appeared all the more acute when considered alongside antinuclear statements from church leaders who saw deterrence as representative of a broader moral crisis in society. Various Christian leaders invalidated nuclear deterrence as a moral posture permitted under the guidelines of just war theory, and in so doing they signaled a new relationship among church, state, and society in the United States and the United Kingdom.

The moral authority of church leaders, combined with the technical expertise of scientists opposed to the arms race, made antinuclear opinions respectable in the political mainstream and underpinned electoral strategies to unseat conservatives in Washington and Whitehall. The defection of the scientific community from the nuclear establishment to the disarmament cause and mass movement politics marked a public turn in science diplomacy. Scientists became toolmakers for the peace movement, providing the expertise that legitimized anti–civil defense practices, NWFZs, and major media critiques of nuclear deterrence. Though antinuclear protestors and scientists shared a common goal and at times similar tactics, the source of their opposition and the lineage of their work differentiated transatlantic protest from public science diplomacy. Scientists—especially those in Pugwash, FAS, UCS, and similar organizations—saw their efforts to halt the arms race as part of a longer diplomatic tradition dating back to the Manhattan Project, in which technical experts drew on their links to political power as they considered the ethical implications of the atomic age. Transatlantic activists, on the other hand, viewed themselves as offspring of the civil rights, women's liberation, workers' rights, and antiwar movements.

Public science diplomacy was particularly focused on SDI and nuclear winter theory because scientists understood that SDI set the conditions for the superpower summits. Those momentous meetings were public diplomacy affairs designed with two goals in mind. First, the United States and Soviet Union had to achieve an agreement that would reduce the destructive capacities of their nuclear arsenals. Second, and perhaps more importantly, they had to persuade American, British, Soviet, NATO, and Warsaw Pact citizens and leaders that the Cold War had actually come to an end. In the Anglo-American context, the latter goal was wholly a task for public diplomacy. Techniques that had initially been refined to counter the innovations of the antinuclear movement were deployed to full effect during the Reagan-Gorbachev summits to promote the idea that a new era of superpower relations had arrived, marking the end of the nuclear 1980s and the Cold War.

The antinuclear ideas of the 1980s—expressed by the antinuclear movement and by Reagan and Gorbachev—produced lasting effects on the form of great power diplomacy. The innovations arising from the competition among the antinuclear movement, public diplomacy, and the Soviet peace offensive ushered in a new era in which public opinion would play a larger role in international relations. Any history that positions think tanks, non-government organizations, civil society groups, scientists, and municipal governments as key actors in international affairs must see the nuclear 1980s as a key inflection point for the growth of their influence. Any story of information diplomacy and information warfare must see the nuclear 1980s as a watershed moment in which technological advancements in communications made local politics into global politics. Even during the decade, interactions among public diplomacy, public science diplomacy, and protest spread beyond nuclear issues to produce changes in other areas, such as the formulation and implementation of U.S. policies toward Latin America, the realization of an international agreement to save the ozone layer, and the founding of the National Endowment for Democracy. The major innovations in public diplomacy practices in the nuclear 1980s also affected the way in which scholars now seek to understand how engagements between governments and international publics condition modern geopolitics.

Yet the nuclear 1980s also remade the theme, institutions, and audience for political communications, leading to a moral divergence between conservatives and liberals in American and British society. Public diplomacy and protest may have resolved the ideological conflict at the heart of the Cold War in favor of the West. But in the West the echoes of nuclear debates reverberate in the culture wars and political polarization that characterize the Anglo-American world in the post-Cold War era.

For a time, the unipolar moment and temptations of a peace dividend created the false impression that the U.S. government should assume a smaller role in shaping international public opinion. American officials had grown confident that the commercial processes unleashed by globalization would ensure the dominance of American cultural exports, while the development of cable television, the Internet, and other media and communications technologies empowered think tanks, nongovernmental organizations, social movements, and corporations to spread American democratic ideals and the gospel of free markets abroad. This view underpinned a 1995 Cato Institute report that disparaged the U.S. government's public diplomacy programs as "Cold War institutional relics" and derided USIA as "an agency in search of a mission."[2] In the late 1990s, federal funding for all public diplomacy programs declined significantly until USIA was abolished altogether in 1999.[3]

The terror attacks of September 11, 2001, revealed the flaw in this thinking but simultaneously led to the readoption of the philosophy that public diplomacy is valuable as an instrument of war, less so as a tool for waging peace. Many foreign policy observers suggested that the failings of American public diplomacy had created the conditions for hostile terror networks to inhabit the Muslim world. The new public diplomacy fostered by the George W. Bush administration had situated the soft power aspect of information management within a military apparatus, most noticeably through the Pentagon's Office of Strategic Information. Framed as a clash of civilizations and an exercise in democracy and freedom promotion, a flurry of public diplomacy initiatives from the U.S. government and recommendations from U.S. and British think tanks revived the Cold War framework and rationale for engaging with foreign publics.[4]

The world is still in the process of surviving the Cold War because that bygone superpower contest continues to define a range of responses to international conflict, especially between great powers. Policymakers, scholars, and the informed public often ask if the economic, military, ideological, and informational challenges to American hegemony now amount to a new Cold War.[5] Proposals to bring back USIA to regain a public diplomacy advantage stem from the complex disinformation environment now being shaped by Chinese and Russian hybrid warfare and by nonstate actors hostile to the western democracies.[6]

However, the United States would do better to move past this Cold War framework. Reconstituting USIA would draw energy away from a more appropriate whole-of-government approach to public diplomacy that would make engagement with foreign publics a priority in all relevant departments. Prominent international issues such as climate change, which touch multiple government entitles, can be better managed by an interagency group structure similar to the one developed by the Reagan administration to win support for its nuclear policies rather than by a reconstituted USIA that would act as a single-source messenger. A whole-of-government approach makes investment in public diplomacy less contingent upon the close relationship between presidents and USIA directors and more likely to remain a budgetary and policy constant rather than a national security instrument to be mobilized in times of conflict and demobilized in times of peace, as was the case in the years after World War I and the Cold War.

Decentralizing public diplomacy allows government departments to select the best possible non-government partners or subnational and supranational government partners to advocate for and listen to foreign publics. In the nuclear 1980s, experts engaged in public science diplomacy made the effectiveness of municipal internationalism a source of resistance to the Cold War as the ordering principle of geopolitics. Their experience offers a roadmap for today's public diplomacy experts who hail the rise of city diplomacy as an essential facet of international affairs, given that an increasing percentage of the world's population resides in urban settings.

British public diplomacy practices have historically been used as a model for U.S. reforms. Since its first post–Cold War reflection in 1995, British public diplomacy has proven to be extraordinarily adept at learning lessons from major geopolitical turning points. The War on Terror, the 2008 financial crisis, and London's pursuit of the Olympics led to the creation of the Public Diplomacy Strategy Board and to the embrace of fast-evolving digital communications platforms. The decentralized crowded-house arrangements of British public diplomacy have ensured two things that U.S. public diplomats have historically valued: transparency and credibility.[7] The independence and integration of British public diplomacy into the core business of diplomacy has achieved another goal long sought by U.S. public diplomats: it has allowed those officials to be in on the takeoffs and not just the crash landings of policymaking and implementation.[8] The importance of public diplomacy in British foreign policy speaks to the high value that the United Kingdom places on soft power, given its limited hard power resources compared to those of the United States. Limited resources, however, have created an exceptionally collaborative public diplomacy philosophy in the United Kingdom. This enthusiasm for working with non-government actors should be embraced by public diplomacy reformers in the United States.

In the twenty-first century, public diplomacy is most effective when it starts with the question "Whom can I empower?"[9] The experience of the nuclear 1980s demonstrates that, if stakeholders can agree on the fundamental challenges facing society, then national governments can resolve existential issues by empowering and listening to social movements, scientists, local governments, and private enterprise to increase their informational authority. Informational authority will, in turn, become more valuable as new information technologies continue to affect political and social realities and adjust our ability to deal with existential threats such as climate change, nuclear war, and global pandemics.

NOTES

Introduction

1. "Great Confrontations at the Oxford Union: Caspar Weinberger vs. E. P. Thompson, February 27, 1984," YouTube video, 57:15, December 21, 2014, https://www.youtube.com; Mark Schacter, "Weinberger Voted Winner of Oxford Debate," *UPI Archives*, February 27, 1984.
2. Caspar Weinberger, memo to Ronald Reagan, February 29, 1984, National Security Council Executive Secretariat, U.K. Country Files, box 46, Ronald Reagan Presidential Library (hereafter cited as RRPL).
3. E. P. Thompson, "A Letter to America," *Nation*, January 24, 1981; Mary Kaldor, "Letter to America," *Nation*, October 10, 2002.
4. R. W. Apple, Jr., "Weinberger Drops Debate at Oxford," *New York Times*, April 20, 1983.
5. Lawrence Wittner, *Toward Nuclear Abolition: A History of the World Nuclear Disarmament Movement, 1971–Present* (Stanford, CA: Stanford University Press, 2003); James Cronin, *Global Rules: America, Britain, and a Disordered World* (New Haven, CT: Yale University Press, 2014); Kyle Havey, *American Anti-Nuclear Activism, 1975–1990: The Challenge of Peace* (New York: Palgrave Macmillan, 2014); Jan Henrik Meyer, "Global Protests against Nuclear Power: Transfer and Transnational Exchange in the 1970s and 1980s," *Historical Social Research* 39, no. 1 (2014): 165–90; Leopoldo Nuti, Frederic Bozo, Marie-Pierre Rey, and Bernd Rother, eds., *The Euromissile Crisis and the End of the Cold War* (Stanford, CA: Stanford University Press, 2015); Vincent Intondi, *African Americans against the Bomb: Nuclear Weapons, Colonialism, and the Black Freedom Movement* (Stanford, CA: Stanford University Press, 2015); Sarah Bridger, *Scientists at War: The Ethics of Cold War Weapons Research* (Cambridge, MA: Harvard University Press, 2015); Paul Rubinson, *Redefining Science: Scientists, the National Security State, and Nuclear Weapons in Cold War America* (Amherst: University of Massachusetts Press, 2016); Jonathan Hogg, *British Nuclear Culture: Official and Unofficial Narratives in the Long Twentieth Century* (London: Bloomsbury Academic, 2016); Daniel Cordle, *Late Cold War Literature and Culture: The Nuclear 1980s* (London: Palgrave Macmillan, 2017); Angela Santese, "Ronald Reagan, the Nuclear Weapons Freeze Campaign, and the Nuclear Scare of the 1980s," *International History Review* 39, no. 3 (2017): 496–520; Eckart Conze, Martin Klimke, and Jeremy Vargon, eds., *Nuclear Threats, Nuclear Fear, and the Cold War of the 1980s* (Cambridge: Cambridge University Press, 2017); William Knoblauch, *Nuclear Freeze in a Cold War: The Reagan Administration, Cultural Activism, and the End of the Arms Race* (Amherst: University of Massachusetts Press, 2018); Christoph Laucht, "The Politics of Uncertainty and the Nuclear Threat in Britain, 1979–1985," *History Compass* 16, no. 12 (2018); Ellen Boucher, "Anticipating Armageddon: Nuclear Risk and the Neoliberal Sensibility in Thatcher's Britain," *American Historical Review* 124, no. 4 (2019): 1225; Andrew Hunt, *We Begin Bombing in Five Minutes: Late Cold War Culture in the Age of Reagan* (Amherst: University of Massachusetts Press, 2021).

6. Kenneth Adelman, "Speaking of America: Public Diplomacy in Our Time," *Foreign Affairs* 4 (Spring 1981): 913.

7. Scott Lucas, "Campaigns of Truth: The Psychological Strategy Board and American Ideology, 1951–1953," *International History Review* 18, no. 2 (1996): 279–302.

8. Nicholas Cull, "'Public Diplomacy' before Gullion: The Evolution of a Phrase," University of Southern California, Center for Public Diplomacy blog, April 18, 2006, https://uscpublicdiplomacy.org.

9. Nicholas Cull, *The Cold War and the United States Information Agency: American Propaganda and Public Diplomacy, 1945–1989* (New York: Cambridge University Press, 2008), xviii.

10. George Creel, *How We Advertised America: The First Telling of the Amazing Story of the Committee on Public Information That Carried the Gospel of Americanism to Every Corner of the Globe* (New York: Harper and Brothers, 1920); Alan Axelrod, *Selling the Great War: The Making of American Propaganda* (New York: Palgrave Macmillan, 2009); Stephen Vaughn, *Holding Fast the Inner Lines: Democracy, Nationalism, and the Committee on Public Information* (Chapel Hill: University of North Carolina Press, 2011); John Maxwell Hamilton, *Manipulating the Masses: Woodrow Wilson and the Birth of American Propaganda* (Baton Rouge: Louisiana State University Press, 2020).

11. Justin Hart, *Empire of Ideas: The Origins of Public Diplomacy and the Transformation of U.S. Foreign Policy* (Oxford: Oxford University Press, 2013).

12. Emily Metzgar, "Public Diplomacy, Smith-Mundt, and the American Public," *Communication Law and Policy* 17, no. 1 (2012): 67–101; Weston R. Sager, "Apple Pie Propaganda? The Smith-Mundt Act before and after the Repeal of the Domestic Dissemination Ban," *Northwestern University Law Review* 109, no. 2 (2015): 511–46.

13. John Lewis Gaddis, "The Cold War, the Long Peace, and the Future," *Diplomatic History* 16, no. 2 (1992): 234–46.

14. Laura Belmonte, *Selling the American Way: U.S. Propaganda and the Cold War* (Philadelphia: University of Pennsylvania Press, 2008), 184.

15. Reinhold Wagnleitner, *Coca-Colonization and the Cold War: The Cultural Mission of the United States after the Second World War* (Chapel Hill: University of North Carolina Press, 1994); Walter L. Hixson, *Parting the Iron Curtain: Propaganda, Culture, and the Cold War, 1945–1961* (New York: St. Martin's Press, 1996); Mary Dudziak, *Cold War Civil Rights: Race and the Image of American Democracy* (Princeton, NJ: Princeton University Press, 2011); Teasel Muir-Harmony, *Operation Moonglow: A Political History of Project Apollo* (New York: Basic Books, 2020).

16. Lois Roth, "Public Diplomacy and the Past: The Search for an American Style of Propaganda," *Fletcher Forum* 8, no. 2 (1984): 365.

17. Kenneth Osgood, *Total Cold War: Eisenhower's Secret Propaganda Battle at Home and Abroad* (Lawrence: University Press of Kansas, 2006), 155.

18. Hallvard Notaker, Giles Scott-Smith, and David J. Snyder, *Reasserting America in the 1970s: U.S. Public Diplomacy and the Rebuilding of America's Image Abroad* (Manchester, UK: Manchester University Press, 2016).

19. Panel on International Information, Education, and Cultural Relations, *International Information, Education, and Cultural Relations: Recommendations for the Future* (Washington, DC: Center for Strategic and International Studies, 1975).

20. Wilson P. Dizard, Jr., *Inventing Public Diplomacy: The Story of the U.S. Information Agency* (Boulder, CO: Lynne Rienner, 2004), 200–210.

21. Olin Robinson et al., *1980 Annual Report* (Washington, DC: U.S. Advisory Commission on Public Diplomacy, 1980), https://www.state.gov.

22. Gregory Tomlin, *Murrow's Cold War: Public Diplomacy for the Kennedy Administration* (Sterling, VA: Potomac, 2016).

23. Strobe Talbott, *Master of the Game: Paul Nitze and the Nuclear Peace* (New York: Knopf, 1988); Paul H. Nitze, *From Hiroshima to Glasnost: At the Center of Decision* (New York: Grove Weidenfeld, 1989); Wilson D. Miscamble, "Rejected Architect and Master Builder: George Kennan, Dean Acheson, and Postwar Europe," *Review of Politics* 58 (Summer 1996): 437–68.

24. David Abshire, "NATO at the Moral Crossroads," *Washington Quarterly* 7, no. 3 (1984): 3.

25. Fred Kaplan, *Wizards of Armageddon* (Stanford, CA: Stanford University Press, 1991); Hugh Gusterson, *Nuclear Rites: A Weapons Laboratory at the End of the Cold War* (Berkeley: University of California Press, 1996); Lynn Eden, *Whole World on Fire: Organizations, Knowledge, and Nuclear Weapons Devastation* (Ithaca, NY: Cornell University Press, 2006); Paul Erickson, Judy Klein, Lorraine Daston, Rebecca Lemov, Thomas Sturm, and Michael D. Gordin, *How Reason Almost Lost Its Mind: The Strange Career of Cold War Rationality* (Chicago: University of Chicago Press, 2013); Paul Erickson, *The World the Game Theorists Made* (Chicago: University of Chicago Press, 2015); Ron Robin, *The Cold War They Made: The Strategic Legacy of Roberta and Albert Wohlstetter* (Cambridge, MA: Harvard University Press, 2016); Simon J. Moody, *Imagining Nuclear War in the British Army, 1945–1989* (Oxford: Oxford University Press, 2020).

26. Michael MccGwire, "Nuclear Deterrence," *International Affairs* 82 (July 2006): 778. Also see Michael MccGwire, "Deterrence: The Problem Not the Solution," *International Affairs* 62 (Winter 1985–86): 55–70.

27. George Orwell, "You and the Atom Bomb," [London] *Tribune*, October 19, 1945.

28. Guy Oakes, *The Imaginary War: Civil Defense and American Cold War Culture* (Oxford: Oxford University Press, 1995); Spencer Weart, *The Rise of Nuclear Fear* (Cambridge: Harvard University Press, 2012); Matthew Grant and Benjamin Ziemann, *Culture, Thought, and Nuclear Conflict, 1945–1990* (Manchester, UK: Manchester University Press, 2016).

29. Nicholas Cull, *Selling War: The British Campaign against American Neutrality in World War II* (Oxford: Oxford University Press, 1996); Andrew Defty, *Britain, America, and Anti-Communist Propaganda, 1945–1953: The Information Research Department* (New York: Routledge, 2004); Lowell Schwartz, *Political Warfare against the Kremlin: U.S. and British Propaganda Policy at the Beginning of the Cold War* (London: Palgrave Macmillan, 2009).

30. Graham Mytton, "Audience Research at the BBC External Services during the Cold War: A View from the Inside," *Cold War History* 11, no. 1 (2011): 49–67; Gordon Johnston and Emma Robertson, *BBC World Service: Overseas Broadcasting, 1932–2018* (London: Palgrave Macmillan, 2019).

31. Cull, *The Cold War and the United States Information Agency*, 14; John Jenks, *British Propaganda and News Media in the Cold War* (Edinburgh: Edinburgh University Press), 100–110.

32. Ronald Reagan, "Address to Members of the British Parliament," speech, Westminster, London, June 8, 1982, https://www.reaganlibrary.gov.

33. William Roger Louis and Hedley Bull, *The "Special Relationship": Anglo-American Relations Since 1945* (Oxford: Clarendon, 1987); David Reynolds, "Rethinking Anglo-American Relations," *International Affairs* 65, no. 1 (1988–89): 89–111; John Baylis, *Anglo-American Relations Since 1939–1980: The Enduring Alliance* (Manchester, UK: Manchester University Press, 1997); John Baylis, "Exchanging Nuclear Secrets: Laying the Foundations of the Anglo-American Nuclear Relationship," *Diplomatic History* 25 (Winter 2001): 33–61; Jenifer Mackby and Paul Cornish, *U.S.-U.K. Nuclear Cooperation after 50 Years* (Washington, DC: Center for Strategic and International Studies Press, 2008); Richard Aldous, *Reagan and Thatcher: The Difficult Relationship* (New York: Norton, 2012); Alan Dobson and Steve Marsh, *Anglo-American Relations: Contemporary Perspectives*

(London: Routledge, 2013); Kristan Stoddart, *Facing Down the Soviet Union: Britain, the USA, NATO, and Nuclear Weapons, 1976–1983* (London: Palgrave Macmillan, 2014).

34. Susanne Schregel, "Nuclear War and the City: Perspectives on Municipal Interventions in Defense (Great Britain, New Zealand, West Germany, USA, 1980–9185)," *Urban History* 42, no. 4 (2015): 564–83; Susanne Schregel, "Global Micropolitics: Toward a Transnational History of Grassroots Nuclear Free Zones," in *Nuclear Threats, Nuclear Fear, and the Cold War of the 1980s,* ed. Eckart Conze, Martin Klimke, and Jeremy Varon (New York: Cambridge University Press, 2017), 214; Andrea Chiampan, "Nuclear Weapons, 'Nuclear Ideas', and Protests: Did They Matter?," in *New Perspectives on the End of the Cold War: Unexpected Transformations?,* ed. Bernhard Blumenau, Jussi M. Hanhimäki, and Barbara Zanchetta (London: Routledge, 2018): 46–68.

35. Matthew Evangelista, *Unarmed Forces: The Transnational Movement to End the Cold War* (Ithaca, NY: Cornell University Press, 1999); John Krige and Kai-Henrick Barth, "Introduction: Science, Technology, and International Affairs," *Osiris* 21 (2006): 1–21; Kai-Henrik Barth, "Catalysts of Change: Scientists as Transnational Arms Control Advocates in the 1980s," *Osiris* 21, no. 4 (2006): 182–20.

36. Ronald Reagan, "Address before the U.S. Advisory Commission on Public Diplomacy," speech, U.S. Department of State, September 16, 1987, https://www.state.gov.

37. E. P. Thompson, "The Ends of the Cold War," *New Left Review* 182 (July–August 1990): 139–46.

38. For the definitions used by the U.S. Advisory Committee on Public Diplomacy, see any of their annual reports from 1982 to 1989, https://www.state.gov.

39. Joseph Nye, Jr., "Public Diplomacy and Soft Power," *Annals of the American Academy of Political and Social Science* 616 (March 2008):101–3.

40. Manuel Castells, "The New Public Sphere: Global Civil Society, Communication Networks, and Global Governance," *Annals of the American Academy of Political and Social Science* 616 (March 2008): 78–93; John Robert Kelley, "The New Diplomacy: Evolution of a Revolution" *Diplomacy and Statecraft* 21, no. 2 (2010): 286–305.

Chapter One: The World Reagan Wanted

1. Martin Schram, "Carter Goes into Debate with Lead in New Poll," *Washington Post,* October 28, 1980.

2. Sean Wilentz, *The Age of Reagan: A History, 1974–2008* (New York: HarperPerennial, 2009), 124.

3. Jimmy Carter and Ronald Reagan, "October 28, 1980 Debate Transcript," https://www.debates.org.

4. Ronald Mason, "The Domestic Politics of War and Peace: Jimmy Carter, Ronald Reagan, and the Election of 1980," in *U.S. Presidential Elections and Foreign Policy: Candidates, Campaigns, and Global Politics from FDR to Bill Clinton,* ed. Andrew Johnstone and Andrew Priest (Lexington: University of Kentucky Press, 2017), 263.

5. Kiron K. Skinner, Serhiy Kudelia, Bruce Bueno de Mesquita, and Condoleezza Rice, *The Strategy of Campaigning: Strategies from Ronald Reagan and Boris Yeltsin* (Ann Arbor: University of Michigan Press, 2007), 202; Shana Kushner Gadarian, "Foreign Policy at the Ballot Box: How Citizens Use Foreign Policy to Judge and Choose Candidates," *Journal of Politics* 72 (October 2010): 1052.

6. Lettow, *Ronald Reagan and His Quest to Abolish Nuclear Weapons (New York: Random House, 2006)*; Martin Anderson and Annelise Anderson, *Reagan's Secret War: The Untold Story of His Fight to Save the World from Nuclear Disaster* (New York: Three Rivers, 2009).

7. Anderson and Anderson, *Reagan's Secret War*, 94.
8. "Reagan's Nuclear War Briefing Declassified," December 22, 2016, National Security Archive, https://nsarchive.gwu.edu.
9. Hal Brands, "The Vision Thing" (Richmond: University of Virginia, Miller Center, January 2016), https://millercenter.org.
10. Jon Nordheimer, "Reagan, in Direct Attack, Assails Ford on Defense," *New York Times*, March 5, 1976.
11. Ronald Reagan, "To Restore America," speech, March 31, 1976, https://www.reaganlibrary.gov.
12. Anne Cahn, *Killing Détente: The Right Attacks the CIA* (University Park: Pennsylvania State University Press, 1998).
13. Kiron Skinner, Martin Anderson, and Annelise Anderson, *Reagan in his Own Hand: The Writings of Ronald Reagan That Reveal His Revolutionary Vision for America* (New York: Free Press, 2001), 110–12.
14. Ibid., 85
15. Ronald Reagan, "Address to the Veterans of Foreign Wars Convention in Chicago," speech, August 18, 1980, http://www.presidency.ucsb.edu.
16. Daniel Yankelovich and Larry Kaagan, "Assertive America," *Foreign Affairs* 59, no. 3 (1980): 696–713; Andrew Z. Katz, "Public Opinion and the Contradictions of Jimmy Carter's Foreign Policy," *Presidential Studies Quarterly* 30 (December 2000): 662–87.
17. Vincent Tinker, "Ronald Reagan, Peace through Strength, 1980," YouTube video, 2:01, December 21, 2008, https://www.youtube.com.
18. Sara A. Mehltretter Drury, "Defining National Security as Peace through Strength: Ronald Reagan's Visionary Rhetoric of Renewal in the 1980 Presidential Campaign," *Argumentation and Advocacy* 51, no. 2 (2014): 87–102.
19. Republican Party platform, Republican National Convention, Detroit, 1980, https://www.presidency.uscb.edu.
20. T. M Nichols, "Carter and the Soviets: The Origins of the U.S. Return to a Strategy of Confrontation," *Diplomacy and Statecraft* 13, no. 2 (2002): 21–42; Olav Njolstad, "The Carter Legacy: Entering the Second Cold War," in *The Last Decade of the Cold War: From Escalation to Conflict Transformation*, ed. Olav Njolstad (London: Routledge, 2005), 163–87.
21. Matthew Glass, *Citizens against the MX* (Chicago: University of Illinois Press, 1993), 1–25.
22. Lawrence Wittner, *Toward Nuclear Abolition: A History of the World Disarmament Movement, 1971–Present* (Stanford, CA: Stanford University Press, 2003), 1–20.
23. Natasha Zaretsky, *Radiation Nation: Three Mile Island and the Political Transformation of the 1970s* (New York: Columbia University Press, 2018); J. S. Walker, *Three Mile Island: A Nuclear Crisis in Historical Perspective* (Berkeley: University of California Press, 2006).
24. David S. Meyer, *A Winter of Discontent: The Nuclear Freeze and American Politics* (New York: Praeger, 1990), 149.
25. Randall Forsberg, "Call to Halt the Nuclear Weapons," speech, April 1980, Institute for Defense and Disarmament Studies.
26. Sean Wilentz, *The Age of Reagan: A History, 1974–2008* (New York: Harper Perennial, 2009), 110.
27. Kyle Longley, Jeremy Mayer, Michael Schaller, and John Sloan, *Deconstructing Reagan: Conservative Mythology and America's Fortieth President* (New York: Routledge, 2006); William Silber, *Volcker: The Triumph of Persistence* (New York: Bloomsbury, 2012); William Steding, *Presidential Faith and Foreign Policy: Jimmy Carter the Disciple and Ronald Reagan the Alchemist* (New York: Palgrave Macmillan, 2014); Aaron Donaghy, *The Second*

Cold War: Carter, Reagan, and the Politics of Foreign Policy (Cambridge: Cambridge University Press, 2021).

28. Tom W. Smith, "The Polls: American Attitudes toward the Soviet Union and Communism," *Public Opinion Quarterly* 47 (Summer 1983): 287–88.

29. Dan Ebener, "Nuclear Freeze Campaign Made in the U.S.A.," *New York Times,* December 12, 1982.

30. Douglas C. Waller, *Congress and the Nuclear Freeze: An Inside Look at the Politics of a Mass Movement* (Amherst: University of Massachusetts Press, 1987), 34–35.

31. Hugh Mehan, Charles E. Nathanson, and James M. Skelly, "Nuclear Discourse in the 1980s: The Unraveling Conventions of the Cold War," *Discourse and Society* 1, no. 2 (1990): 133–38.

32. Henry Nau, "Ideas Have Consequences: The Cold War and Today," *International Politics* 48, nos. 4/5 (2011): 460–81.

33. Raymond Garthoff, *The Great Transition: American-Soviet Relations and the End of the Cold War* (Washington, D.C.: Brookings Institution Press, 2001), 7.

34. Robert C. Rowland and John Jones, *Reagan at Westminster: Foreshadowing the End of the Cold War* (College Station: Texas A&M University Press, 2010).

35. Robert Schmuhl, *Statecraft and Stagecraft: American Politics in the Age of Personality* (Notre Dame, IN: University of Notre Dame Press, 1992), 29.

36. Ronald Reagan, first press conference, January 29, 1981, https://millercenter.org; Ronald Reagan, news conference on arms control with Sam Donaldson, January 29, 1981, Sven Kraemer Files, box 9, folder "NATO TNF," RRPL.

37. John Rosenberg, "To Arms for the Western Alliance: The Committee on the Present Danger, Defense Spending and the Perception of American Power Abroad, 1973–1980," in *Reasserting America in the 1970s: U.S. Public Diplomacy and the Rebuilding of America's Image Abroad,* ed. Hallvard Notaker and Daniel J. Snyder (Manchester, UK: Manchester University Press, 2016), 247–53.

38. Morton Blackwell, "A New Right Foreign Policy Offensive," memo, August 29, 1980, Morton Blackwell Files, box 1, folder "American Security Council and Coalition for Peace through Strength," RRPL.

39. Lawrence Eagleburger and Richard Burt, "U.S.-Soviet Relations Over the Near-Term," memo to Alexander Haig, March 16, 1981, in *Foreign Relations of the United States* (hereafter cited as FRUS), 1981–89, vol. 3, Soviet Union, January 1981–January 1983, doc. 28; Richard Pipes, memo to Richard Allen, February 24, 1981, ibid., doc. 2.

40. Lee Edwards, *Leading the Way: The Story of Ed Feulner and the Heritage Foundation* (New York: Crown Forum, 2013).

41. Ibid.

42. James McGann, *Think Tanks and Policy Advice in the United States: Academics, Advisors, and Advocates* (New York: Routledge, 2007), 8–11.

43. Richard Pipes, "Thoughts on Linkage," memo to Richard Allen, February 17, 1981, *FRUS*, 1981–89, vol. 3, Soviet Union, January 1981–January 1983, doc. 19; Alexander Haig, "U.S.-Soviet Relations over the Near Term," memo to Ronald Reagan, April 2, 1982, ibid., doc. 154.

44. David Shribman, "Group Goes from Exile to Influence," *New York Times*, November 23, 1981.

45. Strobe Talbott, *Deadly Gambits: The Reagan Administration and the Stalemate in Nuclear Arms Control* (New York: Knopf, 1984), 43–52.

46. Helmut Schmidt, "1977 Alistair Buchan Memorial Lecture," *Survival* 20, no. 1 (1978): 3–4.

47. Jim Hoagl, "Ongoing Crisis Forces Iran to Forefront of Four-Power Summit in Guadeloupe," *Washington Post*, January 5, 1979; Pierre Lellouche, "SALT and European Security:

The French Dilemma," *Survival* 22, no. 1 (1980): 2–6; Jimmy Carter, *White House Diary* (New York: Picador, 2011), 272; Thomas K. Robb, *Jimmy Carter and the Anglo-American "Special Relationship"* (Edinburgh: Edinburgh University Press, 2016), 85–88.

48. John Minnion and Philip Bolsover, *The CND Story: The First 25 Years of CND in the Words of the People Involved* (London: Allison and Busby, 1983).

49. Thomas Rid, *Active Measures: The Secret History of Disinformation and Political Warfare* (New York: Farrar, Straus, and Giroux, 2020), 260.

50. E. P. Thompson and Dan Smith, eds., *Protest and Survive* (London: Monthly Review Press, 1980); Minnion and Bolsover, *The CND Story,* 56–80; Wittner, *Toward Nuclear Abolition,* 23, 64–65.

51. Rid, *Active Measures.*

52. Douglas Hurd, "Nuclear Weapons: Public Attitudes," March 5, 1981, Foreign and Commonwealth Office Records (hereafter cited as FCO), ser. 46, folder 2741, National Archives, Kew (hereafter TNA).

53. A. J. D Pawson, "The Soviet Propaganda Campaign on Theatre Nuclear Forces," July 6, 1981, FCO, ser. 46, folder 2756; U.K. Embassy in Washington, "Nuclear Issues," memo to U.K. Foreign and Commonwealth Office, July 10, 1981, ibid.; A. J. D Pawson, "Nuclear Weapons Policy—Public Attitudes," July 23, 1981, ibid.; A. J. D. Pawson, "NPG Staff Discussion on Public Presentation of Nuclear Issues," memo to J. M. Legge, September 18, 1981, ibid.

54. "Charles Z. Wick Obituary" *Independent,* October 23, 2011.

55. Allen Hansen, *USIA: Public Diplomacy in the Computer Age* (New York: Praeger, 1989).

56. G. Lewis Schmidt, interview with John Shirley, November 21, 1989, Foreign Affairs Oral History Project Information Series, Association of Diplomatic Studies and Training (hereafter cited as ADST), https://www.adst.org.

57. Charles Z. Wick, memo to Ronald Reagan, January 24, 1982, Central Intelligence Agency Electronic Reading Room (hereafter cited as CIA-ERR); Charles Z. Wick, memo to William Clark, March 5, 1983, National Security Council Subject Files, box 27, folder "Public Diplomacy," RRPL.

58. Todd Leventhal, "Remembering Herb Romerstein," *Public Diplomacy Council Commentary* (December 2016), https://www.publicdiplomacycouncil.org.

59. John Lenczowski, personal communication, February 5, 2021.

60. Dennis Blair, memo to Richard Allen, May 8, 1981, Dennis Blair Files, box RAC 4, folder "Public Diplomacy March 1981–June 1981," RRPL.

61. Mike Schneider, personal communication, January 18, 2021; U.S. Department of Defense, *Soviet Military Power* (Washington, DC: U.S. Government Printing Office, May 1981), http://insidethecoldwar.org.

62. Fletcher Schoen and Christopher J. Lamb, "Deception, Disinformation, and Strategic Communications: How One Interagency Group Made a Major Difference," occasional paper (Washington, DC: National Defense University Press, 2012).

63. U.S. NATO Mission, "TNF: October 26 SCG, Summary Report," cable to Alexander Haig, October 27, 1981, Sven Kraemer Files, box 4, folder "NATO SCG, October 81," RRPL.

64. Alexander Haig, "Haig Breakfast Memo for the Record," March 26, 1981, *FRUS,* 1981–89, vol. 3, Soviet Union, January 1981–January 1983, doc. 36.

65. Talbot, *Deadly Gambits,* 43–61.

66. National Intelligence Council, "National Intelligence Estimate: Moscow and the Reagan Administration: Initial Assessments and Responses," NIC M 81–10011, September 1981, CIA-ERR.

67. Duncan Clarke, "Arms Control and Foreign Policy under Reagan," *Bulletin of the Atomic Scientists* 37, no. 9 (1981): 12–19.

68. "Meeting between Secretary Haig and Minister Gromyko with Their Delegations," September 23, 1981, William Clark Files, box 3, folder "Haig/Gromyko Meetings," RRPL.

69. "Strategic Forces Modernization Program," National Security Decision Directive 12, October 1, 1981, National Security Decision Directives (hereafter NSDDs), 1981–89, RRPL.

70. Ronald Reagan, "Remarks and a Question-and-Answer Session with Reporters on the Announcement of the United States Strategic Weapons Program," October 2, 1981, American Presidency Project, University of California, Santa Barbara, https://www.presidency.ucsb.edu; Cahn, *Killing Détente*.

71. "Nuclear Weapons Employment Policy," NSDD 13, October 19, 1981, NSDDs, 1981–89, RRPL.

72. Geoffrey Godsell, "Limited Nuclear Warfare Why Reagan Worries Europe," *Christian Science Monitor*, October 21, 1981; Bernard Gwertzman, "Reagan Clarifies His Statement on Nuclear War," *New York Times,* October 22, 1981.

73. Walter Picnus and George C. Wilson, "Nuclear Warning Shot Plan Disputed," *Washington Post,* November 6, 1981.

74. U.S. NATO Mission, "NAC Ministerial Communiqué," memo to U.S. State Department, November 30, 1981, Sven Kraemer Files, box 4, folder "NATO Meetings," RRPL.

75. U.S. Embassy in London, "Anti-Nuclear Weapons Demonstration," memo to U.S. State Department, October 27, 1981, Sven Kraemer Files, box 3, folder "NATO-antinuclear," RRPL.

76. Richard Allen, "Your Meeting with John Lewis: A Few Key Points for the Record," memo to Ronald Reagan, November 18, 1981, National Security Council Executive Secretariat, United Kingdom Country Files, box 45, RRPL.

77. Sven Kraemer, "NPSG—Agenda Item on TNF," memo to Richard Allen, November 5, 1981, Sven Kraemer Files, box 9, folder "NATO TNG IGs," RRPL; Chief of arms control intelligence staff, "National Security Council Meeting on TNF Scheduled for November 12," memo to director and deputy director of Central Intelligence Agency, November 10, 1981, CIA-ERR.

78. Ronald Powaski, *March to Armageddon: The United States and the Nuclear Arms Race, 1939 to the Present* (New York: Oxford University Press, 1989), 197–99.

79. "Theater Nuclear Forces (Intermediate Range Nuclear Forces)," NSDD 15, November 16, 1981, NSDDs, 1981–89, RRPL.

80. National Security Council, "Theater Nuclear Forces; Egypt," meeting minutes, October 13, 1981, National Security Council Executive Secretariat, Meeting Files, 1981–87, RRPL.

81. Ibid.

82. Sven Kraemer, "National Security Council Meeting," memo to Richard Allen, November 10, 1981, National Security Council Executive Secretariat, Meeting Files, 1981–87, RRPL.

83. National Security Council, "Theater Nuclear Forces," meeting minutes, November 12, 1981, in ibid.

84. Ronald Reagan, "Remarks to Members of the National Press Club on Arms Reduction and Nuclear Weapons," speech, November 18, 1981, Washington, DC, American Presidency Project, University of California, Santa Barbara, https://www.presidency.ucsb.edu.

85. Hans M. Tuch, *Communicating with the World: U.S. Public Diplomacy Overseas* (New York: St. Martin's Press, 1990), xi.

86. Caspar Weinberger, "Secretary Weinberger's Meeting with Thatcher," memo to Ronald Reagan through James Nance, December 11, 1981, National Security Council, European Directorate Files, box 91326, RRPL; "Adding up the 'Zero Option' Will Take Time," *New York Times*, November 22, 1981.

87. Richard Burt, personal communication, December 4, 2020.

Chapter Two: Britain's Choice

1. WGBH Television, "Zero Hour: Interview with E. P. Thompson," *War and Peace in the Nuclear Age,* October 15, 1987, WGBH Media Library and Archives, http://openvault. wgbh.org.
2. E. P. Thompson, "Resurgence in Europe and the Role of END," in *The CND Story: The First 25 years of CND in the Words of People Involved,* ed. John Minnion and Philip Bolsover (London: Allison and Busby, 1983), 81.
3. E. P. Thompson and Ken Coates, "Appeal for European Nuclear Disarmament," in *Protest and Survive,* ed. E. P. Thompson and Dan Smith (London: Monthly Review Press, 1980), 163–66.
4. Ken Coates, *No Cruise Missiles, No SS-20s: European Nuclear Disarmament* (Nottingham, UK: Bertrand Russell Peace Foundation, 1980), 3.
5. On specific dimensions of moral traditionalism, see Michael Johnston, "Right and Wrong in British Politics: 'Fits of Morality' in Comparative Perspective," *Polity* 24 (Autumn 1991): 19–20. On the transformation of the British Labour Party, see Eric Shaw, *The Labour Party Since 1979: Crisis and Transformation* (Routledge: London, 2002), 15–17; Andy McSmith, *No Such Thing as Society: A History of Britain in the 1980s* (London: Constable, 2010), 50–51; and Lawrence Black, Hugh Pemberton, and Pat Thane, *Reassessing 1970s Britain* (Manchester, UK: Manchester University Press, 2013), 8–9.
6. Tony Benn and Chris Mullin, eds., *Arguments for Democracy* (London: Cape, 1981).
7. Richard Gozney, "Civil Defense: The Public Line," memo to [unknown first name] Logan, May 1, 1981, FCO, ser. 46, folder 2742.
8. Michael Howard, "Reviving Civil Defense," *Times,* January 30, 1980.
9. WGBH Television, "Zero Hour: Thompson"
10. Thompson and Smith, *Protest and Survive,* 22.
11. Ibid., 26.
12. WGBH Television, "Zero Hour: Thompson."
13. Michael Howard, "Surviving a Protest: A Reply to E. P. Thompson's Polemic," *Encounter* (November 1980): 15–21.
14. David Curtis Skaggs, Jr., *Michael Howard: Military Historian and Strategic Analyst* (Carlisle, PA: U.S. Army War College, June 1983).
15. U.K. Parliament, *Civil Defense Act, 1948,* https://www.legislation.gov.uk.
16. U.K. Home Office, circular no. ES 3/1973, p. 4, TNA.
17. Jacquelyn Arnold, "British Civil Defense Policy in Response to the Threat of Nuclear Attack: 1972–1986" (PhD diss., London Metropolitan University, 2014), 103, 124.
18. Martin Spence, "Hard Rock/Hard Luck Pack," April 28, 1982, Campaign for Nuclear Disarmament Records (hereafter CND Records), ser. 5/6, London School of Economics (hereafter LSE) Special Collections.
19. Duncan Campbell, "World War III: An Exclusive Preview," *New Statesman,* October 3, 1980; Duncan Campbell and Rob Edwards, "Square Leg Caught Out," *New Statesman,* October 3, 1980.
20. British Broadcasting Corporation Television, "If the Bomb Drops," *Panorama,* March 11, 1980.
21. Philip Bolsover, *Civil Defense: The Cruelest Confidence Trick* (1980; Nottingham, UK: Russell, 1982), 22.
22. Joan Ruddock, "Why the 1980 Revival Happened—and Where We Go From Here," in Minnion and Bolsover, *The CND Story,* 96.
23. John Baylis and Kristan Stoddart, "Britain and the Chevaline Project: The Hidden Nuclear Programme, 1967–1982," *Journal of Strategic Studies* 26, no. 4 (2003): 144–46.

24. Len Scott, "Labour and the Bomb: The First 80 Years," *International Affairs* 82, no. 4 (2006): 690.

25. Norman Webster, "Labour Party Votes to Switch on Disarmament," *Globe and Mail*, June 4, 1980; David Griffiths, "CND and the Labour Party," in Minnion and Bolsover, *The CND Story*, 134.

26. WGBH Television, "Zero Hour: Interview with Bruce Kent," *War and Peace in the Nuclear Age*, November 26, 1987, WGBH Media Library and Archives, http://openvault.wgbh.org.

27. Lawrence Wittner, *Toward Nuclear Abolition: A History of the World Disarmament Movement, 1971–Present* (Stanford, CA: Stanford University Press, 2003), 133.

28. Tim Heppell and Andrew Crines, "How Michael Foot Won the Labour Party Leadership," *Political Quarterly* 82, no. 1 (2011): 82.

29. Ibid., 91.

30. Ian Aitken, "Labour Picks Foot to Heal Party Splits," *Guardian*, November 11, 1980.

31. "Work Place Groups in CND Structure," 1981, CND Records, box 4/1/1.

32. Susan Willett, "Conversion Policy in the UK," *Cambridge Journal of Economics* 14, no. 4 (1990): 479–81.

33. Hilary Wainwright, "The Women Who Wire Up the Weapons: Workers in Armament Factories," in *Over Our Dead Bodies: Women against the Bomb*, ed. Dorothy Thompson (London: Virago, 1983), 141.

34. Minnion and Bolsover, *The CND Story*, 133; *The Story of the Lucas Aerospace Shop Stewards Alternative Corporate Plan*, video documentary (Milton Keynes, UK: Open University, 1978), https://www.youtube.com.

35. Suzanne Gordon, "Converting Plants to Peace," *Nuclear Times* (March 1983).

36. "British Unions Plan Conversion of Defense Industries to Alternative Production," *Labour Notes*, June 29, 1983.

37. Peter Shipley, memo to Alan Howarth, October 5, 1981, Conservative Research Department Records (hereafter CRD Records), box 4, folder 18/11, Conservative Party Archives, Weston Libraries Special Collections, Oxford University (hereafter WLSC); Labour Campaign for Nuclear Disarmament, meeting minutes, January 9, 1982, and October 24, 1982, CND Records, ser. 6/4; Bruce Kent, "General Secretary's Report to the CND Conference," November 26, 1982, CND Records, box 1, folder 1/2.

38. Jenny Edwards, "Labour's Pledge—Disarmament," *Sanity* (October–November 1981); Pete Higgins, "The Unions," ibid.

39. Peter M. Jones, "British Defense Policy: The Breakdown of Inter-Party Consensus," *Review of International Studies* 13 (1987): 115–16.

40. Lord Thorneycroft, "Paper on Strategy for Dealing with the Labour Party," October 23, 1980, CRD Records, box 4, folder 16; David Nicholson, "Suggestions for Handling Foot," November 7, 1980, ibid.

41. U.S. Embassy in London, "Labour Party National Executive Adopts Unilateralism," memo to U.S. State Department, July 24, 1981, James Rentschler Files, box 2, RRPL.

42. At times this committee was referred to as the British Atlantic Council.

43. Mr. Reeve, "Public Opinion and Nuclear Weapons Policy," memo to Patrick Moberly, February 13, 1981, FCO Records, ser. 46, folder 2740; Douglas Hurd, "Nuclear Weapons: Public Attitudes," March 5, 1981, ibid., folder 2741; C. R. Dean, "Nuclear Weapons: Public Attitudes," to Mr. Reeve, March 29, 1981, ibid.; Peter Carrington, "Public Opinion and Nuclear Weapons Policy," April 28, 1981, ibid; "Public Opinion and Nuclear Weapons," October 26, 1981, ibid., folder 2745.

44. Peter Shipley, memo to Alan Howarth, September 25, 1981, CRD Records, box 4, folder 18/9.

45. "Chairman's Meeting: Minutes to Discuss the CND Campaign," June 28, 1981, ibid.

46. Ed Feulner, personal communication, November 9, 2020.

47. Peter Shipley, "Joint Studies with Heritage Foundation," July 22, 1981, CRD Records, box 4, folder 18/9.

48. William Clark, "The Institute for European Defence and Strategic Studies" (PhD diss., University of Strathclyde, 2013).

49. Peter Shipley, memo to Scott Hamilton, March 16, 1982, CRD Records, box 4, folder 18/11.

50. Bernard Ingham, minutes about lunch between Margaret Thatcher and Rupert Murdoch, January 4, 1981, Thatcher Correspondence (hereafter THCR), box 1, folder 12/8 f3, Churchill Archive Centre, Cambridge University (hereafter CAC); Clark, "The Institute for European Defence and Strategic Studies."

51. Tony Kerpel, memo to Margaret Thatcher, January 5, 1981, CRD Records, box 4, folder 18/6.

52. Coalition of Peace through Security, "Report of the First Year of Operation," 1982, Morton Blackwell Files, box 4, folder "Coalition for Peace through Security," RRPL.

53. Peter Blaker, memo to Tony Kerpel, September 1981, Sven Kraemer Files, box 3, folder "NATO Countries–UK," RRPL; Peter Blaker, "Public Opinion on Nuclear Weapons," memo to Margaret Thatcher, October 5, 1981, FCO, ser. 46, folder 2745.

54. Coalition of Peace through Security, "Report of the First Year of Operation."

55. Ibid.

56. Sven Kraemer, "Meeting with British Group 'Coalition for Peace through Strength [*sic*],'" memo to Robert Schweitzer, October 1, 1981, Sven Kraemer Files, box 3, folder "NATO Countries–UK," RRPL; Dennis Blair and Jim Rentschler, "Meeting with British Group 'Coalition for Peace through Strength [*sic*],'" memo to Janet Colston, October 2, 1981, ibid.; Coalition of Peace through Security, "Report of the First Year of Operation.

57. Bishop of Salisbury's Working Group, *The Church and the Bomb: Nuclear Weapons and the Christian Conscience* (London: CIO Press, 1982), vi–viii.

58. Frank L. Jones, "'The High Priest of Deterrence': Sir Michael Quinlan, Nuclear Weapons, and the Just War Tradition," *Logos* 16 (Summer 2013): 14–42.

59. Michael Quinlan, *Thinking about Nuclear Weapons* (London: RUSI Defence Studies, 1997).

60. Roger Ruston, *A Say in the End of the World: Morals and British Nuclear Weapons Policy, 1941–1987* (Oxford: Clarendon, 1989), 203.

61. Peter Blaker, "Nuclear Public Relations," memo to Margaret Thatcher, December 21, 1983, Prime Minister Office Records (hereafter PREM), ser. 19/1690 f224, TNA.

62. Michael Foot, *Another Heart and Other Pulses: The Alternative to the Thatcher Society* (London: Collins, 1984), 56–95.

63. Roger Williams, "British Scientists and the Bomb: The Decisions of 1980," *Government and Opposition* 16, no. 3 (1981): 267–92; WGBH Television, "Zero Hour: Thompson."

64. Williams, "British Scientists and the Bomb," 267.

65. Bishop of Salisbury's Working Group, *The Church and the Bomb*, vi–viii.

66. Martin Ryle, "Nuclear Disarmament Democracy and Internationalism," *Radical Philosophy* 29 (Autumn 1981): 6.

67. Benn and Mullins, *Arguments for Democracy*, 101.

68. Mike Pentz, "Scientists against Nuclear Arms," memo to Dorothy Hodgkin, January 8, 1981, Dorothy Hodgkin Personal Papers, folder MS.ENG.C.7955, WLSC.

69. *SANA Newsletter* 3 (February 1982), Dorothy Hodgkin Personal Papers, folder MS.ENG.C.5688, WLSC; "SANER Scientists to Equip Peace Fight," *Morning Star*, March 21, 1981.

70. Pentz, "Scientists against Nuclear Arms."

71. "Inaugural SANA Conference at Open University," March 21–22, 1981, Joseph Rotblat Personal Papers, box 5, folder 6/8/4, CAC.

72. Spence, "Hard Rock/Hard Luck Pack."

73. Paul Bolton, "Education: Historical Statistics," November 27, 2012, House of Commons Library, SN/SG/4252, 20.

74. Jamie Jenkins, "Women in the Labour Market," September 25, 2013, U.K. Office of National Statistics, https://www.ons.gov.uk.

75. Ann Pettitt, *Walking to Greenham: How the Peace Camp Began and the Cold War Ended* (London: Honno, 2008).

76. *The Greenham Factor* (London, 1983); Barbara Harford and Sarah Hopkins, eds., *Greenham Common: Women at the Wire* (London: Women's Press, 1984), 19.

77. Wittner, *Toward Nuclear Abolition,* 131.

78. Peter Shipley, memo to Alan Howarth, October 26, 1981, CRD Records, box 4, folder 18/11.

79. Keith Britto, "CND," memo to Alan Howarth, November 9, 1981, ibid.; Peter Shipley, to memo Alan Howarth, November 6, 1981, ibid.

80. Richard Allen, "Your Meeting with John Louis: A Few Key Points for the Record," memo to Ronald Reagan, November 18, 1981, National Security Council, Executive Secretariat Files, U.K. Country Files, box 45, folder "United Kingdom" RRPL.

81. U.S. Embassy in Paris, "Report of Conversation by Representatives from White House/State Department/ICA," memo to U.S. Information Communication Agency, May 17, 1982, David Gergen Files, box 7, folder "Nuclear Freeze," RRPL.

82. Richard Burt, personal communication, December 4, 2020.

83. Charles Z. Wick, memo to William Casey, Alexander Haig, William Clark, and Caspar Weinberger, March 17, 1982, CIA-ERR.

84. Dean E. Fischer, memo to George Shultz, April 2, 1982, Denis Blair Files, box RAC 4, folder "Public Diplomacy, April 1982," RRPL.

85. Charles Z. Wick, "Public Opinion in Europe," memo to the Special Planning Group, Spring 1982, David Gergen Files, box 8, folder "Public Diplomacy," RRPL.

86. Peter Shipley, memo to Scott Hamilton, March 16, 1982, CRD Records, ser. 4, folder 18/11.

87. Caroline Blackwood, *On the Perimeter* (London: Heinemann, 1984), 26.

88. *The Greenham Factor.*

89. Liza Filby, "God and Mrs. Thatcher: Religion and Politics in the 1980s" (PhD diss., University of Durham, 2010), 12–15.

90. Brian Walden, "Victorian Values," interview with Margaret Thatcher, *Weekend World,* January 16, 1983; Raphael Samuel, "Mrs. Thatcher's Return to Victorian Values," *Proceedings of the British Academy* 78 (1992): 9–29.

91. U.S. Embassy in London, "The President's Visit to London," memo to White House, March 8, 1982, National Security Council, Executive Secretariat Files, U.K. Country Files, box 45, folder "United Kingdom," RRPL.

92. Shipley, memo to Hamilton, March 16, 1982.

93. Charles Z. Wick, memo to Ronald Reagan, April 15, 1982, Michael Deaver Files, box 61, folder, "Wick, Charles Z.," RRPL.

94. Nicholas Henderson, "President Reagan's Visit," memo to U.K. Foreign and Commonwealth Office, February 5, 1982, PREM, ser. 9/942, folder 221; Nicholas Henderson, "President Reagan's Visit," memo to U.K. Foreign and Commonwealth Office, March 8, 1982, ibid., folder 172; Nicholas Henderson, "President Reagan's Visit," memo to U.K. Foreign and Commonwealth Office, March 26, 1982, ibid., folder 69.

95. Michael Schneider, personal communication, January 18, 2021.

96. Robert C. Rowland and John M. Jones, *Reagan at Westminster: Foreshadowing the End of the Cold War* (College Station: Texas A&M University Press, 2010), 64.

97. Ibid., 39.

98. Schneider, personal communication.

99. U.S. Embassy in Paris, to "Report of Conversation from Representatives of White House, State Department, and Information Communication Agency," memo to U.S. Information Communication Agency, May 17, 1982, David Gergen Files, box 7, folder "Nuclear Freeze," RRPL.

100. Rowland and Jones, *Reagan at Westminster*, 48.

101. Gifford Malone, "Function of Diplomatic Organs," in *Public Diplomacy: USA vs. USSR*, ed. Richard Staar (Stanford, CA: Hoover Institution Press, 1986); Fletcher Schoen and Christopher J. Lamb, *Deception, Disinformation, and Strategic Communications: How One Interagency Group Made a Major Difference* (Washington, DC: National Defense University Press, 2012).

102. Ronald Reagan, "Address to Members of the British Parliament," speech, June 8, 1982, London, https://www.presidency.ucsb.edu.

103. Carnes Lord, "In Defense of Public Diplomacy," *Commentary* 77, no. 4 (1984): 42–50.

104. Richard Pipes, "Ash Heap of History: President Reagan's Westminster Address 20 Years Later," speech, June 3, 1982, Heritage Foundation, Washington, DC, https://www.c-span.org.

105. Strategy Board for American Security Council Foundation for Coalition for Peace through Strength, *A Strategy for Peace through Strength* (Boston, VA, 1984), esp., 65, 87, 96, 181.

106. George Urban, *Radio Free Europe and the Pursuit of Democracy: My War within the Cold War* (New Haven, CT: Yale University Press, 1997), 71.

107. Rowland and Jones, *Reagan at Westminster*, 52.

108. BJM Research Partners, "Life in Britain: Exploratory In-Depth Research Findings," August 13, 1982, Conservative Central Office (hereafter CCO Records), Conservative Party Archives, box 180, series 25/1/31, WLSC.

109. Rowland and Jones, *Reagan at Westminster*, 64.

110. "Anti-Reagan Protest Draws 115,000 in London," *UPI*, June 6, 1982. Contemporary analysis indicates that the press underreported the crowd size; see Candy Atherton, "General Election Strategy Reports from Workshops Held at Annual Conference," Winter 1982–83, CND Records, box 1/1/2.

111. Atherton, "General Election Strategy Reports from Workshops held at Annual Conference."

112. Ibid.

113. Matthew Grimley, "Thatcherism, Morality, and Religion" in *Making Thatcher's Britain,* ed. Ben Jackson and Robert Saunders (Cambridge: Cambridge University Press, 2012), 85.

114. David Martin, "The Christian Ethic and Security and Deterrence," in *Unholy Warfare: The Church and the Bomb,* ed. David Martin and Peter Mullen (Oxford: Blackwell, 1983), 96–97.

115. Paul Oestreicher, "Replant the Peace Gospel," *Sanity* (March–April 1981).

116. Pope John Paul II, "Holy Mass of Pentecost: Homily of John Paul II," speech, May 30, 1982, Coventry, UK, http://www.vatican.va.

117. Philip Bolsover, "Briefing—Hard Rock and Square Leg," September 1981, CND Records, box 5/6.

118. Ken Coates, *The Most Dangerous Decade: World Militarism and the New Non-Aligned Peace Movement* (Nottingham, UK: Bertrand Russell House, 1984), 79.

119. *West Yorkshire Peace Newsletter* (December 1981–January 1982), Papers of the Nuclear

Weapons Freeze Campaign (hereafter NWFC Papers), box 1, Western History Manuscript Collection (hereafter WHMC), State Historical Society of Missouri.

120. Philip Bolsover, *Civil Defence: The Cruellest Confidence Trick* (Nottingham: Russell, 1982).

121. Spence, "Hard Rock/Hard Luck Pack."

122. Hard Rock Working Group, meeting minutes, April 27, 1982, CND Records, box 5/6.

123. "SANA and Hard Rock," *SANA Newsletter* 5 (November 1982), Dorothy Hodgkin Personal Papers, folder MS.ENG.C.5688, WLSC; David Caplin [for SANA], "Draft Civil Defense Regulations 1983," October 17, 1983, U.K. Home Office Records (hereafter HO Records), ser. 322, folder 1085, TNA.

124. "SANA and Hard Rock."

125. Owen Greene, Barry Rubin, and Neil Turok, *London after the Bomb: What Nuclear Attack Really Means* (Oxford: Oxford University Press, 1982), 14–16.

126. Ibid., 45–55.

127. Ibid., 51–52, 64–67.

128. Ibid.

129. Robert Poole and Steve Wright, *Target North-West: Civil Defense and Nuclear War in Region 10* (Manchester, UK: Manchester Free Press, 1982); Philip Bolsover, "Brighton Hard Rock," June 1982, CND Records, box 5/6; Azzem Qasrawi, Felicitas Wellhoefer, and Fred Stewart, "Ground Zero: The Short Term Effects of a Nuclear Attack on the West Midlands," Fall 1982, Maurice Wilkins Personal Papers, K/PP178/11/21/1, folder "Scientists against Nuclear Arms, 1987–1990," King's College London Archives (hereafter KCLA).

130. Bolsover, "Brighton Hard Rock;" "SANA and Hard Rock."

131. R. Banks, remarks, U.K. House of Commons debate, Hansard, July 29, 1982, vol. 28, cc. 1422–33.

132. "Hard Luck Pack"; Coates, *The Most Dangerous Decade*, 82–85.

133. Coates, *The Most Dangerous Decade*, 82–85.

134. Ibid., 82–83.

135. William Whitelaw, remarks, U.K. House of Commons debate, Hansard, July 14, 1982, vol. 27, cc. 395W; Margaret Thatcher, remarks, U.K. House of Commons Debate, Hansard, July 15, 1982, vol. 27, cc. 1164–68.

136. William Whitelaw, memo to John Nott, June 1982, HO Records, ser. 322, folder 1021; William Whitelaw, "Exercise Hard Rock and Civil Defense Policy," July 9, 1982, ibid.

137. Labour Campaign for Nuclear Disarmament, meeting minutes, October 24, 1982, CND Records, ser. 6/4; Labour Campaign for Nuclear Disarmament, "A Time of Opportunity: Labour CND Annual Report," 1981, ibid.

138. Bruce Kent, "General Secretary's Report to the CND Conference," November 26, 1982, CND Records, box 1/1/2.

139. Bishop of Salisbury's Working Group, *The Church and the Bomb*, 59–60.

140. Ibid., 60.

141. Ibid., 62, 132.

142. Ibid., 95–98.

143. "Record of Meeting between FCO Secretary Carrington and Free Church Federal Council Delegation," September 22, 1981, FCO Records, 46/2745; Bishop of Salisbury's Working Group, *The Church and the Bomb*, 158–59.

144. John Nott, "Nuclear Issues," October 20, 1982, PREM, ser. 19/979 f349.

145. Caspar Weinberger, "Meeting between Secretary Weinberger and Prime Minster Thatcher," memo to William Clark and George Shultz, September 8, 1982, National Security Council, European and Soviet Directorate Files, box 91330, RRPL; Nott, "Nuclear Issues."

146. "Women and the Beacon of Peace," *Sanity* (February 1983); Maggie O'Kane, "Base Fears: Women at Greenham," *Magill,* December 30, 1983; Ann Snitow, "Holding the Line at Greenham: Being Joyously Political in Dangerous Times," *Mother Jones* 10 (February–March 1985): 30–47.
147. "Women and the Beacon of Peace"; O'Kane, "Base Fears."
148. "Is Fence Cutting Violent?," *Greenham Common Newsletter* (1983), Jayne Nelson Papers (hereafter 7JAN), 2012/16, box 3, LSE Special Collections.
149. Kent, "General Secretary's Report to the CND Conference," November 26, 1982; Bruce Kent, "General Secretary's Report," June 27, 1983, CND Records, box 1/1/2.
150. James Hinton, "A Parliament for Survival; A Note on CND's General Election Strategy," November 1, 1982, CND Records, box 1/4.
151. Neville Pressley, "Parliamentary and Elections Committee: Its Roles and Political Context," 1982, CND Records, ser. 1/7.
152. Francis Pym, "Nuclear Weapons and Public Opinion," memo to Margaret Thatcher, January 7, 1983, PREM, ser. 19/1690, f220.
153. Bernard Ingham, memo to [John] Coles, December 17, 1982, ibid., ser. 19/1690; Bernard Ingham, "Nuclear Weapons and Public Opinion," memo to Margaret Thatcher, January 28, 1983, ibid.
154. Max Beloff, "The Anti-CND Campaign" (part 1), memo to Margaret Thatcher, December 14, 1982, THCR, ser. 1/4/2 f9.
155. Max Beloff, "The Anti-CND Campaign" (part 2), memo to Margaret Thatcher, December 14, 1982, ibid.

Chapter Three: An Antinuclear Awakening

1. On the collapse of the New Deal order, see Steve Fraser and Gary Gerstle, *Rise and Fall of the New Deal Order, 1930–1980* (Princeton, NJ: Princeton University Press, 1990).
2. William Moomaw, "Scientists Diplomats or Diplomat Scientists: Who Makes Science Diplomacy Effective," *Global Policy* 9 (November 2018): 78–80.
3. Theodore Hesburgh, "The Nuclear Dilemma: The Greatest Moral Problem of All Time," speech, May 12, 1988, Eighth Annual Morgenthau Memorial Lecture, Carnegie Council for Ethics in International Affairs, New York City.
4. Marjorie Hyer, "Apostolic Delegate to U.S. Reassigned by Pope," *Washington Post,* June 28, 1980.
5. William Greider, "The Power of the Cross," *Rolling Stone,* April 28, 1983.
6. Jim Castelli, *The Bishops and the Bomb: Waging Peace in a Nuclear Age* (New York: Doubleday, 1983), 13–25.
7. William A. Au, *The Cross, the Flag, and the Bomb: American Catholics Debate War and Peace, 1960–1983* (Westport, CT: Greenwood, 1985), 249.
8. U.S. Conference of Catholic Bishops, "The Gospel of Peace and the Danger of War," statement, February 15, 1978.
9. John Quinn, "Remarks as President of National Council of Catholic Bishops, on President Carter's Decision to Defer Production of Neutron Warheads," statement, April 14, 1978; James Casey, "Another Holocaust? The Nuclear Arms Race," statement, April 29, 1978; Harold Ford and Francis Winters, *Ethics and Nuclear Strategy* (Maryknoll, NY: Orbis, 1977).
10. Kenneth Himes, "Deterrence and Disarmament: Ethical Evaluations and Pastoral Advice," *Cross Currents* 33 (Winter 1983–84): 421–31.
11. U.S. Senate, Committee on Foreign Relations, testimony of John Krol, hearings on SALT II Treaty, 96th Congress, September 18, 1979.

12. Barbara Molony and Jennifer Nelson, *Women's Activism and "Second-Wave" Feminism* (London: Bloomsbury, 2017), 4–5.

13. Carl Sagan, memo to Richard Garwin, June 5, 1984, Seth MacFarlane Collection of the Carl Sagan and Ann Druyan Archive (hereafter MacFarlane Collection), box 818, folder 3, Manuscript Division, Library of Congress; Helen Caldicott, personal communication, September 4, 2017.

14. Randy Kehler, "Draft of Strategy Paper," memo to Freeze Strategy Committee, February 9, 1981, NWFC Papers, box 7.

15. Rod Morris, memo to Randy Kehler, March 11, 1981, ibid.; WGBH Television, "Missile Experimental: Interview with Randy Kehler," *War and Peace in the Nuclear Age*, November 24, 1987, WGBH Media Library and Archives, https://openvault.wgbh.org; Douglas C. Waller, *Congress and the Nuclear Freeze: An Inside Look at the Politics of a Mass Movement* (Amherst, MA: University of Massachusetts Press, 1987), 36–37.

16. Kehler, "Draft of Strategy Paper."

17. Richard Halloran, "Weinberger Begins Drive for Big Rise in Military Budget," *New York Times*, March 5, 1981; Headrick Smith, "How Many Billions for Defense?," *New York Times*, November 1, 1981; William Hartung, *The Economic Consequences of a Nuclear Freeze* (New York: New York Council on Economic Priorities, 1984), 44.

18. Gary Guenther, *The Implications of a Nuclear Arms Freeze for the U.S. Economy in the Short Run* (Washington, DC: Congressional Research Service, August 1982); Gordon Adams, *The Iron Triangle: The Politics of Defense Contracting* (New Brunswick, NJ: Transaction, 1982); Robert W. DeGrasse, Jr., *Military Expansion, Economic Decline: The Impact of Military Spending on U.S. Economic Performance* (New York: Council on Economic Priorities, 1983); Hartung, *The Economic Consequences of a Nuclear Freeze*.

19. Seymour Melman, *Disarmament: Its Politics and Economics* (Washington, DC: American Academy of Arts and Sciences, 1962); Seymour Melman, *The Defense Economy: Conversion of Industries and Occupations to Civilian Needs* (New York: Praeger, 1970); Seymour Melman, *Pentagon Capitalism: The Political Economy of War* (New York: McGraw-Hill, 1970).

20. Milton Katz, *Ban the Bomb: A History of SANE, the Committee for a Sane Nuclear Policy* (New York: Greenwood, 1986), 142

21. "SANE: The Third Decade," n.d., SANE Papers, series G, box 17, Swarthmore College Peace Collection (hereafter SCPC).

22. Steve Ladd, "National Freeze Strategy: Broadening the Base and Increasing Our Political Influence," January 3, 1981, NWFC Papers, box 7; Kehler, "Draft of Strategy Paper"; Corinna Gardner, "The Movement in Black and White," *Nuclear Times* (August–September 1983).

23. Vincent J. Intondi, *African Americans against the Bomb: Nuclear Weapons, Colonialism, and the Black Freedom Movement* (Stanford, CA: Stanford University Press, 2015), 95–96.

24. Nuclear Network, "The Black Participation Project," March 7, 1983, NWFC, box 4; David McReynolds, "Memo on Events in June," January 30, 1982, SANE Papers, series G, box 67.

25. Barack Obama, "Breaking the War Mentality," *Sundial*, March 10, 1983. *Sundial* was Columbia University's student newspaper.

26. Intondi, *African Americans against the Bomb*, 93.

27. "Conference Maps Strategy," *Jobs with Peace Network Newsletter* (Winter–Spring 1983), NWFC Papers, box 4.

28. Manning Marable, "Jobs, Peace, Freedom: A Political Assessment of the August 27 March on Washington," *Black Scholar* 14 (December 1983): 5.

29. Sarah Bridger, *Scientists at War: The Ethics of Cold War Weapons Research* (Cambridge, MA: Harvard University Press, 2015), 194–221.

30. Ann Finkbeiner, *The Jasons: The Secret History of Science's Postwar Elite* (New York: Penguin, 2007), 90–118.

31. Jan Brown et al., *Science against the People* (Berkeley, CA: Berkeley Scientists and Engineers for Social and Political Action, 1972); Kelly Moore, *Disrupting Science: Social Movements, American Scientists, and the Politics of the Military, 1945–1975* (Princeton, NJ: Princeton University Press, 2009), 158–189.

32. "Militarism and Science," special issue, *Science for the People* 13 (July–August 1981); Gail Shields, "The Economic Impact of the MX Missile," *Science for the People* 14 (September–October 1982): 6–12.

33. Richard Garwin, "Are Defense Dollars Good for University Research?," *Sipriscope* (September–October 1982).

34. Ibid.

35. Nathaniel Sheppard, Jr., "Concern Grows over Policy on National Labs," *New York Times*, December 8, 1981.

36. Ruth Adams and Susan Cullen, eds., *The Final Epidemic: Physicians and Scientists on Nuclear War* (Chicago: University of Chicago Press, 1981).

37. Finn Aaserud, interview with Henry Kendall, November 26, 1986, Niels Bohr Library and Archives, American Institute of Physics, College Park, MD, https://www.aip.org.

38. Paul Walker, "Teach-ins on American Campuses," *Bulletin of the Atomic Scientists* 38, no. 2 (February 1982): 10–11; "Nuclear Issues Are on the Agenda of Many Colleges," *Chronicle of Higher Education*, March 23, 1983.

39. Frank Barnaby, "Military Scientists," *Bulletin of the Atomic Scientists* 37, no. 6 (June 1981): 11–12.

40. Kurt Waldheim, *Comprehensive Study on Nuclear Weapons* (New York: Autumn Press, 1981), para. 67.

41. W. K. H. Panofsky, "Science, Technology, and the Arms Build-up," *Bulletin of the Atomic Scientists* 37, no. 6 (June 1981): 48–54.

42. Pope John Paul II, "Science and Conscience," *Bulletin of the Atomic Scientists* 37, no. 4 (April 1981): 7–8.

43. James E. Wood, Jr., "The Nuclear Arms Race and the Churches," *Journal of Church and State* 25, no. 2 (Spring 1983): 219–29.

44. The National Conference of Catholic Bishops and the U.S. Catholic Conference merged in 2001 to form the U.S. Conference of Catholic Bishops.

45. Donald Meyer, *A Winter of Discontent: The Nuclear Freeze and American Politics* (New York: Praeger, 1990), 50–51.

46. George Sommaripa, "National Strategy for Achieving a Nuclear Freeze," November 13, 1981, NWFC Papers, box 7.

47. Jared McBrady, "The Challenge of Peace: Ronald Reagan, John Paul II, and the American Bishops," *Journal of Cold War Studies* 17, no. 1 (2015): 132.

48. Au, *The Cross, the Flag, and the Bomb,* 207.

49. "Religious Perspectives on the Nuclear Weapons Debate: Excerpts from the Bishop's Pastoral Letter on War and Peace, Proposed Third Draft," *Science, Technology, and Human Values* 8 (Summer 1983): 14; Castelli, *The Bishops and the Bomb,* 78–85.

50. McBrady, "The Challenge of Peace," 144.

51. Bradford Hinze, "Whatever Happened to the Way the U.S. Bishops Prepared *The Challenge of Peace?*," *New Theology Review* 21, no. 2 (May 2008): 16–25.

52. Frances Fitzgerald, *Way Out There in the Blue: Reagan, Star Wars, and the End of the Cold War* (New York: Simon and Schuster, 2000); Wittner, *Toward Nuclear Abolition*, 193.

53. Lawrence Feinberg, "GU President Assails Moral Majority and Reagan's Program," *Washington Post,* October 2, 1981.

54. Castelli, *The Bishops and the Bomb*, 40.
55. Mark Shields, "Keeping the Catholics," *New York Times*, February 19, 1982.
56. Herman Kahn, *On Thermonuclear War* (Princeton, NJ: Princeton University Press, 1960); Johnathan Schell, *The Fate of the Earth* (New York: Knopf, 1982).
57. Sharon Ghamari-Tabrizi, *The Worlds of Herman Kahn* (Cambridge, MA: Harvard University Press, 2005), 203–80.
58. Charles Percy Snow, *The Two Cultures* (London: Cambridge University Press, 1959).
59. Jonathan Hogg, *British Nuclear Culture: Official and Unofficial Narratives in the Long Twentieth Century* (London: Bloomsbury Academic, 2016), 137.
60. Peter McGrath, "The Nuclear Book Boom," *Newsweek*, April 12, 1982.
61. WGBH Television, "Missile Experimental: Interview with Douglas Waller," *War and Peace in the Nuclear Age*, November 24, 1987, WGBH Media Library and Archives, http://openvault.wgbh.org.
62. WGBH Television, "Missile Experimental: Randy Kehler."
63. Angela Santese, "Ronald Reagan, the Nuclear Weapons Freeze Campaign, and the Nuclear Scare of the 1980s," *International History Review* 39, no. 3 (2017): 503.
64. Edward Kennedy, memo to Carl Sagan, March 10, 1982, MacFarlane Collection, box 846, folder 3; William Proxmire, memo to Carl Sagan, March 23, 1982, ibid., folder 6; Alan Cranston, record of press conference, March 25, 1982, ibid., box 844, folder 7; Albert Gore, Jr., memo to Carl Sagan, October 4, 1982, ibid., box 846, folder 1.
65. Daniel Akaka, memo to Carl Sagan, March 15, 1982, ibid., box 844, folder 5.
66. See R. P. Turco, O. B. Toon, T. P. Ackerman, J. B. Pollack, and Carl Sagan, "Nuclear Winter: Global Consequences of Multiple Nuclear Explosions," *Science,* December 23, 1983, 1283–92.
67. Patricia Williams, memo to Randy Kehler, March 22, 1983, NWFC Papers, box 2.
68. Peter Perl, "Hundreds Launch 'Ground Zero' Week Here," *Washington Post*, April 19, 1982.
69. William Clark, "Policy Offensive on Arms Control and the Anti-Nuclear Movement," memo to Edwin Meese, James Baker, and Michael Deaver, April 22, 1982, David Gergen Files, box 7, folder "Nuclear Freeze," RRPL.
70. Caroline Rand Heron and William Rhoden, "The Nation in Summary; Welcome to Ground Zero, All You Folks," *New York Times*, April 25, 1982; Waller, *Congress and the Nuclear Freeze*, 69.
71. Stephanie DeAbreu, "Mounting Concern over Nuclear War Begins to Involve Nation's Schools," *Education Week*, April 7, 1982.
72. Robert Devine, "Promoting Nuclear Literacy," *Nuclear Times* (September 1984); John Arnold and Ellen Storey Vasu, "Teaching about Nuclear Disarmament: Attitudes of Middle Level Teachers," *Middle School Research Selected Studies* 13, no. 1 (1988): 1–11.
73. On concerns of early Cold War mothers, see Toshihiro Higuchi, *Political Fallout: Nuclear Weapons Testing and the Making of a Global Environmental Crisis* (Stanford, CA: Stanford University Press, 2020).
74. Several other studies analyzed the views of children, leading to controversy over the validity of the Harvard team's findings. See Michael Kernan, "Children in Fear of Nuclear War," *Washington Post*, October 14, 1983; Fox Butterfield, "Experts Disagree on Children's Worries about Nuclear War," *New York Times,* October 16, 1984; and D. J. R. Bruckner, "Ideas and Trends; Children's Nuclear-War Fears in Dispute, *New York Times,* June 23, 1985.
75. Eric Chivian, John Mack, J. P. Waletzky, C. Lazaroff, R. Doctor, and J. M. Goldenring, "Soviet Children and the Threat of Nuclear War: A Preliminary Study," *American Journal of Orthopsychiatry* 55, no. 4 (1985): 484–502.

76. "The Dirt on T. K. Jones," *New York Times*, March 19, 1982; Robert Scheer, *With Enough Shovels: Reagan, Bush, and Nuclear War* (New York: Random House, 1982).

77. Metta Winter, "Survivalism in the Schools," *Nuclear Times* (March 1983).

78. Educators for Social Responsibility, annual report, 1985, Physicians for Social Responsibility Records, box 48-A, S2, SCPC.

79. Red Cavaney, "Summer Initiatives: An Overview," memo to Michael Deaver, April 16, 1982, Elizabeth Dole Files, box 40, folder "Nuclear Freeze," RRPL.

80. Clark, "Policy Offensive on Arms Control and the Anti-Nuclear Movement."

81. Alexander Haig, "Address to Georgetown University's Center for Strategic and International Studies," speech, April 6, 1982, David Gergen Files, box 7, folder "Nuclear Freeze," RRPL.

82. Reinhold Niebuhr, "Our Moral and Spiritual Resources for International Cooperation," U.S. National Commission for UNESCO Working Paper (Washington, DC: Government Printing Office, 1956), 36.

83. "Minutes of Interagency Coordinating Committee for U.S.-Soviet Affairs Meeting: Overview of U.S.-Soviet Relations," April 26, 1982, *FRUS*, 1981–89, vol. 3, Soviet Union, January 1981–January 1983, doc. 164.

84. Thomas Melady, "Seizing the Peace Initiative in the Catholic Church," memo to James Baker, April 13, 1982, Elizabeth Dole Files, box 40, folder "Nuclear Freeze," RRPL.

85. John A. McCoy, *A Still and Quiet Conscience: The Archbishop Who Challenged a Pope, a President, and a Church* (New York: Orbis, 2015), 25; Jim Wallis, ed., *Peacemakers: Christian Voices from the New Abolitionist Movement* (New York: Harper and Row, 1983), 28.

86. Wittner, *Toward Nuclear Abolition*, 171.

87. "How the 'Peace Bishops' Got That Way," *Washington Post*, December 27, 1981.

88. McBrady, "The Challenge of Peace," 130–31, 148–49.

89. Marie Gayte, "The Vatican and the Reagan Administration: A Cold Warrior Alliance?," *Catholic Historical Review* 97, no. 4 (2011): 713–36.

90. Across the country there were antinuclear demonstrations conducted in solidarity with the SSOD march: for instance, 100,000 people gathered in the Rose Bowl in Pasadena ("100,000 Jam Rose Bowl for Disarmament Rally," *New York Times*, June 7, 1982).

91. Steve Ladd, "National Freeze Strategy: Broadening the Base and Increasing Our Political Influence," January 3, 1981, NWFC Papers, box 7.

92. Paul Montgomery, "Throngs Fill Manhattan to Protest Nuclear Weapons," *New York Times*, June 13, 1982.

93. Paul Bremer, "Public Affairs Strategy in Support of Administration's Nuclear Policy," memo to William Clark, May 5, 1982, William MacFarlane Papers, box 1, RRPL; Red Cavaney, "Nuclear Freeze Private Sector Resources," memo to Robert MacFarlane, April 30, 1982, Sven Kraemer Files, box 6, folder "Nuclear Freeze," RRPL; Morton Blackwell, "Advisor Lists: Limited Government/Conservative Groups," memo to Elizabeth Dole, n.d., Elizabeth Dole Files, box 40, folder, "Nuclear Freeze," RRPL.

94. Cavaney, "Nuclear Freeze Private Sector Resources."

95. Herman Kahn, "Thinking about Nuclear Morality," *New York Times*, June 13, 1982.

96. Ibid.

97. Ernest W. Lefever and Stephen Hunt, eds., *The Apocalyptic Premise: Nuclear Arms Debated: Thirty-One Essays by Statesmen, Scholars, Religious Leaders, and Journalists* (New York: Scarecrow, 1982).

98. Phyllis Schlafly and Chester Ward, *Kissinger on the Couch* (New York: Arlington House, 1975), 753.

99. Lynn Rosellini, "Victory Is Bittersweet for Architect of Amendment's Downfall," *New*

York Times, July 1, 1982; Rosemary Chalk, "Women and the National Security Debate," *Bulletin of the Atomic Scientists* 38, no. 7 (1982): 44–46.

100. Ronald Reagan, "Remarks at the Centennial Meeting of the Supreme Council of the Knights of Columbus," speech, Hartford, CT, August 3, 1982. https://www.presidency.ucsb.edu.

101. Theresa Keeley, *Reagan's Gun-Toting Nuns: The Catholic Conflict over Cold War Human Rights Policy in Central America* (Ithaca, NY: Cornell University Press, 2020).

102. Marjorie Hyer, "Influencing the Catholic Bishops," *Washington Post*, November 15, 1982.

103. Colman McCarthy, "The Crossing of the Bishops: Michael Novak, Catholic Critic: His Journey from McGovern to Reagan," *Washington Post*, May 11, 1983.

104. Nicholas Cull, *The Cold War and the United States Information Agency: American Propaganda and Public Diplomacy, 1945–1989* (New York: Cambridge University Press, 2008), 405.

105. Michael Novak, "American Bishops and Nuclear Disarmament," *Wall Street Journal*, January 14, 1982; Michael Novak, "Arms and the Church," *Commentary* (March 1982): 37–41; Michael Novak, "Arms and the Poor," *National Review*, September 3, 1982; Michael Novak, "A Layman's Dissent," *Time*, November 8, 1982.

106. Rael Jean Isaac and Erich Isaac, "The Counterfeit Peacemakers," *American Spectator*, reprinted in Lefever and Hunt, *The Apocalyptic Premise*, 163.

107. Philip H. Dougherty, "Advertising; *Reader's Digest* Cuts Rate Base," *New York Times*, September 10, 1985.

108. John Barron, "The KGB's Magical War for Peace," September 28, 1982, CIA-ERR.

109. Jack Matlock Files, box 44, folders "World Peace Council" 1–4, RRPL.

110. U.S. Department of State, Bureau of Public Affairs, "Soviet Active Measures: An Update," Special Report 101, (Washington, DC, July 1982).

111. Vladimir Bukovsky, "Better Red Than Dead Is Not Good Enough," *Times*, December 4, 1981; Vladimir Bukovsky, "The Peace Movement and the Soviet Union," *Commentary* (May 1982), https://www.commentary.org.

112. Kiron Skinner, Annelise Anderson, and Martin Anderson, *Reagan in His Own Hand: The Writings of Ronald Reagan That Reveal His Revolutionary Vision for America* (New York: Free Press, 2001), 149–50.

113. Joanne Omang, "Soviet Effort in Nuclear Freeze Rally Cited," *Washington Post*, December 10, 1982.

114. William Clark, "Nuclear Freeze," memo to James Baker, August 16, 1982, David Gergen Files, box 7, folder "Nuclear Freeze," RRPL.

115. Judith Miller, "Nuclear Freeze: Both Sides Term It a Victory," *New York Times,* August 7, 1982; Waller, *Congress and the Nuclear Freeze*, 161.

116. "National Strategy Task Force," Summer 1982, NWFC Papers, box 7; "Freeze Hearings," *Public Interest Report of the Federation of American Scientists* 35 (October 1982); "Model Freeze," *Public Interest Report of the Federation of American Scientists* 35 (December 1982); "Freeze Hearings, Part II," *Public Interest Report of the Federation of American Scientists* 36 (February 1983); "Freeze Hearings, Part III," *Public Interest Report of the Federation of American Scientists* 36 (May 1983).

117. U.S. House of Representatives, Committee on Science and Technology, Subcommittee on Investigations and Oversight, "The Consequences of Nuclear War on the Global Environment," hearing, 97th Cong., 2nd sess., September 15, 1982.

118. Citizen's Congress on National Security, "Issue Brief Four," November 18–20, 1983, MacFarlane Collection, box 808, folder 2.

119. Lawrence Badash, *A Nuclear Winter's Tale: Science and Politics in the 1980s* (Cambridge: MIT Press, 2009), 120.

120. Various firsthand accounts describe Reagan's introduction to strategic defense. See

Edward Teller, *Better a Shield Than a Sword: Perspectives on Defense and Technology* (New York: Free Press, 1987); and Martin Anderson, *Revolution* (New York: Harcourt, 1988).

121. William Clark, "Your Meeting with Edward Teller," memo to Ronald Reagan, September 13, 1982, Edwin Meese Files, box 5, folder "NF-CFOA 415," RRPL; Donald Baucom, interview with George Keyworth, September 28, 1987, in *The Reagan Files: The Strategic Defense Initiative*, ed. Jason Saltoun-Ebin, www.thereaganfiles.com.

122. Edward Teller, memo to Ronald Reagan, July 23, 1982, George Keyworth Files, box 15, folder "Teller Edward," RRPL.

123. "Early Warnings," *Nuclear Times* 1 (October 1982).

124. William Lanouette, "James D. Watkins: Frustrated Admiral of Energy," *Bulletin of the Atomic Scientists* 46, no. 1 (1990): 36–42.

125. Sydell Gold, "Letter from Edward Teller to the President," memo to William Clark, Edwin Meese Files, box 5, folder "NF-CFOA 415," RRPL.

126. Clark, "Your Meeting with Edward Teller."

127. Robert McFarlane, "Report of the Nuclear Arms Control Information Policy Working Group," memo to James Baker, August 27, 1982, David Gergen Files, box 7, folder "Nuclear Freeze," RRPL; Robert Sims, "Nuclear Freeze," memo to David Gergen, September 3, 1982, ibid., box 8, folder "Nuclear Freeze."

128. Thomas Graham, Jr., "Freeze Resolutions and Referenda," memo to Robert Dean, August 17, 1982, Robert McFarlane Files, box 1, folder "Arms Control; INF," RRPL.

129. Mark Niedergang, "Winning the Freeze: A Peace Movement Program for the Future," November 1982, NWFC Papers, box 7.

130. Randy Kehler, "Minutes of the Executive Committee Meeting of August 13, 1982," memo to Executive Committee, September 8, 1982, ibid., box 2; Randy Kehler, "Minutes of the Executive Committee Meeting," September 28, 1982, ibid.

131. Randy Kehler, "Minutes of the Executive Committee Meeting," September 28, 1982, ibid.

132. Kathy Sawyer, "Voter Registration Is Increasing: Reversing Two-Decade Trend," *Washington Post*, December 27, 1983; Rhodes Cook, "Voter Turnout and Congressional Change," *Pew Research Center* (2006), https://www.pewresearch.org.

133. "1982 Election Report," *Peace Pac* (November 1982); "The 1982 Election," *Bulletin of the Atomic Scientists* 39, no. 1 (1983): 56–57; Waller, *Congress and the Nuclear Freeze*, 165.

Chapter Four: Determined to Deter

1. Walter Cronkite, host, "The Great Nuclear Arms Debate," *CBS News*, April 23, 1983, National Security Council Records, European and Soviet Affairs Directorate, box RAC 12, folder "Public Diplomacy 1983," RRPL; William Holstein, "Cronkite Tapes Great Nuclear Debate," *United Press International*, April 22, 1983.

2. Margaret Thatcher, Michael Heseltine, Francis Pym, William Whitelaw, and Cecil Parkinson, "Nuclear Weapons and Public Opinion," record of conversation, January 31, 1983, PREM, ser. 19/1690 f147.

3. Francis Pym, "Nuclear Weapons and Public Opinion," memo to Margaret Thatcher, January 13, 1983, PREM, ser. 19/1690.

4. Francis Pym, "Nuclear Weapons and Public Opinion," memo to Margaret Thatcher, January 7, 1983, ibid.

5. Bruce Kent, "General Secretary's Report to the CND Conference," November 26, 1982, CND Records, box 1/1/2; Greenham Common Women, memo to Campaign for Nuclear Disarmament council, n.d., 7JAN, ser. 2012/16, box 2; "Women Only at Greenham," *Anti-Nuclear Action*, n.d., ibid., box 3; "Debate on Women in the Peace Movement, Part Three," *Sanity* (May 1983).

6. Bernard Ingham, memo to John Coles, December 17, 1982, PREM, ser. 19/1690.

7. Peter Craine, memo to John Coles, December 16, 1982, ibid.

8. Brian Walden, "Victorian Values," interview with Margaret Thatcher, *Weekend World*, January 16, 1983.

9. Margaret Thatcher, "Women in a Changing World," Dame Margery Corbett-Ashby Memorial Lecture, July 26, 1982, CAC.

10. Laura Beers, "Thatcher and the Women's Vote," in *Making Thatcher's Britain*, ed. Ben Jackson and Robert Saunders (Cambridge: Cambridge University Press, 2012), 118–19.

11. Louis Harris Group, "A Survey of Attitudes toward the Family," memo to Conservative Central Office, January 1983, CCO, ser. 180/9/5/4.

12. Leopold Labedz and Melvin Lasky, "Western Europe—US: Visit of EDU Delegation: Outline for a 'Vigorous Information Program,'" January 20, 1983, Walter Raymond Files, box RAC 7, loose materials, RRPL.

13. David Goodall, "Meeting with Roman Catholic Bishops of England and Wales: Nuclear Defense Issues," memo to Foreign and Commonwealth Office, January 14, 1983, THCR, ser. 1/4/7 f4.

14. Ibid.

15. Tanya Ogilvie-White, *On Nuclear Deterrence: The Correspondence of Michael Quinlan* (London: Routledge, 2011), 112–66.

16. Ibid., 142–43; Francis X. Winters, "Nuclear Deterrence Morality: Atlantic Community Bishops in Tension," *Theological Studies* 43, no. 3 (1982): 428–46.

17. Ogilvie-White, *On Nuclear Deterrence*, 149–64.

18. Michael Quinlan, "The Ethics of Nuclear Deterrence: A Criticism of the United States Bishops' Letter," April 16, 1984, PREM, ser. 19/1687 f14.

19. Conservative Research Department, "Alliance Manifesto, 1983," briefing for Margaret Thatcher, May 16, 1983, THCR, ser. 2/7/3/16 f20.

20. Margaret Thatcher, House of Commons parliamentary questions, Hansard, January 18, 1983, vol. 35, cc. 166–70.

21. U.S. Embassy in London, "Public Affairs Handling of Security and Arms Control Issues," memo to U.S. State Department, February 10, 1983, National Security Council, Executive Secretariat, United Kingdom Country Files, box 46, RRPL.

22. U.K. Embassy in Bonn, "Chancellor Kohl's Visit," memo to Foreign and Commonwealth Office, January 26, 1983, PREM, ser. 19/1037 f297; U.K. Embassy in Bonn, "Visit of Chancellor Kohl (and Herr Genscher)," memo to Foreign and Commonwealth Office, February 2, 1983, ibid., ser. 19/1037 f211; U.K. Prime Minister's Office, record of conversation between Margaret Thatcher and Helmut Kohl, February 4, 1983, ibid., ser. 19/1037 f165.

23. U.K. Embassy in Bonn, "Visit of Chancellor Kohl (and Herr Genscher)."

24. Oliver Wright, "Vice President Bush's Visit to London," memo to Foreign and Commonwealth Office, February 4, 1983, PREM, ser. 19/973 f212.

25. U.S. Embassy in Washington, "Public Affairs Handling of Security and Arms Control Issues," memo to U.S. State Department, February 10, 1983, National Security Council, Executive Secretariat, U.K. Country Files, box 46, RRPL.

26. John Vinocur, "Bush Finds Allies Open on Arms Pact," *New York Times*, February 11, 1983.

27. U.K. Embassy in Rome, "Visit of Vice President Bush," memo to Foreign and Commonwealth Office, February 8, 1983, PREM, ser. 19/973.

28. Ronald Reagan, memo to Margaret Thatcher, February 16, 1983, ibid., ser. 19/979.

29. R. B. Bone, "INF," memo to Margaret Thatcher, March 17, 1983, ibid.

30. Mr. Beavan, "Secretary of State's Meeting with Shultz at Palo-Alto on March 3: INF," memo to Foreign and Commonwealth Office, March 4, 1983, ibid.

31. Ronald Reagan, "Remarks at the Annual Conference of the American Legion," speech, February 22, 1983, https://www.reaganlibrary.gov.

32. "Tarzan's War: Minister Felled by Peace Women," *Daily Mirror*, February 8, 1983; "UK Minister Dragged to the Ground: Protestors Besiege Heseltine," *Globe and Mail*, February 8, 1983.

33. Julia Emberley and Donna Landry, "Coverage of Greenham and Greenham as 'Coverage,'" *Feminist Studies* 15, no. 3 (1989): 497.

34. Roger Ruston, *A Say in the End of the World: Morals and British Nuclear Weapons Policy, 1941–1987* (Oxford: Clarendon, 1989),

35. Francis Pym, "Nuclear Weapons and Public Opinion," memo to Margaret Thatcher, January 7, 1983, PREM. ser. 19/1690.

36. Graham Leonard, "The Morality of Nuclear Deterrence," in *Unholy Warfare: The Church and the Bomb,* ed. David Martin and Peter Mullen (Oxford: Blackwell, 1983).

37. Graham Leonard, "A Fragile Peace," in *The Cross and the Bomb: Christian Ethics and the Nuclear Debate*, ed. Francis Bridger (London: Mowbray, 1983), 5–24.

38. Paul Oestreicher, "Lord, make us reject the Bomb—but not yet," *Sanity* (April 1983).

39. Ibid.

40. Francis Pym, memo to the General Synod of the Church of England, February 24, 1983, PREM, ser. 19/1690 f116.

41. David Goodall, "Meeting with Roman Catholic Bishops of England and Wales: Nuclear Defense Issues," memo to Foreign and Commonwealth Office, January 14, 1983, THCR, ser. 1/4/7 f4; Ogilvie-White, *On Nuclear Deterrence*, 149.

42. Basil Hume, "Towards a Nuclear Morality," *Times*, November 17, 1983.

43. Steve Dorril, "American Friends: The Anti-CND Groups," *Lobster* 3 (February 1984).

44. Labour Campaign for Nuclear Disarmament, "Executive Committee Meeting Minutes," March 12, 1983, CND Records, box 6/4; James Hinton, "A Parliament for Survival; A Note on CND's General Election Strategy," November 1, 1982, ibid., box 1/4.

45. Candy Atherton, "General Election Strategy Reports from Workshops held at Annual Conference" (Winter 1982–83), ibid., box 1/1/2.

46. Labour Campaign for Nuclear Disarmament, memo to Campaign for Nuclear Disarmament National Council, June 18, 1983, ibid., box 6/4.

47. Campaign for Nuclear Disarmament, "Meeting Minutes of the CND Council," January 15–16, 1983, ibid., box 1/1.

48. Patrick Mayhew, "Report of the BMA Inquiry into the Medical Effects of Nuclear War," memo to prime minister's staff, March 3, 1983, HO Records, ser. 322/1027.

49. Philip Steadman, personal communication, April 6, 2018.

50. J. A. Howard, "British Medical Association—Inquiry into the Medical Effects of Nuclear War," HO Records, series 322/1027; Mayhew, "Report of the BMA Inquiry into the Medical Effects of Nuclear War"; British Broadcasting Corporation, "BBC Interview with Michael Heseltine," *BBC News*, March 3, 1983, HO Records, series 322/1027.

51. Alun Chalfont, "The Great Unilateralist Illusion," *Encounter* (April 1983): 18–38.

52. Alastair Burnet, interview with Michael Heseltine, April 3, 1983, *TV Eye*, Thames TV.

53. Paul Chilton, *Language and the Nuclear Arms Debate: Nukespeak Today* (Dover, NH: Pinter, 1985), 13.

54. WGBH Television, "Zero Hour: Interview with Michael Heseltine," *War and Peace in the Nuclear Age,* April 11, 1987, WGBH Media Library and Archives, http://openvault.wgbh.org.

55. Ibid.

56. Margaret Thatcher, memo to Ronald Reagan, March 21, 1983, PREM, ser. 19/979; Ronald Reagan, memo to Margaret Thatcher, March 23, 1983, ibid.

57. Margaret Thatcher, memo to Ronald Reagan, March 24, 1983, ibid.; Ronald Reagan, memo to Margaret Thatcher, March 29, 1983, ibid.

58. Ronald Reagan, "National Security Decision Directive (NSDD) 86: U.S. Approach to INF Negotiations," March 28, 1983, National Security Council, Executive Secretariat Records, 1981–87, box RAC 5, RRPL.

59. William Clark, "National Security Planning Group Meeting," March 18, 1983, National Security Council, Executive Secretariat, National Security Planning Group, 1981–87, box 91306, RRPL.

60. WGBH Television, "Zero Hour: Heseltine."

61. R. B. Bone, "Letters from the Public on Nuclear Disarmament," memo to A. J. Coles, March 31, 1983, PREM, ser. 19/1690 f100.

62. WGBH Television "Zero Hour: Heseltine."

63. "Projects Committee Report to National Council," April 16–17, 1983, CND Records, box 5/3; "Human Chain Links Nuclear Sites," *BBC on This Day*, April 1, 1983, http://news.bbc.co.uk.

64. "What Do We Think the Camp Is?: Camp Meeting Minutes," July 21, 1983, 7JAN, ser. 2012/16, box 3.

65. Christopher Moores, "Opposition to Greenham Women's Peace Camps in 1980's Britain: RAGE against the 'Obscene,'" *History Workshop Journal* 78, no. 1 (2014): 207.

66. Olga Maitland and Rosemary Brown, memo to Christian Campaign for Nuclear Disarmament, May 13, 1982, CND Records, box "Christian CND, 1982–1985"; "Peace Pentecost," *Ploughshares: News from Christian CND* (Summer 1983), ibid.; M. A. Pakenham, "Year-End Assessment of Public Nuclear Debate," December 20, 1984, FCO, ser. 46/4188.

67. Moores, "Opposition to Greenham Women's Peace Camps in 1980's Britain," 207.

68. Lois Romano, "Lady for the Defense," *Washington Post*, October 20, 1983; Myra MacPherson, "Lady Olga for Defense," *Washington Post*, July 20, 1986.

69. "Unclassified Summary of Public Positions on INF," January 31, 1983, National Security Council, Subject Files, box 23, RRPL.

70. "Private Sector Initiatives in U.S. Public Diplomacy" (March–April 1983), ibid., box 27.

71. *Nuclear Times,* January 1983.

72. WGBH Television, "Zero Hour: Heseltine."

73. Philip Kawior and Frank Fahrenkopf, "The 1983 British General Election," June 20, 1983, CCO Records, ser. 180/28/1; Peter Cropper, "The General Election Campaign of 1983: A CRD View," June 29, 1983, CRD Records, box 4/30/6.

74. Conservative Research Department, "The Vital Issue," daily notes, no. 7, May 27, 1983, THCR, ser. 2/7/3/22 f55.

75. Dan Smith, "Forward Planning: CND after the Election" (June 1983), CND Records, box 1/1.

76. Meg Beresford, "Report for CND from General Election Unit," June 17, 1983, ibid., box 1/2.

77. W. L. Miller, "There Was No Alternative: The British General Election of 1983," *Parliamentary Affairs* 37, no. 1 (1984): 377.

78. Philip Kawior, "The 1983 British General Election," memo to Frank Fahrenkopf, June 20, 1983, CCO Records, ser. 180/28/1.

79. Conservative Research Department, "People in Glass Houses," May 28, 1983, THCR, ser. 2/7/3/22 f64.

80. Labour won far more seats than the Liberal-SDP alliance did so was not in fear for its status as the official opposition.

81. I. Crewe, "Britain: Two and a Half Cheers for the Atlantic Alliance," in *The Public and Atlantic Defense,* ed. G. Flynn and H. Rattinger (London: Croom Helm, 1985).

82. Of poll respondents, 72 percent named unemployment as the most important issue. See Miller, "There Was No Alternative," 378.

83. Ibid., 365.

84. Adam Roberts, "The Trouble with Unilateralism: The U.K., the 1983 General Election, and Non-Nuclear Defense," *Bulletin of Peace Proposals* 14, no. 4 (1983): 307.

85. MORI, "The Gender Gap," *Ipsos*, July 26, 2001, https://www.ipsos.com.

86. Roger Molander, memo to Randy Kehler, December 7, 1982, NWFC Papers, box 7; WGBH Television, "Missile Experimental: Interview with Randy Kehler," *War and Peace in the Nuclear Age,* November 10, 1987, WGBH Media Library and Archives, http://openvault.wgbh.org; WGBH Television, "Missile Experimental: Interview with Douglas Waller," *War and Peace in the Nuclear Age,* November 24, 1987, ibid.

87. Harry Wren, *Congress Rejects MX Dense Pack Deployment: Prelude to the Strategic Policy Decisions of 1983* (Washington, DC: Library of Congress, Congressional Research Service, April 19, 1983).

88. National Security Council, "START," meeting minutes, April 21, 1982, National Security Council, Executive Secretariat Meeting Files, 1981–87, RRPL.

89. Christopher Paine, "MX: Too Dense for Congress," *Bulletin of the Atomic Scientists 39, no.* 2 (1983): 4.

90. Ibid.

91. Richard Garwin, "Dense Pack—Better than What?," article forwarded to Solly Zuckerman, May 23–24, 1981, Solly Zuckerman Papers, ser. SZ/2/Gen, folder "Garwin," University of East Anglia Special Collections (hereafter Zuckerman Papers).

92. Herbert Scoville, "MX Invites Attack," *New York Times*, December 13, 1982.

93. Wren, *Congress Rejects MX Dense Pack Deployment.*

94. Walter Fauntroy, memo to Randy Kehler, October 31, 1982, NWFC Papers, box 4.

95. Martin Luther King, Jr., Center for Nonviolent Social Change, "Minutes of the National Planning Council," January 13, 1983, ibid.

96. Twentieth-Anniversary Mobilization, "A Call to the Nation" (1983), ibid.

97. Manning Marable, "Jobs, Peace, Freedom: A Political Assessment of the August 27 March on Washington," *Black Scholar* 14 (December 1983): 13.

98. Ibid.

99. Randy Kehler, memo to Nuclear Freeze Strategy Task Force, January 3, 1983, NWFC Papers, box 7; "Draft Strategy Paper for the National Conference 1983," January 5, 1983, ibid.; Randy Forsberg, "Campaign Strategy for 1983," memo to Freeze, January 8, 1983, ibid.

100. David Riley, "Congressional Strategy Opposing First-Strike Weapons," memo to Randy Kehler and Reuben McCornack, January 19, 1983, ibid.; Helen Caldicott, personal communication, April 18, 2018.

101. Edward Teller, memo to Ronald Reagan, July 23, 1982, George Keyworth Files, box 15, folder "Teller, Edward," RRPL.

102. Frances Fitzgerald, *Way Out There in the Blue: Reagan, Star Wars and the End of the Cold War* (New York: Simon and Schuster, 2001), 192–97.

103. Donald Baucom, *The Origins of SDI, 1944–1983* (Lawrence: Kansas University Press, 1992), 358.

104. Ibid.

105. Donald Baucom, interview with George Keyworth, September 28, 1987, in *The Reagan Files: The Strategic Defense Initiative,* ed. Jason Saltoun-Ebin, http://www.thereaganfiles.com.

106. WGBH Television, "Missile Experimental: Interview with James D. Watkins," *War and*

Peace in the Nuclear Age, December 8, 1987, WGBH Media Library and Archives, http://openvault.wgbh.org.

107. Ibid.

108. WGBH Television, "Missile Experimental: Interview with Bud McFarlane," *War and Peace in the Nuclear Age,* December 18, 1987, WGBH Media Library and Archives, http://openvault.wgbh.org.

109. Baucom, *Origins,* 375–80.

110. Ibid.

111. Jeffrey G. Barlow, "The Hard Facts the Nuclear Freeze Ignores," Heritage Foundation, November 3, 1982.

112. Dee Jepsen, "Nuclear Freeze," memo to Red Cavaney, November 16, 1982, Elizabeth Dole Files, box 40, folder "Nuclear Freeze," RRPL.

113. Michael Novak, "Moral Clarity in the Nuclear Age," *Crisis,* March 1, 1983; reprinted, *National Review,* April 1, 1983.

114. Ed Rowny, "START: Congressional Freeze Resolution," memo to U.S. secretaries of state and defense, March 7, 1983, Sven Kraemer Files, box 16, folder "Nuclear Freeze Resolution," RRPL.

115. Ronald Reagan, "Remarks at the Annual Convention of the National Association of Evangelicals," speech, Orlando, FL, March 8, 1983, https://www.presidency.ucsb.edu.

116. Corinna Gardner, "The Movement in Black and White," *Nuclear Times* (August–September 1983).

117. Patricia Williams, "Freeze Coalition Work with Black Communities," memo to Nuclear Weapons Freeze Campaign, National Committee, February 3, 1983, NWFC Papers, box 4.

118. Nuclear Network, "The Black Participation Project," March 7, 1983, ibid.

119. Andrew P. Hogue, *Stumping God: Reagan, Carter, and the Invention of a Political Faith* (Waco, TX: Baylor University Press, 2012); Clyde Haberman, "Religion and Right-Wing Politics: How Evangelicals Reshaped Elections," *New York Times,* October 28, 2018.

120. Robert Freidman, "The Bomb and Jerry Show," *Nuclear Times* (August–September 1983).

121. Ibid.

122. Jerry Falwell, "Nuclear War and the Second Coming of Christ," *Old Time Gospel Hour,* March 20, 1983, https://archive.org; Bill Peterson, "Reagan's Use of Moral Language to Explain Policies Draws Fire," *Washington Post,* March 23, 1983.

123. David E. Anderson, "The Rev. Jerry Falwell, Fundamentalist Leader of the Moral Majority . . . ," *UPI,* March 14, 1983.

124. Robert E. Baldwin, "Peace through Strength: Nuclear Freeze the Big Lie," *Moral Majority Report* (April 1983); Lawrence S. Wittner, *Toward Nuclear Abolition: A History of the World Nuclear Disarmament Movement: 1971–Present* (Stanford, CA: Stanford University Press, 2003), 190.

125. Strobe Talbott, *Deadly Gambits: The Reagan Administration and the Stalemate in Nuclear Arms Control* (New York: Knopf, 1984).

126. Ronald Reagan, "Address to the Nation on Defense and National Security," speech, Washington, DC, March 23, 1983, http://www.atomicarchive.com.

127. WGBH Television, "Missile Experimental: Interview with George Keyworth," *War and Peace in the Nuclear Age,* November 30, 1987, WGBH Media Library and Archives, http://openvault.wgbh.org.

128. Reagan, "Address to the Nation on Defense and National Security."

129. "Excerpts from Mondale's Address to Publishers," *New York Times,* April 27, 1983.

130. Steven Rearden, *Congress and SDIO, 1983–1989* (Fort Belvoir, VA: Defense Technical Information Center, 1992), 50–52.

131. Ibid.

132. Ibid.

133. Ibid.

134. Ibid.

135. Bruce Abell, "Fact Sheet for White House Counsel," memo to George Keyworth, April 28, 1983, George Keyworth Files, box 15, folder, "Teller, Edward," RRPL.

136. Rearden, *Congress and SDIO*, 49.

137. Ibid.

138. Hans Bethe, memo to Ronald Reagan, March 29, 1983, George Keyworth Files, box 11, folder "SDI 1983," RRPL.

139. "Conference Maps Strategy," *Jobs with Peace Network Newsletter* (Winter–Spring 1983), NWFC Papers, box 4; Patricia Williams, "Exit Memo," memo to Randy Kehler, March 23, 1983, ibid., box 2; Jim Lopez, "Minority Update," memo to Pam McIntyre, July 27, 1983, ibid., box 4; Jim Lopez, "Minority Outreach Program within Asian, Hispanic, and Native American Communities," memo to Freeze National Committee, February 1, 1984, ibid.

140. "Conference Maps Strategy."

141. Gardner, "The Movement in Black and White."

142. "26 Groups Join in Campaign for Arms Freeze," *New York Times,* October 17, 1982.

143. Gardner, "The Movement in Black and White."

144. Harold Washington, "The Black Vote: The New Power in Politics," *Ebony* 39, no. 1 (1983): 108–10.

145. Nuclear Network, "The Black Participation Project"; Carl E. Davis, "Fisk University Conference: 'The Arms Race vs. Human Needs: National Dialogue on Jobs, Peace, and Freedom,'" memo to Randy Kehler et al., June 6, 1983, NWFC Papers, box 4; Nuclear Weapons Freeze Campaign, "Including the Third World in U.S. Peace Activism for a Truer View of World Peace," meeting notes, April 28, 1984, ibid.; "Minorities and Arms Control: How the Civil Rights Community Can Help Reduce the Threat of Nuclear War," May 23, 1984, ibid.

146. Bruce Shapiro, "Movement Looks for the Union Label," *Nuclear Times* (April 1983).

147. Marable, "Jobs, Peace, Freedom," 7–8.

148. Gene Carroll, "Update," memo to Freeze activists, May 1, 1983, NWFC Papers, box 4.

149. William Hartung, *The Economic Consequences of a Nuclear Freeze* (New York: New York Council on Economic Priorities, 1984), 1.

150. Ibid., 23–24.

151. Robert W. DeGrasse, Jr., *Military Expansion, Economic Decline: The Impact of Military Spending on U.S. Economic Performance* (New York: Council on Economic Priorities, 1983), 12.

152. Ibid., 14–15.

153. Shapiro, "Movement Looks for the Union Label"; "Freeze Progress Timeline; Art Project '83: Art for a Nuclear Weapons Freeze" (1983), NWFC Papers, box 1.

154. Martin Luther King, Jr., Center for Nonviolent Social Change, "Minutes of the National Planning Council."

155. Kiron K. Skinner, Annelise Anderson, and Martin Anderson, *Reagan: A Life in Letters* (New York: Free Press, 2003), 425–26.

156. Brent Scowcroft, *Report of the President's Commission on Strategic Forces* (Washington, DC: U.S. Government Printing Office, April 6, 1983), 1.

157. Ibid., 25.

158. Ibid., 22–25.

159. N. Stephen Kane, *Selling Reagan's Foreign Policy: Going Public vs. Executive Bargaining* (Lanham, MD: Lexington, 2018), 117–85.

160. "SPG Tasking," memo to SPG principals, April 18, 1983, National Security Council Records, European and Soviet Affairs Directorate, box RAC 12, folder "Public Diplomacy 1983," RRPL.

161. John Kelly, "Public Affairs Strategies for National Security Issues: Basic Audiences and the Priority," memo to Gerald Helman, April 19, 1983, ibid.

162. National Conference of Catholic Bishops, "The Challenge of Peace: God's Promise and Our Response," pastoral letter (Washington, DC: U.S. Catholic Conference, Office of Publication Services, 1983).

163. L. Bruce van Voorst, "The Churches and Nuclear Deterrence," *Foreign Affairs* 61 (Spring 1983): 847–48.

164. National Conference of Catholic Bishops, "The Challenge of Peace," para. 218.

165. Bernard Gwertzman, "Reagan Clarifies His Statement on Nuclear War," *New York Times*, October 22, 1981.

166. National Conference of Catholic Bishops, "The Challenge of Peace," paras. 218–20.

167. Ibid., para. 16.

168. Jared McBrady, "The Challenge of Peace: Ronald Reagan, John Paul II, and the American Bishops," *Journal of Cold War Studies* 17, no. 1 (2015): 132, 136.

169. Jim Castelli, *The Bishops and the Bomb: Waging Peace in a Nuclear Age* (New York: Doubleday, 1983), 137–62.

170. William Au, *The Cross, the Flag, and the Bomb: American Catholics Debate War and Peace, 1960–1983* (Westport, CT: Greenwood, 1984), 249–68.

171. William Greider, "The Power of the Cross," *Rolling Stone,* April 28, 1983.

172. Douglas C. Waller, *Congress and the Nuclear Freeze: An Inside Look at the Politics of a Mass Movement* (Amherst, MA: University of Massachusetts Press, 1987); WGBH Television, "Missile Experimental: Waller."

173. Fred Kaplan, "Does Midgetman Fall Short?" *Nuclear Times* (August–September 1983).

174. Talbott, *Deadly Gambits*, 339.

175. Robert Grey, *Congress, Arms Control, and Weapons Modernization* (Washington, DC: Library of Congress, Congressional Research Service, 1984), 86–109.

176. David Cortright, memo to Randy Kehler, May 27, 1983, NWFC Papers, box 7; Fred Kaplan, "Reagan Gores Liberals on MX," *Nuclear Times* (July 1983).

177. WGBH Television, "Missile Experimental: Interview with Randall Forsberg," *War and Peace in the Nuclear Age,* November 9, 1987, WGBH Media Library and Archives, http://openvault.wgbh.org.

178. WGBH Television, "Reagan Shield: Interview with James Woolsey," *War and Peace in the Nuclear Age,* October 13, 1987, WGBH Media Library and Archives, http://openvault.wgbh.org.

179. Walter Raymond, "Public Diplomacy" (Spring 1983), National Security Council Records, European and Soviet Affairs Directorate, box RAC 12, folder "Public Diplomacy 1983," RRPL.

180. Pat Nieburg and Stanton H. Burnett, "Interview with Stanton H. Burnett, 1990," digital ID mfdip.2004buro5, Library of Congress, https://www.loc.gov.

181. Peter Dailey, "Status Report on INF Activities," memo to William Clark, March 14, 1983, National Security Council Records, European and Soviet Affairs Directorate, box RAC 12, folder "Public Diplomacy 1983," RRPL.

182. Paul Nitze, "INF Arms Reduction and Modernization Issues: Speakers Resource Book" (September 1983), Paul Nitze Papers, box 114, Library of Congress.

183. Robert Armstrong, "Economic Summit: Williamsburg," memo to A. J. Coles, May 24, 1983, PREM, ser. 19/1008 f39.

184. U.K. Embassy in Washington, DC, "Williamsburg: The U.S. Approach," memo to Foreign and Commonwealth Office, May 25, 1983, ibid.; A. J. Coles, "Saturday Evening Dinner: Discussion of Arms Control," memo to Margaret Thatcher, May 26, 1983, ibid., f32.

185. Coles, "Saturday Evening Dinner."

186. U.K. Prime Minister's Office, record of conversation between Margaret Thatcher and Helmut Kohl, May 28, 1983, PREM, ser. 19/1009 f99.

187. U.K. Prime Minister's Office, record of conversation among Margaret Thatcher, Francis Pym, Yasuhiro Nakasone, and Shintaro Abe, May 28, 1983, ibid., f104.

188. Coles, "Saturday Evening Dinner."

189. Ronald Reagan, *The Reagan Diaries,* ed. Douglas Brinkley (New York: HarperCollins, 2007), 156.

190. George P. Shultz, *Turmoil and Triumph: My Years as Secretary of State* (New York: Scribner's, 1993), 356.

191. Ibid., 186.

192. Nitze, "INF Arms Reduction and Modernization Issues."

193. Ronald Reagan, memo to Margaret Thatcher, June 15, 1983, THCR, ser. 3/1/32, part 1, f40.

194. Margaret Thatcher, *The Downing Street Years: 1979–1990* (New York: HarperCollins, 1993), 290.

195. Shailendra Ghorpade, "Sources and Access: How Foreign Correspondents Rate Washington D.C.," *Journal of Communications* 34, no. 4 (1984): 32–40.

196. Gilbert Anderson, "Status Report No. 12—Arms Reductions and Security Issues," memo to Lawrence Eagleburger and Gerald Helman, April 23, 1983, National Security Council, Executive Secretariat Files, box 11, folder "Arms Control-Public Diplomacy," RRPL.

197. Alvin A. Snyder, *Warriors of Disinformation: American Propaganda, Soviet Lies, and the Winning of the Cold War: An Insider's Account* (New York: Arcade, 1997), 40–43.

198. Shultz, *Turmoil and Triumph,* 357.

199. Ibid., 300–301.

200. Robert Kaiser, "Go Ahead, Sucker, Bet on Reagan's Reelection," *Washington Post,* May 22, 1983; Louis Harris, "Early Indications Show Close 1984 Presidential Election," *Harris Survey,* July 11, 1983.

201. William Greider, "March of the Righteous," *Rolling Stone,* October 13, 1983.

202. Richard Wirthlin, "1984 Presidential Vote," memo to Edwin Meese, James Baker, and Michael Deaver, September 2, 1983, Michael Deaver Files, box 65, folder, "Dick Wirthlin, 1983–1984," RRPL.

203. Charles Wick, "Soviet Propaganda Alert No. 15," memo to Michael Deaver, August 10, 1983, ibid., box 61, folder "Wick, Charles Z."

204. U.S. Mission in Geneva, "INF: End of Round V Assessment," memo to U.S. secretary of state, July 14, 1983, National Security Council, Subject Files, box 23, RRPL; Sven Kraemer, "Summary of Ambassador Nitze's Meeting with the President," memo to William Clark, July 22, 1983, ibid.

205. Cliff Groce, interview with Walter Roberts, September 10, 1990, Oral History Project Information Series, https://adst.org.

206. Barbara Gamarekian, "To Nominee for NATO, Timing Seems Right," *New York Times,* July 12, 1983; Nicholas J. Cull, "Public Diplomacy: Taxonomies and Histories," *Annals of the American Academy of Political and Social Science* (616, no. 1 (2008): 38.

207. Cull, "Public Diplomacy," 38–39.

Chapter Five: Arms Control Undone

1. U.K. Prime Minister's Office, record of conversation between Margaret Thatcher and George H. W. Bush, June 24, 1983, PREM, ser. 19/979 f153.

2. Women's Encampment for a Future of Peace and Justice, "Resource Handbook" (New York, 1983), http://bcrw.barnard.edu.

3. Connie McKenna, "The Greenham of America," 7JAN, 2012/16, box 2; "Greenham Goes to Russia: Songbook," ibid.; Jan Beuhler, "The Puget Sound Women's Peace Camp: Education as an Alternative Strategy," *Frontiers* 8, no. 2 (1985): 40–44.

4. Maurice Chittenden and Elizabeth Grice, "Greenham Peace Women Go to War," *Sunday Times*, October 18, 1989.

5. Ronald Reagan, memo to Margaret Thatcher, September 10, 1983, THCR, ser. 3/1/33, part 1, f27; "Minutes of the Full Cabinet Meeting," September 15, 1983, British Cabinet Papers, ser. 128/76 f254, TNA; Margaret Thatcher, memo to Ronald Reagan, September 15, 1983, THCR, ser. 3/1/33, part 1, f45; Ronald Reagan, "Radio Address to the Nation on American International Broadcasting," speech, September 10, 1983, https://www.presidency.ucsb.edu; Ronald Reagan, "Statement on the Joint Congressional Resolution Condemning the Soviet Attack on a Korean Civilian Airliner," speech, September 15, 1983, ibid.; Ronald Reagan, "Radio Address to the Nation on the Soviet Attack on a Korean Civilian Airliner," speech, September 17, 1983, ibid.

6. Alexander Dallin, *Black Box: KAL 007 and the Superpowers* (Berkeley: University of California Press, 1985).

7. Charles Z. Wick, "Foreign Media Reaction to the Downing of the KAL Flight 007," memo to Reagan administration cabinet members, September 2, 1983, General Records, CIA-ERR, https://www.cia.gov; U.S. Information Agency, "The Shootdown of KAL 007: Moscow's Charges—and the Record" (Washington, DC, 1983).

8. Raymond Garthoff, *The Great Transition: American-Soviet Relations and the End of the Cold War* (Washington, DC: Brookings Institution Press, 1994), 127.

9. U.K. Prime Minister's Office, record of conversation between Margaret Thatcher and Helmut Kohl, September 21, 1983, PREM, ser. 19/1036 f54.

10. James Reston, "Washington; Reagan's Public Diplomacy," *New York Times*, September 28, 1983.

11. Ronald Reagan, "Address before the 38th Session of the United Nations General Assembly," speech, September 26, 1983, https://www.reaganlibrary.gov; Ronald Reagan, "National Security Decision Directive (NSDD) 104: U.S. Approach to INF Negotiations—II," September 21, 1983, National Security Council, Executive Secretariat Records, 1981–87, box RAC 6, RRPL.

12. George Urban, *Diplomacy and Disillusion at the Court of Margaret Thatcher: An Insider's View* (London: Tauris, 1996), 34–63; Archie Brown, *The Human Factor: Gorbachev, Reagan, and Thatcher, and the End of the Cold War* (Oxford: Oxford University Press, 2020), 113–27.

13. U.K. Prime Minister's Office, "Policy on East-West Relations," meeting minutes, September 12, 1983, PREM, ser. 19/1155 f38.

14. Michael Heseltine, "Britain and Arms Control," memo to Margaret Thatcher, September 1, 1983, ibid., 19/979.

15. U.K. Prime Minister's Office, record of conversation between Thatcher and Kohl, September 21, 1983; R. B. Bone, "INF," memo to A. J. Coles, September 5, 1983, PREM, ser. 19/979 f65; R. B. Bone, "Mr. Andropov's Message to the Prime Minister on INF," memo to Tim Flesher, August 31, 1983, ibid., f76.

16. Margaret Thatcher, memo to Yuri Andropov, September 27, 1983, THCR, ser. 3/1/33, part 1, f95.

17. William Clark, "Visit of British Prime Minister," memo to Ronald Reagan, n.d., National

Security Council Records, European and Soviet Affairs Directorate, box 90902, folder "Thatcher Visit—September 1983," RRPL.
18. U.K. Embassy in Washington, DC, "Prime Minister's Visit to Washington, September 28–30," October 1, 1983, THCR, ser. 1/10/59 f81.
19. Margaret Thatcher, "Speech at the Winston Churchill Foundation Award Dinner," September 29, 1983, THCR.
20. Urban, *Diplomacy and Disillusion*, 34–63.
21. Ibid., 34–53; Donnie Radcliffe, "Margaret Thatcher, in Her Prime," *Washington Post*, September 30, 1983.
22. Greenham Common Women against Cruise Missiles, "Latest News," 7JAN, 2012/16, box 3; Greenham Common Women against Cruise Missiles, "American Court Case: Press Update," October 23, 1983, ibid.; Greenham Common Women against Cruise Missiles, "American Court Case," November 9, 1983, ibid.
23. Greenham Women against Cruise Missiles v. Reagan, 591 F. supp. 1332 (1984).
24. James M. Markham, "First U.S. Pershing Missiles Delivered in West Germany," *New York Times*, November 24, 1983.
25. Sven Kraemer, "INF—Summary of Round VI," memo to Robert McFarlane, National Security Council Records, Subject Files, box 2, RRPL; William Staples, "Chronologies of US and Soviet Initiatives in INF," memo to Robert Kimmitt, January 17, 1984, ibid., box 24.
26. Charles Stuart Kennedy, interview with David Michael Wilson, January 11, 2001, Pat Nieburg and Stanton H. Burnett, interview with Stanton H. Burnett, 1990, digital ID mfdip.2004bur05, Library of Congress, https://www.loc.gov; Walter Raymond, "USIA Actions in Support of INF Deployment," memo to Robert McFarlane, November 4, 1983, National Security Council Records, Executive Secretariat, box 11, folder "Arms Control-Public Diplomacy 10/07/1983–11/06/1983," RRPL.
27. Alvin A. Snyder, *Warriors of Disinformation: American Propaganda, Soviet Lies, and the Winning of the Cold War: An Insider's Account* (New York: Arcade, 1997), 82.
28. Penny Pagano, "TV Goes Global on WORLDNET," *Los Angeles Times*, March 2, 1985.
29. Hans Tuch, *Communicating with the World: U.S. Public Diplomacy Overseas* (New York: St. Martin's, 1990), 99–105.
30. Charles Z. Wick, "Status Report No. 42—Arms Reduction and Security Issues," memo to Lawrence Eagleburger and Gerald Helman, December 5, 1983, National Security Council Records, Executive Secretariat, box 11, folder "Arms Control—Public Diplomacy 10/07/1983–11/06/1983, RRPL.
31. John Vinocur, "After the Arms Talks," *New York Times*, October 13, 1983.
32. Lynn Rusten, *The Soviet Position in the Strategic Arms Reduction Talks (START) and Soviet Reactions to U.S. Proposals* (Washington, DC: Library of Congress, Congressional Research Service, December 1983), 5; "Hurd Call on [Meeting] General Rowny," March 14, 1983, FCO, ser. 46/3514.
33. Strobe Talbott, *Deadly Gambits: The Reagan Administration and the Stalemate in Nuclear Arms Control* (New York: Knopf, 1984), 342.
34. George Shultz, "Next Steps on Defense against Ballistic Missiles (DABM)," memo to Ronald Reagan, November 28, 1983, National Security Council, Executive Secretariat Records, 1981–87, RRPL.
35. Ronald Reagan, "National Security Decision Directive (NSDD) 85: Eliminating the Threat from Ballistic Missiles," March 25, 1983, ibid., box RAC 5; Ronald Reagan, "National Security Study Directive Number 6–83: Study on Eliminating the Threat Posed by Ballistic Missiles," April 19, 1983, in *The Reagan Files: The Strategic Defense Initiative*, ed. Jason Saltoun-Ebin, http://www.thereaganfiles.com; "Strategic Defense Initiative: SDI Chronology, 1983–1990," March 19, 1990, Digital National Security Archive.

36. James C. Fletcher, "The Strategic Defense Initiative: Defensive Technologies Study" (April 1984), in *Strategic Defense Initiative: Folly or Future?*, ed. P. Edward Haley, Jack Merritt, and Martin C. Needler (London: Routledge, 1986); Fred S. Hoffman, "Ballistic Missile Defense and U.S. National Security: Summary Report: Future Security Strategy Study" (October 1983), in *The Star Wars Controversy: An "International Security" Reader,* ed. Stephen E. Miller and Stephen Van Evera (Princeton, NJ: Princeton University Press, 1986), 3–14.

37. Ronald Reagan, "National Security Decision Directive (NSDD) 98: U.S. Approach to START Negotiations—VI," June 14, 1983, National Security Council, Executive Secretariat Records, 1981–87, box RAC 6, RRPL.

38. Albert Gore, Jr., memo to Robert McFarlane, November 18, 1983, National Security Council Records, Subject Files, box 24, RRPL.

39. R. P. Turco, O. B. Toon, T. P. Ackerman, J. B. Pollack, and Carl Sagan, "Nuclear Winter: Global Consequences of Multiple Nuclear Explosions," *Science,* December 23, 1983, 1283–92.

40. Carl Sagan, "The Nuclear Winter," *Parade,* October 30, 1983, 4–7; Lawrence Badash, *A Nuclear Winter's Tale: Science and Politics in the 1980s* (Cambridge: MIT Press, 2009), 3.

41. Paul Ehrlich, Carl Sagan, Donald Kennedy, and Walter Orr Roberts, *The Cold and the Dark: The World after Nuclear War* (New York: Norton, 1984), xviii.

42. Chaplin Barnes, "Public Relations Plan," memo to steering committee for "The World after Nuclear War: The Conference on Long-Term Worldwide Biological Consequences of Nuclear War," June 21, 1983, Carl Sagan Papers, box 812, folder 5, Library of Congress.

43. Porter, Novelli, and Associates, "The World after Nuclear War: Media Placements," n.d., ibid., folder 6.

44. Albert Gore, Jr., memo to Robert Scrivner, December 17, 1982, ibid., box 808, folder 6; Albert Gore, Jr., to Carl Sagan, December 17, 1982, ibid., box 812, folder 3; Albert Gore, Jr., Mark O. Hatfield, and Charles Matthias, Jr., "Dear Colleague" letter, October 21, 1983, ibid., box 813, folder 2.

45. Carl Sagan, "Nuclear War and Climate Catastrophe: Some Policy Implications," *Foreign Affairs* 62 (Winter 1983): 257–92.

46. Ronald Reagan, "National Security Decision Directive (NSDD) 119: Strategic Defense Initiative," January 6, 1984, National Security Council, Executive Secretariat Records, 1981–87, box RAC 6, RRPL.

47. George Keyworth, "Recommendations from Bill Wilson et al. Pertaining to the New Defence Initiative," memo to Ronald Reagan, July 20, 1983, George Keyworth Files, box 5, folder "Meese Correspondence," RRPL.

48. Reagan, "NSDD 119."

49. U.S. General Accounting Office, "Ballistic Missile Defense: Records Indicate Deception Program Did Not Affect 1984 Test Results," July 21, 1984, National Security Archive; Tim Weiner, "Inquiry Finds 'Star Wars' Tried to Exaggerate Test Results," *New York Times,* July 23, 1994.

50. Ronald Reagan, *The Reagan Diaries* (New York: HarperCollins, 2007), 212.

51. U.S. Department of State, "Six Month Projection on Arms Control Public Diplomacy," January 20, 1984, National Security Council, Executive Secretariat Records, 1981–87, box 11, folder "Arms Control Public Diplomacy 11/30/1983–1/25/1984," RRPL.

52. National Security Council, "Strategic Defense Initiative," meeting minutes, November 30, 1983, ibid.

53. William Casey, "National Intelligence Estimate: Soviet Ballistic Missile Defense," October 13, 1982, Reagan Collection, CIA-ERR.

54. Ronald Reagan, "National Security Decision Directive (NSDD) 116: Strategic Defense Initiative: Congressional and Allied Consultation," December 2, 1983, National Security Council, Executive Secretariat Records, 1981–87, box RAC 6, RRPL.

55. Robert McFarlane, "NSPG Meeting on Soviet Noncompliance with Arms Control Agreements," December 20, 1983, in Saltoun-Ebin, *The Reagan Files*.

56. Garthoff, *The Great Transition*, 318, 370–89, 518.

57. Ronald Reagan, "National Security Decision Directive (NSDD) 121: Soviet Noncompliance with Arms Control Agreements," January 14, 1984, National Security Council, Executive Secretariat Records, 1981–87, box RAC 6, RRPL.

58. Gerard Smith, Paul Warnke, and Herbert Scoville, "Alleged Violations of Arms Control Agreements," January 18, 1984, NWFC Papers, box 1.

59. Bob Helm, "SDI Management," memo to Robert McFarlane, January 27, 1984, National Security Council, Subject Files, box 31, RRPL.

60. George Keyworth, memo to Caspar Weinberger, December 9, 1983, in Saltoun-Ebin, *The Reagan Files*.

61. Caspar Weinberger, *Fighting for Peace: Seven Critical Years in the Pentagon* (New York: Warner Books, 1990), 291–29.

62. Ibid., 294–95.

63. Francis Fitzgerald, *Way Out There in the Blue: Reagan, Star Wars, and the End of the Cold War* (New York: Simon and Schuster, 2000), 256.

64. George P. Shultz, *Turmoil and Triumph: My Years as Secretary of State* (New York: Scribner's, 1993), 249–50.

65. B. G. Cartledge, "Ballistic Missile Defense: UK Policy towards the US Strategic Defense Initiative," PREM, ser. 19/1188 f35; M. A. Pakenham, "Ballistic Missile Defence: UK Policy towards the US Strategic Defence Initiative (SDI)," November 5, 1984, Ministry of Defence Records, ser. 24/2915, TNA (hereafter DEFE).

66. National Security Council Planning Group, meeting minutes, March 27, 1984, National Security Council, Executive Secretariat Records, System Files 1981–87, RRPL.

67. Fitzgerald, *Way Out There in the Blue*, 257.

68. Larry Hyden, "Strategic Defense Initiative," memo to George Keyworth, February 9, 1984, George Keyworth Files, box 11, folder "SDI," RRPL.

69. U.S. Senate, Committee on Foreign Relations, hearing on strategic defense and anti-satellite weapons, hearing no. 98–750, April 25, 1984, 98th Cong., 2nd sess., Library of Congress.

70. George Keyworth, memo to Ronald Reagan, May 25, 1984, George Keyworth Files, box 11, folder "SDI," RRPL.

71. Tom Stoel, memo to Carl Sagan, January 20, 1984, Carl Sagan Papers, box 808, folder 3, Library of Congress; Edith Villastrigo, memo to Carl Sagan, March 4, 1987, ibid., box 692, folder 5; Karen Mulhauser, memo to Carl Sagan, January 23, 1984, ibid., box 808, folder 3; Shirley Golden, memo to Shirley Arden, January 30, 1984, ibid.

72. Tim Wirth, memo to Carl Sagan, May 4, 1984, ibid., box 845, folder 6; Alan Cranston, memo to Carl Sagan, September 7, 1984, ibid., box 844, folder 7; "DNC Platform," 1984, ibid., box 842, folder 4.

73. "U.S.-Soviet Forum on Nuclear Winter," Public Interest Report, *Journal of the Federation of American Scientists* 37 (January 1984): 1.

74. Ibid.

75. Carl Sagan, "Nuclear Winter: A Dialogue between Drs. Sagan and Teller," memo to Edward Teller, May 7, 1984, Carl Sagan Papers, box 845, folder 6, Library of Congress.

76. "Sagan-Teller Debate of May 16," May 24, 1984, ibid., box 890, folder 3.

77. Nils Randlev Hundebøl, interview with Michael MacCracken, April 19, 2013, Niels Bohr Library and Archives, American Institute of Physics, http:/www.aip.org.

78. Michael MacCracken, "More on Confronting Carl Sagan If it Comes to That," memo to Edward Teller, April 30, 1984, Edward Teller Papers, box 492, folder 9, Hoover Institution Library and Archives, Stanford University (hereafter Teller Papers); Michael MacCracken and John Walton, "The Effects of Interactive Transport and Scavenging of Smoke on the Calculated Temperature Change Resulting from Large Amounts of Smoke," *Proceedings of the International Seminar on Nuclear War: The Nuclear Winter and the New Defense Systems: Problems and Perspectives, the Technical Basis for Peace, 19–24 August 1983, Erice, Sicily* (Geneva: World Scientific, 1992); Hundebøl, interview with MacCracken.

79. "Sagan-Teller Debate of May 16."

80. Ibid.

81. Ashton B. Carter, "Directed Energy Missile Defense in Space—A Background Paper," doc. OTA-BP-ISC-26 (Washington, DC: U.S. Congress, Office of Technological Assessment, April 1984).

82. Ibid., 81.

83. Ibid., 20.

84. Ashton B. Carter, memo to Carl Sagan, September 13, 1984, Carl Sagan Papers, box 816, folder 6, Library of Congress.

85. Michael Warner, "Reassessing the Office of Technology Assessment" (Washington, DC: Heritage Foundation, November 7, 1984).

86. Ibid.

87. Richard Garwin and Hans Bethe, "Anti-Ballistic Missile Systems," *Scientific American* 218, no. 3 (1968): 259–68.

88. Union of Concerned Scientists, *The Fallacy of Star Wars: Why Space Weapons Can't Protect Us* (New York: Vintage, 1984); Finn Aaserud, interview with Henry Kendall, November 25, 1986, Niels Bohr Library and Archives, American Institute of Physics, http://www.aip.org.

89. Hans Bethe, Richard Garwin, Kurt Gottfried, and Henry Kendall, "Space-Based Ballistic Missile Defense," *Scientific American* 251 (October 1984): 39–49.

90. William J. Broad, *Star Warriors* (New York: Touchstone, 1986); Naomi Oreskes and Erik M. Conway, *Merchants of Doubt: How a Handful of Scientists Obscured the Truth on Issues from Tobacco Smoke to Global Warming* (New York: Bloomsbury, 2010), 56.

91. "Governor Ronald Reagan Announces Formation of the Science and Technology Task Force," October 20, 1980, Teller Papers, box 282, folder 5.

92. Edward Teller, memo to Richard Allen, November 7, 1980, ibid.

93. Robert Jastrow, William Nierenberg, and Frederick Seitz, memo to John Warner, June 11, 1984, George Keyworth Files, box 11, folder "SDI," RRPL.

94. Sanford Lakoff and Herbert York, *A Shield in Space? Technology, Politics, and the Strategic Defense Initiative:* (Los Angeles: University of California Berkeley Press, 1989), 269.

95. Richard Garwin, memo to John Warner, July 9, 1984, Carl Sagan Papers, box 818, folder 3, Library of Congress.

96. Robert Jastrow, "Why Strategic Superiority Matters," *Commentary* 75, no. 3 (1983): 27–32.

97. Thomas Graham and Bernard Kramer, "The Polls: ABM and Star Wars: Attitudes toward Nuclear Defense, 1945–1985," *Public Opinion Quarterly* 50 (Spring 1986): 125–34.

98. Fitzgerald, *Way Out There in the Blue*, 258–59.

99. Ronald Reagan, *An American Life: The Autobiography of Ronald Reagan* (New York: Simon and Schuster, 2011), 269.

100. Robert Brent Toplin, "Ronald Reagan and the Day the Earth Stood Still," *History News Network* (2008), https://historynewsnetwork.org.

101. Benjamin Fischer, *A Cold War Conundrum: The 1983 Soviet War Scare* (Washington, DC: Center for the Study of Intelligence, 1997).

102. National Security Council Planning Group, "Discussion of Substantive Issues for Geneva," meeting minutes, December 17, 1984, National Security Council, Executive Secretariat, 1981–87, box 91307, RRPL.

103. Barry Sussman and Kenneth E. John, "Washington Post–ABC News Poll," *Washington Post*, January 20, 1984.

104. Everett Carl Ladd, "On Mandates, Realignments, and the 1984 Presidential Election," *Political Science Quarterly* 100 (Spring 1985): 1–25.

105. Ronald Reagan, "Address to the Nation and Other Countries on United States-Soviet Relations," speech, Washington, DC, January 16, 1984, https://www.presidency.ucsb.edu.

106. Carnes Lord, "In Defense of Public Diplomacy," *Commentary* 77 (April 1984): 42–50.

107. Kenneth Adelman, personal communication, November 17, 2020.

108. "Public Diplomacy Action Plan for START and the Nuclear Freeze," July 27, 1983, Sven Kraemer Files, box 6, RRPL.

109. Garthoff, *The Great Transition,* 163.

110. George Keyworth, "SDI and Congressional Campaigns," memo to Mike Schwartz, July 31, 1984, George Keyworth Files, box 12, folder "SDI," RRPL.

111. "Prepared for Peace," advertisement (1984), https://www.youtube.com.

112. Andrew Hunt, *We Begin Bombing in Five Minutes: Late Cold War Culture in the Age of Reagan* (Amherst, MA: University of Massachusetts Press, 2021).

113. David Ryan, "1984, Regional Crises, and Morning in America: The Predawn of the Reagan Era," in *U.S. Presidential Elections and Foreign Policy: Candidates, Campaigns, and Global Politics from FDR to Bill Clinton*, ed. Andrew Johnstone and Andrew Priest (Lexington: University Press of Kentucky, 2017), 271.

114. Daniel Yankelovich and John Doble, "The Public Mood: Nuclear Weapons and the U.S.S.R," *Foreign Affairs* 63 (Fall 1984): 33–46.

115. Eleanor Smeal, "The Women's Trust: A Campaign Organization for the Times" (Summer 1983), NWFC Papers, box 4.

116. Cathy Cevoli, "Will Gender Gap Become a Gulf," *Nuclear Times* (April 1984).

117. Ibid.

118. Arms Control Education Project, "Disarmament Organizers' Meeting," June 8, 1984, NWFC Papers, box 1.

119. Jan Meriwether and Jenny Russell, "Mother's Day, 1984," May 31, 1984, ibid., box 8.

120. "WAND PAC Update" (Fall 1984), ibid.

121. Diane Aronson, memo to Women's Action for Nuclear Disarmament affiliates and special contacts, June 1, 1984, ibid.

122. Carol Cohn, "Sex and Death in the Rational World of Defense Intellectuals," *Signs* 12 (Summer 1987): 714

123. Derrick De Kerckhove, "On Nuclear Communication," *Diacritics* (Summer 1984): 71–81; Paul Chilton, *Language and the Nuclear Arms Debate: Nukespeak Today* (Dover, NH: Pinter, 1985).

124. Cohn, "Sex and Death in the Rational World of Defense Intellectuals," 717–18.

125. "National Women's Conference to Prevent Nuclear War," in *Defense Monitor* (Washington, DC: Center for Defense Information, 1984), Papers of Physicians for Social Responsibility, box 13-A, SCPC.

126. Suzanne Gordon, "From Earth Mother to Expert," *Nuclear Times* (May 1983).

127. "National Women's Conference to Prevent Nuclear War."

128. Phyllis La Farge, *The Strangelove Legacy: Children, Parents, and Teachers in the Nuclear Age* (New York: Harper and Row, 1987).

129. Robert Devine, "Promoting Nuclear Literacy," *Nuclear Times* (September 1984).

130. Cathy Cevoli, "Peace Issues Pick Up Steam," *Nuclear Times* (October–November 1984).

131. Kathleen Frankovic, "The 1984 Election: The Irrelevance of a Campaign," *Political Studies* 18 (Winter 1985): 40.

132. Bella Abzug and Mim Kelber, "Despite the Reagan Sweep, a Gender Gap Remains," *New York Times*, November 23, 1984; Kathleen Frankovic, "The 1984 Election: The Irrelevance of a Campaign," *Political Studies* 18 (Winter 1985): 40.

133. Douglas C. Waller, *Congress and the Nuclear Freeze: An Inside Look at the Politics of a Mass Movement* (Amherst, MA: University of Massachusetts Press, 1987), 294–96.

134. Ibid.

135. David S. Meyer and Thomas Rochon, *Coalitions and Political Movements: The Lessons of the Nuclear Freeze* (New York: Rienner, 1997), 14.

136. Arms Control Education Project, "Impact '84" (Fall 1984), Freeze Voter '84 Records, box 3 SCPC; Council for a Livable World, "Electoral Analysis" (December 1984), NWFC Papers, box 2.

137. Waller, *Congress and the Nuclear Freeze,* 296.

138. Bill Curry, memo to Freeze Voter '84 supporters, November 16, 1984, Freeze Voter '84 Records, box 2, SCPC.

139. National Security Council Planning Group, "Next Steps in the Vienna Process," meeting minutes, September 18, 1984, National Security Council, Executive Secretariat, 1981–87, box 91307, RRPL.

140. Ibid.

141. U.S. Department of Defense, *Soviet Military Power* (Washington, DC: U.S. Government Printing Office, 1981); U.S. Department of Defense, *Soviet Military Power* (Washington, DC: U.S. Government Printing Office); Defense Intelligence Agency, "Soviet Military Power: Strategic Forces," (1983), https://fas.org.

142. National Security Council Planning Group, "Soviet Defense and Arms Control Objectives," November 30, 1984, National Security Council, Executive Secretariat, 1981–87, box 91307, RRPL.

143. National Security Council Planning Group, "U.S. Soviet Arms Control Objectives," December 5, 1984, ibid.

144. National Security Council Planning Group, "Discussion of Substantive Issues for Geneva," December 17, 1984, ibid.

145. Ibid.

146. Ibid.

147. Bob Linhad, "SDI Bible," memo to Robert McFarlane, December 1, 1984, ibid., box 31.

148. Ibid.

149. Zbigniew Brzezinksi, Robert Jastrow, and Max Kampelman, "'Star Wars,' It's Not Just Science Fiction—Why the U.S. Needs Reagan's Space Defense Program," *San Francisco Chronicle*, February 13, 1985, reprinted from *New York Times*, January 1985.

150. Ken Kramer, "Space-Based Defense Possible," *Limon County Leader*, May 28, 1984; Jeremy Stone, "Two Roads to Security," *FAS Public Interest Report* 38 (March 1985): 1–2.

151. Edward Linenthal, *Symbolic Defense: The Cultural Significance of the Strategic Defense Initiative* (Champaign: University of Illinois Press, 1989), 45.

152. George Rathjens and Jack Ruina, "BMD and Strategic Instability," *Daedalus* 114 (Summer 1985): 239.

153. WGBH Television, "One Step Forward: Interview with Sidney Drell," *War and Peace in the Nuclear Age,* December 15, 1987, WGBH Media Library and Archives, http://openvault.wgbh.org.

154. McGeorge Bundy, George F. Kennan, Robert S. McNamara, and Gerard Smith, "The President's Choice: Star Wars or Arms Control," *Foreign Affairs* 63 (Winter 1984): 267.

155. Stone, "Two Roads to Security," 1–2.

156. National Security Council Planning Group, "Discussion of Substantive Issues for Geneva."

157. Ibid.

158. Linhad, "SDI Bible."

159. David Roberts, "SDI," memo to Mr. Crabbie or P. J. Weston, May 31, 1984, FCO, ser. 46/4108; Robin Kenwick, "Non-Paper on DABM," memo to P. J. Weston, December 14, 1983, ibid., ser. 46/3611.

160. F. S. Hoffman, *Ballistic Missile Defenses and U.S. National Security* (Washington, DC: U.S. Department of Defense, October 1983); J. C. Fletcher, "The Technologies of Ballistic Missile Defense," *Issues in Science and Technology* 1 (Fall 1984): 139–94.

161. P. J. Weston, "Ballistic Missile Defense: UK Views," November 10, 1983, FCO, ser. 46/3611.

162. Kenwick, "Non-Paper on DABM"; Charles Hill, "View of Allies on Strategic Defense Initiative," memo to Robert McFarlane, National Security Council, Subject Files, box 32, RRPL.

163. Mr. Roberts, "UK Non-Paper on SDI: Questions, Answers, and Comments," memo to Mr. Soutar, April 5, 1984, FCO, ser. 46/4107.

164. David Roberts, "SDI," memo to John Weston and Mr. Crabbie, May 14, 1984, ibid.; M. A. Pakenham, "Ballistic Missile Defense: UK Policy towards the US Strategic Defense Initiative (SDI)," November 5, 1984, DEFE, ser. 24/2915.

165. Roberts, "SDI.

166. M. A. Pakenham, "DABMS," memo to Mr. Wright, December 30, 1983, FCO, ser. 46/3611.

167. Solly Zuckerman, *Star Wars in a Nuclear World* (London: Kimber, 1986), 148–81, esp. 155.

168. Michael Kandiah and Gillian Staerk, eds., "The British Response to SDI," conference record, Centre for Contemporary British History, University of London, 2005, 51.

169. M. A. Pakenham, "Advanced Defense Technologies/Star Wars," memo to John Weston, December 6, 1983, FCO, ser. 46/3611; John Pike, "The Death Beam Gap: Putting Keegan's Follies in Perspective" (October 1992), https://fas.org.

170. Margaret Thatcher, *The Downing Street Years: 1979–1990* (London: HarperPerennial, 1995), 463.

171. Kandiah and Staerk. "The British Response to SDI."

172. David Caplin, "Civil Defense," memo to Will Hurd, HO Records, ser. 322/1085; David Caplin, personal communication, September 4, 2017.

173. Joseph Rotblat, *Scientists in Quest for Peace: A History of the Pugwash Conferences* (Cambridge: MIT Press, 1972).

174. Pugwash, "Minutes of the Annual General Meeting," March 30, 1982, Dorothy Hodgkin Papers, MS.ENG C. 5864, WLSC; Pugwash Executive Committee, "Statement of the Pugwash Executive Committee on the Pugwash Workshop on Nuclear Forces in Europe," December 20, 1982, Joseph Rotblat Papers, ser. 5/2/7/7, CAC (hereafter RTBT); Pugwash, "Minutes of the 62nd Pugwash Council," July 8–9, 1984, ibid., ser. 5/3/1/43; Joseph Rotblat, "Pugwash Conference on Science and World Affairs: A Brief Description" (May 1985), ibid., ser. 5/2/2/47.

175. Solly Zuckerman, *Monkeys, Men, and Missiles: An Autobiography, 1946–1988* (New York: Norton, 1988).

176. Joseph Rotblat, memo to Solly Zuckerman, November 4, 1987, Zuckerman Papers, ser. SZ/PUG/4/2/7—SZ/PUG/5.

177. Solly Zuckerman, memo to Richard Garwin, August 10, 1984, ibid., ser. SZ/Gen 35, box "Garwin."

178. Ibid.

179. Russell Peterson, memo to Solly Zuckerman, June 19, 1984, ibid., ser. SZ/2/SUB/2/4.

180. Frederick Warner, memo to Solly Zuckerman, March 27, 1984, ibid., ser. SZ/2/SUB/1–10; Solly Zuckerman, memo to Frederick Warner, April 4, 1984, ibid.

181. Michael Andrews, prod., *On the Eighth Day* (London: BBC, 1984), https://www.youtube.com.

182. Mark Harwell, *Nuclear Winter: The Human and Environmental Consequences* (New York: Springer Verlag, 1984), xii.

183. Frederick Warner, memo to Solly Zuckerman, March 20, 1984, Zuckerman Papers, ser. SZ/2/SUB/1–10; Frederick Warner, memo to Solly Zuckerman, June 4, 1984, ibid.

184. Solly Zuckerman, memo to Robert Armstrong, October 12, 1984, ibid.

185. Denis Healey, "Beyond Nuclear Deterrence," speech, Fabian Autumn Lecture, November 26, 1985 (London: Fabian Society, 1986).

186. Mike Pentz and Solly Zuckerman, "Scientists against Nuclear Arms" (January 1981), Zuckerman Papers, ser. SZ/CSA/19/2.

187. Pugwash Executive Committee, meeting minutes, May 19, 1981, Dorothy Hodgkin Papers, MS. ENG. C. 5684, WLSC.

188. Gil Booth, "SANA at UEA," memo to Solly Zuckerman, December 13, 1983, Zuckerman Papers, ser. SZ /CSA/19/2.

189. Campaign for Nuclear Disarmament, "The Nuclear Winter—A Framework for Campaign Planning," February 9, 1984, CND Records, ser. 1/2.

190. Scientists against Nuclear Arms, "The Nuclear Winter Conference: Open University, June 24, 1984," HO Records, ser. 322/1085; Scientists against Nuclear Arms, *SANA Newsletter* 12 (January 1985), ibid.

191. Mike Pentz, *A Change in the Weather: The Nuclear Winter Tour*, unpublished memoir, chap. 46; Linda Pentz Gunter, personal communication, April 15, 2018.

192. Scientists against Nuclear Arms, "The Nuclear Winter Conference."

193. Scientists against Nuclear Arms, *SANA Newsletter*.

194. Norman Myers, memo to Carl Sagan, November 16, 1983, Carl Sagan Papers, box 813, folder 2, Library of Congress.

195. Michael Andrews, "On the Eighth Day," *Natural World,* September 24, 1984.

196. Duncan Campbell, *War Plan UK: The Truth about Civil Defence in Britain* (London: Burnett, 1982).

197. Michael Ancram, remarks, House of Commons debate, Hansard, November 13, 1984, vol. 67, cc. 207W; John Home Robertson, remarks, House of Commons debate, Hansard, January 25, 1985, vol. 71, cc. 1232–40.

Chapter Six: Summits

1. Edwin J. Feulner, Jr., "Public Diplomacy: Lessons from the Washington Summit" (Washington, DC: U.S. Advisory Commission on Public Diplomacy, 1988).

2. M. A. Pakenham, "Ballistic Missile Defense: UK Policy towards the US Strategic Defense Initiative (SDI)," November 5, 1984, DEFE, ser. 24/2915.

3. Record of meeting with Manfred Woerner, January 18, 1985, PREM, ser. 19/1764 f206.

4. "Final Report to the President of the High Frontier Panel," January 8, 1982, National

Security Council, Subject Files, box 13, RRPL; Foreign and Commonwealth Office, "Controls on Anti-Satellite Systems (ASATs)," memo to U.K. Prime Minister's Office, February 20, 1984, PREM, ser. 19/1188 f204.

5. J. Baylis, "British Nuclear Doctrine: The 'Moscow Criterion' and the Polaris Improvement Program," *Contemporary History* 19, no. 1 (2005): 53–65; K. Stoddart, "Maintaining the 'Moscow Criterion': British Strategic Nuclear Targeting," *Journal of Strategic Studies* 31, no. 6 (2008): 897–924.

6. U.K. Prime Minister's Office, "Policy on East-West Relations," meeting minutes, September 12, 1983, PREM, ser. 19/1155 f38.

7. R. B. Bone, "Contacts with the Soviet Union," memo to A. J. Coles, June 4, 1984, ibid., ser. 19/1394 f408; U.K. Embassy in Moscow, "Your Visit to Moscow: 1–3 July: General Impressions," memo to Foreign and Commonwealth Office, July 3, 1984, ibid., ser. 19/1394 f371; Richard Owen, "The Golden Boy's First Challenge," *Times*, December 13, 1984.

8. Colin Budd, "Gorbachev's Visit," memo to C. D. Powell, December 4, 1984, PREM, ser. 19/1394 f198.

9. Owen, "The Golden Boy's First Challenge."

10. U.K. Embassy in Moscow, "Gorbachev's Visit," memo to Foreign and Commonwealth Office, December 10, 1984, PREM, ser. 19/1394 f131.

11. L.V. Appleyard, "Gorbachev's Visit: UK Objectives," memo to C. D. Powell, November 19, 1984, ibid., ser. 19/1394 f260.

12. C. D. Powell, "Record of the Meeting between the Prime Minister and Mr. Gorbachev," December 16, 1984, ibid., ser. 19/1394 f56.

13. Ibid.; also see Archie Brown, *The Gorbachev Factor* (New York: Oxford University Press, 1996), 37.

14. John Cole, interview with Margaret Thatcher, December 17, 1984, British Broadcasting Corporation, https://www.margaretthatcher.org.

15. U.K. Embassy in Washington, "Gorbachev's Visit to Britain: US Press Coverage," memo to Foreign and Commonwealth Office, December 19, 1984, PREM, ser. 19/1394 f29.

16. Margaret Thatcher, "Meeting with President Reagan: Gorbachev," memo to Ronald Reagan, December 22, 1984, ibid., ser. 19/1394 f9.

17. Ibid.

18. "Record of Thatcher-Reagan Meeting," December 22, 1984, National Security Council Records, European and Soviet Affairs Directorate, box 90902, folder "Thatcher Visit, RRPL; U.K. Prime Minister's Office, "No. 10 Record of a Meeting between the Prime Minister and President Reagan," December 22, 1984, THCR, ser. 1/10/78 f79; "Press Conference after Camp David Talks," December 22, 1984, ibid., Central Office of Information transcript.

19. Mr. D. Fewtrell, "Meeting with Dumas: Paris—SDI/EUREKA Summary," memo to Foreign and Commonwealth Office, May 21, 1985, FCO, ser. 46/4632.

20. "Record of Thatcher-Reagan Meeting," December 22, 1984; U.K. Prime Minister's Office, "No. 10 Record of a Meeting between the Prime Minister and President Reagan," December 22, 1984; "Press Conference after Camp David Talks," December 22, 1984.

21. Ronald Reagan, "National Security Decision Directive (NSDD) 172: Presenting the Strategic Defense Initiative," May 30, 1985, National Security Council, Executive Secretariat Records, 1981–87, box RAC 6, RRPL.

22. Lawrence Wittner, *Toward Nuclear Abolition: A History of the World Nuclear Disarmament Movement, 1971–Present* (Stanford, CA: Stanford University Press, 2003), 132–38.

23. Geoffrey Darnton, *London Nuclear Warfare Tribunal: Evidence, Commentary, and Judgment* (Stockholm: Myrdal Foundation, 1989), sec. 1.1.

24. U.K. Embassy in Washington, "The Prime Minister Visit, Defense Subjects, Strategic Defense Initiative," memo to Foreign and Commonwealth Office, February 25, 1985, FCO, ser. 46/4629.

25. Margaret Thatcher, address to Joint Houses of Congress, February 20, 1985, THCR, Central Office of Information transcript.

26. Steven Steiner, "SDI Public Diplomacy in Europe," memo to John Poindexter, February 11, 1985, National Security Council, Executive Secretariat, System Files, box RAC 4, folder "SDI and Public Diplomacy in Europe," RRPL.

27. U.K. Embassy in Moscow, "Record of Meeting between the Prime Minister and Vice President Bush," memo to Foreign and Commonwealth Office, March 13, 1985, PREM, ser. 19/1656 f75.

28. C. D. Powell, "Meeting between the Prime Minister and the General Secretary," memo to L. V. Appleyard, March 13, 1985, ibid., ser. 19/1646 f37.

29. Jeremy Stocker, *Britain and Ballistic Missile Defense, 1942–2002* (London: Routledge, 2004), 147–48.

30. Paul Nitze, "On the Road to a More Stable Peace," speech to the Philadelphia World Affairs Council, February 20, 1985.

31. Geoffrey Howe, "Defense and Security in the Nuclear Age," *Journal of the Royal United Services Institute for Defense Studies* 130 (June 1985): 3–8.

32. "Howe's UDI Speech from SDI," *Times*, March 18, 1985; George F. Will, "Papier-Mache Secretary," *Washington Post*, March 24, 1985.

33. George Shultz, memo to Geoffrey Howe, March 26, 1985, PREM, ser. 19/1444 f92.

34. Alun Chalfont, *Star Wars: Suicide or Survival* (Boston: Little, Brown, 1985).

35. Memo of George Keyworth and Alun Chalfont meetings, February 13–20, 1985, George Keyworth Files, box 20, folder "United Kingdom," RRPL; Alun Chalfont, memo to George Keyworth, March 20, 1985, ibid.; George Keyworth, "Draft Copy of Corward for Lord Chalfont's Pro-Star Wars Book," June 13, 1985, ibid.; George Keyworth, memo to Ronald Reagan, December 5, 1985, ibid.

36. David Fishlock, "Conversion of a Star Wars Sceptic," *London Financial Times,* March 14, 1985.

37. Herbert Meyer, "Thatcher and SDI," memo to William Casey, January 4, 1985, George Keyworth Files, box 20, folder "United Kingdom," RRPL; David Hart, "SDI and the ABM Treaty: Gallup Poll Findings," May 28, 1985, ibid.

38. George Keyworth, memo to Charles Price, June 10, 1985, ibid.; Michael Pakenham, "Your Meeting with David Hart and Dr. George Keyworth," memo to [first name unknown] Thomas, June 12, 1985, FCO, ser. 46/4632.

39. Robert Stella, memo to George Keyworth, July 26, 1985, George Keyworth Files, box 20, folder "United Kingdom," RRPL.

40. Christian Campaign for Nuclear Disarmament, "Peace Pentecost 1986" (April 1986), CND Records, ser. 1993/9/5.

41. George Keyworth, "Presidential Meeting with Prince of Wales," memo to Robert McFarlane, October 1, 1985, George Keyworth Files, box 20, folder "United Kingdom," RRPL.

42. U.K. Embassy in Lisbon, "Secretary of States' Bilateral Meeting with Shultz: Tete-a-tete," memo to Foreign and Commonwealth Office, June 5, 1985, PREM, ser. 19/1655 f55.

43. U.K. NATO delegation, "North Atlantic Ministerial Meeting: SDI," memo to Foreign and Commonwealth Office, June 7, 1985, FCO, ser. 46/4632.

44. Serge Schmemann, "Gorbachev to Visit Paris before Meeting Reagan," *New York Times*, July 4, 1985.

45. William Eaton, "Gorbachev, in Paris, Plans to Reveal Details of Soviet Nuclear Proposals Today," *Los Angeles Times*, October 3, 1985.

46. Tom Korologos, "Summitry," memo to Robert McFarlane, Jack Matlock Files, box 44, folder "Summit 1986—U.S. Advisory Commission on Public Diplomacy," RRPL.

47. Robert McFarlane, "President Reagan's Negotiations with Gorbachev in Geneva," memo to Robert Armstrong, November 4, 1985, PREM, ser. 19/1693 f271.

48. James Markham, "Gorbachev Opens in Paris to Mixed Reviews," *New York Times*, October 6, 1985.

49. U.K. NATO delegation, "Soviet Nuclear Arms Control Counter-Proposals: Briefing of the Council by Nitze," memo to Foreign and Commonwealth Office, October 9, 1985, PREM, ser. 19/1693 f319.

50. Solly Zuckerman, memo to Richard Garwin, June 3, 1985, Zuckerman Papers, ser. SZ/2/Gen 35, box "Garwin.".

51. Scientists against Nuclear Arms and Council for a Livable World, "Star Wars: A Policy Discussion of the Strategic Defense Initiative," October 16, 1985, European Nuclear Disarmament Records (hereafter END Records), ser. 15/12, LSE; Pugwash, "47th Pugwash Symposium: Strategic Defenses: Technological Aspects; Political and Military Implications," December 5–8, 1985, RTBT, ser. 5/2/2/47.

52. Solly Zuckerman and Richard Garwin correspondence, Zuckerman Papers, ser. SZ/GEN/35, folder "Garwin."

53. Campaign for Nuclear Disarmament Executive Committee, meeting minutes, August 3, 1985, CND Records, ser. 1/2.

54. Jo Thomas, "100,000 in London Protest Arms Race," *New York Times*, October 27, 1985.

55. U.S. Advisory Commission, "Report on Public Diplomacy" (1986), CIA-ERR.

56. Geoffrey Howe, "Geneva Arms Control Talks: Western Strategy," memo to Margaret Thatcher, September 6, 1985, PREM, ser. 19/1660 f282.

57. White House, record of conversation among Margaret Thatcher, Ronald Reagan, and aides, October 23, 1985, National Security Council, Executive Secretariat Records, Peter Sommer Files, box RAC 4, RRPL; U.K. Mission to New York, "President Reagan's Meeting with Allied Leaders," to Foreign and Commonwealth Office, October 24, 1985, PREM, ser. 19/1655 f20.

58. George Shultz, "Your Meeting with Prime Minister Margaret Thatcher," memo to Ronald Reagan, October 22, 1985, National Security Council, System Files, box RAC 8508455, RRPL.

59. Alexander Yakovlev, "About Reagan," memo to Mikhail Gorbachev, March 12, 1985, in *The Last of the Superpower Summits: Reagan, Gorbachev and Bush: Conversations that Ended the Cold War*, ed. Svetlana Savranskaya and Thomas Blanton (Baltimore: Central European Press, 2016), 25.

60. Melvyn P. Leffler, *For the Soul of Mankind: The United States, the Soviet Union, and the Cold War* (New York: Hill and Wang, 2008), 339–41.

61. Mikhail Gorbachev, memo to Ronald Reagan, June 22, 1985; Mikhail Gorbachev, memo to Ronald Reagan, September 12, 1985; Mikhail Gorbachev, memo to Ronald Reagan, October 12, 1985; Ronald Reagan, memo to Mikhail Gorbachev, October 22, 1985; Ronald Reagan, memo to Mikhail Gorbachev, October 31, 1985; Ronald Reagan, memo to Mikhail Gorbachev, November 1, 1985; all in *The Reagan Files,* ed. Jason Saltoun-Ebin, http://www.thereaganfiles.com.

62. Anatoly S. Chernyaev, diary entry, July 1, 1985, in "The Diary of Anatoly S. Chernyaev, 1987," trans. Anna Melyakova, ed. Svetlana Savranskaya, National Security Agency Archives, https://nsarchive2.gwu.edu.

63. On Shevardnadze's early life, influences, and rise in the Soviet hierarchy, see Melvin Goodman and Carolyn Ekedahl, *The Wars of Eduard Shevardnadze* (Sterling, VA: Potomac, 2001), 7–28.

64. George P. Shultz, *Turmoil and Triumph: My Years as Secretary of State* (New York: Scribner's, 1993), 586.
65. Roderic Lyne, "Making Waves: Mr. Gorbachev's Public Diplomacy, 1985–1986," *International Affairs* 63 (Spring 1987): 205.
66. "An Interview with Mikhail Gorbachev," *Time*, September 9, 1985.
67. "Are Media Setting Up Reagan on the Summit?," *Human Events*, September 14, 1985.
68. Ronald Reagan, "Radio Address to the Nation and the World on the Upcoming Soviet–United States Summit Meeting," November 9, 1985, https://www.reaganlibrary.gov; Gerald M. Boyd, "Reagan, in Speech to Soviet Public, Says Aim Is Peace," *New York Times*, November 10, 1985.
69. National Security Council, "Soviet Foreign Minister Shevardnadze's Visit," meeting minutes, September 20, 1985, in Saltoun-Ebin, *The Reagan Files*.
70. Ronald Reagan, "Gorbachev," personal memo (November 1985), in Savranskaya and Blanton, *The Last of the Superpower Summits*, 44; Shultz, *Turmoil and Triumph*, 597.
71. "The Spirit of Geneva," *New York Times*, November 22, 1985; Douglas MacArthur II, "Perspectives on Geneva Summits: 1985 and 1955," *Christian Science Monitor*, December 4, 1985; Jeremy Stone, "Summit: No Results but Good Prospects," *FAS Public Interest Report* 38 (December 1985): 1.
72. "Dinner Hosted by the Gorbachevs," memo, November 19, 1985, National Security Agency Archives, https://nsarchive2.gwu.edu.
73. "Summary of the President's NATO Consultations: Special Session of the North Atlantic Council," November 21, 1985, Robert E. Linhard Files, box OA 92178, folder "Geneva Summit Records: November 19–21," RRPL.
74. Michael Deaver, *Different Drummer: My Thirty Years with Ronald Reagan* (New York: HarperCollins, 2009), 118; also see Leffler, *For the Soul of Mankind*.
75. U.K. Prime Minister's Office, record of conversation among Margaret Thatcher, Geoffrey Howe, and George Shultz, December 10, 1985, PREM, ser. 19/1655 f6.
76. "Dinner Hosted by the Gorbachevs."
77. "Reagan-Gorbachev Summit: Meeting Three," memo, November 19, 1985, Jack Matlock Files, box 92137, RRPL; "Summary of the President's NATO Consultations: Special Session of the North Atlantic Council."
78. "Strategic Defense Initiative Chronology: 1983–1990," March 19, 1990, Digital National Security Archive. Other major allies also agreed to participate in SDI research, including Israel in May 1986 and Japan in July 1987.
79. "Letter to Secretary General Gorbachev," *Public Interest Report of the Federation of American Scientists* (December 1985).
80. Mikhail Gorbachev, memo to Ronald Reagan, January 14, 1986, in Saltoun-Ebin, *The Reagan Files*.
81. John F. Burns, "Andropov Offers Ban on Space," *New York Times*, April 28, 1983.
82. Frank Von Hippel and Tomoko Kurokawa, "Citizen Scientists: Frank Von Hippel's Adventures in Nuclear Arms Control," *Journal for Peace and Nuclear Disarmament* 3, no. 1 (2019): 1–32.
83. U.S. Department of State, *Active Measures: A Report on the Substance and Process of Anti-U.S. Disinformation and Propaganda Campaigns* (Washington, DC: U.S. Government Printing Office, August 1986); U.S. Arms Control and Disarmament Agency, *The Soviet Propaganda Campaign against the U.S. Strategic Defense Initiative* (Washington, DC: U.S. Government Printing Office, August 1986).
84. Mikhail Gorbachev, *On My Country and the World* (New York: Columbia University Press, 2000), 230.

85. U.K. Embassy in Moscow, "Gorbachev's Statement on Arms Control," memo to Foreign and Commonwealth Office, January 16, 1986, PREM, ser. 19/1693 f231; U.K. Embassy in Washington, "Gorbachev's Proposals on Arms Control," memo to Foreign and Commonwealth Office, January 22, 1986, ibid., ser. 1693 f226; Foreign and Commonwealth Office, "Gorbachev's Proposals on Arms Control," memo to Charles Powell, January 24, 1986, ibid., ser. 19/1693 f208.

86. National Security Planning Group, "Arms Control: Responding to Gorbachev," meeting minutes, February 3, 1986, CIA-ERR.

87. Edwin J. Feulner, Jr., et al., "1986 Annual Report" (Washington, DC: U.S. Advisory Commission on Public Diplomacy, April 16, 1986).

88. Savranskaya and Blanton, *The Last of the Superpower Summits*, 125; Mikhail Gorbachev, "Tasking for Assistants for International Issues," March 20, 1986, National Security Archive.

89. U.K. Embassy in Washington, "U.S./Soviet Nuclear Arms Control Negotiations: U.S. Approach to Geneva Round IV," memo to Foreign and Commonwealth Office, January 16, 1986, PREM, ser. 19/1759 f299; U.K. Embassy in Washington, "Gorbachev's Proposals on Arms Control," memo to Foreign and Commonwealth Office, January 22, 1986, ibid., ser. 1693 f226; "Arms Control Support Group Paper for Senior Arms Control Group OWL," January 25, 1986, National Security Archive.

90. George Shultz, "Responding to Gorbachev's Arms Control Proposals," memo to Ronald Reagan, January 29, 1986, National Security Archive.

91. Caspar Weinberger, "Choosing a Response to Gorbachev Proposal," memo to Ronald Reagan, January 31, 1986, ibid.

92. Kenneth Adelman, "Responding to Gorbachev's January Proposal," memo to Ronald Reagan, January 29, 1986, ibid.

93. "USIA Conference on Public Diplomacy," March 3–4, 1986, Jack Matlock Files, box 44, folder "USIA Conference on Public Diplomacy," RRPL.

94. U.S. Embassy in London, "Public Diplomacy Activities of Ambassador Matlock," memo to U.S. Information Agency (March 1986), ibid., folder "USIA Conference on Public Diplomacy, London"; Jack Matlock, "USIA Conference on Public Diplomacy," memo to Rodney McDaniel, March 18, 1986, ibid.

95. National Security Planning Group, "Arms Control: Responding to Gorbachev."

96. Michael Donley and Linton Brooks, "Hoffman Memorandum Re: Long-Term Strategy, Policy, and Programs," memo to John Poindexter, June 11, 1986, National Security Archive.

97. Ronald Reagan, "Address to the Nation on National Security," February 26, 1986; Ronald Reagan, "Radio Address to the Nation on the Strategic Defense Initiative," July 12, 1986; Ronald Reagan, "Radio Address to the Nation on House of Representatives Defense Authorization Bill," August 12, 1986; all in http://www.presidency.ucsb.edu.

98. Peter Westwick, "Space-Strike Weapons and the Soviet Response to SDI," *Diplomatic History* (November 2008): 957.

99. Andrei Grachev, *Gorbachev's Gamble: Soviet Foreign Policy and the End of the Cold War* (Cambridge: Polity, 2008), 85.

100. European Nuclear Disarmament, "Anti-Star Wars Campaign Meeting," February 5, 1986, END Records, ser. 15/13.

101. Pugwash, "Meeting and Statement of Pugwash Council on the 34th Pugwash Conference: 1984 and Beyond: Science, Security, and Public Opinion," July 9–14, 1984, RTBT, ser. 5/2/1/34; A. E. Laurence, memo to Joseph Rotblat, July 16, 1984, ibid., ser. 5/6/8/3; B. T. Feld, "Summary of Proposals by Council Members for Improving the Quality of Pugwash Conferences," memo to Martin Kaplin, October 17, 1986, Dorothy Hodgkin Personal

Papers, MS.ENG.C.5684, WLSC; "Pugwash at Thirty: Reviving," *Public Interest Report of the Federation of American Scientists* (October 1987).

102. Susanne Schregel, "Global Micropolitics: Toward a Transnational History of Grassroots Nuclear Free Zones," in *Nuclear Threats, Nuclear Fear, and the Cold War of the 1980s,* ed. Eckart Conze, Martin Klimke, and Jeremy Varon (New York: Cambridge University Press, 2017), 214.

103. *Nuclear Times* (October 1983). Missoula, Montana, had declared itself a nuclear-free zone in 1978 in response to concerns about nuclear power.

104. *Nuclear Times* (May 1983).

105. Bruce Kent, "Annual Report to CND Annual Conference," November 23–25, 1984, CND Records, ser. 2/4.

106. Luis Li, "State Sovereignty and Nuclear Free Zones," *California Law Review* 79 (July 1991): 1171.

107. Educators for Social Responsibility, "Annual Report" (1985), Papers of Physicians for Social Responsibility, box 48-A S2, SCPC.

108. Jerry Thornton, "City Becomes Largest U.S. Nuclear-Free Zone," *Chicago Tribune,* March 24, 1986; Andrew Malcolm, "Chicago Declares Itself Nuclear Weapon-Free Zone," *New York Times,* March 13, 1986.

109. U.S. Department of State, Bureau of Intelligence and Research, Office of Active Measures Analysis and Response, "Soviet Influence Activities: A Report on Active Measures and Propaganda, 1987–1988" (Washington D.C.: U.S. Government Printing Office August 1989), 56.

110. British Pugwash Group, "Acceptability of SDI Research Contracts," April 14, 1986, RTBT, ser. 5/6/5/15.

111. Greater London Council, "Can Star Wars Defend Europe?," symposium, February 25, 1986, RTBT, ser. 5/6/6/1.

112. Technology groups included the British Society for Social Responsibility in Science, Computing and Social Responsibility, Engineers for Nuclear Disarmament, Electronics for Peace, London New Technology Network, Medical Campaign against Nuclear Weapons, SANA, and Verification Technology Information Centre. See Neil Kinnock, "Coalition against Star Wars," press release, June 26, 1986, END Records, ser. 15/12.

113. Ibid.

114. Space Watch, "Minutes of Anti-Star Wars Meeting," March 12, 1986, ibid., ser. 15/13.

115. Ibid.

116. Memo of conversation between Ronald Reagan and Margaret Thatcher, May 4, 1986, National Security Council, System Files, RRPL.

117. National Security Planning Group, "U.S.-Soviet Relations," meeting minutes, June 12, 1986, in Saltoun-Ebin, *The Reagan Files.*

118. Jack Matlock, "A Strategy for U.S.-Soviet Relations," memo to John Poindexter, May 7, 1986, National Security Archive.

119. "U.S. to Break SALT II Limits Friday," *Washington Post*, November 27, 1986.

120. Mikhail Gorbachev, memo to Ronald Reagan, September 15, 1986, in Saltoun-Ebin, *The Reagan Files.*

121. Memo of conversation between Reagan and Thatcher, May 4, 1986; U.K. Prime Minister's Office, "Record of Conversation between Thatcher and Soviet Ambassador," April 30, 1986, PREM, ser. 19/3548 f131.

122. U.K. Embassy in Washington, "Secretary of State's Meeting with Weinberger," memo to Foreign and Commonwealth Office, September 10, 1986, PREM, ser, 19/1759 f246.

123. Margaret Thatcher, memo to Ronald Reagan, October 6, 1986, ibid., ser. 19/1759 f146.

124. Kenneth Adelman, *Reagan at Reykjavik: 48 Hours That Ended the Cold War* (New York: Broadside, 2014), 35–36.

125. U.K. Embassy in Washington, "U.S./Soviet Relations: Arms Control Issues in Congress," memo to Foreign and Commonwealth Office, October 10, 1986, PREM, ser. 19/1695 f285.

126. Robert Samuel, "Conservative Intellectuals and the Reagan-Gorbachev Summits," *Cold War History* 12, no. 1 (2012): 144–47.

127. "Reagan-Gorbachev First Meeting in Reykjavik," October 11, 1986, Jack Matlock Files, Box 92140, RRPL.

128. Ibid.

129. Ibid.; "Reagan-Gorbachev Second Meeting in Reykjavik," October 11, 1986, Jack Matlock Files, box 92140, RRPL.

130. U.S. Department of State, "Reagan-Gorbachev Meetings in Reykjavik, October 1986. Third Meeting," October 12, 1986, National Security Archive.

131. Ibid.

132. "Reagan-Gorbachev Fourth Meeting in Reykjavik," October 11, 1986, Jack Matlock Files, box 92140, RRPL.

133. Beth Fischer, *The Myth of Triumphalism: Rethinking President Reagan's Cold War Legacy* (Lexington: University of Kentucky Press, 2020) , 71–73.

134. Anthony Eames, "A Corruption of British Science: The Strategic Defense Initiative and British Technology Policy," *Technology and Culture* 62, no. 3 (2021): 812–38.

135. "Reagan-Gorbachev Fourth Meeting in Reykjavik."

136. Shultz, *Turmoil and Triumph*, 774–75; Brown, *The Gorbachev Factor*, 232–33; Leffler, *For the Soul of Mankind*, 393–94; James Graham Wilson, *The Triumph of Improvisation: Gorbachev's Adaptability, Reagan's Engagement, and the End of the Cold War* (Ithaca, NY: Cornell University Press, 2014), 111–15.

137. John Poindexter, "Why We Can't Commit to Eliminating all Nuclear Weapons within 10 Years," memo to Ronald Reagan, October 16, 1986, Alton Keel Files, box 3, folder "Reykjavik Briefing," RRPL.

138. U.S. Embassy in Moscow, "Your Meeting with Shevardnadze," memo to U.S. Department of State, October 31, 1986, *FRUS*, 1969–76, vol. 6, Soviet Union, October 1986–89, doc. 4.

139. Charles Powell, memo to Margaret Thatcher, October 14, 1986, PREM, ser. 19/1695 f227.

140. Ray Moseley and George de Lama, "Star Wars Sinks Arms Deal," *Chicago Tribune*, October 13, 1986; "Gorbachev Speech Blames U.S. for Cost of Arms Race," *Los Angeles Times*, October 15, 1986; Gary Lee, "Gorbachev Blames Reagan," *Washington Post*, October 15, 1986; Michael Mandelbaum and Strobe Talbott, "After the Summit: Reykjavik and Beyond," *Foreign Affairs* 65, no. 2 (1986).

141. William Greider, "Reagan Flubs Reykjavik Summit," *Rolling Stone*, December 4, 1986.

142. Marcus Witcher, *Getting Right with Reagan: The Struggle for True Conservatism: 1980–2016* (Lawrence: University of Kansas Press, 2019), 122–44.

143. U.S. Arms Control and Disarmament Agency, *The Soviet Propaganda Campaign against the US Strategic Defense Initiative.*

144. Adam Clymer, "Summit Aftermath: What the Public Thinks; First Reaction: Poll Shows Arms control Optimism and Support for Reagan," *New York Times*, October 16, 1986.

145. Richard Staar, *Public Diplomacy: USA versus USSR* (Stanford, CA: Hoover Institution Press, 1986).

146. Ibid., 233.

147. Ibid., 135.

148. Ibid., 232.

149. Steven Weisman, "Gorbachev Calls for 'Star Peace,'" *New York Times*, November 28, 1986.

150. U.S. Department of State, *Soviet Influence Activities*.

151. Staar, *Public Diplomacy*, 50–100.

152. Ronald Reagan and Margaret Thatcher, teleconference, October 13, 1986, National Security Council, System Files, RRPL.

153. Ibid.

154. U.K. NATO delegation, "Reykjavik Summit: NAC Briefing by Shultz," memo to Foreign and Commonwealth Office, October 12, 1986, PREM, ser. 19/1759 f96.

155. Foreign and Commonwealth Office, "Arms Control: European Approach," exchange of memos with Charles Powell, November 19, 1986, ibid., ser. 19/1695 f40.

156. "Soviet Ambassador's Call on the Prime Minister," November 10, 1986, ibid., ser. 19/3548 f123.

157. U.S. delegation to Vienna, memo to U.S. State Department, November 6, 1986, National Security Council, European and Soviet Directorate Files, box 90902, RRPL.

158. Margaret Thatcher, "Press Conference after Camp David Talks," November 15, 1986, THCR, Central Office of Information transcript; U.K. Embassy in Washington, "Camp David: Arms Control," memo to Foreign and Commonwealth Office, November 16, 1986, PREM, ser. 19/1695 f82; Margaret Thatcher, memo to Mikhail Gorbachev, November 25, 1986, ibid., ser. 19/3548 f96.

159. Mikhail Gorbachev, "About Shultz," speech to Soviet Politburo, April 16, 1987, trans. Svetlana Savranskaya, in "The INF Treaty and Washington Summit: 20 Years Later," National Security Archive, electronic briefing book 238.

160. Karen DeYoung, "Thatcher Gives British Soviets British-Style 'Glasnost,'" *Washington Post*, March 30, 1987; Howell Raines, "Thatcher's Visit: Glasnost in Action?," *New York Times*, April 3, 1987; Steven Rosenberg, "The Thatcher Interview That Shocked the World," https://www.bbc.co.uk.

161. Mikhail Gorbachev, "Once Again on the Outcomes of Margaret Thatcher's Visit," speech to Soviet Politburo, April 16, 1987, trans. Svetlana Savranskaya, in "The INF Treaty and Washington Summit."

162. Margaret Thatcher, memo to Ronald Reagan, April 1, 1987, National Security Archive; "Prime Minister's Visit to Moscow," April 6, 1987, THCR, ser. 1/10/117 f39.

163. Soviet Politburo, "About the Conversation with Shultz," discussion, April 16, 1987, trans. Svetlana Savranskaya, in "The INF Treaty and Washington Summit."

164. Charles Z. Wick, memo to Ronald Reagan, July 22, 1987, National Security Council, System Files, RRPL; Charles Z. Wick, "Public Diplomacy for INF," memo to Frank Carlucci (Spring 1987), ibid.

165. Charles Z. Wick, memo to Ronald Reagan and Frank Carlucci, May 27, 1987, ibid.

166. Wick, "Public Diplomacy for INF."

167. John Kordek, "Director Wick's Trip to London" (July 1987), National Security Council, System Files, RRPL.

168. Scientists against Nuclear Arms, "Putting It Across," annual conference, April 25–26, 1987, Maurice Wilkins Papers, ser. K/PP178/11/21/1, folder "Scientists against Nuclear Arms, 1987–1990," King's College London, College Archive.

169. Matthew Evangelista, *Unarmed Forces: The Transnational Movement to End the Cold War* (Ithaca, NY: Cornell University Press, 1999), 249–340; David Reynolds, "Science, Technology, and the Cold War," in *The Cambridge History of the Cold War: Endings*, ed. Melvyn P. Leffler and Odd Arne Westad (Cambridge: Cambridge University Press, 2010), 378–99; Alison Kraft, Holger Nehring, and Carole Sachese, "The Pugwash Conferences and the Global Cold War: Scientists, Transnational Networks, and the Complexities of Nuclear Histories," *Cold War Studies* 20 (Winter 2018): 4–30.

170. "Ten Days in a Changing Moscow," *Public Interest Report of the Federation of American Scientist* 40 (March 1987); Frank Von Hippel, "A U.S. Scientist Addresses Gorbachev," *Bulletin of the Atomic Scientists* 43, no. 4 (1987): 12–13; Evangelista, *Unarmed Forces*, 249–322.

171. Anatoly S. Chernyaev, diary entry, June 14, 1987, in "The Diary of Anatoly S. Chernyaev, 1987."

172. Soviet Politburo, "On Soviet-American Relations and Negotiations on Nuclear and Space Armaments," discussion, February 26, 1987, trans. Svetlana Savranskaya, in "The INF Treaty and Washington Summit."

173. Soviet Politburo, "About the Conversation with Shultz."

174. Soviet Politburo, "On Soviet-American Relations and Negotiations on Nuclear and Space Armaments."

175. Shultz, *Turmoil and Triumph*, 901–24, 983–1015.

176. Sidney Blumenthal, "Richard Perle: Disarmed but Undeterred," *New York Times*, November 23, 1987.

177. Soviet Politburo, "About the Conversation with Shultz."

178. Memo of conversation between George Shultz and Eduard Shevardnadze, September 15, 1987, *FRUS*, 1969–76, vol. 6, Soviet Union, October 1986–89, doc. 67.

179. Memo of conversation between Mikhail Gorbachev and George Shultz, October 23, 1987, trans. Svetlana Savranskaya, in "The INF Treaty and Washington Summit."

180. Brown, *The Gorbachev Factor*, 130–54, 163, 212–51.

181. William Webster and Robert Gates, "Gorbachev's Gameplan: The Long View," November 24, 1987, *FRUS*, 1969–76, vol. 6, Soviet Union, October 1986–89, doc. 103.

182. Memo of conversation between Ronald Reagan and Mikhail Gorbachev, December 8, 1987, in "The INF Treaty and Washington Summit."

183. U.S. State Department, "Secretary's 12/11 NAC Briefing on Washington Summit," December 11, 1987, in ibid.

184. As early as 1989, Thomas Risse-Kappen sought to counter the rapid rise of peace through strength as a coherent grand strategy narrative; see his "Did 'Peace through Strength' End the Cold War? Lessons from INF" *International Security* 16, no. 1 (2001): 162–88.

185. Tuch, *Communicating with the World*, 161.

186. Marvin Stone, "Proposed Summit Public Affairs Calendar for Principals," memo to Colin Powell and Thomas Griscom, November 18, 1987, National Security Council, Coordination Office Files, box 22, folder "Summit—Public Diplomacy," RRPL; Edwin J. Feulner, Jr., "Public Diplomacy: Lessons from the Washington Summit" (Washington, DC: U.S. Advisory Commission on Public Diplomacy, 1988).

187. Kiron Skinner, Annelise Anderson, and Martin Anderson, *Reagan: A Life in Letters* (New York: Free Press, 2003), 418–21.

188. Jack Nelson, "Reagan Seeks to Calm His Right-Wing Critics: Conservatives Say He's Abandoned His Ideals over Arms Control, Central America Initiative," *Los Angeles Times*, September 6, 1987.

189. Hedrick Smith, "The Right against Reagan," *New York Times*, January 17, 1988.

190. Ibid.

191. Peter Grier, "Treaty Critics Aim beyond Ratification: Conservative Objections to the INF Pact Could Frame the Debate over Cuts in Long-Range Missiles," *Christian Science Monitor*, February 3, 1988.

192. "Appeasement Is as Unwise in 1988 as in 1938," *Washington Times*, January 25, 1988.

193. Smith, "The Right against Reagan."

194. White House, "First Plenary, Moscow Summit," May 30, 1988, National Security Archive.

195. George Shultz, "My April Trip to the Soviet Union," memo to Ronald Reagan, April 12, 1988, *FRUS*, 1969–76, vol. 6, Soviet Union, October 1986–89, doc. 141.

196. U.S. Department of State, "The Secretary's Meeting with Gorbachev," April 22, 1988, ibid., doc. 147.

197. Ibid.

198. George Shultz, "Shevardnadze Visit," memo to Ronald Reagan, n.d., ibid., doc.140.

199. David K. Shipler, "Meeting in Moscow; An Opportunity to Talk the Cold War to Death," *New York Times,* May 22, 1988.

200. James Wilkinson, "Agreements Concluded to Date at Moscow Summit," memo to Michael Armacost, May 31, 1988, in "The Moscow Summit 20 Years Later," National Security Archive, electronic briefing book 251.

201. Joseph G. Whelan, *The Moscow Summit 1988: The Last Gorbachev-Reagan Negotiating Encounter* (Washington, DC: Library of Congress, Congressional Research Service, June 29, 1989), 89–396.

202. Mikhail Gorbachev, "On Reagan's Visit to Moscow," speech to Soviet Politburo, June 6, 1988, trans. Svetlana Savranskaya, in "The Moscow Summit 20 Years Later."

203. Ronald Reagan, "Remarks to Members of the Royal Institute of International Affairs in London," June 3, 1988, https://www.presidency.ucsb.edu.

204. David S. Painter and Thomas S. Blanton, "The End of the Cold War," in *A Companion to Post-1945 America*, ed. Jean-Christophe Agnew and Roy Rosenzweig (New York: Blackwell, 2006): 479–80.

205. Don Oberdorfer, "Thatcher Says Cold War Has Come to an End," *Washington Post,* November 18, 1988.

206. Daniel Yankelovich and Richard Smoke, "America's 'New Thinking,'" *Foreign Affairs* 67 (Fall 1988): 1.

207. Ibid., 1–17.

208. See, for example, John Lewis Gaddis, "Hanging Tough Paid Off," *Bulletin of the Atomic Scientists* 45 (January 1989): 11–14. For an early rebuke of the Reagan victory narrative, see Daniel Deudney and G. John Ikenberry, "Who Won the Cold War?," *Foreign Policy* 87 (Summer 1992): 123–38.

209. Jay Winik, "The Neoconservative Reconstruction," *Foreign Policy* 73 (Winter 1988–89): 140. Also see Jay Winik, *On the Brink: The Dramatic Behind the Scenes Saga of the Reagan Era and the Men and Women Who Won the Cold War* (New York: Simon and Schuster, 1996).

210. For other adherents to the Reagan victory school, see Peter Schweizer, *Reagan's War: The Epic Story of His Forty Year Struggle and Final Triumph over Communism* (New York: Doubleday, 2002); John Lewis Gaddis, *The Cold War: A New History* (New York: Penguin, 2006); and Paul Kengor, *The Crusader: Ronald Reagan and the Fall of Communism* (New York: HarperPerennial, 2007).

211. Edwin J. Feulner, Jr., et al., "1989 Annual Report" (Washington, DC: U.S. Advisory Commission on Public Diplomacy, December 1, 1988).

212. Melvyn P. Leffler, "Ronald Reagan and the Cold War: What Mattered Most," *Texas National Security Review* 1 (May 2018): 77–89.

213. Adelman, *Reagan at Reykjavik,* 261.

214. Joseph G. Whelan, *Soviet Diplomacy Behavior, 1979–1988: New Tests for U.S. Diplomacy* (Washington, DC: Library of Congress, Congressional Research Service, August 1988); Whelan, *The Moscow Summit 1988.*

Conclusion: Surviving the Cold War

1. Elizabeth Kastor, "For Wick, Cheers from the Chief," *Washington Post*, November 18, 1988.

2. Roger Pilon, *The CATO Handbook for Congress* (Washington, DC.: CATO Institute, 1995), 307–8.

3. Susan Epstein, *U.S. Public Diplomacy: Background and the 9/11 Commission Recommendations* (Washington, DC: Library of Congress, Congressional Research Service, 2006).

4. Liam Kennedy and Scott Lucas, "Enduring Freedom: Public Diplomacy and U.S. Foreign Policy," *American Quarterly* 57, no. 2 (2005): 309–33; [classified author], *Public Diplomacy: A Review of Past Recommendations* (Washington, DC: Library of Congress, Congressional Research Service, 2005).

5. Penny Von Eschen, *Paradoxes of Nostalgia: Cold War Triumphalism and Global Disorder Since 1989* (Durham, NC: Duke University Press, 2022).

6. Christopher Paul and Matt Armstrong, "The Irony of Misinformation: USIA Myths Block Enduring Solutions," *1945*, July 6, 2022, https://www.19fortyfive.com; Matthew Armstrong, "No We Do Not Need to Revive the U.S. Information Agency," *War on the Rocks*, November 12, 2015, https://warontherocks.com.

7. Ali Fischer, "Four Seasons in One Day: The Crowded House of Public Diplomacy in the United Kingdom," in *The Routledge Handbook of Public Diplomacy*, ed. Nancy Snow and Nicholas Cull (London: Routledge, 2020), 243–54.

8. James Pammet, *British Public Diplomacy and Soft Power: Diplomatic Influence and Digital Disruption* (London: Palgrave Macmillan, 2016), 4.

9. Nicholas Cull, *Public Diplomacy: Foundations for Global Engagement in the Digital Age* (Medford, MA: Polity, 2019), 58.

INDEX

ANTHONY EAMES is director of scholarly initiatives at the Ronald Reagan Presidential Foundation and Institute and teaches for George Washington University's Elliott School of International Affairs. He earned his PhD from Georgetown University and has spoken and published widely on nuclear and national security issues, including in the *Journal of Military History, Technology & Culture*, and *War on the Rocks*. He is also the coauthor of *Sharing Nuclear Secrets* (2023). Anthony currently resides in Washington, D.C., where he enjoys the great cycling trails and the beauty of the mid-Atlantic with his wife, son, and dog, but he remains a proud Chicago native. When he is not thinking about nuclear issues, he is dreaming of deep-dish pizza, the Chicago Bulls of the 1990s, and the shores of Lake Michigan in the summertime.